CASS SERIES: STUDIES IN INTELLIGENCE
(Series Editors: Christopher Andrew and Michael I. Handel)

Also in this series

Codebreaker in the Far East
by Alan Stripp

War, Strategy and Intelligence
by Michael I. Handel

A Don At War
(revised edition) by Sir David Hunt

Controlling Intelligence
edited by Glenn P. Hastedt

Security and Intelligence in a Changing World: New Perspectives for the 1990s
edited by A. Stuart Farson, David Stafford and Wesley K. Wark

Spy Fiction, Spy Films and Real Intelligence
edited by Wesley K. Wark

From Information to Intrigue: Studies in Secret Service Based on the Swedish Experience 1939–45
by C.G. McKay

Dieppe Revisited: A Documentary Investigation
by John P. Campbell

The Australian Security Intelligence Organization: An Unofficial History
by Frank Cain

Intelligence, Defence and Diplomacy: British Policy in the Post-war World
edited by Richard J. Aldrich and Michael F. Hopkins

Intelligence and Strategy in the Second World War
edited by Michael I. Handel

POLICING POLITICS: SECURITY INTELLIGENCE AND THE LIBERAL DEMOCRATIC STATE

PETER GILL

FRANK CASS

First published 1994 in Great Britain by
FRANK CASS & CO. LTD.
Gainsborough House, Gainsborough Road,
London E11 1RS, England

and in the United States of America by
FRANK CASS
c/o International Specialized Book Services, Inc.,
5804 N.E. Hassalo Street, Portland, Oregon 97213-3644

British Library Cataloguing in Publication Data
Gill, Peter
  Policing Politics: Security Intelligence
  and the Liberal Democratic State.
  (Studies in Intelligence Series)
  I. Title II. Series
  327.1

Library of Congress Cataloging-in-Publication Data
Gill, Peter, 1947–
  Policing politics : security intelligence and the liberal
democratic state / Peter Gill.
      p.   cm. -- (Cass series--studies in intelligence)
  Includes bibliographical references and index.
  ISBN 0–7146–3490–5 -- ISBN 0–7146–4097–2 (pbk.)
  1.   Intelligence service--Great Britain.   2.   Secret service--Great
Britain.   I. Title.   II. Series.
JN329.I6G54   1994
327.1'241--dc20   93–31498
                                                                     CIP

ISBN 0 7146 3490 5 (hardback)
ISBN 0 7146 4097 2 (paperback)

*Printed in Great Britain by
Bookcraft Ltd.
Midsomer Norton, Bath*

For Pen, with all my love

Contents

Figures and Tables

Acknowledgements

Many people have contributed to the writing of this book over a long period of time, most of them unknowingly. The issues discussed here first intrigued me as a student and teacher of United States politics when revelations of FBI abuses developed from a trickle to a flood in the early 1970s. Reading the reports of the congressional investigations provided me with a first overview of the operations of the secret state. Working as a research and information officer for Merseyside Police Authority in the mid-1980s provided more immediate experience of certain aspects of state information policies. During this period I benefited greatly from working with Margaret Simey, John George and Richard Kinsey.

The research which was specifically oriented to this book was aided greatly by the Canadian High Commission in London who awarded me a personal research grant in 1988. I am very grateful to all those who provided me with help and hospitality on my subsequent trips to Canada in 1988 and 1989; in particular, Stuart Farson. Stuart also read and commented helpfully on the first brief draft of the book. I would like to thank also Tony Bunyan and Richard Norton-Taylor, who have both provided help and good ideas; Gillian Hall for being a supportive colleague; Robina Dexter for casting her lawyerly eye over one chapter for me; and Phil Cubbin for assistance with some of the figures. The School of Social Science at the (then) Liverpool Polytechnic provided me with some relief from teaching for one term in 1991, which gave me more space than normally exists in the (now) 'new' universities in which to write.

Martyn Nightingale and Joe Sim both read the penultimate

draft and made many helpful suggestions. Now that the account-
ants and bureaucrats are taking over higher education, our discussions came as a breath of fresh air. I would express particular
gratitude to Joe. He read two drafts of the book, commenting
extensively each time, and provided continuing support and
encouragement as the writing proceeded. But, in addition, he
has been a great friend and colleague as we have attempted
jointly to keep particular parts of the educational show on the
road at 'the John' during the last two years.

Finally, I want to thank the family. With book-writing I suspect
it is like divorce: it is the children who suffer. There have been
times when Ell and Rob would have liked to do something else,
but sometimes the word processor was taken over by Batman and
Sir Perceval, so I hope it was not all bad! Despite having her own
creative interests during the period when most of the book was
written, Pen has been unstinting in her support. I thank her for
her specific help on the book, but I am in debt to her for much
more than that.

Pete Gill, Liverpool, 1993

PERMISSIONS

The author and publisher are grateful to the following publishers
for permission to quote extracts from published work:

Houghton Mifflin Company, New York, for permission to quote
from *Secrecy and Democracy* by Admiral Stansfield Turner.
Copyright © 1985 by Stansfield Turner. All rights reserved.

International Thomson Publishing Services Limited, Andover,
for permission to quote from *The Ties that Bind* by J.T. Richelson
and D. Ball, published by Unwin Hyman, 1990.

Penguin USA for permission to quote from *Spycatcher* by Peter
Wright, published by Penguin Viking in 1987.

Abbreviations

ACLU	American Civil Liberties Union, US
ACSI	Advisory Committee on Security Intelligence (recommended by McDonald Commission but not implemented), Canada
ALP	Australian Labour Party
ASIO	Australian Security Intelligence Organisation
ASIS	Australian Secret Intelligence Service
BPP	Black Panther Party, US
BT	British Telecom
CANZAB	Canada, Australia, New Zealand, America, Britain – network of counter-intelligence organisations set up in 1960s
CASIS	Canadian Association for Security and Intelligence Studies
CI	Counter-Intelligence
CIA	Central Intelligence Agency, US
CND	Campaign for Nuclear Disarmament, UK
COINTELPRO	Counter-Intelligence Programmes 1956–71 in FBI, US
CPGB	Communist Party of Great Britain
CSIS	Canadian Security Intelligence Service
DCI	Director and Co-ordinator of Intelligence, Northern Ireland
DIS	Defence Intelligence Staff, UK

DSD	Defence Signals Directorate, Australia
DSS	Department of Social Security, UK
EC	European Community
FBI	Federal Bureau of Investigation, US
FISA	Foreign Intelligence Surveillance Act, US
FLQ	Quebec Liberation Front
FOI	Freedom of Information
GAO	General Accounting Office, US Congress
GCHQ	Government Communications Headquarters, UK
GPU	Soviet Security Service, prior to 1922
GRU	Soviet Military Intelligence Agency
HUMINT	Human Intelligence (information from human sources)
IBA	Independent Broadcasting Authority, UK
IG	Inspector General
IOB	Intelligence Oversight Board, US
IRD	Information Research Department, UK
JIC	Joint Intelligence Committee, UK
JIO	Joint Intelligence Organisation, Australia and UK
KGB	Committee for State Security, USSR
MfS	Ministry for State Security, German Democratic Republic
MI5	Military Intelligence 5, Security Service, UK
MI6	Military Intelligence 6, Secret Intelligence Service, UK
MIS	Ministerial Committee on Intelligence, UK
NATO	North Atlantic Treaty Organisation
NCCL	National Council for Civil Liberties (now, Liberty), UK

NCIS	National Criminal Intelligence Service, UK
NDP	New Democratic Party, Canada
NIE	National Intelligence Estimate, US
NIO	Northern Ireland Office
NSA	National Security Agency, US
NSID	National Security Intelligence Directorate, RCMP, Canada
ONA	Office of National Assessments, Australia
OPR	Office of Professional Responsibility, Justice Department, US
PFIAB	President's Foreign Intelligence Advisory Board, US
PFLP	Popular Front for the Liberation of Palestine
PIRA	Provisional Irish Republican Army
PLO	Palestine Liberation Organisation
PRO	Professional Responsibility Office, FBI, US
PSIS	Permanent Secretaries Committee on Intelligence, UK
PTA	Prevention of Terrorism Act, UK
RAP	Analysis and Production Branch, CSIS, Canada
RCMP	Royal Canadian Mounted Police
RUC	Royal Ulster Constabulary
SAVAC	Iranian security service under the Shah
SB	Special Branch, UK
SIGINT	Signals Intelligence
SIRC	Security Intelligence Review Committee, Canada
SIS	Secret Intelligence Service, UK
SIS	Security Intelligence Service, New Zealand
Stasi	State Security Service, German Democratic Republic
TARC	Target Approval and Review Committee, CSIS, Canada
TCG	Tasking and Co-ordination Group, Northern Ireland

UKUSA   1947 security agreement between US, UK, Australia, Canada and New Zealand, dividing the world into areas of SIGINT responsibility

Introduction

Perhaps the most significant international event of the last decade has been the end of the 'cold war' which, since 1947, had been the primary factor in determining the foreign policies of the Western industrialised states. It also had a profound effect on the domestic politics of these nations, leading to, among other things, the vetting of recruits to state employment, the surveillance of dissenting political movements and strenuous efforts by governments to minimise access to state information. The collapse of the regimes of Eastern Europe was nowhere more spectacular than among their own security agencies, for example the ransacking of the offices of the Stasi in the former German Democratic Republic in January 1990. In the Soviet Union the KGB had embarked upon a process of *glasnost*, through giving interviews to the Western media, until its involvement in the coup attempt of August 1991 led to its break-up into smaller agencies within the republics into which the Soviet Union divided.

The impact on the intelligence services of the West has been less dramatic; indeed they have attempted to convey the impression of business as usual. Uncertainty is the enemy of security, so the irony of the post-cold war era is that the collapse of the bi-polar certainties of the cold war has produced greater uncertainties in a world of more fragmented international politics. This will lead to politicians demanding ever more information and a potentially healthy future for the agencies which provide it. Clearly this involves a search for new targets. Some of these remain the traditional military ones, for example, Iraq, while the upheavals of the international political economy have brought a shift of intelligence resources to the gathering of economic information.[1] 'Subversion' has to some degree been substituted by 'terrorism' as a primary target of security intelligence agencies, both foreign and domestic, since serious political violence is seen as having, depending on local circumstances, both foreign and domestic roots. Another newer target is drugs-trafficking.

This book has been written against that background and is concerned with the organisation of the domestic security intelligence agencies in the United Kingdom, especially the Security Service and police Special Branches.[2] It examines what is known or has been alleged about, first, the effectiveness of these agencies in achieving their objective of 'good intelligence' and, second, the extent to which their activities abuse the political rights of individuals and organisations. *Glasnost* is coming only lately and gently to these agencies. In December 1991, when Stella Rimington was named as the new Director General of the Security Service she was the first to have her name officially released by the Home Office – which would, however, provide no photograph. Therefore the press were obliged to buy or steal copies of the only known photograph of her, first published in 1986 in a profile in the *New Statesman* about her role as head of the Security Service division responsible for the surveillance of trade unions.[3]

Previous British writing about intelligence has been dominated by historical approaches and has focused less on the domestic than on the foreign agencies.[4] The analysis here is different. It starts with a 'problem'. Recent discussion and debate of domestic security intelligence matters in the UK has shown, first, that rather little is actually known (as distinct from alleged) and, second, that what indications there are point to an almost total absence of political control, let alone democratic oversight of these agencies. Stated baldly, the problem is that there is some evidence that these agencies, at best, fail to provide effective security intelligence and at worst, actively undermine the liberal democratic political process.

As will be seen from the Notes, the sources for the book are primarily secondary – academic and journalistic – plus official reports. The approach here has not been to trawl such primary sources as there are for fresh revelations about security intelligence operations, and I have no sources among present or former officers. Therefore the study is 'interpretive': it attempts

2

to organise what we do know about the UK security intelligence agencies and their equivalents elsewhere. Together with this, the concepts and methods of social science are used in order to develop a systematic framework for the comparative analysis of security intelligence agencies. However, the aim of the book is not to produce a solely academic treatise, but to make the case for a full inquiry into security intelligence in the UK as the necessary prelude for any changes in this crucial yet hidden aspect of the operations of the modern state.

Chapter 1 discusses a range of writings on security intelligence in the UK to illustrate both the extent and limits of what is known and to summarise some of the major allegations that have been made as to abuses of power by the agencies. In the light of this, the book's research strategy is elaborated. A central aspect of the approach is to make use of what is known about security intelligence matters from the extensive inquiries and research which have taken place in other countries in order to develop what might be seen as an agenda for an inquiry in the UK.

In Chapter 2 the applicability of concepts of information, power, law and the state to the analysis of security intelligence matters is considered. A multi-level model of the state is developed. This provides a means of analysing the relationship between, first, security intelligence agencies and other state institutions, in which the key concept is autonomy, and, second, security intelligence agencies and society, in which the key concept is penetration. Different degrees and combinations of autonomy and penctration will give rise to various 'types' of agency. These provide a means of comparing agencies over time and between states.[5]

One of the major reasons why domestic security intelligence agencies have been found to have abused their power is that their tasks have been extremely ill-defined, or not defined at all. Governments have often preferred not to know who was being targeted and how, or they have been happy to acquiesce in the agencies' own definitions of 'subversives' or other deviants requiring surveillance. In Chapter 3 the importance of defining the security intelligence mandate is examined, particularly for those categories of 'threat' which are not defined in law, such as 'subversion'.

In Chapters 4 and 5 the discussion of the ways in which agencies penetrate society is organised by means of the notion of the 'intelligence process': targeting, techniques of information-gathering – overt and covert – the analysis of information (or 'production of intelligence'), the dissemination of intelligence, and the use of countering techniques, for example, disruption.

In Chapter 6 organisational aspects of domestic security intelligence are discussed. Is there a need for a specialised agency separate from the police? What is the relationship between 'law enforcement' and 'security intelligence'? How autonomous from ministerial direction and control are, or should be, the agencies? How, if at all, are government intelligence priorities transmitted to the agencies? There is also consideration of the agencies' resources – budgets and personnel, the problems of recruitment to a 'closed' agency, and the significance of organisational culture and communications.

Chapters 7 and 8 discuss oversight. Some general principles are established and are then used to examine the main alternative mechanisms which have been adopted in the UK and elsewhere at different levels of the state. The object here is not to argue that any particular foreign experiment will be appropriate to the UK – political institutions cannot be simply transplanted into different systems – but is to provide some comparative context for a discussion of what would be appropriate for the UK.

Finally, Chapter 9 presents the concluding argument that not enough is known about security intelligence processes in the UK, either by the public or by policy-makers outside the agencies themselves. The agenda for an inquiry is considered, bearing in mind that the motive for state inquiries is often to provide reassurance to the public that something is being done, rather than actually to have a real impact. Different possible forms of inquiry are considered. The inquiry's terms of reference should be wide and should include examination of the serious allegations made as to abuses of power by security intelligence agencies, the effectiveness of the agencies' functioning, and, in the light of their findings in these areas, proposals for future control and oversight procedures.

Since different writers on intelligence matters sometimes use different terminology to describe the same phenomenon, it will be useful before we go any further to make clear in

4

what sense certain key terms are being used throughout this analysis. In general 'information' is used to describe those pieces of knowledge, reports, publications, gossip, warnings, tip-offs and indiscretions which provide the raw material for collection agencies. 'Intelligence' describes the product of the process by which information is gathered, processed and analysed.

So we are concerned with the collection of information and production of intelligence by various state agencies but we are more interested in some of these than others. First, all state and non-state actors collect information relating to their 'environment' in an attempt to prepare themselves better for advancing or defending their interests. In the state sector, for example, military forces seek to produce intelligence on the capabilities of actual or potential adversaries, while, in the private sector, corporations do the same. Second, the state sector includes agencies for the production of foreign intelligence, which has been defined as 'information . . . on the capabilities, intentions and activities of foreign powers, organisations or their agents'.[6] This relates to various perceived threats – military, political or economic – (see Chapter 3 for full discussion) and may be gathered abroad or at home. These varieties of intelligence are discussed only incidentally here.

The main concern here is with what is variously described in the literature as counter-intelligence (CI), domestic intelligence or security intelligence. The first of these describes states' attempts to counter the intelligence-gathering efforts of others. For example, (foreign) CI has been defined officially in the US as 'activities conducted to protect the United States and United States' citizens from espionage, sabotage, subversion, assassination or terrorism'.[7] Harry Ransom defined CI similarly as being directed against 'hostile foreign intelligence operations' but added:

> In essence it is a police function. More specifically its purpose is to protect information against espionage, to guard personnel against subversion, and to secure installations or material against sabotage.[8]

Roy Godson of the Consortium for the Study of Intelligence suggested CI be described as 'the identification, neutralization and, under certain conditions, manipulation of other countries' intelligence services'.[9] The main feature common to these definitions is that CI is concerned with foreign threats. Therefore in the US, whence those definitions of CI emanate, there has been a tendency to distinguish 'domestic intelligence' from CI.[10]

For example, Abram Shulsky defines the state's concern with domestic intelligence as being:

> with threats against its ability to govern, or its very existence, that arise from individuals or groups within the nation's borders. Such threats could come from groups that seek to overthrow the government by illegal means, that seek to use violence to change government policies, or that seek to exclude from the body politic members of a given ethnic, racial, or religious group.[11]

The US Comptroller General similarly defined it as 'gathering information on individuals within the United States who allegedly attempt to overthrow the government or deprive others of their civil liberties or rights'.[12] Richard Morgan defined the term as 'information-gathering and record keeping which is unrelated to a particular, known crime and is directed at persons and groups engaged in political activity'.[13] All these definitions include, implicitly or explicitly, the political nature of the targets of domestic intelligence. It is this factor which leads some analysts to describe domestic intelligence agencies as 'political police',[14] and is what distinguishes it from 'criminal' or law enforcement intelligence. The intelligence process is much the same for domestic and criminal intelligence; it is likely to be the specific targets which are different.

This book is primarily concerned with domestic intelligence but the term 'security intelligence' is preferred since, as its usage has developed in Canada in particular, the phrase most accurately conveys the areas of state intelligence activity to be discussed. Security intelligence is sometimes defined more narrowly as referring just to the security of the information, property and personnel of an agency but here the term 'protective security' will be used to describe these functions. In the analysis that follows, security intelligence is used as a generic term to describe the state's gathering of information about and attempts to counter perceived threats to its security deriving from espionage, sabotage, foreign-influenced activities, political violence and subversion. Accordingly, security intelligence agency is the term used to describe the specific bodies established by the state to carry out this function.

For too long state security intelligence activity, even in self-proclaimed liberal democracies, proceeded unchecked. During the last 20 years efforts have been made in many countries to bring the 'secret state' to account. This book seeks to show why such democratisation is required in the UK and how it might be achieved.

NOTES

1. R. Whitaker, 'Security and Intelligence in the Post-Cold War World', in R. Miliband and L. Panitch (eds), *New World Order?* (London: Merlin Press, 1992), pp. 111–30.
2. These agencies provide the primary institutional focus of the book. Other agencies, for example, SIS and GCHQ, include security intelligence functions within their broader mandate to collect foreign intelligence, but they do not receive detailed attention here.
3. *New Statesman*, 5 December 1986, p. 14; *New Statesman and Society*, 20 December 1991, p. 7.
4. K.G. Robertson, 'Editorial Comment: An Agenda for Intelligence Research', *Defense Analysis*, 3(2), 1987, p. 96.
5. Cf. G. Hastedt, 'Towards the Comparative Study of Intelligence', *Conflict Quarterly*, XI(3), 1991, pp. 55–72.
6. Executive Order of the President 11905, 18 February 1976.
7. Ibid. Different definitions of CI, from both before and after 1975, are discussed in N.S. Miler, 'Counterintelligence at the Crossroads' in R. Godson (ed.), *Intelligence Requirements for the 1980s: Elements of Intelligence* (Washington DC: National Strategy Information Center, revised edition, 1983), pp. 45–51.
8. H.H. Ransom, *Central Intelligence and National Security* (Cambridge, MA: Harvard University Press, 1958), p. 13.
9. R. Godson, 'Elements of Intelligence: an Introduction', in Godson (ed.), supra (note 7), p. 7.

10. For example, the Consortium for the Study of Intelligence published a separate volume on 'Domestic Intelligence' in their Intelligence Requirements series: National Strategy Information Center, Washington DC, 1986.

11. A.N. Shulsky, *Silent Warfare: Understanding the World of Intelligence* (Washington DC: Brassey's (US) Inc., 1991), p. 4.

12. Report to the House of Representatives Committee on the Judiciary, *FBI Domestic Intelligence Operations – Their Purpose and Scope*, 24 February 1976, quoted in R.E. Morgan, *Domestic Intelligence: Monitoring Dissent in America* (Austin: University of Texas Press, 1980), p. 169.

13. Morgan, ibid, p. 9.

14. For example, T. Bunyan, *The History and Practice of Political Police in Britain* (London: Quartet Books, 1977); A.T. Turk, *Political Criminality: The Defiance and Defense of Authority* (London: Sage Publications, 1982), pp. 122–3.

1

What Do We Know and How Do We Know It?

The existing literature on security intelligence matters in the UK is both less extensive than in North America and, qualitatively, has contributed less to the development of a systematic body of knowledge. No attempt is made to discuss all the published work on the domestic security intelligence agencies in the UK. The objective is to provide an overview of the main contributions to what we know in order to establish a context for our analysis.

In a 1980 book review, Harry Ransom identified four main categories of the extensive literature on intelligence matters which had appeared in the United States since 1974. First, memoirs of former intelligence officers had been published with the help of the agencies themselves and had been subject to pre-publication review and consequently 'sanitised'. Second, 'whistleblowing exposés' had been written by disgruntled former intelligence officers, reformist journalists or activists. Third, attempts to analyse intelligence activities had been made by social scientists working primarily from non-secret sources; and fourth, there were a large number of congressional or executive branch studies, hearings and reports.[1] For reasons that will become apparent, it would be artificial to impose precisely the same categories on the UK literature but the same broad categorisation can be usefully employed.

'INSIDER' ACCOUNTS

The first group in the UK – the memoirs of former intelligence officers – is small; the main reason for this is that governments in general have taken the view that the publication of any insider accounts of security intelligence are, in the words of the Official Secrets Act 1989, 'damaging'.[2] Therefore there has been no development of systematic procedures for pre-publication review such as exist in the US. For example, between January 1977 and March 1983, 170 authors submitted 430 items for approval to the Publications Review Board, and none was completely prohibited. On the other hand, some authors have ignored these procedures, for example Frank Snepp with his highly critical account of the CIA in Vietnam, *Decent Interval*.[3] Such works as have emerged with official blessing in the UK have done so on an erratic basis. For example, Lord Ismay, Churchill's Minister of Defence, is said to have given semi-official blessing to the publication in 1953 of *The Man Who Never Was* by writing an introduction to it.[4] In general the powerful have been relatively prepared to see officials publish stories of (successful) wartime operations compared with the complete embargo that has been placed on writing about peacetime security operations.

The first main example of the former was J. C. Masterman's *The Double Cross System*. Masterman was one of a group of mainly Oxford academics recruited to MI5 from 1940 onwards who worked in B.1.A, the section concerned with double agents. Specifically, Masterman chaired the Twenty (XX) Committee which co-ordinated the efforts of all the intelligence departments in running the system by which German agents were discovered, and in some cases 'turned' to feed disinformation back to Germany. As he left the Security Service in 1945 Masterman was asked to write a report on the double-cross system, with access to all the relevant documents and, at that time, no thought of publication.[5] The result is a detailed discussion of the theory and the practice of the double-cross system, the objectives of which were:

1. To control the enemy system, or as much of it as we could get our hands on
2. To catch fresh spies when they appeared
3. To gain knowledge of the personalities and methods of the German Secret Service
4. To obtain information about the code and cypher work of the German service

10

5. To get evidence of enemy plans and intentions from the questions asked by them
6. To influence enemy plans by the answers sent to the enemy
7. To deceive the enemy about our own war plans and intentions.[6]

Most of the report consists of a detailed discussion of specific operations between 1941 and 1945, but Masterman also ventures some more general observations on the value of counter-espionage measures, including their relevance in peacetime. Given the success of the double-cross system against Germany, he argues, perhaps not surprisingly, that the only safe rule of conduct for any nation is to adopt counter-espionage against any other country, friend or enemy, which indulges in espionage, and that the key to success is a 'carefully cultivated double agent system'.[7] It is impossible to say, of course, whether the system was as successful as Masterman argues, because, for example, of the problems in quantifying how much of the disinformation fed back to Germany actually reached the decision-makers.[8]

When the study was eventually published in 1972 Masterman acknowledged that his initial proposal 'some years ago' was 'premature' but that government permission had now been granted.[9] Apparently, Masterman had approached several directors-general of the Security Service without success, but once Masterman informed the then Home Secretary, Reginald Maudling, that the book had been accepted for publication in the US, he was invited to see both Maudling and the Foreign Secretary. Eventually publication with few changes was authorised whereupon HMSO appeared to claim all the royalties. They finally accepted 50 per cent.[10] It is interesting to consider why another Conservative government, 15 years later, did not adopt a similar strategy to deal with Peter Wright's intended publication of *Spycatcher*.[11]

In this category also is the work of R.V. Jones, though it derives from his time with the SIS rather than MI5. *Most Secret War* was published in 1978 as an account of British scientific intelligence during the war. Jones solved the problem of access to materials by taking with him at the end of the war the 60 wartime reports he had written. The government initially told him that nothing could be published but after 'much haggling with the

Cabinet Office, MI6 and the D-Notice Committee' an acceptable text was negotiated.[12] When Jones published his more wide-ranging *Reflections on Intelligence* in 1989 his Acknowledgements made clear the extent of official co-operation he had received from the UK government: 'Repeated encouragement has come from many authorities in the United States . . .'[13]

There is one example of security intelligence history which was written with the full co-operation of the authorities. Hinsley and Simkins wrote the fourth volume of the official history of *British Intelligence in the Second World War*. The first three volumes dealt with the influence of intelligence on strategy and operations while the fourth, entitled *Security and Counter-Intelligence*,[14] dealt with counter-espionage, protective security, and deception operations in Britain and overseas. The authors say that no constraints were imposed on them during the research, but they distinguish, as did the government, between two types of source. Records of the service intelligence directorates which would be placed in the Public Records Office could be referred to in footnotes, but a second type of record could be consulted but not referred to as a source. These were the 'domestic' files of, for example, the Security Service, 'which are unlikely to be opened in the Public Record Office'.[15] Otherwise, the authors say, they were restricted in their use of records only to the extent that secrecy about intelligence techniques and regarding individuals remained essential. Thus, as history, this remains a partial account, and one whose publication was blocked for nearly ten years by Prime Minister Margaret Thatcher.[16] The book sits somewhat uneasily in this category because it is much more than a personal memoir and, having been written by two historians, might be seen as belonging to the third category. But both authors were 'insiders': Harry Hinsley spent the war at the Government Code and Cypher School at Bletchley, while from 1945 to 1971 Anthony Simkins, according to the flyleaf, 'was attached to the War Office and the Ministry of Defence'. Thus while official sanction could be given to a book discussing explicitly MI5 activities during the war, the fact that one of the authors served in MI5 thereafter still had to remain a secret! Simkins in fact was Deputy Director-General when he retired in 1971.

The memoir with the most spectacular impact was *Spycatcher*. Before this was published, Peter Wright's views had been anonymously canvassed via Chapman Pincher in 1981 and 1984 (see below). In 1984 Wright himself appeared on a Granada TV programme broadcast on 16 July – *The Spy Who Never Was*. In this, Wright recounted some of his major allegations regarding Hollis and his revelations of MI5 operations against the Communist Party and investigations of Harold Wilson. No attempt was made by the government to stop the programme. Wright's determination to produce his own book was apparently based on the failure of earlier revelations to stir the authorities into action. It was compounded by the trials of Geoffrey Prime (1983) and Michael Bettaney (1984) which convinced him that Soviet penetration continued unabated and, perhaps, of the inadequacy of the pension he claimed he was receiving from the Security Service. For its part the government's case, pursued against the publisher Heinemann in the Australian courts, was that the book would damage liaison between the Security Service and its allies, might encourage others to write their memoirs, might assist terrorists and, by a process of collateral verification, might assist Soviet intelligence.[17] The government's case was unsuccessful, largely because the inconsistencies of previous official policy regarding publication of security intelligence material were ruthlessly exposed by the defence.[18]

The other book which is worthy of note since it echoes a number of the themes of this discussion is *Inside Intelligence* by Anthony Cavendish. He makes it clear that his objective in writing the book was to defend the reputation of Maurice Oldfield against the smear that he had been a practising homosexual.[19] Cavendish himself served in the SIS only briefly between 1948 and 1953 but his friendship and regular contact with Oldfield continued until the latter's death in 1981. Oldfield became Chief of the SIS in 1973 and retired in 1978. Then, in October 1979 he was appointed to be Intelligence Co-ordinator in Belfast, as part of an effort to resolve the 'intelligence wars' in Northern Ireland, but by June 1980 he was forced to leave the post because of illness. From 1973 onwards, it is said, Oldfield was subjected to bureaucratic and then personal attack, primarily orchestrated by MI5, which perceived itself as having most to lose from SIS involvement in Northern Ireland and, later, Oldfield's co-ordinating activities. Some of these smears found their way into the public domain via Chapman Pincher.[20]

Cavendish also endured a lengthy legal battle before his book was finally published in 1990. He started writing it shortly after Oldfield's death, abandoned it when SIS made their displeasure clear, and then completed it after further smears against Oldfield appeared in 1987. SIS again told Cavendish that it could not be published, whereupon he had 500 copies printed and circulated to the 'Establishment' as 'Christmas cards' in December 1987. For the next 18 months a variety of legal battles were fought in England and Scotland as the government sought to prevent further publication, but they finally lost when the House of Lords rejected the government case against a number of newspapers which had printed extracts.[21]

'USUALLY RELIABLE SOURCES'?

One consequence of successive governments refusing to countenance former officials publishing their memoirs has been the growth of a minor cottage industry of writers producing agency histories which are clearly based on 'insider' sources. To the extent that officials and former officials have been disinclined to try to publish their own work, they have made use of various writers to bring their arguments into the public domain. An early example of the genre was *MI5* published in 1963 and written by a journalist, John Bulloch. It was primarily concerned with the period of MI5's establishment in 1909 through the First World War and was written as a tribute to Vernon Kell who was Director-General from 1909 to 1940.[22] Since Kell died in 1942 he did not provide Bulloch with material, but his widow did and her help is acknowledged by the author. Given this, it is perhaps not surprising that the book is entirely uncritical of the Security Service – it concentrates on the counter-espionage activities of the Service and sees great strength in the fact that the organisation was still essentially the same in 1963 as it had been when Kell brought it to 'fighting strength' at the start of the First World War.[23] In adopting such an uncritical stance the author gave several hostages to fortune. For example, in discussing Kell's recruitment principle that 'no one should be accepted who was not of pure British stock', Bulloch accepts that this might seem somewhat 'Blimpish' but argued that the policy clearly worked because of the absence of defectors or leaks from the Security Service, as compared with other intelligence agencies.[24] Subsequently, of course, we were to learn of Blunt.

Somewhat unusually, the book indicates that it was 'Reprinted before publication April 1963'. This was the result first of the publisher's being contacted by the secretary of the D-Notice Committee and then of a meeting between author, publisher, the Home Secretary and Roger Hollis, then Director General of MI5. The authorities argued that the publication would be contrary to the 'public interest' rather than to the Official Secrets Act, and it was agreed that the government would pay the costs of replacing some pages and rebinding. The book then sold a great deal more copies than had been anticipated, although nothing on the scale of *Spycatcher*.[25]

In praising MI5, Bulloch commented that he had never received a story, or even a hint of a story from them.[26] Other authors who were to publish material relating to MI5 in subsequent years appear to have been luckier. One of these was Chapman Pincher, for many years a journalist on the *Daily Express* who clearly had a number of contacts within the intelligence agencies well before becoming the conduit through which Peter Wright sought initially to make his case regarding Soviet penetration of the Security Service. In his first book on these matters, *Inside Story*, published in 1978, Pincher recounts how he had been briefed in February 1956 by the head of MI5's legal department. He was told that there would be a continuing KGB exercise using Burgess and Maclean's appearance in Moscow to ferment distrust between the USA and UK services, and a story was duly published. Pincher claims to have been astute enough to perceive (perhaps with the benefit of hindsight) that what the authorities were really concerned about was the naming of further moles,[27] but the problem for the journalist relying on leaks and secret briefings from within security intelligence agencies is that it will be frequently impossible to find collateral for stories. Sometimes they might receive accurate information; at others it is likely to be disinformation.[28]

Inside Story was not concerned solely with MI5 and nor were Pincher's subsequent books; their primary concern was with the penetration of the British Security and Secret Intelligence

Services by their Soviet counterparts. *Their Trade is Treachery*, published in 1981 and then *Too Secret Too Long*, in 1984, derived primarily from Pincher's contact with Peter Wright and the latter's determination to put his case before the public. Some hint of what was to come had been provided in *Inside Story* which contained the first of what were to become three main versions of Wright's story regarding the plot to destabilise the Labour government of 1974–76.[29] This version was about

> One senior MI5 officer [who] had become so incensed by the activities of two particular ministers that he decided it was urgently in the national interest for them to be exposed, irrespective of what his Director-General, then Sir Michael Hanley, or the Prime Minister might decree.[30]

Realising that such action would at the least end his career, the officer, so the story went, attempted to secure his future prospects with a job offer from the City. When any promise failed to materialise 'the MI5 officer completely lost heart and kept both his silence and his job'.[31]

After his retirement in 1976, Wright's silence lasted until Thatcher's Commons statement on the Blunt affair in November 1979. He was specifically concerned that the Prime Minister had been wrongly briefed by the Security Service, and prepared a dossier entitled 'The Security of the UK against the assault of the Russian Intelligence Service', which he hoped to deliver via Lord Rothschild to the PM. He was persuaded instead to pass the material to Chapman Pincher who, it was suggested, would be most likely to be able to secure publication of the material. The issue of how the government of the day determined that they would not seek to prevent the publication of *Their Trade is Treachery* became a central plank in the defence strategy to defend the eventual publication of *Spycatcher* in 1986.[32]

It is clear that the development of Wright's argument complemented Pincher's own beliefs regarding both the extent of Soviet penetration and the fact that its occurrence had been concealed from the public, and this was the prime purpose of the book. Pincher said that he had wanted for some time to give the general public the fullest possible details of the appalling penetration of Whitehall, including the security and intelligence services, by Soviet spies and saboteurs . . . Here it is.[33]

However, if it had been Wright's intention to provoke an inquiry into his allegations, then publication of *Their Trade is Treachery* will have disappointed him because Pincher said in the final chapter of the first version of the book:

> To anyone who has the genuine interests of MI5 and the Secret Service at heart, as I hope they have, there are basic objections to an outside inquiry of any kind.[34]

Instead, part of the official reaction to the publication of the book was the establishment of a Security Commission (see Chapter 7) inquiry. Its report was not published but the government issued a statement incorporating some of the Security Commission's recommendations, mainly relating to minor changes in the positive vetting system.[35]

Despite this, Pincher and Wright continued to co-operate, and in 1984 *Too Secret Too Long* was published, in which Pincher provided a more detailed exposition of the arguments relating to Soviet penetration. Pincher had now changed his mind on the subject of oversight and argued that more effective secrecy would be aided by

> the setting up of an independent body with powers to oversee certain aspects of the work of the secret services and to report on them in detail to the Prime Minister and, in secure terms, to Parliament.[36]

Efficiency rather than any concern for the propriety of security intelligence operations was clearly Pincher's main concern, but he argued also that effective oversight would offer the only deterrent

> to another outrageous situation – the extent to which Parliament and the public have been systematically misled

17

by official statements and reports on security and espionage affairs.[37]

This is pretty rich given that Pincher claims in a later work that he, rather than Wright or anybody else in MI5, was the origin of Wilson's fears that there was a plot to destabilise his government.[38] Given Pincher's admitted role as a front for Security Service 'information policies', this claim should be treated sceptically.

In view of the partisan nature of Pincher's books, specifically regarding Hollis, it is not surprising that an opposing faction began to respond, and in the process of defending Hollis, to identify another former MI5 official as the 'mole'. Rupert Allason, under the pen name Nigel West, wrote *MI5*, first published in 1981, and *A Matter of Trust: MI5 1945–72* first published in 1982. Allason and his researchers over a period of about three years contacted former members of the Security Service and the other UK agencies, a number of MI5's wartime double-agents, FBI, CIA, assorted Chief Constables, foreign embassies and others in order to obtain the information for the books. There are no acknowledgements in the second book, so presumably the list in the first covered both. Allason is more explicit than Pincher about the methods by which he set about gathering his information and he has set out also to provide a somewhat more systematic view of the Security Service. For example he started by establishing organisation charts for the Service which were eventually published in both books, along with, in most cases, the names of branch heads at different times.

Some names were removed from *A Matter of Trust* after the government obtained an *ex parte* injunction against the book. No threat was apparently made to prosecute Allason under the Official Secrets Act but, when the government saw that any civil action against the book would be defended, it backed off, having obtained just the exclusion of some names.[39] It was a curious episode: the D-Notice Committee was offered a copy of the manuscript but, before they had replied, the Attorney General applied for the injunction, MI5 having meanwhile obtained its own copy! The D-Notice Committee accepted the offer on the very day the injunction was granted and therefore could not be

18

provided with a copy! Needless to say, the main effect of all this was to ensure yet greater sales for the book and the paperback edition included a new Introduction quoting proudly from the government's affidavit requesting the injunction.[40]

The first of the books dealt with the period from MI5's origins until 1939, with the outbreak of war and Kell's dismissal, and with the war itself. Although the discussion ends in 1945 there is a Postscript which discusses some implications of the exposure of Anthony Blunt and then makes some critical comments about Pincher's *Their Trade is Treachery*. Pincher was right, says 'West', to say that Hollis had been the subject of an investigation by the Fluency Committee, which was established as a joint MI5/MI6 committee to investigate the penetration of the two services in the wake of Philby's defection and Golitsin's initial allegations. However, 'West' continued, Pincher was wrong to say that Burke Trend, the Cabinet Secretary, had been called in to investigate Hollis further and also wrong to claim that Trend's report had concluded that Hollis 'was the likeliest suspect' for a Soviet agent within MI5.[41] In *A Matter of Trust*, 'West' gave more detailed attention to the issue of Soviet penetration and repeated his argument that the evidence produced by the 'molehunters' on the Fluency Committee was 'inconclusive'.[42] By 1987, however, when *Molehunt* was published, Allason took a stronger line and identified an alternative mole to Hollis, the Pincher-Wright candidate. Allason identified Graham Mitchell, who first worked in counter-subversion when he joined MI5 in 1939, was Director of D Branch (counter-espionage) after the war until 1956 when he was promoted to Deputy Director-General where he remained until his early retirement in 1963.[43] While acknowledging that the case against Mitchell is equally circumstantial to that against Hollis, 'West' argues it is more substantial.[44] If one leaves aside the apparently chimerical search for the elusive 'fifth man' (more recently 'identified' by Andrew and Gordievsky as John Cairncross[45]) there is useful material in the work of each of these authors. Given their willingness to act as conduits for particular partisan views of the history of security intelligence operations in the UK, however, their work must be handled carefully.

Finally in this category, Rupert Allason, this time under his own name, also wrote a history of the Metropolitan Police Special Branch published in its centenary year.[46] This is another very useful albeit uncritical book which, compared with those on the Security Service, rests more on material excavated from the Public Records Office. It makes use also of the help of former branch officers, including two retired heads.[47] One of these, Leonard Burt, Commander of the Branch between 1946 and 1958, went so far as to write the Foreword to the book, but there is not the same sense here of sources pursuing intra-organisational battles.

CRITICAL ACCOUNTS

Ransom's second category was that of 'whistleblowing' exposés, written by disgruntled former intelligence professionals, reformist journalists or activists. Since the motivations of these various groups, and of individuals within any group, can diverge widely, it is not entirely useful to see them as simply one category. We discussed some 'disgruntled' insiders above. What distinguishes Wright and Cavendish, apart from their desire to attack or defend particular colleagues, is that their right-wing politics led them only reluctantly into opposition to the Conservative governments of the day. Neither was proposing major changes to control and oversight structures for security intelligence; rather, they argued that specific governments had been too weak to root out enemies of the state, or to defend particular officers from bureaucratic attack. Yet, clearly, the implications of their analysis for the problems to be found within the security intelligence agencies might be more far-reaching than their own analysis envisaged.

Fred Holroyd's critical account indicates the present impossibility of obtaining serious inquiries into the abuse of intelligence and subsequent countering operations. Fred Holroyd's *War Without Honour* was published in 1989, although it was not the first time his allegations had been voiced.[48] Holroyd had joined the Army in 1960 and first went to Northern Ireland as a Military Intelligence Officer in 1973 where, during 1974–75 he became aware of a variety of dirty tricks engaged in by the Army, MI5, MI6 and the RUC, on both sides of the border. These ranged from the 'professionally disreputable to murder'.[49]

After a few months he was recruited by MI6[50] and during 1975–76 became embroiled in the intelligence war by which

MI5 was seeking to take over the Northern Irish 'turf' from MI6. When Holroyd had been recruited by MI6 he had gone to seek the approval of his commanding officer 'Colonel D'. 'D' approved Holroyd working for SIS as long as he gave 'D' a copy of everything that passed his way. Subsequently Holroyd discovered that 'D' was actually working for MI5, as was his successor as Holroyd's army boss. Holroyd draws an interesting and important distinction between the *modi operandi* of the two agencies at the time. While acknowledging that MI6 was 'certainly capable of running some dubious operations', for example, organising the Littlejohn brothers' bank robberies in 1972, that agency defined the 'name of the game [as] essentially persuasion, penetration, information'. This involved taking a long-term view that ultimately a political settlement would be required and therefore alienation of the Republican community was pointless. In contrast, the agent handlers brought in by MI5, including some from the SAS, pursued a policy that involved coercing and blackmailing sources into carrying out deniable operations out of fear of exposure. Such a policy, said Holroyd, had only short-term pay-offs, if any, and no long-term gains at all.[51] Holroyd may have been a little kind to MI6 inasmuch as the SAS has, since 1945, been the sharp end of MI6 operations rather than MI5's; but there is evidence that the use of aggressive counter-insurgency techniques by mixed 'pseudo-gangs' of army personnel, loyalist paramilitaries and 'turned' Republicans dated from 1972[52] when, it is said, MI5 appeared in the province.[53]

Later in 1975 Holroyd was removed from Northern Ireland on the pretext that he had suffered a breakdown, and was subjected to a period of 'Army psychiatry' at Netley, Hampshire. Just before he resigned from the Army in 1976 he began a long campaign to air his complaints regarding security force actions in Northern Ireland.[54] Eventually, in 1987 he was offered £150,000 compensation by the Ministry of Defence for his lost career, but, despite being broke, he turned the offer down because it was conditional on withdrawing support from Colin Wallace[55] whose own allegations were entirely consistent with Holroyd's. Mark Urban, a journalist with a brief army background, assesses the claims of both Holroyd and Wallace (see below) in a recent book, *Big Boys' Rules*. He concludes that much of what they say is true, particularly regarding the 'turf wars' and smearing of politicians. However, he argues that, on the basis of his own research, their claims of widespread collusion between security forces and Loyalist death squads are unproven.[56] John Stalker's investigation of the RUC[57] is examined in detail in Chapter 5.

Finally, brief mention is merited of one who has tried over many years and failed to get his views published: Jock Kane. He had worked in GCHQ and since 1973 had sought to expose what he saw as the security weaknesses and corruption in GCHQ which made it highly vulnerable to penetration. After taking early retirement, Kane's views were published in a *World in Action* programme and the *New Statesman* in 1980,[58] and in 1983 Robert Hale were about to publish his book. Special Branch officers seized all the copies of the book (and went to the US to reclaim copies of the manuscript) but Kane was never prosecuted under the Official Secrets Act; instead an injunction was obtained against publication on the basis of the civil law of confidence (as would be attempted subsequently against Peter Wright). To date the proceedings are going nowhere, while the injunction lasts the government achieves its aim.[59]

As with Wright and Cavendish, it is important to note that in the case of Holroyd, Stalker and Kane, the allegations against the abuse of the security intelligence process are based not upon any general critique of state power, but on two separate concerns, both of which are central to this analysis. First, there is the question of the effectiveness of the security intelligence process and the extent to which the secrecy within which it is shrouded is maintained mainly to prevent revelations of the sheer bureaucratic ineptitude to which the process is prone; and, second, the extent to which the lack of democratic control of the process has led to systematic abuse of power by the state.

The second group of works within this 'critical' category have been written by various journalists and activists whose perspective has been much more to expose security intelligence abuses as part of a civil libertarian critique of the state. The first attempt to describe the domestic security intelligence apparatuses of the state in the UK, and to do so within a general explanatory theory, was Tony Bunyan's *The History and Practice of the Political Police in Britain*, first published in 1976. The book is important because it set out the 'interdependent matrix'[60] of the state institutions engaged in countering political movements: it discussed first the political uses of the law, including the Official Secrets Acts, conspiracy, and emergency powers, and then the uniformed police, Special Branch and MI5. It examined also the techniques of surveillance used by these agencies and the private security industry.

Subsequent work in the UK has not always attempted to build on Bunyan's systematic analysis of these matters. David Leigh's *The Frontiers of Secrecy* published in 1980 is primarily 'a polemic against secrecy in British life'.[61] The strength of the book is that it covers a wide spectrum of the different ways in which information control contributes to the very limited public awareness of how power is exercised in Britain. It discusses how the Official Secrets Acts, classification procedures, D-Notices, contempt of court, and the Lobby system all contribute to this process and examines the role of the security intelligence agencies in jury-vetting. The British system is contrasted unfavourably with those elsewhere, for example, in Sweden, the US and Canada, where freedom of information laws exist. Although Leigh draws brief comparisons between the role of 'ministerial responsibility' in Britain and the 'separation of powers' in the US, he does not really provide an adequate analytical context for the debate. This would need more detailed analysis of the relationship between the centralisation of state power and information control in Britain.

Whereas secrecy provides a major background variable to all discussion of domestic security intelligence matters, employment vetting is just one of the tasks of security intelligence agencies. It has received more exposure than some other aspects of security intelligence operations in large part because it requires the Security Service to communicate with other organisations, some in the private sector, and the possibility of information becoming available consequently increases. *Blacklist*[62] provides the most comprehensive overview of vetting in Britain because it covers not just specific MI5 and Special Branch operations on behalf of the state, but examines vetting in the private sector and, importantly, the interaction between state and private sectors. The main central service for the latter since 1919 has been the Economic League and this is the subject of detailed scrutiny in the book *The Economic League: The Silent McCarthyism*, published by the Civil Liberties Trust in 1989, which builds on the material in *Blacklist*. The League was formed in 1919 under the tutelage of 'Blinker' Hall who had just retired as Director of Naval Intelligence. At this time Hall was supporting Basil Thomson, head of Special Branch, in his post-war effort to establish a new peacetime intelligence service which would have domestic subversion as its main target (see Chapter 6).[63] This book is complemented by Ian Linn's examination of the history and present practice of the state in vetting its own employees,[64] including brief comparative information on procedures in Australia, Canada and Sweden.

There is one other book which should be noted here: *In Defence of the Realm?*[65] by Richard Norton-Taylor, the *Guardian* journalist, places present security intelligence operations in the context of the 'closed world' of the executive-dominated British political process in Britain. In addition to special branches and the Security Service, he looks also at the roles of MI6 and GCHQ and the significance of the *network* of agencies. Again, there is brief consideration of practice elsewhere in Europe, North America and Australia and, finally, a consideration of the case for greater accountability of the security intelligence agencies. The proposals made are considered in more detail in Chapters 7 and 8 below.

Finally in this category there are three books which, taken together, comprise the most systematic statement of the case that groups within the security intelligence agencies, particularly the Security Service, directed their information-gathering and disseminating practices against a number of elected politicians, especially during the 1970s and particularly against Harold Wilson. Paul Foot's *Who Framed Colin Wallace?* (1989) examines in great detail the career and trials of Colin Wallace. He started work as a public relations officer for the Army in Northern Ireland in 1968, was promoted to information officer in 1970 and commissioned into the UDR in 1972. Until 1974 Wallace was involved in successive disinformation campaigns directed at the paramilitary groups in Northern Ireland, but during that year he became increasingly critical of the changing direction that disinformation policy was taking. Specifically, not long after MI5 had taken over control of intelligence in Northern Ireland from MI6 in 1973, an information offensive called 'Clockwork Orange' was initiated. The initial objective was to expose the personal vulnerabilities of paramilitary commanders through the construction of mythical stories. Most of the original material was provided by intelligence agencies. From 1974, however, the information that Wallace received from MI5 increasingly concerned the alleged financial and sexual vulnerabilities of British politicians.[66] In October 1974 he declined to work further on Clockwork Orange and a month later wrote a memo complaining about the continuing lack of police action regarding the Kincora Boys' Home. It had been known to the police and MI5 that workers at the home, who were senior Protestant paramilitaries, had been subjecting inmates to sexual abuse, but instead of action being taken against the workers (this did not happen until the case was publicised in 1980), the knowledge had been used as a device to gather information from those involved and to sow dissension between different Protestant groups.[67]

In December 1974 Wallace was told he was to be removed from Northern Ireland for a new job in Preston. In February 1975 he was suspended from duty for 'leaking' an army document (something he had spent several years doing as part of his job) to a journalist when he left for Preston. He was dismissed from the Army, but reinstated after he appealed. Subsequently, after he had resigned from the Army, Wallace met the Conservative Member of Parliament, Airey Neave, who asked for and was given some of his disinformation material which Neave used later in a speech. In 1980 Wallace was working as a local government public relations officer in Sussex when Jonathan Lewis, the husband of a colleague with whom Wallace's relationship had 'gone some way beyond mere friendship', was found dead.[68] Although the police initially said that foul play was not suspected, six weeks later Wallace was charged with murder. He was subsequently convicted of manslaughter and sentenced to ten years' imprisonment. He was paroled in December 1986. Foot's book is not just an exposé of the disinformation policies employed in Northern Ireland by the military and intelligence agencies, including the shifting of the target of disinformation policy in 1974 towards the Labour Party, but also presents the case that Wallace was framed for the death of Lewis. Pincher had referred obliquely to Wallace in 1978.[69] Subsequently, citing his unofficial briefings on the case, Pincher insists that Wallace was a fantasist who was removed from Northern Ireland because he was out of control.[70]

David Leigh's *The Wilson Plot* and Steve Dorril and Robin Ramsay's *Smear!* both examine in detail the attempts to discredit Harold Wilson which were allegedly orchestrated by the Security Service. Although it was the few pages Peter Wright devoted to this subject in *Spycatcher* which first gave massive publicity to the idea of such a 'plot', both these books tell us a great deal more about it, and point out that Wright himself gave several versions of what happened in the 1970s (see Chapter 5 below for detailed discussion).[71] One difference between these books is that while Leigh makes only two references to Northern Ireland, Dorril and Ramsay give much greater significance to events there. While Leigh's examination of the Wilson plot rests primarily on the supposed Soviet subversion of the Labour Party, this provides just one thread in Dorril and Ramsay's analysis. The other major strand in *Smear!* is the whole area of counter-insurgency thinking which grew in influence from the later 1960s onwards. This inspired policy in Northern Ireland after 1975[72] and came to feature also in the conspiracy theories of the Right regarding British politics during the 1970s. The person who has given such an argument a great deal more credence now than it would have enjoyed some years ago is, of course, Colin Wallace who has provided, for the first time, primary evidence of MI5 material[73] which, Dorril and Ramsay argue, shows that

> the secret state and its allies had embarked not just on a campaign against the Labour government, but against the whole of the liberal-left of British politics. The ambition shining through Wallace's version of MI5's thinking between the elections of 1974 is nothing less than the realignment of British domestic politics along hard Right lines.[74]

Despite the subsequent triple general election success of Margaret Thatcher, this might seem something of an overstatement. There is a danger that this argument provides a 'mirror-image' of the fantasy on the Right during the 1970s that rising industrial militancy presaged the 'realignment of British politics' along Soviet lines, but clearly the Rightists installed within the secret state were in a powerful position at least to set about achieving part of their ambition by discrediting the parties representing the major alternatives. The significance of the political climate in the 1970s is discussed further in Chapter 2.

ACADEMIC WRITINGS

Ransom's third category of literature was written by 'social scientists attempting to analyse objectively' aspects of intelligence activities, working primarily from non-secret sources. In 1986 he published a further review primarily of American works in this category.[75] The main contributions in Britain have come from two academic specialisms: historians and lawyers. Work on intelligence from the main social science disciplines – politics and sociology – is extremely thin on the ground.

The first comprehensive examination of 'The Making of the British Intelligence Community', to quote the sub-title, was Christopher Andrew's *Secret Service*. Dealing briefly with nineteenth-century developments, including the birth of Special Branch,[76] the bulk of the book deals with the main intelligence services from 1909 to 1945. More attention is given to foreign intelligence but there are also useful accounts of major aspects of domestic security intelligence, including the roles of and rivalry between MI5 and Special Branch during and after the First World War, the course of security intelligence in Ireland between 1914 and 1922, and domestic security operations against 'subversion' and fascism in the 1930s. Andrew notes at the outset that 'Whitehall has done what it can to discourage serious study of the making of the British intelligence community'[77] so this is an important book because it does represent a major breach in what for years had been a complete unwillingness among academics – historians and others – to study secret intelligence processes, either in their own right or as part of broader attempts to explain political processes and state power.

The mine of usual sources for the historian is even smaller for the post-war period than for earlier ones, and there is only one chapter in the book dealing with the post-1945 period. Andrew points out correctly that an overall assessment of this period is impossible because those parts of the record which do become public are unlikely to be representative of the whole.[78]

27

He refers briefly, however, to Wilson's suspicions regarding MI5 but dismisses them:

> A prime minister who after eight years in office entertains suspicions, however improbable, that his own security service is plotting against him scarcely merits confidence in his administration.[79]

This emphasis on the earlier period is seen also in the work of the main historian of the development of the domestic security intelligence agencies in Britain, Bernard Porter. In *The Origins of the Vigilant State*, he traces the history of the Metropolitan Special Branch until 1914. His main argument is that, first, the founding of a political police in Britain was delayed for longer than elsewhere because

> the necessary relationship between government and people within a liberal capitalist economy, left no room, in the mid-Victorians' eyes, for counter-subversive measures.[80]

As Porter notes, this attitude combining rather than separating notions of economic and political freedom cannot be said to be true in the late twentieth century.[81] Porter shows how, by a combination of factors, the Special Branch slowly evolved from a generalised mistrust of secret, or even plain-clothes policing, into what was to become a political police. He identifies causes of this development in changes in personnel, secrecy and the fact that the Branch's early targets were primarily within the 'foreign fringes' of domestic British politics, specifically Irish nationalists and European anarchists. Thus the probability, as Porter puts it, that Special Branch at this time employed improper and illegal methods, including the use of *agents provocateurs*, gave rise to less controversy than when it started to target Britons after the First World War.

Porter's *Plots and Paranoia* (1989) takes a rather longer period – from 4,000 BC to AD 1988 – although the last 200 years provide the bulk of the material. Again concentrating on domestic security intelligence activities, Porter seeks to discuss 'the available evidence in its context'[82] and tries to analyse rather than simply provide a description of events. The Epilogue to the book presents some highly relevant observations on the problems of method in writing about intelligence, including the problems deriving from the (part-intentional, part-unintentional) falsification of the historical record. Both these books are written from the perspective of a liberal distaste for 'secret police' and point very clearly to the danger that the 'medicine' they provide might have effects as damaging as the 'disease' against which they are dispensed.[83] However, they do not relate the position of the security intelligence agencies adequately to the broader question of the position of the state and its relations with its UK subjects.

D.G.T. Williams's *Not in the Public Interest* provides the earliest example of academic work by a lawyer in the area of secrecy and internal security. The first part of the book deals with the origins and scope of the Official Secrets Acts, classification procedures and similar secrecy within local government, as well as the problems of censorship and D-Notices that have been encountered by the press. Williams also examines most of what was then known about MI5 including aspects of its counter-subversion and counter-espionage roles during and between the world wars and the main post-1945 security scandals from May and Fuchs to Vassall and Profumo. There is a section on security vetting and on the extent to which the courts provide a check on executive secrecy. Throughout, the discussion is thorough and the criticisms of British practice are carefully understated, for example: 'Where issues of executive secrecy crop up, the courts have on the whole been sympathetic to the claims of the executive'.[84] The extent to which this represented an academic voice in the wilderness at a time when so few academics were concerned to study such questions is demonstrated by the fact that Williams's conclusion remains as valid a quarter of a century on:

> The public interest has many facets, and it would be deplorable if the assessment of the public interest were to become the exclusive province of the executive itself. Secrecy and security have to be balanced against the legitimate demands for an informed public opinion which is, when all is said and done, the essential element in a country which claims to be democratic.[85]

Michael Supperstone's *Brownlie's Law of Public Order and National Security*[86] presents the 'black letter' law on treason, sedition, official secrecy, vetting, and interception of communications. It goes beyond a discussion purely of legal formulations as evidenced by the fact that there are five pages on the Security Service which, at the time of publication, had no legal charter. Also of interest is that British practice with respect to secrecy, security intelligence, and freedom of expression, is contrasted with the legal situation in the United States. In 1987 Supperstone published a further article[87] which again provided an interesting discussion going well beyond the purely formal aspects of the law, considering developments relating to the control and accountability of security intelligence in North America and concluding that a public debate on the best legislative and administrative framework 'to facilitate the conduct of proper intelligence activities' is required.[88]

Another work by a lawyer which is worthy of mention, and which might otherwise have been included in the exposé category is Geoff Robertson's *Reluctant Judas*.[89] This concerns the case of Kenneth Lennon who was shot in 1974, just two days after he had confessed to workers at the National Council for Civil Liberties that he had been acting as an informer and *agent provocateur* for Special Branch. Robertson examines critically the roles of police, prosecutors and press and shows the impact on the criminal justice process of the perceived needs of 'national security'.

Next are three books by lawyers, the common theme of which is state secrecy. James Michael's *The Politics of Secrecy*[90] examined not only the extent of secrecy in Britain but included three chapters looking at practice elsewhere. References to the security intelligence agencies in this book are incidental rather than central to the argument. In John Baxter's *State Security, Privacy and Information*[91] both the state's protection of its own information and its ability to invade citizens' privacy are covered. As far as information-gathering is concerned, Baxter concentrates on technical means rather than the most frequently used means of open sources and informers (see Chapter 4), which does give a somewhat skewed view of the state's activities. The third book, Patrick Birkinshaw's *Reforming the Secret State*[92] is more concerned with the legal technicalities of, first, the Official Secrets Act 1989 and, second, the Security Service Act

1989 but, as with Michael's book, he places the analysis within the comparative framework of foreign, especially US, practice. These two Acts, it might be mentioned, are also well reviewed by lawyers, but with a clear eye on the political context, respectively in S. Palmer, 'Tightening Secrecy Law'[93] and I. Leigh and L. Lustgarten, 'The Security Service Act, 1989'.[94]

In a brief article in 1987 Ken Robertson compared the nature of recent US work on intelligence matters with that in the UK: he made a number of important points and commented that:

> The relative neglect of intelligence by British political scientists, international relations experts and lawyers is staggering compared with their US counterparts.[95]

This remains the case. The work by lawyers referred to above is primarily concerned with issues of state secrecy and addresses intelligence questions only incidentally and that small body of work which does address intelligence directly appeared after 1987. Robertson, a sociologist, has made one of the few efforts to bring a social scientific perspective to the study of intelligence, for example, his piece on 'The Politics of Secret Intelligence – British and American Attitudes',[96] but, as if to reinforce the basic point, the journal he edited and in which this piece appears incorporates a majority of articles written by historians.

OFFICIAL REPORTS

Ransom's fourth category was the body 'of congressional and executive branch studies, hearings and reports' on intelligence matters. In the US there has been a large number of these and they reflect 'the compromises of facts and values required by the American competitive political process'.[97] The body of such reports in the UK is much smaller and provides a much more limited overview of the world of intelligence. If the American reports reflect the compromises required by a competitive political process, the limited nature of the British reports reflects the lack of any serious competitor to the centralised power of the executive branch. There is a detailed discussion in Chapter 9 of what is required by way of a proper inquiry into the security intelligence agencies; for now, suffice to say that one has to bear in mind what role state inquiries in general are intended to play. Discussing tribunals of inquiry, which have tended to be established to investigate improprieties or negligence in public life, Wraith and Lamb noted that discovering what happened and making recommendations to prevent recurrences is secondary to the primary aim of restoring public confidence and satisfying the public that a proper investigation had been made.[98]

Two additional themes run through the history of government inquiries and reports into security intelligence matters, only some of which are reviewed here. The first is the crucial nature of the terms of reference plus the influence of the inquiries' own decisions as to how to conduct their task; and the second is the extent to which inquiries have been misled by the security intelligence agencies concerned. Lord Denning's inquiry into the Profumo affair provides an early example of these themes. Part of the problem was in the nature of the inquiry established: it was non-statutory and Denning was to sit alone and in secret. Thus, as he described it, he 'had to be detective, inquisitor, advocate and judge and it has been difficult to combine them'.[99] 'Impossible' might have been more accurate. Denning's report did provide some service to students of security intelligence because, for the first time, some history of MI5's relationships with ministers was provided, including the 1952 Maxwell-Fyfe Directive.[100] However, it has been suggested that while Denning was told by MI5 that Ward was acting for them in a 'honey-trap' operation targeted at Ivanov, the Russian naval attaché, he chose not to mention this in his report. Instead this concentrated far more on blackening Ward's name in the context of allegations about call-girl rings and sexual perversions.[101] Alternatively, it has been argued that, despite Denning's claim to have been given full access to MI5's files and memoranda, he was misled.[102] If MI5 did not actually lie, it told only part of the story – in Robert Armstrong's words, it was 'economical with the truth'.

Even before the full extent of the inadequacies of Denning's Profumo Report were acknowledged, concern about the inquiry was partly responsible for the establishment in 1964 of the Security Commission, which has produced 15 reports since then into known or possible breaches of security (see Table 9.1 p. 329 for list). Reflecting the ultimate responsibility of the Prime Minister in matters of security intelligence, the Commission is activated as and when the PM determines; that is, it performs no permanent oversight function, and only abbreviated versions of its reports have been published. In a recent article about the Commission, one of its secretaries is quoted as describing its work as 'a constant process of challenging management to justify their decision'.[103] Yet one has to doubt the extent to which outsiders, without specialised help and only on an occasional basis, are able to have a serious impact on procedures. There might even be some doubt as to how hard they try. For example, the inquiry after the conviction of Geoffrey Prime began by interviewing the Director of GCHQ and then, we are told, 'talked with anyone else who might help decide what went wrong, including junior co-workers'.[104] One other person who surely could have thrown a great deal of light on Prime's ability to remove documents from GCHQ over a long period of time was Jock Kane who had been campaigning on the issue for years (see above) but he was not interviewed by the Commission.[105] Others suggest that the Commission can be simply misled by the Security Service, or, at least, can have its inquiries 'guided' by MI5 into channels which will do minimum damage.[106]

Another example of both themes is provided by the D-Notice affair in 1967. An article by Chapman Pincher appeared in the *Daily Express* outlining the process by which international telegrams were intercepted by the Post Office and made available to the intelligence services. An outraged Prime Minister established a committee of three Privy Councillors to investigate the alleged breach of a D-Notice and damage to national security.[107] A major reason for the government's concern was that any inquiry be limited since otherwise it might threaten to expose the UKUSA network of interception including the US National Security Agency (NSA) and GCHQ, still unacknowledged in Britain at this time. Thus official witnesses were induced to lie to the Committee under pressure from GCHQ and the Security Service and any references to GCHQ by witnesses were immediately jumped on by Lord Radcliffe, the Chair of the Committee. All the historical elements are present in this case: limited terms of reference, self-denial by the inquiry members and misleading evidence given by the security intelligence agencies.[108]

An excellent example of the 'self-denying ordinance' is provided by the one example of a legislative foray into the task of inquiring into security intelligence matters – the House of Commons Home Affairs Select Committee's inquiry into police Special Branches (1985). When the Committee first discussed the possibility of inquiring into Special Branches, it was warned by the then Home Secretary, Leon Brittan, that, because of the problems officers would have in giving detailed evidence, it 'could turn out to be a bit of a blind alley'.[109] And so it was to prove, if not for quite the reasons the Home Secretary predicted. The Committee decided at the outset not to investigate individual cases and to take all oral evidence in public. The eventual Report, which was not endorsed by the Labour minority, indulged in some dubious logic by saying that it could not investigate complaints or Special Branch working methods because they would have cast light on Security Service methods which would have 'assisted those opposed to the safety of the state'.[110] By accepting the taboo that secrecy must be absolute, the Committee therefore denied itself any chance of actually finding answers to the allegations that had been made about Special Branches. As the Church Committee had pointed out in 1975 in relation to US intelligence, relying on high-level briefings (as the Home Affairs Committee did) will simply not get at the necessary information; for that, access to documents and rank-and-file operatives is necessary.[111]

Finally, the Franks Committee inquiry into the Falklands invasion is relevant, not because of its specific subject matter, which was foreign and military rather than domestic security intelligence, but because it was established with five privy councillors, four from the Lords and one from the Commons, who were given complete access to intelligence reports, assessments and officers. This has been cited as a possible precedent for future Parliamentary review of the intelligence services.[112] However, it should be noted that although the Committee made some important recommendations about aspects of the intelligence process, particularly assessment, it remained coy on other questions. For example, its discussion of the Joint Intelligence Organisation and Committee refers only to the 'security and intelligence agencies' in general as participating in the process.[113]

What has not appeared in the UK is anything which reports on the security intelligence agencies to the extent that judicial and legislative inquiries have elsewhere; for example: Justice Hope's Royal Commission reports in Australia;[114] Justice McDonald's Royal Commission reports in Canada;[115] and the Senate Select Committee to Study Governmental Operations with respect to Intelligence Activities.[116] Taken together, the material provided by these inquiries demonstrates how important they can be in opening up the secret state to accountability and offering a rich source of material to help to frame the questions which should be asked in any such inquiry in the UK.

A RESEARCH STRATEGY

Researching and writing about security intelligence matters is fraught with difficulties;[117] doing so with respect to the UK is yet more so. Why? Researchers depend on information about their subject matter, and information on these matters is difficult to come by; therefore there may just be very little to go on. However the issue is as much qualitative as quantitative: any information which can be obtained has to be treated sceptically. As we have seen, this is the case whether the information is gleaned from official records, from the reported reminiscences of former intelligence officers, or from the mouths of those officers themselves. For various reasons all these sources are prone to different forms of inaccuracy – incompleteness, or partiality – but what they have in common is that the agencies concerned have a professional interest in the manipulation of information and its use as a tool in their trade. While all departments of state gather information and use information policies as adjuncts to their executive tasks, the gathering, analysis and use of information is the very *raison d'être* of the security intelligence agencies. Thus writing about the security intelligence world might be likened to attempting a large jig-saw puzzle when the picture on the box is incomplete, you have only a fraction of the pieces you need and some of those may well be from another puzzle altogether.

This problem with the quality and quantity of information available to researchers is aggravated in the case of the UK by the particularly secretive traditions of the state in the UK.

35

These traditions derive from the concentration of power in central institutions which is manifested in and legitimated by the concepts of parliamentary sovereignty and ministerial responsibility.[118] Whatever democratisation of the state has taken place during the last 200 years – for example, the extension of the franchise and growing involvement of organised groups in the policy process – it has occurred within a relatively unchanging climate of belief that the central state itself should remain the arbiter of what information is and is not published about its activities. Since this traditional state prerogative was first challenged during the second half of the nineteenth century, successive Official Secrets Acts have attempted to maintain central control of information processes. Hitherto in the UK there simply has been no alternative centre of political power that might have challenged this control. For example, there are no other units of government with autonomous political/constitutional authority, nor has the legislative assembly mounted a challenge because of its subordination to the executive via the system of majority party rule. Since governing parties have defined their interest as continuing control of the information process, secrecy is the 'cement' of the constitution.[119] Announcements by John Major after his election victory in 1992 that his government intends to provide more information about its activities does not change this.

These factors may well explain the relative lack of serious academic work into this question in the UK and perhaps it is right to leave the ground for future historians who can at least make use of the official papers when they are released in 30, 50, or 100 years' time, if ever or whenever some slip past the weeders and turn up in the Public Record Office.[120] But this would leave a serious gap in our contemporary political analysis of an important aspect of the state's operations since 'security intelligence' or 'political policing' goes to the very heart of the relationship between the state and its people – most accurately described as 'subjects' rather than 'citizens' in the UK.[121] This concerns the integrity of the democratic process itself; for example, the question of whether the state can contemplate its own transformation by its people without suppressing them in the name of 'national security'. Therefore it is argued here that such questions are simply too important for contemporary politics and political analysis to be left to the burrowings of future historians.

But if we are to attempt the puzzle, then how are we to proceed? Chambliss and Seidmann[122] suggest a useful methodology for law and society research. It begins, they say, with a 'discontent', or the identification of a particular problem. Second, alternative possible explanations for the problem must be prepared, making use of 'heuristics' (ways of finding out) drawn from past experience. These give us preliminary guides for tackling the problem under review. Third, once those possible explanations which fit the available information least well have been eliminated, those that are left can be used to construct alternative solutions to the problem. Finally, the selected solution must be implemented, and, over time, monitored and evaluated. In this way information is generated which can be used to test the preceding process. Such a methodology has a number of important features. First, it rejects the commonly expressed idea of a division between 'pure' and 'applied' research; 'problem-solving' or 'policy' research constitute parts of the same enterprise as 'academic' or 'theoretical' research. Second, a set of 'categories' or vocabulary will be required to guide empirical investigation in such a way that explanation is aided. Third, the approach requires an explicit perspective which depends on 'personal consciousness'; that is the researcher must make clear her or his 'domain assumptions' (in Gouldner's phrase) so that they can be challenged by others.[123]

This present work is actually capable of attempting only part of such a research cycle regarding security intelligence agencies in the UK, but also makes suggestions as to the ways in which the cycle might be completed. First, what is the problem? As we have seen throughout this chapter, during the last 15–20 years a series of allegations have been made by a variety of people – some security intelligence 'insiders', some not – about a number of security intelligence activities in the UK ranging from the unethical to the illegal. Some of these allegations are of conduct which was arguably more 'subversive' of the democratic process than anything targeted as such by the Security Service during this period. At one level, there has been the surveillance of trade unionists and peace campaigners, and the use of information gathered from such surveillance in campaigns of disinformation and disruption by the state.[124] At another level disinformation campaigns are said to have been directed at a democratically elected government.[125] At yet another level there are the allegations of extreme countering policies amounting to the summary execution of people believed to be engaged in serious political violence against the state.[126]

Second, what alternative possible explanations for these allegations can be proposed? Four main ones can be found scattered though the literature on the subject: that the allegations are false and come from former intelligence officers who are seeking to make money by writing scurrilous books or to settle old organisational scores; that the allegations are false and are made by those who for political reasons are setting out to discredit the state; that the allegations are true but that they reflect a legitimate use of state power in order to protect democratic decision-making structures and citizens from attack; or, finally, that the allegations are true and represent an illegitimate use of state power which represents a serious threat to democratic rights to life, privacy and freedom of speech.

How can we test these alternatives for 'best fit'? Bearing in mind that security intelligence agencies are part of the state bureaucracy, we can refer to what is known about the operations of such bureaucracies. For example, at the most general level what is the relationship between the bureaucracy and the social, political and economic structure? Regarding specific organisations, reference may be made to the different models of decision-making, the relationship between rules and discretion, between policy and implementation and between different groups or sub-cultures of officials.[127]

Acknowledging that in important respects security intelligence agencies are different from other state bureaucracies, we can also examine what has been ascertained elsewhere about such agencies.[128] In a number of other countries thorough inquiries have published much of their findings so that it is possible to create a clear model of the intelligence process as it operated within these agencies.[129] Of course, it is not possible to conclude that just because a security intelligence agency operates in a particular way in country A that it will do so in precisely the same way in country B, but we are interested in asking questions about the operation of the security intelligence agencies in the

UK rather than constructing the definitive account thereof, which would be impossible at this stage. Therefore, it is entirely legitimate to make use of foreign work, especially that based on agencies operating within political frameworks which are not totally dissimilar, for example the 'Washminster' systems of Australia and Canada. Richelson and Ball refer to a 'distinct pattern' of security intelligence activities in the UKUSA countries.[130]

The third and fourth parts of the research cycle cannot be completed by the present work; indeed, it is a central argument here that insufficient information is available at present to allow for movement on to the third stage. Inevitably this analysis concentrates on what is known (or alleged). The proposal for an inquiry is, in large part, an acknowledgement that much remains unknown.[131] Chapter 9 provides a detailed argument about the type of inquiry (and research) that will be required in order finally to identify the best of the possible 'explanations' defined above, and then to propose solutions to the problem. A once-and-for-all inquiry, however, could not be the end of the story because monitoring and evaluation of the implementation of the proposals would be required.

Two other features of the adopted methodological approach require comment here. As far as possible the analysis avoids unnecessarily complex jargon, but in key areas a specific vocabulary of social science concepts is required in order to make sense of the data and to avoid reliance on commonsense meanings of words which can cause confusion. So, in the next chapter, key concepts – information, power, law, autonomy, penetration – are elaborated and a 'dual' or 'Gore-Tex' model of the state developed.

Finally, the author needs to make clear his perspective on these matters: it is that there is inadequate democratic control of state structures in the UK, particularly of the security intelligence agencies, and that this poses such a threat to democratic forms that it requires fundamental change. I am a social scientist, not an intelligence-insider nor a government policy-maker. However, this analysis is addressed to all these groups and to anybody concerned about the ineffectiveness and/or unaccountability of the 'secret state'. These groups have diverse interests and I appreciate the danger of falling between stools, but this diversity should not be exaggerated.[132] Chapter 2 is concerned primarily with the kind of theoretical questions which interest academics more than practitioners but the intention is not to engage in arcane theoretical debate. Rather, the discussion aims to provide a more rigorous framework for the consideration of the comparative empirical material regarding security intelligence which appears in the subsequent chapters. Simply accumulating 'facts' without such a framework can be highly misleading, both for intelligence and academic analysts.

I have much sympathy with the argument that political and social science are held in little general regard partly because of their unwillingness to tackle 'problems'; therefore they are perceived as 'irrelevant'. This analysis is an attempt to deal 'directly and theoretically' with the problem of domestic security intelligence agencies, to confront the analytical issues necessary to understand them and, I hope, to contribute to some resolution of the problem.[133]

NOTES

1. H.H. Ransom, 'Being Intelligent about Secret Intelligence Agencies', *American Political Science Review*, 74(1), March, 1980, pp. 141–2.
2. Secretary of State for the Home Department, *Reform of Section 2 of the Official Secrets Act 1911*, Cm 408, June 1988, p. 10.
3. D. Hooper, *Official Secrets: The Use and Abuse of the Act* (London: Secker & Warburg, 1987), pp. 295–6, 326.
4. N.H. Pearson, Foreword, in J.C. Masterman, *The Double-Cross System in the War of 1939 to 1945* (London: Yale University Press, 1972, History Book Club Edition, undated) p. x.
5. Ibid, p. xv.
6. Ibid, p. 58.
7. Ibid, pp. 34–5.
8. For example, see H.H. Ransom, 'Strategic Intelligence and Foreign Policy', *World Politics*, 27, 1974, pp. 135–6.
9. Masterman, supra (note 4), p. xvii.
10. Hooper, supra (note 3), pp. 196–7.
11. P. Wright, *Spycatcher* (New York: Viking Penguin, 1987).
12. Hooper, p. 199. R.V. Jones, *Most Secret War* (London: Hamish Hamilton, 1978).

13. R.V. Jones, *Reflections on Intelligence* (London: Heinemann, 1989) pp. vii–viii. See also pp. 61–4 for discussion of another episode showing the bizarre 'procedures' through which authors had to go to publish material.
14. F.H. Hinsley and C.A.G. Simkins, *British Intelligence in the Second World War, Vol. 4: Security and Counter-Intelligence* (London: HMSO, 1990).
15. Ibid, p. x.
16. *The Guardian*, 5 April 1990, p. 19.
17. Hooper, supra (note 3), pp. 310–12.
18. For different perspectives on the trial see R.V. Hall, *A Spy's Revenge* (Harmondsworth: Penguin, 1987); C. Pincher, A *Web of Deception: the Spycatcher Affair* (London: Sidgwick & Jackson, 1987); and M. Turnbull, *The Spycatcher Trial* (London: Heinemann, 1988).
19. A. Cavendish, *Inside Intelligence* (London: Collins, 1990), pp. xii–xiii.
20. Ibid, pp. 162–72; see also R. Deacon, *'C': a Biography of Sir Maurice Oldfield* (London: Futura Publications, 1985), pp. 221–61.
21. Cavendish, supra (note 19) pp. xi–xiv; see also N. Walker, 'Spycatcher's Scottish Sequel', *Public Law*, Autumn 1990, pp. 354–71.
22. J. Bulloch, *MI5: the Origin and History of the British Counter-Espionage Service* (London: Arthur Barker Ltd., 1963), p. 10.
23. Ibid, pp. 189–90.
24. Ibid, p. 186.
25. Hooper, supra (note 3), pp. 214–15.
26. Bulloch, supra (note 22), p. 187.
27. C. Pincher, *Inside Story* (London: Book Club Associates, 1978), pp. 76–7.
28. Elsewhere Pincher recounts other occasions on which he wrote stories at the behest of MI5. For an example from 1961 see C. Pincher, *Their Trade is Treachery* (London: Sidgwick & Jackson, 1982), pp. 263–4.
29. S. Dorril and R. Ramsay, *Smear! Wilson and the Secret State* (London: Fourth Estate, 1991), pp. 246–7 and see discussion in Chapter 5.
30. Pincher, supra (note 27), p. 170. In *The Truth About Dirty Tricks* (London: Sidgwick & Jackson, 1991), p. 151, Pincher apologises for his error in retelling this 'plot' story in 1978.
31. Ibid, 1978, p. 18.

32. Pincher, supra (note 18), pp. 1–66 provides his *post hoc* account of the publication of *Their Trade is Treachery*. See note 18 for other references.
33. Pincher, supra (note 28), p. ix.
34. Ibid, p. 262.
35. *Statement on the Recommendations of the Security Commission*, Cmnd 8540 (London: HMSO, May 1982); see also Pincher, supra (note 18), p. 69.
36. C. Pincher, *Too Secret Too Long* (London: Sidgwick & Jackson, 1984), p. 4.
37. Ibid.
38. Pincher, supra (note 30), 1991, p. 67.
39. Hooper, supra (note 3), pp. 212–13.
40. N. West, *A Matter of Trust: MI5 1945–72* (London: Coronet Books, 1983), pp. 9–10.
41. N. West, *MI5: British Security Service Operations 1909–1945* (London: Granada, 1983), pp. 433–4. Eunan O'Halpin describes this book as 'unsatisfactory and inaccurate' in 'Financing British Intelligence: the Evidence up to 1945', in K.G. Robertson (ed.) *British and American Approaches to Intelligence* (Basingstoke: Macmillan, 1987), p. 215 note 27.
42. West, supra (note 40), p. 189.
43. N. West, *Molehunt: the Full Story of the Soviet Spy in MI5* (London: Coronet Books, 1987), p. 19.
44. Ibid, p. 44.
45. C. Andrew and O. Gordievsky, *KGB: The Inside Story of its Foreign Operations from Lenin to Gorbachev* (New York: Harper Perennial, 1991), p. 216.
46. R. Allason, *The Branch: a History of the Metropolitan Police Special Branch 1883–1983* (London: Secker & Warburg, 1983).
47. Ibid, p. xii.
48. For example, see *Lobster*, No. 11, 1986. F. Holroyd, *War Without Honour* (Hull: Medium Publishing Co., 1989).
49. Holroyd, ibid, p. 70.
50. Ibid, pp. 40–42.
51. Ibid, pp. 89–94.
52. R. Faligot, *Britain's Military Strategy in Ireland* (London: Zed Press, 1983), pp. 33–8.
53. Dorril and Ramsay, supra (note 29), p. 217.
54. See Holroyd, supra (note 48), pp. 152–3, for chronology.

55. Ibid, Preface.
56. M. Urban, *Big Boys' Rules: The Secret Struggle against the IRA* (London: Faber and Faber, 1992), pp. 50–57. In similar vein see M. Dillon, *The Dirty War* (London: Arrow Books, 1990), pp. 188–208.
57. J. Stalker, *Stalker* (London: Harrap, 1988).
58. *New Statesman*, 16 May 1980, pp. 738–44; 23 May 1980, pp. 774–6.
59. Hooper, supra (note 3), pp. 206–9.
60. T. Bunyan, *The History and Practice of the Political Police in Britain* (London: Quartet, 1977), Preface.
61. D. Leigh, *The Frontiers of Secrecy: Closed Government in Britain* (London: Junction Books, 1980), p. ix.
62. M. Hollingsworth and R. Norton-Taylor, *Blacklist: The Inside Story of Political Vetting* (London: Hogarth Press, 1988).
63. M. Hollingsworth and C. Tremayne, *The Economic League: The Silent McCarthyism* (London: National Council for Civil Liberties, 1989), pp. 5–6.
64. I. Linn, *Application Refused: Employment Vetting by the State* (London: Civil Liberties Trust, 1990).
65. R. Norton-Taylor, *In Defence of the Realm? The Case for Accountable Security Services* (London: Civil Liberties Trust, 1990).
66. P. Foot, *Who Framed Colin Wallace?* (London: Pan Books, 1990), pp. 41–2.
67. Ibid, pp. 115–46; see also Urban, supra (note 56), pp. 56–7.
68. Foot, supra (note 66) p. 193.
69. Pincher, *Inside Story*, p. 197.
70. Pincher, *The Truth About Dirty Tricks*, pp. 159–80.
71. D. Leigh, *The Wilson Plot: The Intelligence Services and the Discrediting of a Prime Minister 1945–1976* (London: Heinemann, 1988), p. xv. Dorril and Ramsay, supra (note 29).
72. Faligot, supra (note 52), p. 21.
73. Dorril and Ramsay, supra (note 29), p. 257.
74. Ibid, p. 273. Pincher argues against giving Wallace's evidence any credibility: *The Truth About Dirty Tricks*, pp. 159–80.
75. H.H. Ransom, 'Review Essay', *American Political Science Review*, 80(3), September, 1986, 985–91.
76. C. Andrew, *Secret Service: the Making of the British Intelligence Community* (London: Heinemann, 1985), pp. 18–20.

77. Ibid, p. xv.
78. Ibid, p. 499.
79. Ibid, p. 502.
80. B. Porter, *The Origins of the Vigilant State* (London: Weidenfeld & Nicolson, 1987), p. 182.
81. Ibid, p. 183. See also A. Gamble, *The Free Economy and the Strong State* (Basingstoke, Macmillan, 1988), pp. 31–7.
82. B. Porter, *Plots and Paranoia: A History of Political Espionage in Britain 1790–1988* (London: Unwin Hyman, 1989).
83. Ibid, p. 234.
84. D.G.T. Williams, *Not In The Public Interest* (London: Hutchinson, 1965), p. 191.
85. Ibid, p. 216.
86. M. Supperstone, *Brownlie's Law of Public Order and National Security* (London: Butterworths, 1981).
87. See Robertson, supra (note 41), pp. 218–43.
88. Ibid, p. 235.
89. G. Robertson, *Reluctant Judas: The Life and Death of the Special Branch Informer, Kenneth Lennon* (London: Temple Smith, 1976). For details of this case see Chapter 4.
90. J. Michael, *The Politics of Secrecy* (Harmondsworth: Penguin, 1982).
91. J.D. Baxter, *State Security, Privacy and Information* (Hemel Hempstead: Harvester Wheatsheaf, 1990).
92. P. Birkinshaw, *Reforming the Secret State* (Milton Keynes: Open University Press, 1991).
93. S. Palmer, 'Tightening Secrecy Law: the Official Secrets Act 1989', *Public Law*, Summer, 1990, pp. 243–56.
94. I. Leigh and L. Lustgarten, 'The Security Service Act, 1989', *Modern Law Review*, 52(6), 1989, pp. 801–36.
95. K.G. Robertson, 'Editorial Comment: An Agenda for Intelligence Research', *Defense Analysis*, 3(2), 1987, pp. 95–101.
96. In Robertson, supra (note 41), pp. 244–72.
97. Ransom, supra (note 1), p. 142.
98. R.E. Wraith and G.B. Lamb, *Public Inquiries as an Instrument of Government* (London: Allen & Unwin, 1971) p. 212.
99. Cmnd 2152, London: HMSO (September 1963), §5.
100. Ibid, §§ 235–41.
101. P. Knightley and C. Kennedy, *An Affair of State* (London: Jonathan Cape, 1987), p. 250.

102. A. Summers and S. Dorril, *Honeytrap* (London: Coronet Books, 1988), pp. 115–16, and see further discussion in Chapter 9.
103. I. Leigh and L. Lustgarten, 'The Security Commission: constitutional achievement or curiosity?' *Public Law*, Summer, 1991, pp. 224–5, and see further discussion in Chapter 7.
104. Leigh and Lustgarten, ibid, p. 221.
105. Channel 4, *After Dark* broadcast 16 July 1988.
106 Leigh and Lustgarten, 'The Security Commission', pp. 222–6.
107. *Report of Committee of Privy Councillors into 'D' Notice Matters*, Cmnd 3309 (London: HMSO, June, 1967).
108. Dorril and Ramsay, supra (note 29), pp. 143–5; Pincher, supra, (note 36) pp. 589–95.
109. *The Guardian*, 24 January 1984, p. 4.
110. Fourth Report from the Home Affairs Committee, *Special Branch*, House of Commons Paper 71 (1984–85), p. v.
111. Final Report of the Select Committee to Study Governmental Operations with respect to Intelligence Activities (hereafter Church Committee), *Intelligence Activities and the Rights of Americans*, Book II, United States Senate (1976), p. 9, note 7.
112. Andrew, supra (note 76), p. 505.
113. Cmnd 8787 (London: HMSO, 1983), p. 95.
114. Justice R.M. Hope, *Royal Commission on Intelligence and Security* issued five reports during 1976–77. Especially relevant here is the Fourth report: *Australian Security Intelligence Organisation* (Canberra: Australian Government Printing Service, 1977). R.M. Hope, *Protective Security Review* (Canberra: A.G.P.S., 1979). R.M. Hope, *Royal Commission on Australia's Security and Intelligence Agencies*, was re-established in 1983 and published eight reports during 1984–85 including: *Report on the Australian Security Intelligence Organization* (Canberra: Commonwealth Government Printer, 1985).
115. Commission of Enquiry Concerning Certain Activities of the Royal Canadian Mounted Police (hereafter McDonald), First Report, *Security and Information* (1979), Second Report, *Freedom and Security under the Law* (1981), and Third Report, *Certain RCMP Activities and the Question of Governmental Knowledge* (Ottawa: Minister of Supply and Services, 1981).
116. The Church Committee published seven main reports during 1975–76. They were: Interim Report, *Alleged Assassination Plots Involving Foreign Leaders* (Washington DC: US Government

Printing Office 1975); Final Report (Washington, DC: US Government Printing Office, 1976), The Final Report consisted of: Book 1, *Foreign and Military Intelligence*; Book II, *Intelligence Activities and the Rights of Americans*, supra. (note 111); Book III, *Supplementary Detailed Staff Reports on Intelligence Activities and the Rights of Americans*; Book IV, *Supplementary Detailed Staff Reports on Foreign and Military Intelligence*; Book V, *The Investigation of the Assassination of President John F. Kennedy: Performance of the Intelligence Agencies*; Book VI, *Supplementary Reports on Intelligence Activities*.

117. Ransom, supra (note 1) p. 141.

118. K.G. Robertson, *Public Secrets* (Basingstoke: Macmillan, 1982), pp. 22–35; I. Harden and N. Lewis, *The Noble Lie: the British Constitution and the Rule of Law* (London: Hutchinson, 1988), Ch. 4.

119. Harden and Lewis, ibid, p. 143.

120. Some Metropolitan Police Special Branch records were turned up at the Public Records Office by a historian in the 1970s, but after reference to them was published they were removed. For full details see R. Harrison, 'New Light on the Police and Hunger Marchers', *Bulletin of the Society for the Study of Labour History*, 37, Autumn 1978, pp. 17–49.

121. T. Tant, *Constitutional Aspects of Official Secrecy and Freedom of Information: An Overview* (University of Essex, 1988), Essex Papers in Politics and Government p. 7.

122. W. Chambliss and R. Seidmann, *Law, Order and Power* (Palo Alto: Addison-Wesley, 1982).

123. Ibid, pp. 15–18. By way of comparison G.F. Rutan suggests that intelligence teaching and research has been conducted within one of three frameworks: historical, structural-functional, and participant interview. *Political Science Methodologies Utilized in the Contemporary Study of State Intelligence Organizations and Functions*, paper prepared for panel on 'Study of Intelligence: Comparative Methodologies', at International Studies Association Conference, Vancouver (March, 1991).

124. Norton-Taylor, supra (note 65), pp. 81–90.

125. Leigh, supra (note 71), especially Ch. 11; Dorril and Ramsay, supra (note 29) *passim*.

126. H. Kitchin, *The Gibraltar Report* (London: Liberty, 1989); Stalker, supra (note 57).

127. For example, see C. Ham and M. Hill, *The Policy Process in the Modern Capitalist State* (Brighton: Wheatsheaf, 1984), *passim*.

128. Cf Supperstone, supra (note 87), pp. 228–9 and see discussion of these organisational questions in Chapter 6.

129. See notes 114–16 above for detailed references to these inquiries.

130. J.T. Richelson and D. Ball, *The Ties That Bind* (Boston: Unwin Hyman, 2nd edition, 1990), p. 306.

131. Cf C. Andrew, 'Historical Research on the British Intelligence Community,' in R. Godson (ed.), *Comparing Foreign Intelligence* (Washington DC: National Strategy Information Center, 1988), p. 55.

132. Cf G.T. Marx, *Undercover: Police Surveillance in America*, Twentieth Century Fund Book (Berkeley: University of California Press, 1988), p. xxiv.

133. Cf D. Held and A. Leftwich, 'A Discipline of Politics?' in A. Leftwich (ed.), *What Is Politics? The Activity and its Study* (Oxford: Basil Blackwell, 1984), pp. 139–59.

2

The State and Security Intelligence: Concepts and Models

One of the investigative tools used by social scientists is the concept – a term or idea, usually abstract, which is defined in such a way as to facilitate study. When investigating new 'territories' it is most useful to start with concepts which have been used in cognate areas in order to make the most of previous experience and to reduce the chances of re-inventing the methodological wheel. There are three main concepts considered here: information, power and law. These are logically interrelated and are central to the study of the state and security intelligence, but for the purpose of this chapter they are initially discussed separately.

INFORMATION

What do we know about information processes generally, about the gathering of information and its dissemination, particularly within and between bureaucracies? Information processes within organisations have been studied primarily with a view to explaining and/or improving the decisions that those organisations then make. Developed from assumptions of rational individual choice, the model of the organisation is of one that calculates the costs and benefits of gathering more information in terms of its impact on decisions. Therefore, Feldman and March suggest,

> relevant information will be gathered and analysed prior to decision-making; information gathered for use in a decision will be used in making that decision; available information

will be examined before more information is requested or gathered; needs for information will be determined prior to requesting information; information that is irrelevant to a decision will not be gathered.[1]

The authors suggest that a review of the literature reveals a quite different picture as to the 'weak link' between information and decisions. They note:

> most organisations and individuals often collect more information than they use or can reasonably expect to use in the making of decisions. At the same time, they appear to be constantly needing or requesting more information, or complaining about inadequacies in information.[2]

Several reasons for this are advanced. First, because of organisational or human limitations the organisation may not be able to process what it has and overload contributes to a breakdown in the information process. Second, limitations on analytical skill or co-ordination between analysts and gatherers leads to the collection of the wrong kind of information. Third, a related point, there may be systematic bias towards collecting more information than is optimal from the point of view of decision-makers, for example because the two functions of collection and decision are separated. Fourth, the decision theory perspective is misleading because often organisations are monitoring their environment for early warning of surprises rather than with respect to specific decisions.

> Organisations gather gossip – news that might contain something relevant but usually does not – in situations in which relevance cannot be specified precisely in advance.[3]

Fifth, given the context of conflicts of interest and power within which it is gathered, the information is subject to 'strategic misrepresentation' which compromises the value of information to the decision-maker, stimulates the oversupply of information and leads to a 'competition among contending liars'.[4] A number of these features can be seen to be endemic within security intelligence agencies, as we shall see in Chapter 6.

Organisational structure provides the context for information processes. Hierarchical organisations, it is suggested, may be effective in dividing up tasks and processing instructions downwards, but they are less adapted to providing adequate mechanisms for the collection and processing of information within the organisation.[5] More specifically, research has shown that there is a systematic tendency for information to be distorted as it is passed upward. This occurs partly because of the need to synthesise in order to prevent overload at the top, and partly as subordinates emphasise what they think their superiors want to hear. Finally,

> As this compounded distortion proceeds upwards through several levels of the organisation, the possibilities of superiors knowing what is actually going on becomes very slight.[6]

Such is life for the mushroom men and women who remain happy by being kept in the dark and fed manure! Within police organisations such problems are aggravated by the presence of semi-military disciplinary codes.[7] Supervision of the rank-and-file in policing is carried out predominantly by reading the reports of actions carried out; direct supervision is a rarity. For the rank-and-file this places a premium on 'getting the story right' in the paperwork, which results in highly distorted views of events reaching management.

The relatively small size of many security intelligence agencies and the nature of their task – collecting and analysing information rather than implementing executive policies – may enable them to avoid certain pathologies of hierarchical organisation. Further, 'need-to-know' principles also imply more decentralised procedures, yet these, in turn, may give rise to different distortions of internal information processes. These are discussed in more detail in Chapter 6. Given that the central mandate of security intelligence agencies *is* to gather information and that their 'decisions' regarding countering operations will often consist of disseminating information, it makes sense to view these agencies as pre-eminently concerned with information control.

In suggesting a framework for the analysis of this phenomenon, Wilsnack defined information control as 'the processes used to make sure that certain people will or will not have access to certain information at certain times.[8] Some have argued that the growth in importance of information control as a means of deploying power came as traditional modes of authority based on obedience and coercion were replaced by more bureaucratic/rationalist modes,[9] but other authors have noted that the origins of state secrecy go further back: to the principle of *arcana imperii*, or 'mysteries of state' when the aura of sacredness was transferred from religious officials to secular leaders which was at its strongest in the absolute monarchies of the seventeenth century.[10]

As far as the UK is concerned, the parliamentary revolt against the absolute monarchy did not, as in the USA, lead to a republican scepticism of the central state but concerned itself more with questions of who would rule rather than how they would do it. Thus parliamentarism sustained the tradition of strong government in the UK[11] and the subsequent development of more sophisticated structures of state secrecy during the nineteenth and early twentieth centuries was the product of the attempts of successive governments to maintain control of information in the context of both democratisation and bureaucratisation.[12] The extension of the franchise was, again, more a question of extending slowly the numbers of people who were allowed to contribute to the choice of who would rule and meant that the governing elite sought to protect more effectively the sanctity of their deliberations as to the 'national interest'. A firmer grasp also had to be exerted over the bureaucracy as ministerial responsibility to parliament for decisions led governments to tighten their grip on what information the state released.[13] Even that classic of state secrecy, the British Official Secrets Act 1911, might be seen less as a reaction to a 'spy scare' than 'as part of a deliberate policy to control the civil service, and to restrict access to public information'.[14]

Wilsnack identifies four key processes of information control: espionage, secrecy, persuasion and evaluation. All these provide indicators to significant parts of the present analysis. Espionage is defined as 'the process of obtaining information from people who do not want you to have that information'.[15] This is helpful since it is a more inclusive definition than is sometimes assumed in discussions of 'spying' as between states and companies. Of particular importance to this consideration of domestic security intelligence is the fact that the term can cover both the efforts of the security intelligence agencies to 'penetrate' the society in its search for information on perceived threats, and the efforts of outsiders to obtain information on the activities of these agencies. This might include the counter-intelligence efforts of insurgent or violent groups, but can also include the efforts of outside investigators on 'oversight' bodies or journalists to obtain information regarding abuses of power. In other words, democratic espionage.

For example, the US Freedom of Information Act (FOIA) (as amended in 1974) and the Privacy Act 1974 provided fresh legal support for those citizens seeking information regarding abuse of power by intelligence agencies. In 1979 the FBI was just one of a number of agencies to appear before a congressional subcommittee to testify that the acts had combined to become a threat to sensitive sources and operations. Specifically the Bureau referred to cases of potential agents and informers refusing to co-operate because they feared exposure. A few months before the hearings, Director William Webster had claimed that 16 per cent of all FOIA requests were from prisoners seeking to identify informers in their cases.[16] But just as states will seek to protect their informers from 'citizens' espionage' by restricting the impact of laws such as the FOIA, so they will make use of other laws to identify those 'citizens' agents' who blow the whistle on state abuse. In October 1991 Channel 4 televised a programme in the UK based on allegations that there had been widespread collusion between the security forces and Loyalist paramilitaries in a campaign of political assassination of Republicans in Northern Ireland. The Royal Ulster Constabulary (RUC) obtained a court order under the Prevention of Terrorism Act (PTA) requiring Channel 4 to disclose its evidence but, when this did not include the identity of its main source, Channel 4 was charged with contempt of court and eventually fined.[17]

'Secrecy' is defined by Wilsnack as 'the process of keeping other people from obtaining information you do not want them to have'.[18] This is, in one sense, the reverse side of espionage: the attempts by states and by other groups and individuals to maintain the secrecy of their own activities. In each of these cases there may be entirely legitimate reasons for secrecy. In the case of the state, Sissela Bok identifies three legitimate arguments for administrative secrecy: the impossibility of making policy completely in the open, the need for 'surprise' in the implementation of policy, for example, criminal investigations and interest rate changes, and 'privacy' considerations, that is, that the state holds much sensitive information about individuals which should not be made public.[19] On the other hand, as Max Weber pointed out:

> . . . the most decisive means of power for officialdom is the transposition of official knowledge into secret knowledge, by means of the notorious concept of the 'official secret'. This is simply a way of securing the administration against external control.[20]

For individuals, some degree of secrecy/privacy is essential in order to maintain self-integrity and identity. Within groups, the determination to achieve secrecy involves a secondary process of procedures to achieve security of communications between group members; within states these take the form of, for example, elaborate classification procedures for documents. In the UK virtually all documents fit within one of four classifications: Top Secret, Secret, Confidential or Restricted, while the US does not use the last category.[21]

'Persuasion' is defined as 'the process of making sure that other people obtain and and believe information you want them to have'.[22] The debate about states and information has too often been seen as essentially a question of secrecy; the strength of this framework of 'information control' is that it gives equal attention to 'persuasion' or what might be described as 'information policy'. Wilsnack points out that it is necessary to distinguish between 'education' (if the communicator believes the information) and 'deception' (if s/he does not). In practice this distinction might be less clear-cut since skill in public relations consists of choosing that information which imparts the best view of state performance, avoids demonstrable untruths (which is risky) and is perhaps best described as 'being economical with the truth'. For example, Tony Poveda contrasts the FBI's relatively open news management policies under Director Clarence Kelley between 1973 and 1976 with the more restrictive ones under William Webster between 1977 and 1980.[23]

Even 'education' can be damaging; for example, information released by state officials about individuals may be true but can be immensely damaging to that individual. Bok points out that publicity can be used as a tool of injustice and be manipulated to skew public opinion.[24] The temptations of deception are clear; perhaps the risks involved are less obvious to those tempted to use them. In wartime the use of deception appears to be highly legitimate but what about its use against domestic groups such as the PIRA when, it might be argued, the alienation resulting in key groups of the domestic population outweighs any gains in the destabilising of the insurgents? This is discussed further in Chapter 5. Even more controversial would be the use by the state of deception techniques against domestic groups indulging in peaceful campaigning activity, such as the special group – DS-19 – set up in the Ministry of Defence in 1983 to issue propaganda against the peace movement. The main weapon used was a letter from Michael Heseltine, then Minister of Defence, to Conservative candidates which purported to reveal communist domination of CND. This was concocted from a mixture of known and false information provided by Stanley Bonnett who had just been pressured to resign from his job with CND. He was paid over £2,000 by Special Branch officers.[25] See Chapter 4 for discussion of informers.

Apart from the specific costs of particular campaigns of 'disinformation', it is important to note also the potential long-term damage done to political discourse which, though not necessarily intended by the state, could certainly be foreseen.[26] The use of deception by the state can easily set up spirals of disinformation, mistrust, and counter-rumours which become entirely self-defeating and which can lead to a major deterioration in the legitimacy of the state.[27]

Wilsnack's fourth category – evaluation – is defined as 'the process of making sure that you learn more from the information you have obtained than just what other people want you to know'.[28] As secrecy was the other side of espionage, this is the other side of persuasion and represents the attempt to see through attempts at deception or disinformation. As we shall see later, evaluation is incorporated into this analysis as one aspect of the 'intelligence process' which is examined in detail in Chapters 4 and 5. The other features of Wilsnack's analysis which are particularly relevant are the arguments that these four information control processes tend to reinforce one another within 'social units', and to lead to collaboration between 'units' which have common or parallel interests. On the other hand, the processes can counteract each other as between social units which are in competition or conflict.[29] As far as security intelligence agencies as 'social units' are concerned, this can provide a useful tool in exploring the conditions under which, for example, different agencies may be able to collaborate, while on other occasions, they will apparently engage in the kind of 'turf wars' which characterised the early days of the relationship between the new Canadian Security Intelligence Service and the RCMP (see Chapter 6), and which also characterised the situation in Northern Ireland particularly between 1972 and 1981.[30]

As a general proposition it is clear that information control systems have a tendency to get out of control as secrecy and deception invite espionage by others, followed by security measures to counteract the espionage, and measures and counter-measures escalate.[31] Understanding this process is crucial to the effort to exert greater accountability of information control processes, especially those in security intelligence agencies. The problems of control and oversight are discussed in Chapters 7 and 8. Since information control processes do not operate in a vacuum, however, next it is necessary to consider power.

POWER

Since the basic mandate of all security intelligence agencies is to defend the parent state against threats to its integrity and autonomy, or, in other words, its ability to exercise power, it may seem obvious to point out the centrality of power but it is important to discuss this explicitly because much of the writing on security intelligence tends to overemphasise the concepts of information and law, at the expense of power. Not surprisingly, official inquiries in North America and Australia concentrated, at least initially, on the allegations of abuses which led to their establishment and on new structures, laws and procedures which might prevent their recurrence. Their reports concentrated therefore on the practicability of forms of control and oversight of security intelligence operations, and much of the associated academic literature followed suit. The missing ingredient in much of this was some more explicit discussion of the significance of power.

The political analysis of power is complex and only some of the theoretical and methodological debates concerning its study can be discussed here. The main strategy for the analysis of political power has conceived of power as sovereignty:

> . . . power as a locus of will, as a supreme agency to which other wills would bend, as prohibitory; the classic conception of power as zero-sum; in short, power as negation of the power of others.[32]

Given this concern with sovereignty, and the fact that the modern nation state is its present embodiment, much analysis of power has therefore centred on the state. However, theoretical perspectives on the state have varied widely as to what aspects of state power they considered worthy of study, the methodologies they applied and the nature of the evidence they gathered.[33] One of the most significant contributions to the debate between different approaches was Stephen Lukes's *Power: A Radical View*[34] in which he identified three 'dimensions' of power analysis. The first, the pluralist, is criticised for its insistence that only those exercises of power which are actually observable could be incorporated into an analysis of power. It is not that pluralists deny the possibility of power being exercised covertly, it is rather that they see no sound methodology for studying it.[35] The second dimension identified by Lukes was the position developed by Bachrach and Baratz in their US work which attacked the pluralists' insistence on observability. They showed that a key feature of power was the ability of some groups to prevent issues from even reaching the political agenda and thus they were able to prevent any observable decision being made at all. Lukes, while recognising this 'elitist' position as an advance on pluralism, still criticised it because it required some behavioural reference point. Researchers would still be concerned to find examples of actual behaviour, for example, 'deciding not to decide', in order to sustain what was called the 'second face of power'.[36]

Lukes instead proposed his own third dimension of power which accepted the essentially contested nature of power as a concept, and was a radical, rather than a liberal or reformist, view of power. He argued this was superior because it incorporated also the possibility of exercises of power in which the objects of the power might remain ignorant that power had actually been exercised over them. Thus Lukes was making use of notions of hegemony and false consciousness to explain the very absence of conflict which the first two dimensions might take as evidence of some genuine value-consensus.

Relating these debates to the study of security intelligence agencies, one can see that pluralist insistence on the accurate reconstruction of open decision-making that leads to actions will not get us very far, dealing as we are with agencies that regard maximum secrecy as an indispensable condition for operating at all! However, there are occasions on which actual exercises of power by such agencies have been observed and some of their members have subsequently spoken about those operations, for example, the appearance in court in Gibraltar of members of the Security Service and the SAS after the shooting of three IRA members in 1988. While making due allowance for the fact that such public presentations of decision-making will be highly partial, they may provide some opportunity for the application of pluralist methods.

On the face of it, the analysis of 'non decision-making' might appear more likely to apply to security intelligence agencies since their decisions are made covertly. The problem is that if there is no actual operation as a result of the decision, or there is one which is kept secret, then the complete lack of access to internal decision procedures will mean that nothing will be known. The problem for both the pluralist and elitist methodologies is that their inductive approach is simply inapplicable to these agencies in the UK as things stand. Following the discussion at the end of Chapter 1, what is much more likely to bear fruit is the use of induction to develop from the empirical material gathered by inquiries into security intelligence operations elsewhere a general model which can then be applied deductively, as it were, to the UK.

Stewart Clegg has traced the view of power as 'sovereign' from Thomas Hobbes through to Lukes[37] and contrasts it with another tradition. As a servant of state power, Hobbes was concerned with 'what power is' and provided a rationalised account of what state power could produce – order. By contrast, Machiavelli, writing 100 years earlier, was not the servant of a strong unified state, did not seek to produce a model of order and was concerned with the strategies and organisation which were most likely to secure power in an ever-changing political landscape. Machiavelli was concerned with 'what power does'. So, while Lukes is seen by Clegg as representing the modern apotheosis of the Hobbesian sovereign, where the power 'extends even into the other's thoughts and consciousness',[38] Machiavelli's modern follower is Foucault, for whom the focus must be on the concrete details of how power is exercised.[39] Foucault wrote:

> I would say that we should direct our researches on the nature of power not towards the juridical edifice of sovereignty, the state apparatuses and the ideologies which accompany them, but towards domination and the material operators of power, towards forms of subjection and the inflections and utilisations of their localised systems, and toward strategic apparatuses. We must eschew the model of the Leviathan in the study of power. We must escape from the limited field of juridical sovereignty and state institutions, and instead base our analysis of power on the study of the techniques and tactics of domination . . .[40]

Thus Foucault is concerned with much more than state power; he is concerned, rather, with the 'micro-techniques' of power which normalise the population through central processes of surveillance in a variety of technical, bureaucratic and legal ways.[41] But although Foucault criticises the 'excessive value attributed to the problem of the state' he also says:

> We need to see things not in terms of the replacement of a society of sovereignty by a disciplinary society and the subsequent replacement of a disciplinary society by a society of government; in reality one has a triangle, sovereignty-discipline-government, which has as its primary target the population and as its essential mechanism the apparatuses of security.[42]

Despite seeking to keep the state within his analytical frame, Foucault has been criticised by others, for example by Poulantzas, who argues,

> . . . he also underestimates the role of the state itself, and fails to understand the function of the repressive apparatuses (army, police, judicial system, etc.) as means of exercising physical violence that are located at the heart of the modern State. They are treated instead as mere parts of the disciplinary machine which patterns the internalisation of repression by means of normalisation.[43]

This would appear to lead to a significant difference between their conceptions of the relationship between the state and security. For Foucault security is a specific principle of political method and practice which is distinct from but may combine with law, sovereignty and discipline within various government structures. Security is aimed at 'the ensemble of the population' and becomes, from the eighteenth century onwards, increasingly the dominant component of modern government,[44] or what he refers to elsewhere as 'governmentality'.[45] One of the main mechanisms of security is liberty:

> Hence liberty is registered not only as the right of individuals legitimately to oppose the power, the abuses and usurpations of the sovereign, but also now as an indispensable element of governmental rationality itself.[46]

For Poulantzas, on the other hand, the state is a prime cause of insecurity because its laws, injunctions, prohibitions and censorship organise the conditions for repression and the means by which it is imposed. 'In this sense, law is *the code of organized public violence*.'[47] Yet the difference between Foucault and Poulantzas should not be exaggerated. Though coming from different directions, both give the state a key role in unifying the various, dispersed patterns of domination in capitalist society.[48]

It is argued here that examining precisely those forms of surveillance characteristic of state security intelligence agencies remains important as a hitherto unexplored part of the terrain. In part, this can be seen as complementing other studies of the micro-techniques of power through surveillance which characterise areas of society such as the school, the workplace and the prison. With particular respect to crime, the state in the Middle Ages operated on the principle of deterring deviants by means of 'discretionary terror'. In the late eighteenth century this was challenged from various scientific and religious perspectives which saw the possibility of reforming them. But if deviants were not to be deterred then more effective means of apprehending them were required. Contemporaneously industrialisation and urbanisation under capitalism was producing a 'society of strangers'[49] and the only means of controlling the population – especially the 'dangerous classes' – was an increased capacity for surveillance. This involves potentially both the collection and accumulation of information and the exercise of supervision,[50] or, in other words, countering operations. In the UK these were to be provided, first, by a new professionalised and bureaucratised police and later by specific security intelligence agencies.

Part of the 'problem' identified at the end of Chapter 1 was the apparent continuation of repressive actions by state agencies which make it clear that techniques of surveillance are not the sole components of modern state power. Power is central to the understanding of security intelligence agencies whether one adopts the view of 'sovereign power' as exercised by the state or the more pluralistic view of an interplay between power and resistance, particularly within organisations.[51] This can be seen by considering a recent attempt to develop a scheme for classifying security intelligence agencies in which Keller suggests three main types: respectively, the 'bureau of domestic intelligence', the 'political police' and the 'independent security state'.

The first of these has the following characteristics: the bureau has limited and specific powers derived from a charter or statute, its primary function is to gather information relating to the criminal prosecution of security offences and it does not conduct aggressive countering operations against citizens or political groups. The second type – political police – is distinguished from the first in that it enjoys greater autonomy from democratic policy-making and is more insulated from legislative and judicial scrutiny. It is more responsive to the groups in power and derives its powers and responsibilities from more loosely defined delegations of executive power. It may also gather political intelligence unrelated to specific offences and conduct aggressive countering operations against political opposition. The independent security state is characterised by a lack of external controls: it is different from the political police because its goals will be determined by officials within the agency and may not coincide with those of the political elite. Its funding and policies remain hidden from the rest of the policy-making process, and the targets of its information-gathering and countering activities are authorised by the agency itself, not elected officials. This third type, Keller says, constitutes a security state within a state.[52]

While each of these clearly gather information, do they all exercise power in relation to the citizenry? For Keller, the third clearly does because it operates covert counter-intelligence programmes, for example the disruption of targeted groups, but the first type apparently does not because it 'passively' collects and analyses information, while the second adds more aggressive information-gathering techniques.[53] Whether or not these are considered to be exercises of power will depend on the way in which power is conceptualised. In the second case aggressive information-gathering, for example bugging, infiltration of informers, though possibly *intended* as only information-gathering techniques can actually have the impact of causing others to change their behaviour, perhaps withdrawing from political activity through fear, and thus meet the criteria of an exercise of power even by the behaviourist standards of observable effects.[54] To see the first type of security intelligence agency as 'exercising' power requires a different formulation of power, one that would be closer to Foucault's view of power 'as a constant surveillance constituting a new discipline of norms and behaviour'.[55] Here the security intelligence agencies are part of a wider variety of 'authorities', and their specific role is the surveillance of the population for evidence of particular forms of resistance and deviance.

LAW

In considering the third concept, law, it will be useful to consider, first, its relation to policing since this has been discussed more extensively than its relation to security intelligence. This can be modelled quite briefly: the criminal law provides a resource for the police which they can use in pursuance of their basic mandate of order maintenance and crime control. Knowing what the law is, however, cannot explain police behaviour because officers will frequently have a variety of options, all of which are equally 'lawful'. Therefore, in order to explain police behaviour, one needs recourse to other concepts: the need, for example for information, to maintain 'authority' or exercise power. Looking more broadly at the role of 'rules' rather than 'the law', then it has been suggested that there are three kinds of these for police. Working rules are those internalised by police officers which become guiding principles of how they actually do the job; inhibitory rules are not internalised but are taken into account and may discourage officers from certain actions in case they are exposed and disciplined; and presentational rules which are those used to give an acceptable appearance to 'outsiders' of the actions which police take. Most of this last group derive from the criminal law.[56]

Therefore law is a potential causal influence on police behaviour and the legal context must be taken into account in explaining particular decisions alongside more informal factors such as subcultures and personal interactions.[57] But, McBarnet argued, if police behaviour deviates from the rhetoric of legality and due process then we cannot assume that it does so despite the law but, instead, must ask to what extent this deviation is institutionalised within formal law itself.[58] In the case of policing, she concludes, the answer to this question is positive:

> Any gap between how the police should behave according to democratic principles and how they do is not simply a by-product of informal abuse and non-legal motivations among the police themselves, the administrators of justice; it exists in the law as defined in court decisions and statutes by the judicial and political elites of the state. Deviation from legality is institutionalised in the law itself.[59]

In other words the law is, literally 'two-faced', it provides a resource for police whether they are acting within or without the boundary of legality, and may also provide a check, internally or externally imposed, on police behaviour.

Does the police–law relationship help us to understand the security intelligence–law relationship? The relationship between security intelligence and police agencies is close, both theoretically and in practice, although the contrary is often argued. De Sola Pool, for example, argues that the intelligence function is confounded with police tasks because the two have often been merged organisationally despite their lack of a conceptual link. He acknowledges that the police need intelligence to function effectively but argues that the police activities of a SAVAC or of a GPU have nothing to do with helping statesmen (*sic*) understand what is going on in the political process.[60] Such a dichotomy only makes sense if intelligence is regarded as an entirely passive function (as in Keller's domestic intelligence bureau above) while policing is seen as an entirely repressive function based on notions of sovereign power. It is suggested here that it will be far more fruitful to see both intelligence and policing as ranging from the 'passive' to the 'active'; both functions include more or less active methods of gathering information and executive action (power). What the state asks of both its security intelligence operatives and its police officers is information which can provide assistance in the maintenance of control in order to achieve desired policies.

Even if one accepts that there is a strong conceptual link between the two, it is not being argued here that they are simply the same nor does it necessarily follow that there should be an organisational combination of police and intelligence. These questions are addressed in Chapter 6. One significant point concerns the extent to which the organisational mandate is related directly to law. While the police mandate can be related entirely to the criminal law, only part of the security intelligence mandate can. Yet order maintenance remains a more fundamental objective of police than law enforcement: asked about this in 1986, the then Chief Constable of West Midlands, Geoffrey Dear, replied:

> They're both important, but I suppose in the final analysis it's got to be the maintenance of public order, or the prevention of disorder. You could encapsulate the whole thing, I suppose, in a not entirely flippant way, by saying

that crime can go through the roof and no-one is too worried about it. But a serious and continuing outbreak of public disorder will bring governments down and chief constables will be lost and out of a job very quickly.[61]

There is other evidence also of the low proportion of police work which contributes towards the actual prosecution of offenders.[62] But if the link between policing and the law is less than commonly supposed, it is still greater than that between security intelligence and the law. For now suffice to say that, in the UK, part of the security intelligence mandate is defined in criminal law, for example, terrorism, sabotage, and espionage, but another part – 'subversion' – is not. (See detailed discussion in Chapter 3.) Still, the point remains that the prime concern of security intelligence agencies is information-gathering, not prosecution, and therefore its targeting of people and groups will be based on the perceived need for information, not whether there is likely to be some immediate 'result', as is more likely to be a priority for the police. John Oseth sees this as 'an important analytical and practical distinction between CI [counter-intelligence] and law enforcement operations',[63] but where police and security intelligence agency share the same objective, say, the prevention of serious political violence, then the difference may be slight.[64]

In any event it remains crucial to consider the framework of law and rules within which security intelligence agencies operate. This is because liberal democracies base their claim to political superiority in large part upon the subordination of 'mere will or power' to the processes of law. If the security intelligence agency does not conduct itself within a framework of law then it may well come to constitute the antithesis of liberal democracy (as in Keller's independent security state). Thus, as has been persuasively argued by Brodeur,[65] the issue of the legal mandate of a police or security intelligence agency is as significant as external oversight mechanisms in minimising their abuse of power. While it is naive to assume that a formal legal mandate will be translated unchanged into the working rules of security intelligence officers, it can provide inhibitory rules which may lead officers to restrict their activity, compared with the situation in which there is no legal mandate at all. Even Poulantzas, who, as we saw above, is primarily concerned with the historical part played by law in repression and violence, acknowledged also that law could act as a limitation upon arbitrary state action, could regulate the exercise of state power and organise the structure of 'real rights' which dominated classes might win.[66]

The law will be similarly two-faced in the case of security intelligence. While Brodeur is right to point to the potential of law as a check on abuse, it must also be acknowledged that, compared with 'conventional' laws, 'political crime' laws are distinguished by their 'explicit politicality, their exceptional vagueness, and their greater permissiveness'.[67] For example, it has been argued that the act of establishing a legal mandate for security intelligence which incorporates notoriously ambiguous concepts such as 'subversion' is *more* dangerous (to citizen rights) because it provides a cloak of legality and increased legitimacy for the agencies.[68] An example of the greater 'permissiveness' of such laws is provided by the UK Prevention of Terrorism Act. Compared with some piece of 'conventional' law such as the Theft Act, which simply criminalises a variety of forms of behaviour, the PTA first criminalises some forms of behaviour and then, crucially, gives greater powers to the police to gather information from people about those forms of behaviour. For example, police may detain people for questioning at ports and for longer periods subsequent to arrest, and a legal duty to provide information to authorities is imposed on people. Information so gathered may contribute to a variety of countering actions, from, relatively rarely, arrests and prosecutions to more direct countering methods (see Chapter 5). This 'permissiveness' may be further augmented: 'the higher interest of the State (*raison d'Etat*)', argues Poulantzas, will mean that the gaps, blanks and 'loopholes' that exist in all juridical systems do so not as oversights but as 'express devices that allow the law to be breached'.[69] This is the context within which the UK Security Service Act 1989 needs to be considered. (See discussion in Chapter 8.)

To the extent that security intelligence officers will attempt to maximise the permissive and minimise the restrictive, it might be argued that attempts to lay more legal requirements on them will simply lead to yet more devious behaviour on their part to avoid the rules. Taken to their logical end such arguments negate any attempts at reducing the abuse of power by state agencies. Even if this position is not accepted, it should still be noted that attempts to limit agencies' activities may increase their tendency to subcontract operations to other state agencies or private operatives. The 'privatisation' of state functions may take place both officially and unofficially. This does indicate just how carefully future legal frameworks must be considered.

While 'law' may restrict 'power', it may also facilitate it, but this applies equally to laws which provide the security intelligence mandate and those relating to control and oversight – the law will be inherently ambiguous in both cases. Unless it is held that law is *only* a legitimating gloss on power, it cannot logically be argued that the law can operate only 'permissively' for the agencies and only 'restrictively' for the overseers, nor vice versa, as some insiders might fear; the law is a potential resource for both. As Stephen Sedley points out in a recent discussion of the relationship between law and state power, the law

> can sometimes bridge the cleft between the rhetoric of justice, which courts cannot jettison at will, and the exercise of state power; and it can on occasion deflect the Orwellian boot as it descends on the upturned face.[70]

Harry Ransom has also pointed to the need for students of intelligence 'to know more about knowledge and power, information and action'.[71] The mutual dependence of the two has been argued most strongly by Foucault:

> . . . there is no power relation without the correlative constitution of a field of knowledge, nor any knowledge that does not presuppose and constitute at the same time power relations.[72]

But if the concern is not just to explain the intelligence process and its relation with power, but also to control or oversee it, then the relationship of these two with law becomes equally important. As we have seen, law and power can both be characterised as double-edged, and each both supports and, sometimes, can provide a check on the other. The connections between these three – information, power and law – are central to developing the argument into a model of the state which will enhance our examination of domestic security intelligence and it is to this we now turn.

MODELLING THE STATE

Information, power and law are central to the state, as can be seen by the following:

> The emergence of the modern nation-state can . . . be identified in terms of a combination of four attributes: the concentration of political authority; citizenship as the political basis for the relationships between rulers and ruled; administration by public bureaucracy rather than by patronage; and administration of society through bureaucratic surveillance.[73]

J. A. Tapia-Valdes develops three main types of state as defined in terms of national security policies. The first of these is based on Dahl's notion of polyarchy which is characterised by the following: freedom to form and join organisations, freedom of expression, right to vote, eligibility for public office, political competition for support, alternative sources of information, free and fair elections, and government policy-making institutions controlled by elected officials.[74] Here, says Tapia-Valdes, national security policy-makers are forced to balance security needs with pluralistic interests and expectations.[75] More specifically, suggests Dahl, military and police organisations must be subject to civilian control and those civilians themselves must be subject to control by the institutions of polyarchy.[76]

Tapia-Valdes's second type is where 'national securitism' develops when 'the acuteness and persistence of the political conflict forces the government continually to resort to its emergency powers'.[77] Here the gap between the official political discourse (polyarchy) and the actual policies of the government creates a purely formal democracy. The government's legitimacy is at stake, rights are restricted, political conflict is 'militarised' and the national security establishment receives powers usually only applicable during an exceptional state of emergency. This is similar to Poulantzas's notion of 'authoritarian statism' in which the balance of coercion and consent is tilted more towards the former while 'maintaining the outer forms of democratic class rule intact'.[78] Note that, in line with the earlier discussion of power, the extra powers may reflect additional laws relating either to the imposition of the 'sovereign will', for example facilitating arrests and convictions, and/or additional powers of surveillance, and information-gathering such as powers to compel information, detain suspects longer or increase the use of other surveillance techniques.

The third type is characterised as the 'garrison state'[79] in which militarism is institutionalised and the military and/or police monopolise all political activity, opposition is outlawed, and ruling groups retain power by extra-legal means. Slightly adapting Tapia-Valdes's terms, therefore, we can talk of a polyarchical state, a national security state, and a garrison state. What is needed is a classification that can help to identify the differences both between states and within them. Regarding the latter, a model is needed to trace the shifts which can occur both between different locations (for example, Britain compared with Northern Ireland) and functional sectors of the state. There are several academic traditions on which we can draw.

THE STRONG STATE?

One major academic strand derives from international relations, specifically since 1945, and the development of the 'cold war' which saw the growth of large and permanent intelligence and military organisations locked into an international structure of nation-states, for example NATO and UKUSA.[80] Because of the accompanying developments of secrecy, vetting, militarism and authoritarianism, it has been suggested that this led to a 'challenge' to liberal democracy (polyarchy).[81] As we shall see this might be characterised more strongly as a shift to a national security state.

In a comprehensive review of the relationship between the state and the question of security, Buzan criticises the approaches to be found in both political science and sociology as being too 'inward-looking', concentrating on the distinction between state and society and the interaction between them. He criticises also the 'billiard ball' model of the realists in international relations because it ignores questions of domestic structure. Arguing that, for the purposes of security analysis, states have to be conceptualised broadly enough to encompass their internal dynamics and their interactions with each other, he proposes a tripartite model consisting of 'the idea', the institutional expression and the physical base of the state.[82] The main sources of the 'idea' of the state are to be found in the concept of nation and the organising ideology – the main significance of this is to point out that the concept of the state cannot be simply conflated with its institutional apparatuses.[83] Buzan explores the many dimensions of possible discontinuities between nations and states[84] and the ambiguous and indeterminate nature of most organising ideologies, for example 'Islam' and 'democracy'. As a result, sweeping criteria of acceptable levels of security can be established which 'can give rise to a dangerous streak of absolutism in national security policy'.[85]

Since institutions can to some extent replace ideas in constituting the state, if not in the very long term, Buzan acknowledges that there might appear to be a sliding scale of substitutability between ideas and institutions; for example, a strong state apparatus might compensate for a weak organising ideology (or legitimacy), but he argues that the two should be seen as complementary, tending to stand and fall together. Institutions are much more tangible than ideas as an object of security and consequently are more vulnerable to physical threats, but Buzan draws an important distinction between 'governing institutions' and the 'continuity of the state'. Within nations it is possible for the former to change without necessarily threatening the latter. However, it is also noted that governments frequently fall into the temptation of conflating their own security with that of the state in the context of domestic politics. The invocation of 'national security' enables the government, for example, to identify domestic opponents with some foreign threat and to make greater use of 'legitimate' violence.[86]

Finally, noting the impossibility of devising some universally applicable definition for 'national security', Buzan suggests that the key distinction to be made is between weak and strong states:

> . . . weak or strong states will refer to the degree of
> socio-political cohesion; weak or strong *powers* will refer

to the traditional distinction among states in respect of their military and economic capability in relation to each other.[87]

The main feature of weak states is their high level of concern with domestic security threats; they have insufficient political and societal consensus to enable them to eliminate the large-scale use of force and they are characterised by one or more of the following: high levels of political violence, a conspicuous role for the political police in the everyday life of citizens, major political conflict over the nature of the organising ideology, a lack of coherent national identity or the presence of contending national identities, lack of clear and observed hierarchy of political authority, and a high degree of state control over the media.[88] On the other hand, strong states have a single source of authority commanding broad legitimacy, and national security is primarily about protecting the state from outside threats and interference.

> The weaker a state is, the more ambiguous the concept of national security becomes in relation to it. To use the term in relation to a very weak state . . . paves the way for the wholesale importation of national security imperatives into the domestic political arena, with all the dangers of legitimised violence that this implies. The security of governments becomes confused with the security of states, and factional interests are provided with a legitimacy which they do not merit.[89]

This approach would clearly be highly appropriate to the large-scale comparison of different states and, in our case, their domestic security intelligence agencies, and there are undoubtedly insights here which will inform our consideration of the state in the UK. However, for the more detailed examination of any particular state, and a different view of what constitutes a strong state – we should consider approaches from other, more 'inward-looking' disciplines, as Buzan characterised them.

The most influential work here is Hall *et al.* in which post-war British history (and specifically the origin of 'mugging' as a moral panic) are examined from the Gramscian perspective of a developing crisis in hegemony. This is

> . . . a profound rupture in political and economic life, an accumulation of contradictions . . . [a] moment when the whole basis of leadership and cultural authority becomes exposed and contested.[90]

The principal way in which this is registered is in 'a tilt in the operation of the state away from consent towards the pole of coercion'.[91] Hall *et al.* argue that the late 1960s represented, in Britain and in other Western countries, a watershed after which the societies became increasingly polarised into 'authority' and its 'enemies'.[92] By 1971 the re-emergence of industrial militancy and the armed insurrection occurring in Northern Ireland coincided with earlier factors (such as student militancy, immigration, crime and 'permissiveness') to bring about 'the mobilisation of legal instruments' all aimed at producing the disciplined society.[93] Between 1972 and 1974

> . . . the 'crisis' came finally to be appropriated – by governments in office, the repressive apparatuses of the state, the media and some articulate sectors of public opinion – as an interlocking set of planned or organised *conspiracies*.[94]

From the perspective of the state, which, within representative liberal democracy has assumed the role of the organiser of conciliation and consent, its actions are 'legitimate'. Therefore any attacks on the consensus are attacks on the state itself and can only be explained by conspiracies. Because class conflicts have been reconciled by the state

> . . . conflict *must* arise because an evil minority of subversive and politically motivated men enter into a conspiracy to destroy by force what they cannot dismantle in any other way.[95]

This leads to the specification of a state of legitimate coercion or of a 'law-and-order society' in which

. . . the pendulum within the exercise of hegemony tilts, decisively, from that where consent overrides coercion, to that condition in which coercion becomes, as it were, the natural and routine form in which consent is secured.[96]

This is all highly resonant with significant political and legal developments since the 1960s, and is clearly reminiscent of Tapia-Valdes's typology. Hall *et al.* are clearly not arguing that Britain has gone as far as the garrison state[97] but their law-and-order society represents a move away from polyarchy towards the national security state.

I would suggest, however, that this characterisation is not as helpful as it might appear. First, the notion that the state came to see dissent as conspiratorial in the 1970s ignores the fact that police and security intelligence agencies have always viewed dissent and disorder as originating in conspiracies of violent minorities. Specifically, the main target of security intelligence agencies (in the UK and elsewhere) since 1917 has been the Communist Party which, despite its partially open political activities, had always been viewed as essentially a foreign-directed conspiracy aimed at the subversion of domestic political organisations, especially trades unions and the Labour Party.[98]

Second, referring back to the last quote from Hall, in certain aspects of state activity, for example military and public order policing, coercion has always been the 'natural and routine form' by which the state has attempted to secure its position. Overall, the problem here, I suggest, is with seeing the state as a homogeneous institution which 'tilts' in one direction or another. We shall return to this argument below.

A more recent contribution to this debate is *The Coercive State* written by Paddy Hillyard and Janie Percy-Smith. The authors' aim is to challenge the assumption that Britain is a democracy by examining not only those state activities which are overtly coercive but also those welfare activities which, they say, have to be demystified before their coercive nature can be seen. They establish a stricter definition of democracy than Dahl's polyarchy: it involves popular participation on an equal basis in decision-making (which is presumably more than just the right to vote and stand for office in competitive elections), access to information, accountability of those to whom responsibility is delegated, maximum opportunity for scrutiny of their decisions and respect for individual and collective liberties. Contending that the British state falls far short of such standards (which is hardly disputable) they argue that the state is 'better characterised as coercive'. Even allowing for the fact that the authors say that their method is descriptive rather than analytic, this does not seem very helpful since all dictionaries incorporate notions of force in their definitions of coercive. Even at a descriptive level, force is not a feature of 'exclusive decision-making and administration', 'few opportunities for popular participation' and 'very limited access to information' which are just some of the features of what the authors describe as the coercive state.[99] Given that the ultimate ability to use force/coercion is the *sine qua non* of all states, it is not helpful to describe any particular state as 'The Coercive State' (since it does not help us to distinguish it from any other state), particularly when some of its characteristics are clearly non-coercive!

On the face of it there is some significant contradiction between different approaches to the analysis of the state, power and security, which, while examining the same phenomena, for example the increasing concern of the state with domestic security, can characterise this as, on the one hand, a 'weakening' of the state and, on the other, a 'strengthening' of the state in a more authoritarian or coercive direction. In part, this problem is more apparent than real but, finally, it does reflect the different value-assumptions of different analytical perspectives. Any reduction in 'socio-political cohesion' will lead to what Buzan refers to as a 'weakening of the state' and might be compared with the notion of a 'crisis in hegemony' as used by Hall *et al*. In both cases the state becomes more concerned with the surveillance and countering of domestic security threats and, as such, is more likely to be characterised as an 'authoritarian' or 'national security' state. Still further weakening might lead to the imposition of a garrison state in which, from Buzan's perspective, socio-political cohesion would be at its lowest and the coercive apparatuses of the state would be its main manifestation.

Where the value-differences emerge is in the interpretation which is to be placed upon the absence of physical force in the relations between a state and its population. In Buzan's strong states, national security is mainly about ensuring the independence, identity and way of life from external threats, though it will still have to guard against threats of internal subversion.[100] The evidence for the existence of such a state is, in large part, the absence of the use of physical force by the state against its own population. For other writers, however, the absence of physical force does not necessarily indicate greater consent but, rather, the replacement of force by other, more manipulative techniques which may actually be more effective than force, for example the use of welfare regulations as suggested by Hillyard and Percy-Smith. In some cases this has gone so far as to suggest that modern power may rest entirely on internalised consent, for example Lukes's third dimension, while others have criticised the extent to which the role of violence in grounding power in those states which Buzan would consider to be 'strong' has been underestimated.[101]

Christopher Dandeker provides some synthesis of approaches which emphasise either the state's external or internal relations. He talks of the development of the 'security state' which emerged due to the combined external pressures of war and internal demands of democratisation. Included among the foundations of this state was internal civil and industrial unrest which gave rise not only to specific institutions of surveillance and control but also to a variety of welfare bureaucracies and corporatist structures, for example nationalised industries, aimed at the better regulation of the economy and society.[102]

In order to clarify the similarities and differences of these various views of state power, use can be made of the game metaphor. As we saw above (p. 56), the traditional 'sovereign' view of power is zero- (or constant) sum. Here, power is seen as essentially negative or repressive: in any power relationship the gains of one side equal the losses of the other. For example, if the state gains power, citizens suffer an equal loss of power. In a non-zero- (or, variable) sum relationship all parties may enjoy gains (or losses). This has been most associated with functionalist views of a general value-consensus in which the interests of all can be advanced by the use of power.[103]

Now, the work of Dandeker and of Hillyard and Percy-Smith is based to some extent on the 'non-sovereign' view of power we have identified and which is associated with Foucault's work. He saw power as a 'positive, creative' force which should not be seen as simply negative and repressive.[104] As

Jessop notes, both Foucault and Poulantzas treat power in this way.[105] Poulantzas rejects specifically the idea that his view of power is constant sum, for example that a loss of power by the bourgeoisie will be matched by an equal increase in the power of the working class. But he rejects this view also because he argues that the line demarcating domination and subordination does not entail the existence of a dichotomy between two groups exchanging constant sum power. Rather, he sees social formations as being more complex and comprising numerous dominant and subordinate classes, fractions of classes and groups.[106] Clearly, therefore, Poulantzas is rejecting the idea of a two-person game, as is Foucault with his concern with the 'micro-physics of power'; but is their view of power best characterised as variable or constant sum?

Their view of power is quite different from the functionalist view of power as working for the objectives of the integrated social whole.[107] Power is 'creative' only in the sense that new discourses, forms of control and deviance will be generated; for example, the creation of 'subversives' in the early twentieth century as a group requiring specific surveillance by security intelligence agencies. Crucially, these theories remain concerned with domination and subordination – remember that Foucault's concern with 'liberty' and 'security' is only within the context of domination – therefore it remains most helpful, at least at the simplest level of the game metaphor, to view them as n-person constant sum. This distinguishes them from views of 'sovereign' power (two-person constant sum) and from a functionalist view (n-person variable sum). The emphasis in n-person constant sum games is on strategies of power and coalition-building: that is, precisely those techniques of power which are at the centre of Foucault's and Poulantzas's work. It is this shift from the two-person (state versus society) to the n-person (variety of state and non-state players) view of constant sum power which is seen as most helpful to the development here of a model of the state and security intelligence.

THE DUAL STATE?

Rather than assuming, or trying to establish, that the state as a *whole* is or is not authoritarian, coercive, or weak, I would suggest, adopting the n-person game metaphor, that it will be more useful to see the state as an entity which *always* operates on different levels. Clearly, the choice of perspective is crucial to the analysis that will follow. We have already seen Buzan's point that, in connection with studies of the state, sociologists and political scientists have *chosen* to concentrate on the relation between state and society, while many international relations theorists, at least those of the realist school, have *chosen* to concentrate on the relations between states. What has characterised much of this work is the fact that the state is seen as a unified 'actor'. This approach was criticised by Graham Allison in his well-known analysis of the Cuban missile crisis, *Essence of Decision*. He noted:

> In spite of significant differences in interest and focus, most analysts and ordinary laymen [*sic*] attempt to understand happenings in foreign affairs as the more or less purposive acts of unified national governments.[108]

In criticising this Rational Actor or 'Classical' model, Allison elaborated two main alternatives, the Organizational Process and Bureaucratic Politics models. Elements of both are present in the analysis in the following chapters. For example, aspects of the internal organisation and standard operating procedures of security intelligence agencies which are examined in Chapter 6 are central to understanding their actions; similarly, the idea of the 'intelligence process' which organises the material in Chapters 4 and 5. More recently, Bob Jessop, concluding a collection of his essays, suggested that research into the state should include an exploration of how the boundaries of the state are established through specific practices. It should not be assumed, he wrote, that the 'core' of the state 'is a unified, unitary, coherent ensemble or agency'. Rather,

> In many cases we can expect to find several rival emergent 'states' corresponding to competing state projects with no overall coherence to the operations of the state system.[109]

Explorers of the terrain of security intelligence have already discovered such phenomena. In the United States, David Wise and Thomas Ross characterised 'The Invisible Government' as the 'loose amorphous grouping of individuals and agencies drawn from many parts of the visible government'. Although centred on the intelligence community, it extended also into the private sector.[110] Later, discussing the origins of the Watergate affair, Alan Wolfe identified the emergence since about 1960 of two states: the first, formal and legal, which contained all the elements of liberal democracy, and exercised a symbolic importance; the second state was covert, unaffected by changes in elected officials and unconcerned with constitutional niceties. Initially concerned primarily with foreign affairs, the 'vigilantes' of the covert state later turned their attention more to domestic politics. Overall, he argued, Kennedy, Johnson and Nixon all showed that they were prepared to break any laws that stood in the way of the national interest as they perceived it and relied upon a covert state subject only to its own discretion to achieve that end.[111]

E. P. Thompson, the British historian, writing in 1978, developed a similar theme regarding the UK:

> . . . the growth of an unrepresentative and unaccountable state within the State has been a product of the twentieth century. Its growth was, paradoxically, actually aided by the unpopularity of security and policing agencies; forced by this into the lowest possible visibility, they learned to develop techniques of invisible influence and control.[112]

Thompson identifies a number of causal factors; for example, two world wars accustoming people 'to arguments of national interest', and facilitating much interchange between academics and intelligence agencies; the retreat from empire, leaving security, military and police agencies with colonial experience looking for new fields of application; and the legacy of 'McCarthyism' in Britain which, while not producing anything as stringent as the *Berufsverbot* in West Germany, resulted, through the positive vetting system in a 'moderate' orthodoxy in the higher reaches of the civil service.[113] Dorril and Ramsay make use of a similar notion to Thompson's with the concept of a 'permanent government' in Britain in their discussion of the discrediting of Harold Wilson.[114]

Writing about the development of counter-insurgency thinking and, more specifically, its application to the domestic politics of Western states, Schlesinger has also pointed out that any theory of state power 'must also consider the possibility that sectoral repression exists despite the existence of democratic forms'.[115] I would suggest that the idea of 'sector' is synonymous with that of 'levels' of the state. Sim *et al.* also refer to different levels of the state in their criticism of notions of 'authoritarian drift':

> . . . the state comprises a series of relations which exist at different levels. It is its very complexity, encompassing contradictory elements, which enables opposition to emerge within the state while defending established positions through internal alliances.[116]

The rules, policies and practices relating to information, power and decision-making at the different levels of the state are frequently quite different; indeed each of these has its own discourse.[117] So, within the 'secret state' there is a predominant 'insider' view concerned more with the need for effective operations and a view of law and oversight mechanisms as inhibiting these, while outside and in the public discourse there is likely to be more concern with the propriety of operations, and with legal rights.[118]

A number of factors explain how these different levels and their discourses continue along their contradictory paths. Part of the answer lies in secrecy; people may well be aware of the liberal democratic rhetoric of the public discourse, but they will not be aware of the specific details of operations carried out by agencies. As long as these remain secret their only connection with law will be with the 'Ways and Means Act'; it will only be if those operations become public that it will become necessary to provide *post hoc* rationalisations of the actions that were taken. Indeed, the specific rules, if any, by which such actions were undertaken, for example the use of 'deadly force' by soldiers or police, may themselves be state secrets.[119] Another part of the answer parallels Doreen McBarnet's exploration of how the law simultaneously sets out to achieve crime control while maintaining the ideology of due process of law. Part of her explanation is structural:

The doctrine of the separation of powers provides a multi-headed state and with it the potential to extol the rhetoric in one sector and deny it in another;[120]

and part lies in techniques of judicial reasoning. Specifically, judges will routinely reiterate the rhetoric of due process in general but will decide particular cases in ways which deny that due process to individuals.[121] The separation of these levels and discourses is also maintained by a number of other mechanisms explored in Chapter 6, for example, the 'need-to-know' and 'plausible deniability'.

AUTONOMY, PENETRATION AND THE GORE-TEX STATE

Before developing the model of a dual or multi-level state for the purposes of analysing security intelligence, we need to consider two further concepts: autonomy and penetration. Autonomy encompasses the relationship between internal security agencies and the state. It raises the question of how independent from external influences security intelligence agencies are in terms of their policies and practices. Does the government (elected ministers in a liberal democracy or other ruling group elsewhere) control the agency, or is the agency essentially autonomous in terms of its targets, its methods of gathering information and its use of countering methods? Tapia-Valdes, for example, incorporates the 'autonomy of the national security establishment'[122] as one variable in classifying types of national security policies. Similarly, Wilsnack, in his discussion of information control processes, notes that relatively dominant groups may use interlocking information control processes specifically 'to minimise their vulnerability to outside influence',[123] in other words to guard their autonomy. The concept of autonomy is also central to Keller's typology of security intelligence agencies. He sees the autonomy of security agencies as measured by their activity which is not controlled or regulated by statute or by any formal executive or judicial policy instrument.[124]

The term 'penetration' is used to describe the relation between the agency and the society, again incorporating considerations of information, power and law. Albeit a 'masculinist' term, it does convey a sense of internal security agencies attempting, sometimes against resistance, sometimes unheeded, to gather information and exercise power within a particular context of law and rules which facilitate the state's efforts to maintain security and order.[125]

Combining the idea of the 'dual state' and these two concepts suggests a model of the state analogous to Gore-Tex. This is a fabric (worn in wet weather by rich runners and other sportspersons) which is covered in a PFTE membrane (that is, there are two *levels* to the fabric). Each pore of the membrane is many times smaller than a drop of water yet many times larger than a molecule of sweat and therefore sweat and body heat can escape while the rain is kept out. So it is with the 'secret state': the barriers of secrecy between it and both other parts of the state and then with society at large cannot normally be penetrated from outside by the 'rain' of public inquiry (represented by the broken arrows in Figure 2.1), but those barriers do not inhibit the 'sweat' of the secret state itself from penetrating outwards into the rest of the state and society in its search for information and its implementation of countering techniques (unbroken arrows in Figure 2.1).

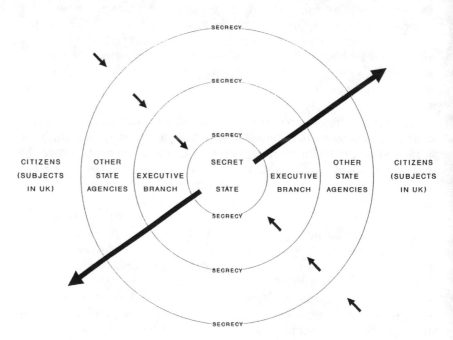

Figure 2.1 The Gore-Tex State

For the purposes of the present analysis three levels of the state are identified. The first, the 'secret state' includes the security intelligence agencies and related bodies such as the JIC and the NSC. The second level is the executive branch which incorporates both the government, or 'political executive', and the permanent bureaucracy. The third level will include legislative assemblies, the judiciary and other bodies appointed by the executive but formally operating independently thereof. The fourth level of analysis, outside the state, is society made up of citizens or, in the UK, subjects.[126]

Wilsnack's discussion of information control processes can also be incorporated into the analysis. Viewed from the perspective of the 'secret state', or inner circle, 'espionage' is the process by which the state penetrates into society in order to gather information, and 'evaluation' is one specific aspect of that process. 'Persuasion' is that aspect of the state's penetration which is concerned with 'information policy', with getting its preferred view of events across, whether this is believed to be accurate or known to be false. 'Secrecy' is the process by which the inner circle seeks to guard its autonomy against encroachments from outer circles. In other words, the model is 'panoptic' – the system of surveillance laid down in modern institutions such as prisons, in which the subject of control is seen without seeing, while the agents of control see without being seen.[127]

This model can also provide a different perspective on the earlier discussion of debates about the shift toward an authoritarian state in Britain; put simply, the developments noted by Hall *et al.* might be seen as the extension to other state agencies of the policies and practices which have been employed by the 'secret state' since its origins.

This model of the Gore-Tex state is one which can be utilised to examine any state; its applicability is not limited just to liberal democracies. What it does not provide, however, is a more specific means for comparing different security intelligence agencies or the same agency at different times. Keller's autonomy/insularity dichotomy provides a useful tool for the analysis of the relation between security intelligence agencies and the rest of the state.[128] However, in order to bring the society into the picture, it is useful to develop Keller's idea of the 'mode of intelligence activity'[129] into the broader concept of penetration.

This gives us a richer variety of 'ideal-types' of security intelligence agencies to further the analysis of the contents of the inner state circle. At one extreme in Figure 2.2 is the independent security state. Here the security intelligence agency is formally embedded within the state yet is actually autonomous of the government and the rest of the state machine while penetrating deeply into social life in its search for information and, probably, its countering activities – a 'strong' Gore-Tex. At the other end is the domestic intelligence bureau which is subject to firm ministerial control and is not permitted to penetrate far into society, relying primarily on open source material and not engaging in countering activities – a 'weak' Gore-Tex.

Between these two is the political police, which enjoys greater autonomy than the bureau from ministerial control and the freedom to employ more extensive information and countering techniques, but which is still subject to greater external control than the independent security state. Where actual security intelligence agencies could be located is an empirical question; indeed, the same agency may be found at different points at different times. While it may seem unlikely that many agencies would locate at C or G, the possibility of either an autonomous agency which exercises high self-restraint or one which is subject to strict ministerial control and is highly penetrative is not excluded.

PENETRATION

		HIGH	MEDIUM	LOW
	HIGH	A Independent Security State	B	C
AUTONOMY	MEDIUM	D	E Political Police	F
	LOW	G	H	I Domestic Intelligence Bureau

Figure 2.2   A Typology of Security Intelligence Agencies

CONCLUSION

The objective of this chapter has been to consider those theoretical and conceptual questions needed to develop a model of security intelligence. This can be used heuristically to suggest avenues of inquiry in order to gain a better understanding of, and democratise the agencies in, the UK. Central to the model will be the practices and processes of information control, power and law. Information control processes of espionage, secrecy and persuasion are central to the questions both of what security intelligence agencies do and of how they might be controlled and subjected to democratic oversight. Since the concern in this analysis is not simply to understand the security intelligence process but also to control it, questions of law arise, specifically the potential and limits of law as a means of controlling the agencies. The power of the agencies needs to be analysed both from the traditional perspective that their information-gathering provides the basis for a range of executive countering actions, from disruption to lethal force, and from the more recent perspective that surveillance itself constitutes a form of power.

Since security intelligence agencies are embedded within the state the model must deal with the interaction of these concepts both within the state and in terms of the state–society relationship. Different types of state – polyarchy, national security, garrison – were identified but in using those categories it is important to note the heterogeneity of the state. Not only might a state move between those categories through time, but different levels or sectors of the state might simultaneously be categorised differently. Specifically it is argued that the state–society relationship should be seen not in terms of a two-person game, but as a *n*-person game dominated by strategic practices of information control and power as between various agencies operating at different levels of the state and outside groups.

The two main concepts within which these practices might be summarised are autonomy and penetration. The first incorporates those processes by which the secret state agencies resist the encroachment of other state agencies and citizens, while the second covers the variety of techniques by which the secret state carries out its surveillance and supervision of other agencies and society in general. The interaction of autonomy and penetration provide the basis for two separate models (though they can be combined). The first, the Gore-Tex state – incorporates the information control and power process as between various levels of the state and society. The second provides, more specifically,

83

for different types of security intelligence agencies which can be used both in the assessment of what UK agencies have been in the past and what they should be in the future.

NOTES

1. M.S. Feldman and J.G. March, 'Information in Organizations as Signal and Symbol', in J.G. March (ed.), *Decisions and Organizations* (Oxford: Basil Blackwell, 1989), p. 411.
2. Ibid, p. 414.
3. Ibid, p. 416.
4. Ibid, p. 417.
5. D. Beetham, *Bureaucracy* (Milton Keynes: Open University Press, 1987), p. 17.
6. B.G. Peters, *The Politics of Bureaucracy* (New York: Longman, 2nd edition, 1984), p. 136.
7. D. Bradley, N. Walker and R. Wilkie, *Managing the Police: Law, Organisation and Democracy* (Brighton: Wheatsheaf, 1986), pp. 120–41, discuss the problems inherent in police hierarchies.
8. R.W. Wilsnack, 'Information Control: A Conceptual Framework for Sociological Analysis', *Urban Life*, 8(4), 1980, pp. 467–99.
9. R. Lowry, 'Towards a Sociology of Secrecy and Security Systems', *Social Problems*, 19(4), Spring 1972, p. 438.
10. S. Bok, *Secrets: Concealment and Revelation* (Oxford: Oxford University Press, 1986). R.A. Chapman, 'Introduction', in R.A. Chapman and M. Hunt, *Open Government: a Study of the Prospects of Open Government within the Limitations of the British Political System* (London: Croom Helm, 1987), p. 17.
11. T. Tant, *Constitutional Aspects of Official Secrecy and Freedom of Information: An Overview* (University of Essex: Essex Papers in Politics and Government, 1988), p. 11.
12. For example, see C. Dandeker, *Surveillance, Power and Modernity: Bureaucracy and Discipline from 1700 to the Present Day* (Cambridge: Polity Press, 1990), pp. 17–18.
13. Tant, supra (note 11), pp. 3–16; K.G. Robertson, *Public Secrets* (Basingstoke: Macmillan, 1982), Ch.4.
14. Robertson, ibid, p. 63.
15. Wilsnack, supra (note 8), p. 470.
16. J.M. Oseth, *Regulating United States Intelligence Operations: A*

Study in Definition of the National Interest (Lexington: University Press of Kentucky, 1985), pp. 135–7.

17. *The Guardian*, 29 July 1992, p. 1; 1 August 1992, p. 1.
18. Wilsnack, supra (note 8), p. 471.
19. Bok, supra (note 10), pp. 175–6.
20. Quoted in D. Beetham, *Max Weber and the Theory of Modern Politics* (London: George Allen & Unwin, 1974), p. 74. J. Orman, *Presidential Accountability: New and Recurring Problems* (New York: Greenwood Press, 1990), pp. 47–9 offers a costs/benefits calculus for presidential secrecy regarding national security.
21. Chapman and Hunt, supra (note 10) pp. 18–21 provides an interesting account of how UK and US procedures were approximately standardised after 1945. I. Linn, *Application Refused* (London: Civil Liberties Trust, 1990), p. 17 provides current UK definitions of these classifications.
22. Wilsnack, supra (note 8), p. 473.
23. T.G. Poveda, *Lawlessness and Reform: the FBI in Transition* (Pacific Grove, CA: Brooks/Cole Publishing Co., 1989), pp. 81–4.
24. Bok, supra (note 10), p. 174.
25. *The Observer*, 3 March 1985; *City Limits*, 7–14 August 1986.
26. Bok, supra (note 10), p. 189.
27. D. Wise, *The Politics of Lying: Government Deception, Secrecy, and Power* (New York: Random House, 1973) is a detailed account of the impact of the 'credibility gap' on US politics. See also Orman, supra (note 20), pp. 50–54 regarding presidential deception.
28. Wilsnack, supra (note 8), p. 475.
29. Ibid, pp. 477–86.
30. For a general discussion of this within and between UKUSA nations see J.T. Richelson and D. Ball, *The Ties That Bind: Intelligence Co-operation between the UKUSA Countries* (Boston: Unwin Hyman, 2nd edition, 1990), pp. 239–61.
31. Bok, supra (note 10), pp. 177–8; Lowry, supra (note 9), pp. 439–40; Wilsnack, supra (note 8), pp. 493–4.
32. S.R. Clegg, *Frameworks of Power* (London: Sage, 1989), p. 4. Pp. 1–20 provide a good summary of the major debates regarding the analysis of power.
33. P. Dunleavy and B. O'Leary, *Theories of the State: The Politics of Liberal Democracy* (Basingstoke: Macmillan, 1987), pp. 340–41.
34. S. Lukes, *Power: A Radical View* (London: Macmillan, 1974),

pp. 11–33; Clegg, supra (note 32), p. 90 provides a useful diagram summarising these dimensions.

35. N.W. Polsby, 'Empirical Investigations of Mobilisation of Bias in Community Power Research', *Political Studies*, XXVII(4), December 1979, 527–49.

36. Lukes, supra (note 34), pp. 19–20.

37. Clegg, supra (note 32), pp. 153–9.

38. Ibid, pp. 5–6.

39. For example, see G. Turkel, 'Michel Foucault: Law, Power and Knowledge', *Journal of Law and Society*, 17(2), Summer 1990, p.190; S. Hall, 'Introduction', in D. Held *et al.* (eds), *States and Societies* (Oxford, Martin Robertson, 1983), p. 247.

40. M. Foucault, 'Power, Sovereignty and Discipline', in Held *et al.* (eds), ibid, p. 310.

41. Clegg, supra (note 32), p. 191.

42. M. Foucault, 'Governmentality', in G. Burchell *et al.* (eds), *The Foucault Effect: Studies in Governmentality* (London: Harvester Wheatsheaf, 1991), pp. 102–3.

43. N. Poulantzas, *State, Power, Socialism* (London: Verso, 1978), p. 77.

44. C. Gordon, 'Governmental Rationality: An Introduction', in Burchell *et al.* (eds) supra (note 42), p. 20.

45. Foucault, supra (note 42), p. 102.

46. Foucault, 1978, quoted in Gordon, supra (note 44), pp. 19–20.

47. Poulantzas, supra (note 43), p. 77, emphasis in original.

48. B. Jessop, *State Theory: Putting Capitalist States in Their Place* (Cambridge: Polity Press, 1990), p. 235.

49. M. Ignatieff, 'State, Civil Society and Total Institutions: A Critique of Recent Social Histories of Punishment' in S. Cohen and A. Scull (eds), *Social Control and the State* (Oxford: Martin Robertson, 1985), pp. 75–105, especially p. 87.

50. Foucault has been criticised for not distinguishing adequately between the different control practices of different institutions compared with, say, Weber, who was more specific about the development of bureaucratic modes of surveillance in relation to struggles between classes, groups and states. Dandeker, supra (note 12), pp. 37–9, 114–23.

51. Clegg, supra (note 32), pp. 182–93. M. Poster, *Foucault, Marxism and History* (Cambridge: Polity Press, 1984), p. 88, note 18.

52. W.W. Keller, *The Liberals and J. Edgar Hoover: Rise and Fall of a Domestic Intelligence State* (Princeton: Princeton University Press, 1989), pp. 13–16.
53. Ibid, p. 156.
54. Cf Posby, supra (note 35).
55. Clegg, supra (note 32), pp. 173–4.
56. D.J.Smith and J. Gray, *Police and People in London, IV: The Police in Action* (London: Policy Studies Institute, 1983), pp. 169–71.
57. D.J. McBarnet, 'Arrest: the Legal Context of Policing', in S. Holdaway (ed.), *The British Police* (London: Edward Arnold, 1979), p. 27.
58. Ibid, p. 28.
59. Ibid, p. 39.
60. I. de Sola Pool, 'Approaches to Intelligence and Social Science', in R.L. Pfaltzgraff, Jr. *et al.* (eds), *Intelligence Policy and National Security* (Basingstoke: Macmillan, 1981), p. 39.
61. Brass Tacks, *Arms of the Law,* broadcast on BBC2, 17 July 1986.
62. For example, see R. Kinsey, *Merseyside Police Officers Survey* (Liverpool: Merseyside County Council, 1985), pp. 42–53.
63. Oseth, supra (note 16), p. 22.
64. S. Farson, 'Security Intelligence Versus Criminal Intelligence: Lines of Demarcation, Areas of Obfuscation, and the Need to Re-evaluate Organizational Roles in Responding to Terrorism', *Policing and Society* 2(1), 1991, pp. 84–5.
65. J.-P. Brodeur, 'Legitimising Police Deviance' in C. Shearing (ed.), *Organisational Police Deviance* (Toronto: Butterworths, 1981) pp. 153–4.
66. Poulantzas, supra (note 43), pp. 76–91.
67. A.T. Turk, *Political Criminality: The Defiance and Defense of Authority* (Beverley Hills: Sage, 1982), p. 54.
68. For example, see E. Grace and C. Leys, *The Concept of Subversion*, paper delivered at SIRC Conference, Queen's University, Ontario, February 1988.
69. Poulantzas, supra (note 43), pp. 84–5, emphasis in original.
70. S. Sedley, 'Law and State Power: A Time for Reconstruction', *Journal of Law and Society*, 17(2), 1990, p. 238.
71. H.H. Ransom, 'Being Intelligent about Secret Intelligence Agencies', *American Political Science Review*, 74(1), March 1980, p. 148.

72. Quoted in Turkel, supra (note 39), p. 179.
73. Dandeker, supra (note 12), p. 56.
74. R.A. Dahl, *Modern Political Analysis* (Englewood Cliffs: Prentice-Hall International, 5th edition, 1991), pp. 72–4.
75. J.A. Tapia-Valdes, 'A Typology of National Security Policies', *Yale Journal of World Public Order*, 9(10), 1982, p. 17.
76. Dahl, supra (note 74), p. 82.
77. Tapia-Valdes, supra (note 75), p. 21.
78. S. Hall, 'Authoritarian Populism: Reply to Jessop', *New Left Review*, 152, 1985, p. 117. See also Poulantzas, supra (note 43), pp. 203–16.
79. Tapia-Valdes, supra (note 75), p. 28.
80. For example, see Richelson and Ball, supra (note 30).
81. T. McGrew, *Global Challenges to Democratic Government*, Block 4, D308, Democratic Government and Politics (Milton Keynes: Open University Press, 1987), pp. 61–4.
82. B. Buzan, *People, States and Fear: An Agenda for International Security Studies in the Post-Cold War Era* (Hemel Hempstead: Harvester Wheatsheaf, 2nd edn, 1991), pp. 59–65.
83. Ibid, p. 70.
84. Ibid, pp. 70–75.
85. Ibid, p. 81 and see discussion in Chapter 3 of the problem of ambiguous definitions of 'national security'.
86. Ibid, pp. 84–90.
87. Ibid, p. 97, emphasis in original.
88. Ibid, pp. 99–100.
89. Ibid, p. 102.
90. S. Hall *et al., Policing The Crisis: Mugging, the State and Law and Order* (Basingstoke: Macmillan, 1978), p. 217.
91. Ibid.
92. Ibid, pp. 243–51.
93. Ibid, p. 284.
94. Ibid, p. 309, emphasis in original.
95. Ibid, p. 310, emphasis in original.
96. Ibid, p. 320.
97. See ibid, pp. 320–21.
98. See B. Porter, *Plots and Paranoia* (London: Unwin Hyman, 1989), *passim*.
99. P. Hillyard and J. Percy-Smith, *The Coercive State: The Decline of Democracy in Britain* (London: Fontana, 1988), pp. 14–16.

100. Buzan, supra (note 82), p. 103.
101. For example, Poulantzas, supra (note 43), p. 79.
102. Dandeker, supra (note 12), pp. 102–7.
103. For example, T. Parsons, 'On the Concept of Political Power', *Proceedings of the American Philosophical Society*, 107, 1963, pp. 232–62.
104. Poster, supra (note 51), p. 83.
105. Jessop, supra (note 48), p. 226.
106. N. Poulantzas, *Political Power and Social Classes* (London: New Left Books, 1975), p. 119.
107. Ibid, p. 118.
108. G.T. Allison, *Essence of Decision: Explaining the Cuban Missile Crisis* (Boston: Little, Brown, 1971), pp. 4–5.
109. Jessop, supra (note 48), p. 366. Buzan also talks of 'many layers of sub-state actors' existing within the state, supra (note 82), p. 349.
110. D. Wise and T.B. Ross, *The Invisible Government* (London: Mayflower, 1968), p. 9
111. A. Wolfe, 'Extralegality and American Power', *Society*, March/April 1976, p. 46. Similarly, M.G. Raskin discusses the national security state as the US version of the 'Dual State': 'Democracy Versus the National Security State' in *Law and Contemporary Problems*, 40(3), 1976, p. 202.
112. E.P. Thompson, *The Secret State*, State Research Pamphlet No. 1 (London: Independent Research Publications, 1979), p.9.
113. Ibid, pp. 9–10.
114. S. Dorril and R. Ramsay, *Smear! Wilson and the Secret State* (London: Fourth Estate, 1991), pp x–xi
115. P. Schlesinger, 'On the Shape and Scope of Counter-Insurgency Thought', in G. Littlejohn *et al.* (eds), *Power and the State* (London: Croom Helm, 1978), p. 125.
116. J. Sim *et al.*, 'Introduction: Crime, the State and Critical Analysis', in P. Scraton (ed.), *Law, Order and the Authoritarian State* (Milton Keynes: Open University Press, 1987), p. 62.
117. S. Farson, 'Propriety, Efficacy and Balance: A Preliminary Appraisal of Canada's "New", "Improved" Administrative Security Program', in P. Hanks and J.D. McCamus (eds), *National Security: Surveillance and Accountability in a Democratic Society* (Cowansville, Québec: Les Editions Yvon Blais, 1989), pp. 129–30.
118. Ibid, and P. Gill, 'The Evolution of the Security Intelligence

Debate in Canada since 1976', in A.S. Farson *et al.* (eds), *Security and Intelligence in a Changing World: New Perspectives for the 1990s* (London: Frank Cass, 1991), pp. 89–91.

119. Cf Poulantzas, supra (note 43), pp. 89–90. Mark Urban provides an illustration of the way in which the 'Yellow Card' in Northern Ireland will be used by soldiers as 'presentational rules', *Big Boys' Rules* (London: Faber and Faber, 1992), p. 72.

120. D.J. McBarnet, *Conviction: Law, the State and the Construction of Justice* (Basingstoke: Macmillan, 1981), p. 159.

121. Ibid.

122. Tapia-Valdes, supra (note 75), p. 16.

123. Wilsnack, supra (note 8), p. 491.

124. Keller, supra (note 52), p. 21. This aspect of security intelligence is discussed in detail in Chapter 6 and is augmented by Keller's companion concept of 'insularity' which 'refers to the ability of the agency to carry out programs without interference from societal and state actors that assuredly would exert countervailing force in its absence.' (Ibid, p. 20.) This 'ability' is subsumed here within 'autonomy' and is discussed in detail in Chapters 7 and 8.

125. Dandeker, supra (note 12), p. 43 and Gurr, 'War, Revolution, and the Growth of the Coercive State', *Comparative Political Studies*, 21(1), April 1988, p. 56 provide just two of many examples of the use of this term to describe states' attempts to control their societies.

126. These four levels correspond to the categories identified by former Director of the CIA, Stansfield Turner, as those which focused the intelligence debate in the US in the 1970s. Oseth, supra (note 16), p. 182.

127. Dandeker, supra (note 12), p. 25. Cf also Gary Marx who discusses the shift towards a 'maximum-security society'. One aspect of this – 'a transparent or porous society' – clearly facilitates penetration by the state. *Undercover: Police Surveillance in America* (Berkeley: University of California Press, 1988), pp. 220–21. The many theoretical and empirical questions discussed in this book are considered further in the articles published together in *Crime, Law and Social Change*, 18(1–2), September 1992: *Special Issue: Issues and Theories on Covert Policing*.

128. See note 124.

129. Keller, supra (note 52), pp. 16–17.

3

Defining the Security
Intelligence Mandate

We saw in the last chapter how a number of key concepts may be utilised in the study of security intelligence. In this chapter we see how other concepts are equally crucial in explaining what security intelligence agencies actually do. Both sets of concepts are seen to be 'essentially contested' – those employed by security intelligence agencies as part of their mandate are no more capable of purely 'scientific' elucidation than are those employed by social scientists. The analysis in this chapter centres on national security, which provides the most general security intelligence mandate, and two more specific ones, subversion and terrorism. Espionage and sabotage are other specific mandates but they are not discussed here in detail because, apart from limitations of space, they are more likely to be defined in the criminal law and are subject to less 'contestation'.[1] The course of political battles over the definition of the core security intelligence mandate provides a good indicator of the relative strengths of the various political forces engaged in the (potential) control and oversight of the agencies concerned.

The question of mandate is examined before organisational questions of security intelligence because any inquiry should ask whether there is, in fact, a need for a specific domestic security intelligence agency separate from police. It is important to examine, first, just what threats to the state and nation are seen to exist, and only then to discuss what organisational arrangements should be made for gathering information and countering those threats.

THE CONCEPT OF NATIONAL SECURITY[2]

Until the 1970s the security intelligence agencies of North America and the UK possessed either no formal mandates or ones developed entirely within the executive arm of the state. Even where they did exist their dominant characteristic was considerable vagueness and ambiguity. The overarching concept is 'national security', but initially let us consider briefly the notion of security. First, a cautionary word: because the evidence regarding security is so ambiguous and confusing

> analysis is plagued by questions which have either no clear answer or several equally plausible ones. Where such questions exist, the way is clear for the politicisation of the security policy process, as different interests seek to make their view prevail.[3]

Conversely, it might be argued, a lack of political debate on these questions could reflect a state dominant to an unhealthy degree. Tapia-Valdes offers the following:

> In a general sense, 'security' is an individual or collective feeling of being free from external dangers or threats, whether physical, psychological or psycho-sociological, which could jeopardise the achievement and preservation of some objectives considered essential, such as life, freedom, self-identity and well-being. This notion of security implies freedom from uncertainty. Such a state of affairs has an ideal existence only.[4]

But complete freedom from uncertainty may be far from 'ideal': more accurately such a hypothetical situation might be characterised as an 'ideal-type', because of the fundamental paradox of security. R.N. Berki discusses social, moral and political paradoxes[5] but they come together as follows: no individual is capable of achieving complete security for himself (though inequality ensures that some are able to purchase more than others) and therefore all depend on some collectivity to enhance their personal security.

92

Theoretically, the two extreme possibilities are the state and the community. The first is the Hobbesian idea of the Leviathan which individuals 'contract' to obey in order to escape the state of nature in which life is 'nasty, brutish and short'. The second is the anarchist idea of the freely associating community in which there is no coercion. Either complete subordination to the state in the first instance, or complete incorporation within the community in the second amounts to a complete loss of individuality. Thus, the individual has no autonomy or power *vis-à-vis* the state or community. For the individual the situation of complete security is simultaneously one of total insecurity. Put another way, if the state is so powerful as to be able to protect its citizens against all threats to their security, the state itself will constitute a massive threat to that security.

In actuality the situation will be less stark: even if Foucault sees security as the central component in the dominance of modern government he sees also that resistance is inherent to that domination,[6] while, for Buzan, 'the grounds for disharmony between individual and national security represent a permanent contradiction'.[7]

Buzan develops his earlier analysis of the tripartite structure of states – the idea, the physical base and the institutional expression (see discussion above in Chapter 2) – and distinguishes between vulnerabilities and threats. Vulnerabilities are relatively easy to establish in terms of the strength or otherwise of the ideological, physical and institutional bases of the state and one kind of national security policy would be for the state to seek to reduce its vulnerabilities.[8] Threats, however, are harder to pin down, first, because of problems of perception. Actual threats may not be perceived at all, while those threats that dominate perception may have little substantive reality. Second, there is the problem of distinguishing between those threats which might cause serious harm to national security and those which are simply the routine uncertainties of life in a competitive international political economy. In those cases where, accidentally or by design, particular problems are labelled as security threats, the political process, as we have already discussed in the last chapter, can be seen to shift away from 'constitutional practices' towards authoritarianism,[9] or, as Tapia-Valdes would have it, from polyarchy towards 'national securitism',[10] or, as is suggested here, where the traditional methods of the security state spread wider throughout the rest of the state apparatus.

There is, not surprisingly given its contested nature, little consensus as to what national security is, though many definitions have been offered.[11] One characteristic that appears more or less universally is the notion of military threat, but what is then added to the definition depends, at least in part, on from where the person offering the definition is coming. For example, the US Department of Defense limits its definition to questions of military and diplomatic advantage over other nations[12] while political scientist Richard Ullman refers very broadly to the quality of life and the integrity of the pluralistic political process:

> A threat to national security is an action or sequence of events that (1) threatens drastically and over a relatively brief span of time to degrade the quality of life for the inhabitants of a state, or (2) threatens significantly to narrow the range of policy choices available to the government of a state or to private, non-governmental entities (persons, groups, corporations) within the state.[13]

While some define national security positively – for example, 'the ability of a nation to pursue successfully its national interests, as it sees them, any place in the world'[14] – most define it 'negatively' as it were, in terms of threats, as does Ullman, above.

Buzan identifies five main threats,[15] The first, military, is, as we have seen, the central traditional concern of national security and can cause serious harm to all components of the state. The second, political, is more directly relevant to our concern with domestic security since it is more likely to emanate from within the state and is most likely to be directed at the organising ideology and institutions of the state. The labelling of political movements as threats to national security may, of course, tell us as much about the state applying the label as about anything intrinsic to the movement. For example, a 'liberal' political movement might be seen by an authoritarian or monarchist state as constituting a threat to national security, while a 'liberal' state will in turn label a communist or religious fundamentalist

94

movement as such a threat. The third, societal, can be difficult to disentangle from political, for example, where the movement involves attacks on national identities.

The fourth, economic, is, suggests Buzan, the most difficult to deal with in the context of national security. In one sense this is because the idea of an economic threat to national security is a contradiction in terms, particularly where the state supports the pre-eminence of a market economy. Uncertainty, competition, and risk, are all indispensable conditions of the market place which is alleged to be the most superior method of organising production and distribution. Therefore 'threat' to national economic actors may be no more than a reflection of their inferior performance, and to attempt to protect them would be simply to distort the operations of the market. Decisions as to when such threats do become questions of national security are, therefore, highly political questions, and Buzan recommends that efforts to elevate particular economic issues onto the national security agenda should be treated with suspicion as a matter of course.[16] Robin Robison, who recently resigned from his position within the Joint Intelligence Committee, said that one of the reasons for his disenchantment was the fact that he was analysing and disseminating purely economic intelligence to the private sector in a way which did not seem to him to be anything to do with national security.[17]

Three main linkages are identified as indicating more genuine economic threats to national security: where it involves the supply of strategic materials which in turn affects the military threat,[18] where it concerns the overall power of the state within the international political system and where economic threats directly impact on domestic stability. In the last case, contemporary social structures in industrialised societies which have developed with increasing prosperity may rely on a continuation of trade and interdependent economic relations. Where these structures are seen to be threatened then harm to national security is more likely to be perceived, For example, the impact in the UK of the 1973–74 oil price increases and a coincident reassertion of the labour movement were both economic threats giving rise to the perception of some that national security was under threat. Indeed, John Davies, a member of the Heath Cabinet at the time, reportedly said to his wife and children in 1973 'that we should have a nice time, because I deeply believed then that it was the last Christmas of its kind we would enjoy'.[19]

The fifth threat, and the most recent to be acknowledged, is the ecological, aspects of which are now seen as the consequence of human action, even if only some instances, for example, pollution across frontiers, can be dealt with by the action of individual states. More often such threats can be dealt with only by collective action.[20]

In the foregoing discussion no distinction is made between foreign and domestic threats; indeed Buzan's five types are clearly derived primarily from the much larger literature regarding foreign threats. Can the same five adequately cover the more specific question of domestic, or internal, security? The military threat is less applicable; for example, Tapia-Valdes draws a distinction:

> The internal side of national security has to deal with rather non-conventional threats, different from actual warfare operations and linked, by its nature, to the ideological characteristic of contemporary belligerent conflicts. These non-conventional threats are those jeopardising internal order, domestic peace and governmental effectiveness.[21]

The lower significance of conventional military threats is probably the greatest distinction to be drawn between domestic and foreign security concerns. Armed force against a state from within is likely to be paramilitary rather than military and to be characterised by the state as terrorism (see discussion below pp. 123–6).

Otherwise, political, societal and economic are likely to characterise the main sources of domestic 'threat'; in addition the possibility of domestic ecological threats will have to be considered. Needless to say, distinguishing domestic from foreign threats may be easier from an analytical than a practical point of view, particularly with growing interdependency. However, the effort does need to be made, since surveillance of domestic political movements has frequently been conducted on the pretext of searching for evidence of covert foreign influence.

In examining the question of when threats might legitimately become issues of national security, Buzan suggests the key factor is their intensity,[22] and this would be equally the case for domestic and for foreign threats. Intensity would include: the threat's specificity, its nearness in space and time, its probability, the weight of its consequences (trivial or serious), and whether or not perceptions of a particular threat are amplified by previous experience. The complexity of the process of assessing threats is compounded as threats begin to interact with countermeasures taken to meet them. For example, the propensity of security officials to play safe by thinking in 'worst-case' terms can result in both the overestimation of the intensity of any threat and an overreaction in terms of countering policies. Given the bureaucratisation of security intelligence within contemporary states, this may also place security agencies in a strong position in domestic budget processes. A classic illustration of this in the domestic security area would be the FBI under J. Edgar Hoover. Hoover's success in protecting the autonomy of the FBI and its resource base can be argued to have been built upon his success in convincing Congress and the public, first, that American communists constituted a serious threat to the national security of the US, and, second, that only the FBI could effectively counter that threat.[23]

Given that broad definitions of national security can pervert the democratic political process, the implications for policy of this conceptual complexity are twofold. First, clear criteria are required for determining how information is to be gathered as to what threats exist, and then criteria need to be established for assessing which threats are of sufficient intensity to require countering action. Chapters 6 and 7 consider the mechanisms required for this, bearing in mind that explicit countering actions are not the only potential threat to the democratic process; that can arise also from the use of surveillance techniques which can amount to disruption and the 'chilling' of rights. A brief consideration of the history of recent national security policy in various countries, however, will demonstrate that such clear criteria have not been employed. Rather, what is manifest is that the term has been used to increase the discretionary power available to political executives.

NATIONAL SECURITY IN THE UNITED KINGDOM

In the UK, the term national security has often been utilised by governments to justify going beyond normally permissible limits in the investigation of citizens' activities. Officially:

> This term has been in general use for many years in a variety of contexts and is generally understood to refer to the safeguarding of the state and the community against threats to their survival or well-being. I am not aware that any previous Administration have thought it appropriate to adopt a specific definition of the term.[24]

So the government wishes to retain as broad a definition as possible, and to ensure that only ministers can decide what is and is not a matter of national security. For example, in the 1984 Data Protection Act, which gives individuals certain rights to see and have corrected data held about them on computers, the phrase 'national security' is used as one of the reasons for exempting computer systems from subject access: Clause 27 reads:

> (1) Personal data are exempt from the provisions of Part II of this Act (ie registration and supervision of computer systems) and of sections 21–24 above (ie right of data subject to inspect, have rectified and be compensated for mistakes) *if the exemption is required for the purpose of safeguarding national security*. (Emphasis added)

Subsection (2) goes on to say that in any case of dispute as to whether the exemption is required:

> . . . a certificate signed by a Minister of the Crown certifying that the exemption is or at any time was so required *shall be conclusive evidence of that fact*. (Emphasis added)

Therefore, there can be no judicial review of a decision to define data as exempt because of national security: national security is what Her Majesty's Government say it is.

As to the problem of the ease with which governments confuse their own 'security' with that of the state, in the UK this 'confusion' has become official policy. In the White Paper issued on the interception of communications which was a prelude to the legislation aimed at providing minimal compliance with the European Court of Human Rights' decision in *Malone* (see discussion in Chapter 4), it was stated:

> The Secretary of State may issue warrants on grounds of national security if he considers that the information to be acquired under the warrant is necessary *in the interest of national security* either because of terrorist, espionage or major subversive activity, or *in support of the Government's defence and foreign policies*.[25] (Emphasis added)

The 1989 Security Service Act also widened the overall mandate of the Security Service from that which had pertained under the Maxwell-Fyfe Directive: the Service is to protect against the specific threats of espionage, sabotage, terrorism, the activities of foreign agents and subversion, but in general its function is 'the protection of national security' and 'to safeguard the economic well-being of the UK against threats posed by the actions or intentions of people abroad'.[26] Given the breadth of the official definition of 'national security' it is difficult to imagine a more permissive mandate for the Security Service, and one which can provide no realistic guidance to the specific threats which should be targeted. When this provision was criticised during debate on the bill, the Home Secretary made it clear that the government did not want to exclude anything which might in the future be deemed to be a threat to 'national security'.[27]

The most recent example in the UK of the extensive executive discretion contained within the national security concept concerned those detained and deported in connection with the Gulf War in 1991. Sixty-seven Iraqis and seven Iraqi diplomats were ordered out of the country before the war began, a further 35 were detained at Rollestone army camp on Salisbury Plain, and more than 50 other Arabs were detained under the 1971 Immigration Act. Attempts to contest some of these detentions and proposed deportations judicially failed in the Court of Appeal when the Master of the Rolls, Lord Donaldson, ruled that the courts could not interfere in cases of national security unless the Home Secretary had acted in bad faith.[28] Here, the court applied the Wednesbury rules, meaning that the courts do not exclude totally the possibility that they might challenge a ministerial definition of national security but would do so only if it were such as no reasonable minister could make – for example, because s/he had improper motives or took into account irrelevant considerations.[29]

The only recourse left to detainees was to put their case before the 'Three Wise Men' whose sole power is to make recommendations to the Home Secretary. After their first 14 recommendations, Kenneth Baker, then Home Secretary, confirmed nine deportations and revoked five. In 1991 the three were: Lord Justice Lloyd, also the Commissioner under the Interception of Communications Act and, in 1992, appointed as Chair of the Security Commission; Sir Robert Andrew, formerly permanent secretary both at the Home and Northern Ireland Offices; and David Neve, a former immigration appeals tribunal president. The detainees cannot be told any of the evidence on which they have been detained and have no right to legal representation. Therefore, possibly appearing with a friend, the detainees have to attempt to prove the negative that they have no connection with any terrorist organisations, the names of which they may not know. Some detainees were permitted to produce several witnesses, others only one, and the questions addressed by the panel ranged from those that might be seen to be legitimately concerned with national security – for example, 'How often did you visit the Iraqi Embassy?' – to those tending to the McCarthyite – 'What is your position on the Palestine question?', 'Have you expressed views on the Gulf crisis?', 'What have you talked about with your wife?' An internal Home Office inquiry by Sir Philip Woodfield, the Security Service staff counsellor, accepted the Service's arguments that they had been right to err on the side of caution in identifying those to be detained.[30]

NATIONAL SECURITY IN THE UNITED STATES

Harold Relyea summarises the developing usage of 'national security' in the United States from the time of the debate about ratification of the Constitution when John Jay wrote about 'security for the preservation of peace and tranquillity, as well as against dangers from *foreign arms and influence*, as from dangers of the *like kind* arising from domestic causes'.[31] Examining the *US Legal Code* for 1970, Relyea found that about 240 of 390 references to national security were descriptions of grants to the President of extensive discretionary authority:

> In none of these instances was *national security* defined, but the cumulative effect, nevertheless, was one of giving the Executive Branch overwhelming latitude to determine *national security* and, accordingly, what actions could appropriately be taken regarding it.[32]

Regarding domestic security, Watergate revealed the extent to which this condition had reached an apotheosis in the 1970s. The congressional inquiries which, first, culminated in the impeachment and resignation of Richard Nixon and then investigated the FBI and CIA, gave the starkest examples of the use and abuse of the notion of national security.

For example, as the cover-up of the initial Watergate burglary began to unravel in the Summer of 1973, John Dean, counsel to the President, who was involved in most of the discussions regarding the original break-in at the Democratic Party headquarters, and the subsequent attempts within the White House to cover up its involvement, realised he needed a lawyer and went to Charles Shaffer. As part of a strategy by Dean to get immunity from prosecution in return for giving the prosecutors information regarding the involvement of the most senior members of Nixon's personal staff, Haldeman and Ehrlichman, he gave Shaffer a copy of the Huston Plan.[33]

This plan derived from White House dissatisfaction during 1969–70 with the information that was available on domestic dissenters and, in particular, on the extent of their supposed foreign support. Within the intelligence community there were other frustrations, particularly with Hoover who since the mid-1960s had become increasingly resistant to the FBI being involved in the more penetrative information-gathering methods. At a meeting in June 1970 Nixon ordered the intelligence community to provide a compete review of intelligence collection procedures, the restraints on these and options for relaxing them. Nixon said:

> The government must know more about the activities of these groups, and we must develop a plan which will enable us to curtail the illegal activities of those who are determined to destroy our society.[34]

Tom Huston was the White House staffer designated to co-ordinate the response from the intelligence community. Described by Hoover as a 'hippie intellectual',[35] Huston believed that the need for unrestricted government information-gathering on the New Left was justified because it was capable of producing a climate of fear in the country which would bring out all the repressive demagogues in the US. Thus, 'The Huston Plan would halt repression on the Right by stopping violence on the Left'.[36] A series of meetings produced a set of options for increased intelligence-gathering which Huston translated into a set of recommendations that the President relax restrictions on communications intelligence, electronic surveillance, mail coverage, surreptitious entries, development of campus informants and use of military undercover agents.

The President initially approved this but a few days later, after representations from the Attorney General, John Mitchell, Nixon reversed his position and withdrew the Plan. Mitchell's opposition had been primed by Hoover's unhappiness with a plan which contained a number of elements he saw as threatening to the FBI. First, that removing restrictions on information-gathering increased the risk of adverse publicity on Bureau operations; and also that the proposal for a permanent inter-agency assessment committee would infringe traditional Bureau prerogatives in the area of domestic security intelligence.

Being directed against American citizens, most of the proposals in the Huston Plan would have involved illegal activities, and his initial issuing of the Plan was part of the second Article of Nixon's impeachment by the House of Representatives in 1974.[37] Therefore it is somewhat ironic that the President was himself deceived by the intelligence agencies both before and after the Plan's emergence. The initial meetings did not disclose that the CIA had a continuing illegal mail-opening programme (with which the FBI was co-operating) nor the FBI's own counter-intelligence programmes, known as COINTELPRO. The President's withdrawal of the Huston Plan had little impact on the agencies: for example, the CIA mail-opening programme continued, as did COINTELPRO, the National Security Agency expanded its collection of Americans' international communications, and the FBI intensified its campus surveillance by lowering the age of informants to 18.[38]

Shaffer was unwilling to get involved with such material, so Dean raised the stakes:

> I just wanted you to know that national security is like executive privilege. It's vague, and you can use it for anything. Because I'm going to tell you another thing that's considered national security at the White House. Hunt, Liddy and those same Cubans who're in jail broke into Daniel Ellsberg's psychiatrist's office out in California. They wanted to get some dirt on Ellsberg to destroy him in the press. How's that?[39]

In March 1973 Dean told Nixon of the break-in at Dr Fielding's office, and that there was evidence to implicate John Ehrlichman. At a meeting on 21 March Nixon, Haldeman and Dean discussed how disclosure might be prevented:

> **Dean**. You might, you might put it on a national security ground, basis, which it really, it was.
> **Haldeman**. It absolutely was.
> **D**. And just say that, uh . . .
> **President**. Yeah.
> **D**. . . . that this is not, you know, this was –
> **P**. Not paid with CIA funds.
> **D**. Uh . . .
> **P**. No, seriously. National security. We had to get information for national security grounds.
> **D**. Well, then the question is, why didn't the CIA do it or why didn't the FBI do it?
> **P**. Because they were – We had to do it, we had to do it on a confidential basis.
> **H**. Because we were checking them?

P. Neither could be trusted.

H. Well, I think –

P. That's the way I view it.

H. That has never been proven, There was reason to question their . . .

P. Yeah.

H. . . . position.

P. You see really, with the Bundy thing and everything coming out, the whole thing was national security.

D. I think we can probably get, get by on that.[40]

Here, clearly, is an example not just of a government failure to distinguish its own political security from national security, but rather of a conscious effort to use the national security blanket to conceal its own illegal behaviour.

NATIONAL SECURITY IN CANADA

It is interesting to contrast the unlimited executive discretion regarding national security in the UK and US with the effort that has been made during the last decade in Canada to provide some more specific definition of what, in policy terms, national security is to mean to the security intelligence agencies. It will be useful first to sketch the background to this effort.

From its nineteenth-century origins until 1984, the organisation of domestic security intelligence work in Canada was the responsibility of the Royal Canadian Mounted Police (RCMP), although the question of removing this work from the RCMP had been raised previously on several occasions, most notably in a Royal Commission Report in 1969.[41]

In March 1976 an RCMP officer standing trial in Quebec for the bombing of a private residence, for which he had been dismissed from the force, claimed that he had been involved in other operations, including a break-in and theft of organisational records from the offices of the Agence de Presse Libre du Quebéc (APLQ) in October 1972. The RCMP assured the government that these were isolated instances but during the following months further allegations were made. After the Quebec provincial government set up an inquiry in June 1977, the federal government appointed its own in an effort to keep more control over the process.

The Federal Commission, headed by Justice David McDonald, issued their First Report dealing with the Official Secrets Act and freedom of information in security matters in October 1979. The Second Report, containing the main brunt of their findings and recommendations, was received by the government in January 1981, and published the following August. The Commission provided a detailed analysis of a variety of activities which it found to be illegal, 'not authorised or provided for by law', or, if lawful, inappropriate: break-ins, electronic surveillance, mail interception, access to confidential information held by other government departments, and undercover operations.[42]

For the future, McDonald proposed a range of measures designed as a coherent system which, he said, should be judged as a whole. The primary functions of the security intelligence agency should be the collection and analysis of information and the reporting of it to agencies with relevant executive responsibilities. The agency, which should be separate from the RCMP and have no police powers, should combine open and covert collection methods, the latter subject to proper controls. The agency should have a statutory mandate regarding its functions, powers and subjection to government direction and control. The agency's operations should be subject to independent outside review.

The government's first attempt at legislation watered down a number of McDonald's proposals regarding oversight and met with a highly critical reception. A committee of the Canadian Senate recommended significant changes, most of which were accepted by the government and a revised bill was passed in June 1984.[43] The Canadian Security Intelligence Service Act as passed placed greater legal restraints on the new Canadian Security Intelligence Service (CSIS), which was to be established separately from the RCMP. It was made subject to greater ministerial control by the Solicitor General than the government had planned in 1983, and a two-part review process was enacted. First, an Inspector General, who is responsible to the Minister, monitors and reviews the operational activities of the CSIS; second, a Security Intelligence Review Committee (SIRC), appointed by government and opposition parties, has the mandate 'to review generally the performance by the Service of its duties and functions',[44] to investigate complaints made against CSIS, and hear appeals against refusal of security clearances. SIRC's Annual Report must be tabled in the Commons by the Solicitor General. (See Chapter 8 for details.)

Also, and most importantly from our present point of view, the Act provided for the first time a statutory definition of what constituted 'threats to the security of Canada'.

> In this Act . . . ' threats to the security of Canada' means
> (a) espionage or sabotage that is against Canada or is detrimental to the interests of Canada or activities directed toward or in support of such espionage or sabotage,
> (b) foreign influenced activities within or relating to Canada that are detrimental to the interests of Canada and are clandestine or deceptive or involve a threat to any person,
> (c) activities within or relating to Canada directed toward or in support of the threat or use of acts of serious violence against persons or property for the purpose of achieving a political objective within Canada or a foreign state, and
> (d) activities directed toward undermining by covert unlawful acts, or directed toward or intended ultimately to lead to the destruction or overthrow by violence of the constitutionally established system of government in Canada,

but does not include lawful advocacy, protest or dissent, unless carried on in conjunction with any of the activities referred to in paragraphs (a) to (d).[45]

These are usually referred to as the espionage, foreign influence, terrorism and subversion sections respectively.

Section 2 of the CSIS Act provides a 'negative' definition of national security in terms of threat, and, subsequently, the government announced in 1989 its five priority national security concerns on which the CSIS should concentrate its security intelligence effort. The first was public safety, covering the safety of air and other transport from terrorist threats;

second, was the integrity of the democratic process, specifically, clandestine attempts to influence Canadian policy-making and violent attempts to bring about political change. The third priority was the security protection of classified information and government installations; fourth was to be economic security, for example, the area of clandestine technology transfer; and fifth, international peace and stability, specifically involving the analysis of foreign threats to Canada's security. Regarding the last of these it needs to be remembered that Canada has no specific foreign intelligence service on a par with the SIS or CIA.[46] In March 1992 the Canadian Solicitor General made the first of what was to be an annual statement on national security, but it was, if anything, less specific then the 1989 statement.[47]

Within the general concept of national security there are more specific concepts which have provided rationales for security intelligence activities. The one that has been most extensively used and abused during the twentieth century is subversion. The term has had an even longer historical pedigree (for example, the proclamations of Henry VIII that Catholics were subversive), but the lack of clear definition enabled the concept to become a catch-all term legitimating surveillance.[48]

'SUBVERSION' IN CANADA

McDonald was critical to varying degrees of a wide range of RCMP surveillance policies which had been based on the concept of 'domestic subversion':

> separatism and national unity, surveillance on university campuses, the Extra Parliamentary Opposition, political parties, labour unions, blacks, Indians and right wing groups.[49]

In his detailed discussion of the problem of defining 'subversion' in such a way that it would not be confused with 'legitimate dissent', McDonald pointed to the problems which develop either when the security services have no official mandate or when a mandate is defined so that it simply gives official sanction to existing service practices. The first of these prevailed until 1974 when the implementation of the Official Secrets Act 1973 provided the first brief legislative authorisation for the use of intrusive techniques of intelligence-gathering in the case of 'subversive activity'. The second situation came about after the issue of the first Cabinet Directive on 'The Role, Tasks and Methods of the RCMP Security Service' in 1975. The RCMP's extension of its operations against subversion since the 1960s and the Watergate revelations in the US during 1973–74 apparently led the Security Service itself to request a clearer government mandate.[50]

Paragraph (iii) of the 1975 Directive was particularly relevant to 'subversion':

> activities directed toward accomplishing governmental change within Canada or elsewhere by force or violence or any criminal means.

This had appeared in s16 of the Official Secrets Act but the RCMP had still felt unduly constrained and therefore the following was added as section (vi) of the 1975 Directive:

> the use or the encouragement of the use of force, violence or any criminal means, or the creation or exploitation of civil disorder, for the purpose of accomplishing any of the activities referred to above;

that is, for example, espionage, terrorism, sabotage, governmental change. In a letter explaining the purpose of the Directive to the senior officers in the Security Service, however, the Director General still felt the need to reassure them that it was 'business as usual':

> While at first glance the ingredients of our guidelines appear to be strict legal precepts, they are not . . . [The Security Service] will continue to monitor traditional areas of interest – such as Communists, Trotskyists, Marxists, separatists, bloc revolutionaries, native extremists, right-wing extremists and revolutionaries from other countries resident in Canada.[51]

As far as McDonald was concerned, both those definitions were too broad and likely to attract security intelligence surveillance to matters that were essentially a police responsibility.[52]

McDonald recommended that 'threats to the security of Canada' in relation to which the security intelligence agency would be authorised to gather intelligence should consist of four categories of activity, and this categorisation is the one that was eventually enacted in the 1984 Act (see above). First, espionage and sabotage, second, clandestine foreign interference, third, serious political violence and terrorism, and fourth,

> revolutionary subversion, meaning activities directed towards or intended ultimately to lead to the destruction or overthrow of the democratic system of government in Canada.[53]

For this fourth category McDonald recommended that only non-intrusive methods be used to collect intelligence on those who were targeted on the basis of this section alone.

Overall, the government retained McDonald's four categories but section 2[d] of the government's first Bill changed the definition of subversion without actually employing the term:

> activities directed toward undermining by covert unlawful acts, or directed toward or intended ultimately to lead to the destruction or overthrow of, the constitutionally established system of government in Canada.

The first point made by critics of the Bill was that 'covert unlawful' applied only to 'undermining' and therefore entirely peaceful and lawful activities; 'intended ultimately . . . to lead to overthrow' would have come within the counter-subversion framework.[54] This was so, but it is not obvious that McDonald's proposal would have avoided this problem since it established neither 'illegal' nor 'violent' standards for 'subversion'.

A second and more convincing criticism was that substituting the 'constitutionally established system of government in Canada' for the 'democratic system' would have included (peaceful) separatist movements and suggested something of a failure to absorb the lessons of the 1970s![55] The Senate Committee supported the government's position on not employing McDonald's 'democratic system of government' on the grounds that 'democratic' was too elastic in meaning to be of help in statutory definitions, but argued that the reference to 'destruction or overthrow' should be qualified by the inclusion of 'by violence'.[56]

The government accepted the Senate's advice so that the final version of 2[d] reads:

> activities directed towards undermining by covert unlawful acts, or directed toward or intended ultimately to lead to the destruction or overthrow by violence of, the constitutionally established system of government in Canada.

Neither the government nor the Senate agreed with McDonald's recommended prohibition of intrusive techniques in subversion investigations.

Although subsection 2[d] does restrict the notion of subversion to matters of unlawfulness or violence, it can still be argued to be 'incredibly broad and indefinite'. Specifically, the phrase 'intended ultimately to lead to' appears to cast the net so widely as to catch all those protesters who may possibly be interested ultimately in overthrowing the government. If this is so, then it derives from the security intelligence perception that one failure to identify someone who is a threat is far worse than a score of cases identifying as threats those who are not.[57]

Therefore much would depend on how this definition was actually applied and how effectively the new oversight mechanism would be in restraining the new CSIS. In 1987, SIRC, having carried out research into the activities of CSIS's counter-subversion branch, concluded that individuals were targeted mainly because of their relationship with some domestic political group, and that CSIS overestimated the influence of such groups and the likelihood of violence. SIRC concluded that the valid work of this branch was actually concerned with two main threats, foreign manipulation and political violence. Therefore, said SIRC, the branch should be closed and this work split between the counter-intelligence and counter-terrorism branches.[58] In the context of further evidence that CSIS seemed to have left the RCMP in name only, the government set about implementing these proposals during the same year.[59] This naturally raised the question of whether section 2[d] should be retained at all.

Having disbanded the Counter-Subversion Branch, the Minister gave no immediate indication that he believed the mandate should be amended:

> There still exist within Canada today, groups and individuals who undertake 'activities directed toward or intended *ultimately* to lead to the destruction or overthrow by violence of the constitutionally established system of government in Canada'. The government has the legal responsibility to investigate such groups and individuals if strictly necessary.[60]

However, no indications have been given as to what kind of activities are envisaged here. It is only the very long term which appears to require this section, since activities 'directed toward . . . serious violence' are already covered in 2[c] (it is difficult to imagine that 'non-serious' violence could be enough to overthrow the Canadian state), and foreign influence is covered in 2[b]. The first section of 2[d] – 'activities directed toward undermining by covert unlawful acts' – seems redundant: the only peaceful (otherwise 2[c] is applicable) acts which are unlawful and which might constitute a threat to national security would be a civil disobedience movement. Since a covert civil disobedience movement is a contradiction in terms, it would properly be subject to normal police procedures. This seems to leave the only active part of the definition as that referring to 'intended ultimately to lead . . .' and this is precisely that most future-oriented of 'threats' which historically has given rise to the diversion of resources to the blanket surveillance of revolutionary rhetoric as a substitute for making realistic threat assessments.

Citing similar arguments in its identification of issues for the five-year parliamentary review of the 1984 Act, which took place during 1989–90, SIRC recommended that 2[d] be repealed.[61] The Special Review Committee of the Commons followed suit though its Report noted that this subsection was one of the most controversial issues the Committee had addressed and the recommendation was not unanimous.[62] Noting this, the government argued that there had been no real evidence of a problem with CSIS's use of 2[d] since those identified at the time of the transition from the RCMP. These initial problems had been dealt with by ministerial directives limiting counter-subversion investigations to open sources unless the minister specifically authorised otherwise.[63] So ended the latest episode in the Canadian debate about the definition of this particular contested concept but because of the inherent ambiguity of legal language in statutes and because of the tendency inherent in security intelligence agencies to interpret their mandates broadly (often from the highest of motives, sometimes not) there will remain a constant tension between the agency and its external reviewers from which precise definitions in particular cases will result.

'SUBVERSION' IN AUSTRALIA

In Australia, too, there have been several efforts in recent years at defining subversion more narrowly. Some aspects were similar to the Canadian context but there were significant differences: inquiries were not sparked off, as they were in North America, by a sudden series of allegations of widespread abuse by the security agencies. Rather they reflected the culmination of a long-running political battle between the Australian Labour Party (ALP) and the security intelligence agencies. The Australian Security Intelligence Organisation (ASIO) was established in 1949, taking over the 'political policing' role from the Commonwealth Investigation Service, mainly because of Anglo-American pressure on the then government to be firmer with the Communist Party of Australia and, specifically, as a result of MI5 telling the government that decrypts of cables from the new Soviet Embassy indicated that there was a ring of Soviet spies in the Department of External Affairs.[64]

The main seeds of Labour suspicion were planted in 1954 when Vladimir Petrov defected from the Soviet embassy where he had worked and from where he had been supplying ASIO with information since 1951. This occurred just before a federal election and was believed by the ALP to have shifted the tide of opinion against them, costing them victory. The Commission which examined the defection and the material Petrov brought with him failed to uncover any spies or produce any prosecutions and the suspicion about ASIO's motives remained within the

ALP. ASIO was sufficiently concerned about this feeling to request to be placed on a statutory footing in 1956 and this was done in a short Bill which endowed the Director General with total control of the organisation. In the early 1970s the ALP, in opposition, only narrowly failed to adopt as party policy the dissolution of ASIO, and when it returned to power matters came to a head. The Attorney General, Senator Lionel Murphy, believing that ASIO was not providing him fully with information on the activities of a small right-wing group of Croatian extremists, flew to Melbourne with Commonwealth Police briefed to accompany him into ASIO's headquarters to secure the material. The incident was well covered by the media who had got wind of the visit, hereafter named the 'Murphy Raid'.[65]

The Prime Minister, Gough Whitlam, appointed Justice R. M. Hope in mid-1974 to investigate not only ASIO but also the Australian Secret Intelligence Service (ASIS), the Joint Intelligence Organisation (JIO) (responsible for providing intelligence assessments to the Defence Department and the military) and the Defence Signals Directorate (DSD), which was the Australian arm of the UKUSA SIGINT network. The inquiry was thus more wide-ranging than the Canadian McDonald inquiry but only a summary of Hope's third report was published, that in 1977. Hope was apparently impressed by ASIS and DSD, but far less so with ASIO which was found to have poor management and leadership, low morale and a tendency to investigate subversion beyond what was required to obtain security intelligence.[66] The ASIO Act 1979 followed, though not from Whitlam's government, with a clearer statement of the functions and scope of ASIO's work. Cain argues that this Act expanded considerably ASIO's powers,[67] though since there had been no previous public statement of their powers, it is hard to see why this should be so. Rather, the Act clearly placed on a legal basis those powers which ASIO had traditionally exercised covertly. Thereby, it could be said, it added to the legitimacy of the organisation and, as Cain argues, made it that much more difficult for any future government to disband the organisation. Its mandate was defined in terms of espionage, sabotage, subversion, active measures of foreign intervention and terrorism. Intrusive information-gathering measures would require ministerial, not judicial warrants, and the Director General became subject to general ministerial directions. However, unlike in Canada, there were specific areas in which the Director General would remain independent: targeting and dissemination of intelligence to other agencies.

Since the ALP was in opposition at the time of the 1979 Act and succeeded in making only marginal amendments to the government's proposal, the new legislation did not completely allay the suspicions of ASIO and these were further compounded in 1983 when one of Justice Hope's earlier, secret, reports was leaked to the press. The ALP, now back in government, was also concerned to deal with ASIO warnings to the Prime Minister, Bob Hawke, that David Combe, a former Labour Party official, was now liaising with a Soviet diplomat over a trade deal, and was at risk of being drawn into an espionage network. The government had the diplomat deported and banned all Cabinet contacts with Combe, but once the affair became public and it seemed as though the government might have overreacted, Justice Hope was called back to conduct another inquiry. Since Combe was not found to have done anything wrong, the likeliest explanation of this is that ASIO, like MI5 in its view of Harold Wilson, saw participation in trade with the Soviet Union as adequate evidence of disloyalty. The final impetus to further reform was given by a bungled training operation in which armed and masked agents of the ASIS held up hotel staff and were themselves arrested by Victoria state police in November 1983.

Hope made a number of structural recommendations which are examined in Chapter 7. Regarding subversion, in his first Commission Hope noted that there was an inherent danger that investigations could infringe basic democratic rights if dissent or non-conformity were mistaken for subversion, and therefore proposed that the definition be confined to activities involving violence or illegality.[68] The Australian Security Intelligence Organisation Act, 1979 implemented the following definition:

> 5.(1) For the purposes of this Act, the activities of persons . . . that are to be regarded as subversion are –
> (a) activities that involve, will involve or lead to, or are intended or likely ultimately to involve or lead to, the use of force or violence or other unlawful acts (whether

by those persons or by others) for the purpose of overthrowing or destroying the constitutional government of the Commonwealth or of a State or Territory;

(b) activities directed to obstructing, hindering or interfering with the performance by the Defence Force of its functions or the carrying out of other activities by or for the Commonwealth for the purposes of security or the defence of the Commonwealth; or

(c) activities directed to promoting violence or hatred between different groups of persons in the Australian community so as to endanger the peace, order or good government of the Commonwealth.

Foreign-related activities were dealt with elsewhere. A further examination of the question led Justice Hope to recommend in his 1985 Report not only that this definition should be further narrowed but that the term 'subversion' should be dropped.[69] Therefore, in the ASIO Amendment Act, 1986, we find the following:

'politically motivated violence' means –

(a) acts or threats of violence or unlawful harm that are intended or likely to achieve a political objective, whether in Australia or elsewhere, including acts or threats carried on for the purpose of influencing the policy or acts of a government, whether in Australia or elsewhere;

(b) acts that –

(i) involve violence or are intended or are likely to involve or lead to violence (whether by the persons who carry on those acts or by other persons); and

(ii) are directed to overthrowing or destroying, or assisting in the overthrow or destruction of, the government or the constitutional system of government of the Commonwealth or of a State or Territory.[70]

The first point to note is that the term 'politically motivated violence' replaced both subversion and terrorism as the object of security concern.[71] The second is that Hope tackled the critical point which has given rise to the open-endedness of subversion as a concept, that is the inclusion of the term 'ultimately' as contained, for example, in both McDonald's recommendation and the current CSIS Act definition in section 2[d]. Hope argued that the definition should not include 'ultimately'

> as it points to, and indeed encourages, an approach that it does not matter how distant in the future the projected violence may occur.[72]

'SUBVERSION' IN THE UNITED STATES

President Roosevelt's initial request to Hoover in 1936 for more systematic intelligence about 'subversive activities in the United States, particularly Fascism and Communism' did have a degree of statutory authorisation dating from the Justice Department appropriations statute enacted before the First World War. However, it appeared to go beyond the Attorney General's order to Hoover in 1924 that the activities of the FBI 'be limited strictly to investigations of violations of law'.[73] Yet Hoover advised the President that there was sufficient statutory authority for development of FBI information-gathering regarding subversion as well as espionage and sabotage.[74] As the Church Committee documented in great detail, this was the basic authorisation upon which the FBI, at least until Hoover's death in 1972, based its information-gathering by mail-opening, wiretapping, electronic surveillance, break-ins and a variety of countering programmes (COINTELPROs) against groups including the Communist Party, civil rights and anti-war movements, and the Ku Klux Klan.

Before the Church Committee had reported its conclusions on its investigation of the FBI, Attorney General Levi issued new guidelines to govern what were now called 'Domestic Security Investigations'. These avoided the use of the term 'subversion' and were to be conducted

> to ascertain information on the activities of individuals, or the activities of groups, which involve or will involve the

116

use of force or violence and which involve or will involve the violation of federal law, for the purpose of:
1. overthrowing the government of the US or the government of a state; . . .
3. substantially impairing for the purpose of influencing US government policies or decisions:
    (a) the functioning of the government of the US;
    (b) the functioning of the government of a State; or
    (c) interstate commerce . . .[75]

The Church Committee reported that it sought to impose special restrictions on the conduct of those investigations which had involved the most flagrant abuses in the past – preventive intelligence investigations and civil disorders assistance – and to provide a clear statutory foundation for those investigations believed to be appropriate and for which there was no legal authority. The Committee argued that preventive intelligence investigations should be limited to those involving terrorist or espionage activities and that civil disorders assistance should be limited to those which were so serious as to possibly require federal troops. The Committee said that FBI officials had read Attorney General Levi's new guidelines as authorising the continued investigation of 'subversives' which they were anxious to prevent since their examination had

> found the term to be so vague as to constitute a license to investigate almost any activity of practically any group that actively opposes the policies of the administration in power.[76]

Citing the evidence of both the abuse of rights and the inefficiency of FBI investigations based on 'soft' evidence, the Committee argued that Bureau resources would be better directed at terrorism and hostile foreign intelligence activity and that, for the Bureau to open a full investigation into either, there should be a substantial indication of either type of activity *in the near future*.
Therefore the Committee recommended that the FBI should be permitted to investigate any American or foreigner to obtain

evidence of criminal activity where there was 'reasonable suspicion' that s/he had committed, was committing or was about
to commit a specific act violating a federal statute pertaining
to domestic security.[77] Based on the Supreme Court decision
in *Terry* v. *Ohio* (1968) this was taken to mean 'specific and
articulable facts . . . taken together with rational inferences
from those facts'.[78] Also, the Committee recommended that the
Bureau should be able to conduct a preliminary investigation of
any American or foreigner where it had a specific allegation or
specific or substantiated information that the subject would soon
engage in terrorist or hostile foreign intelligence activity, such an
investigation not normally exceeding 30 days.[79]

The Guidelines for Domestic Security Investigations were not
changed by the Attorney General in response to the Church
Report, and the latter provided much of the input into the effort
to pass through Congress a comprehensive charter for FBI and
other intelligence activities during the Carter administration.
That effort did not succeed and the election of Reagan as
President in 1980 reflected the shift in the political climate away
from concern with security intelligence abuses in the mid-1970s
to the apparent ineffectiveness of security intelligence in the
late 1970s. This was given substance when revised guidelines
were issued to the FBI by Attorney General Smith in 1983.
In line with the Reagan administration's thinking these are
generally acknowledged to have relaxed the restrictions on FBI
investigations.[80] They authorise the initiation of an investigation

> when the facts or circumstances reasonably indicate that
> two or more persons are engaged in an enterprise for the
> purpose of furthering political or social goals wholly or in
> part through activities that involve force or violence and a
> violation of the criminal laws of the US.[81]

Compared with the Levi guidelines these speak much more
vaguely of 'furthering political or social goals' and whereas
the 1976 version had incorporated the standard proposed by
Church that 'specific articulable facts' were required before a
full investigation could be commenced, the 1983 version stated
that 'reasonable indication' meant that the Bureau 'may take into

account any facts or circumstances that a prudent investigator would consider'.[82] The guidelines go on to state that 'mere hunch' is insufficient and that there must be some objective basis for initiating the investigation, but this is explicitly a weaker standard than that applied in 1976. It is important to note, however, that even this weaker 1983 version still contains the twin standards of force and illegality that are also included in Canada and Australia.

'SUBVERSION' IN THE UNITED KINGDOM

By contrast, in the UK the debate has taken a different direction, though debate might be too strong a word to describe a process which has been so dominated by executive pronouncements. It has been suggested[83] that the first non-statutory charter for the security service was written by a civil servant, Sir Findlater Stewart who was chairman of the Home Defence Committee at the end of the Second World War. Dated 27 November 1945, this Report has not been published, but Lord Denning made reference to it in his Report on the Profumo affair. The purpose of the Security Service, said Findlater Stewart 'is defence of the realm and nothing else'.[84] Denning did not report on the extent to which, if at all, Findlater Stewart elaborated on this.

In 1952 the Home Secretary, David Maxwell-Fyfe, produced a directive which was also not published until Lord Denning reproduced it in his Report. This provided the following mandate for the Security Service:

> Its task is the Defence of the Realm as a whole, from external and internal dangers arising from attempts at espionage and sabotage, or from actions of persons and organisations whether directed from within or without the country, which may be judged to be subversive of the State.[85]

'Subversion' was not defined, and had no legal definition elsewhere, but Denning offered one: subversives were people who 'would contemplate the overthrow of government by unlawful means'.[86] Frank Kitson, seconded by the British Army to

119

Oxford University for a year to develop his theories of counter-insurgency, adopted a broader definition that would have included also actions directed at forcing governments 'to do things which they do not want to do'[87] and, although he did retain an 'illegality' criterion, he argued this could involve strikes and protest marches. This seems to have been nearer than Denning had come to what the Security Service deemed most useful but there was no 'legality' criterion contained in the very broad definition announced in a House of Lords debate on 'subversive and extremist elements' introduced by Lord Chalfont in 1975. The then Labour minister, Lord Harris of Greenwich, defined subversive activities as those

> which threaten the safety or well-being of the state and which are intended to undermine or overthrow parliamentary democracy by political, industrial, or violent means.[88]

This definition had in fact been adopted earlier, probably when the first guidelines for Special Branch were issued by the Home Office in 1970.[89] The Labour members of the Home Affairs Committee inquiry into police Special Branches proposed that Denning's 1963 version be adopted.[90] The majority report of the Committee expressed itself satisfied with the 1975 definition. Emphasising that activities had to both threaten the safety of the state *and* seek to undermine parliamentary democracy, they claimed that this exempted lawful and non-violent activities. But the majority then contradicted itself by arguing that it would not be in the public interest to prevent the police from investigating such activities even if they were not unlawful![91]

The same official wording was maintained in essence in section 1 of the 1989 Security Service Act:

> 1(2) The function of the Service shall be the protection of national security and, in particular, its protection against threats from espionage, terrorism and sabotage, from the activities of agents of foreign powers and from actions intended to overthrow or undermine parliamentary democracy by political, industrial or violent means.

This definition clearly includes political and industrial activity which is both peaceful and lawful. Pressed in the House of Commons on the inadequacy of this, the Home Secretary responded with an 'interpretation' of the definition which excluded those

> who have views on the structure or organisation of Parliament, or if they are involved in seeking to change industrial practices in this country or to negotiate a better deal if they are members of trade unions, or if they seek to challenge or change the government's policies relating to defence, employment, foreign policy or anything else.[92]

But he said this was not a declaration of ministerial policy and nor would it be incorporated into the Bill.[93]

In contrast with definitions pertaining in the US, Canada and Australia, the UK version establishes neither violence nor unlawfulness as necessary components of subversion. All the external inquiries into security intelligence in those other countries have shown how this facilitates the illegitimate surveillance of lawful and peaceful political activity. As the then Home Secretary, Merlyn Rees, said in the Commons in 1978:

> The Special Branch collects information on those who I think cause problems for the State.[94]

Serious efforts have been made in North America and Australasia to apply stricter definitions of the domestic security intelligence mandate. Agencies have reorganised predominantly around the twin mandates of foreign influence (often referred to as counter-intelligence) and serious political violence (usually referred to as counter-terrorism). As we have seen, the question has consequently been raised as to whether a counter-subversion mandate should be retained at all.

There has been, as in Canada, the general 'insider' preference for keeping it so as to maximise the permissiveness of the mandate, but another, more specific, argument was made in the 1980s. In essence the theme was the Soviet use of 'active measures' as part of its continuing foreign policy strategy:

> Active measures may entail influencing the policies of another government, undermining confidence in its leaders and institutions, disrupting relations between other nations, and discrediting and weakening governmental and non-governmental opponents. This frequently involves attempts to deceive the target (foreign governmental and non-governmental elites or mass audiences), and to distort the target's perceptions of reality.[95]

In one sense the argument seems trivial; the Soviet Union does, or did, what all countries try to do – through propaganda and persuasion to advance its perceived national interests – but in another sense the argument is far from trivial because its logic is that nobody should be immune from surveillance. If the perceptions of the target of these 'active measures' are sufficiently distorted then they will become the *unwitting* agent of Soviet influence and to that extent unable to convince the domestic security intelligence service that they should be immune from surveillance.[96] At this point we truly enter the 'wilderness of mirrors', because the very lack of evidence as to, for example, the existence of foreign-inspired or home-grown subversion will be taken, not as disconfirmation of the hypothesis that subversion is a real problem, but as an indication of the extremes of deception and subtlety the subversive and/or the controlling state will go to in order to maintain secrecy.[97] This is the context in which phrases such as 'intended ultimately' become so dangerous because they enable the security intelligence agency to conclude that because belief x is consistent with the foreign policy of country y which is considered to be a threat to national security, then any actions taken consistent with x may be 'intended ultimately to lead . . . to overthrow' and thus justify surveillance.[98] It is not obvious that such arguments have ended with the collapse of the Soviet Union.

It is not surprising that officials and executive politicians prefer to maintain relatively vague, very long-term-oriented mandates for their security intelligence services – 'just in case' – but strong arguments can be made against institutionalising such permissiveness both on the grounds of principle – defending liberties – and pragmatically on the grounds of saving resources. This is an issue for the inquiry which is discussed in Chapter 9.

'TERRORISM'

The current US definition of domestic security investigations discussed above is actually entitled 'Domestic Security/Terrorism Investigations'. Similarly, Australia now talks of 'politically motivated violence' to include both what would have been referred to before 1985 as subversion and 'terrorism'. In North America, Australasia and the UK after 1945 'counter-subversion' was the major programme within the domestic security agencies of those countries, and the main target was domestic communist parties. A variety of factors since the late 1960s has led to a shift in emphasis away from that area: initially the growth of the 'New Left' led to some reorientation of resources away from the Communist Party, but counter-subversion remained the theme. However, the Watergate-related controversies in the US, and the McDonald and Hope commissions in Canada and Australia respectively contributed to a shift of security intelligence resources away from what had been widely criticised as the surveillance of legitimate political activity.

Instead the security intelligence agencies concentrated more upon terrorism. To some extent this reflected real concerns – the rise of the PLO, the Weather Underground in the US, the activities of the Red Brigades (Italy) and Baader Meinhof (Germany), and the rise of the PIRA in Northern Ireland. However, there are also arguments that the growth of terrorism has been used by security intelligence agencies as a rationalisation for the continuation of counter-subversion strategies.[99]

In Canada, the abolition of the counter-subversion branch in CSIS could have meant that improper surveillance would 'get lost' in the counter-terrorism branch. Within CSIS there has been a shift of resources towards the counter-terrorism programme[100] but SIRC has made no specific comment indicating that it believes that there has simply been a shift of old counter-subversion targets to counter terrorism. When the counter-subversion branch was first wound up provision was made for the residue of cases, which were neither transferred to counter-terrorism nor counter-intelligence nor closed, to be maintained by the Analysis and Production Branch (RAP) on the basis of open sources only. Subsequently, in its annual report for 1989–90 SIRC found that files in this residue remained as a result of continued *per se* targeting (that is, a person becoming a target purely by reason of association with a group) rather than on the basis of an assessment as to whether or not the individual was a threat. Therefore SIRC recommended that the residue be disposed of, either by way of file closures or reallocation to counter-terrorism or counter-intelligence.[101] If CSIS wished to maintain any targets traditionally examined under the counter-subversion mandate then this would be the point at which they would be reclassified under the counter-terrorism mandate.

The actual definition of terrorism used in Canada is:

> activities within or relating to Canada directed toward or in support of the threat or use of acts of serious violence against persons or property for the purpose of achieving a political objective within Canada or a foreign state.[102]

The Parliamentary Review Committee of the CSIS Act recommended that this definition be narrowed by the addition of the word 'directly' before the phrase 'relating to Canada' and by deleting the words 'directed toward or', so as to make the definitions less vague.[103] The government saw no need to make these amendments.[104]

The official definition of the term in the UK, as given in the Prevention of Terrorism Act, is:

> the use of violence for political ends, and includes any use of violence for the purpose of putting the public or any section of the public in fear.

The Canadian definition, with its restriction to 'serious violence' is the most specific of those under review here; the other three all refer in one form or another to 'violence' for political 'ends' 'objectives' or, as in the US, are more specific as to the potential targets of the violence. The significance of the definitions lies in what activities are drawn within the net of surveillance and subsequently as targets for countering action. It is the second of these points that crucially distinguishes terrorism from subversion. Most individuals and groups traditionally targeted solely as 'subversive' were usually involved in political protest or industrial action and the countering options were relatively limited to, say, harassment and disruption. By and large, security intelligence agencies contented themselves with amassing yet further information about attendance at meetings and marches.

Terrorism, on the other hand, as Ron Crelinsten has pointed out, involves not just terrorists and counter-terrorists in a reciprocal relationship in which each reacts to the other or attempts to impose change on the other but also a unique triangular form of political communication. The triangle results from the directing of political violence at two distinct targets: the first are the victims of the violence, the second are the targets of the demands, or the wider audience who may, through fear of victimisation, accede to demands. 'Terrorism' is, therefore, a form of political communication, whether employed by state or non-state actors,[105] and definitions of the term are part of the process of communication. Crelinsten develops his model of the mirror relationship between controllers and the controlled right across the spectrum of both control behaviour – from social control through education to military counter-insurgency operations – and insurgent behaviour – from expressive protests to insurrection. He suggests that there are 'zones of ambiguity' at key points along the spectrum where qualitative changes in the behaviour of controllers or controlled occur. From the point of view of security intelligence, determining these transition points is, he says, precisely the problem of threat assessment;[106] when, for example, does legal political dissent become criminal? For the controllers, on the other hand, when does a criminal justice model of obtaining information by legitimate surveillance in order to make arrests give way to a counter-insurgency model of obtaining information by illegitimate means for use in countering operations from disruption to summary execution?

Precisely this kind of shift may be seen to have occurred in the UK in 1992. The prime responsibility for security intelligence regarding the PIRA in Britain was transferred from the Metropolitan Police Special Branch to the Security Service. This is discussed more fully in Chapter 6; for the present, note that if the production of security intelligence by police aimed at prosecution is seen as inadequate then one reason for shifting the responsibility to the Security Service is to gain more countering 'options'. Therefore this could herald a shift to more 'direct' countering methods such as have been made use of in Northern Ireland itself (see Chapter 5).[107]

CONCLUSION

Having considered these problematic concepts which provide the main guidance, at a general level, as to what security intelligence agencies should be doing, or actually do, it is important to note that some recent efforts have been made to define also what they should not be doing. The Church Committee included in one of its final recommendations the following passage:

> In no event should the FBI open a preliminary or full preventive intelligence investigation based upon information that an American is advocating political ideas or engaging in lawful political activities or is associating with others for the purpose of petitioning the government for the redress of grievances or other such constitutionally protected purpose.[108]

Neither the Attorney General's guidelines of 1976 nor 1983 incorporated such a sentiment.

New Zealand was the first to legislate such a clause in 1977 after an inquiry by the Chief Ombudsman into the domestic agency there, the Security Intelligence Service.[109] Canada followed suit, on the recommendation of McDonald, and the final part of Section 2 of the CSIS Act says that 'threats to the security of Canada'

> does not include lawful advocacy, protest or dissent, unless carried on in conjunction with any of the activities referred to in paragraphs [a] to [d].

(These are espionage, sabotage, clandestine foreign influence, serious violence or subversion: see p. 106 above full text of

126

Section 2). The first phrase was as recommended by McDonald[110] but the second phrase unfortunately weakens the overall impact and might be seen as redundant since those activities can be investigated in any case. In Australia the ASIO Amendment Act 1986 incorporated a similar section to the Canadian, and one which was less qualified:

> This Act shall not limit the right of persons to engage in lawful advocacy, protest or dissent and the exercise of that right shall not, by itself, be regarded as prejudicial to security, and the functions of the Organisation shall be construed accordingly.[111]

The UK Security Service Act 1989 contains no such clause.

The significance of this question of the legal mandate for a security intelligence agency is not that there is some immediate translation of law into organisational practice; a restricted legal mandate is not a sufficient condition for the control of such agencies and for minimising their abuses of power. But it is a necessary condition for several important reasons: first, for any realistic assessment to be made of the organisation's effectiveness, second, for the development of self-restraint on the part of officers, and third, to establish a base upon which effective oversight procedures can be built. It is also important to establish clearly what are the 'threats' or potential 'harms' to security and public order in order to avoid the problem of trying to achieve the impossible – *total* security or order, both of which 'cures' are likely to be considerably worse than the 'disease' of insecurity or disorder.

New statutory mandates may, after all, establish new legal authority for security intelligence where there had been none. Indeed, such mandates may be sponsored precisely to head-off movements for more radical change. President Gerald Ford made such a proposal to Congress,[112] and both the Canadian government's first CSIS bill in 1983 and the UK Security Service Act 1989 are arguably examples of this. Clearly, the broader they are defined the more problematic they are in terms of democratic control.

As we have seen, both Australia and Canada have inquired into precisely what threats to the national security are potentially so harmful that the extraordinary powers granted to (or assumed by) security intelligence agencies will be justified. How such an inquiry might proceed in the UK is discussed in the final chapter of this book.

NOTES

1. R. Thomas, *Espionage and Secrecy* (London: Routledge, 1991) provides a highly detailed legal account of the application of s.1 of the Official Secrets Act 1911 to these offences in the UK.
2. 'Nation' and 'state' are separate identities. During the cold war, Western states described their security intelligence agencies as protecting 'national' rather than 'state' security. In part this reflected the Western ideal that the liberal state was a better reflection of the nation than were east European regimes, but the fact remains that the security of state institutions was, and is, the central concern of such agencies.
3. B. Buzan, *People, States and Fear* (Hemel Hempstead: Harvester Wheatsheaf, 2nd edition, 1991), pp. 347–8.
4. J.A. Tapia-Valdes, 'A Typology of National Security Policies', *Yale Journal of World Public Order*, 9(10), 1982, p. 11 note 7.
5. R.N. Berki, *Security and Society: Reflections on Law, Order and Politics* (London: J.M. Dent and Sons, 1986), pp. 28–43.
6. For example, C. Taylor, 'Foucault on Freedom and Truth', in D.C. Hoy (ed.), *Foucault: A Critical Reader* (Oxford: Blackwell, 1986) pp. 94–5.
7. Buzan, supra (note 3), p. 54.
8. Ibid, p. 112.
9. Ibid, p. 116.
10. Supra (note 4), p. 21.
11. H.C. Relyea, 'National Security and Information', *Government Information Quarterly*, 4(1), 1987, pp. 12–4 and Buzan, supra (note 3), pp. 16–17 provide numerous examples.
12. Quoted in Relyea, ibid, pp. 12–13.
13. Quoted in Buzan, supra (note 3), p. 17.
14. P. Hartland-Thunberg, quoted in ibid, p. 16.
15. Ibid, pp. 112–41, on which this discussion is based.
16. Ibid, p. 131.

17. *World in Action*, broadcast 15 July 1991. See also *Financial Times*, 15 June 1992, p. 1.
18. See, for example, Thomas, supra (note 1), pp. 47–50 regarding the applicability of s.1 of the Official Secrets Act 1911 to economic and technological information.
19. S. Dorril and R. Ramsay, *Smear!* (London: Fourth Estate, 1991), p. 230.
20. For example, see J.T. Matthews, 'Redefining Security', *Foreign Affairs*, 68(2), Spring 1989 pp. 162–77.
21. Supra (note 4), p. 13 note 12.
22. Supra (note 3), pp. 134–42.
23. M. Edelman, *The Symbolic Uses of Politics* (Urbana: University of Illinois Press, 1976), pp. 69–72 (originally published 1964). F.M. Sorrentino, *Ideological Warfare: the FBI's Path Toward Power* (Port Washington, New York: Associated Faculty Press, 1985) develops a similar argument regarding the use of symbolism and ideology by the FBI to enhance its power. See also W. Pincus, 'The Bureau's Budget: A Source of Power', in P. Watters and S. Gillers (eds), *Investigating the FBI* (Garden City, NY: Doubleday, 1973), pp. 64–83.
24. D. Hurd, House of Commons Debates (hereafter HC Deb.) Hansard, 23 March 1984, col. 591.
25. Home Office, *The Interception of Communications in the United Kingdom*, Cmnd 9438 (London: HMSO, February 1985), p. 9, emphasis added.
26. Security Service Act, 1989, s.1.
27. HC Deb. 17 January 1989, cols. 213–14.
28. *Ex parte* Cheblak, *The Guardian*, 7 February 1991, p. 39.
29. H W.R. Wade, *Administrative Law* (Oxford: Clarendon Press, 6th edition, 1988), pp. 407–10.
30. *The Guardian*, 2 February 1991, p. 4, 7 February 1991, p. 24, 18 March 1991, p. 16; *The Independent On Sunday*, 3 February 1991, p. 18; *The Independent*, 16 December 1991, p. 1; Liberty, *Agenda*, Spring 1991, p. 3 lists the questions asked at one of these hearings.
31. Quoted in Relyea, supra (note 11), p. 15, emphasis in original.
32. Ibid, p. 19, emphasis in original.
33. Church Committee, *Final Report, Book III, Supplementary Detailed Staff Reports on Intelligence Activities and the Rights of Americans* (Washington DC: US Government Printing Office),

pp. 921–82 gives the details. For a more critical review of Dean's own role in White House intelligence-gathering and his tactics in exposing the Huston Plan see L. Colodny and R. Gettlin, *Silent Coup: The Removal of a President* (New York: St. Martin's Paperback, 1992), pp. 100–2.

34. Church Committee, ibid, p. 937.
35. Ibid, p. 939.
36. Ibid, p. 955.
37. Final Report of the Committee on the Judiciary, House of Representatives, *Impeachment of Richard M. Nixon, President of the United States* (New York: Bantam Books, 1975), p. 5.
38. Church Committee, supra (note 33), p. 980.
39. J. Dean, *Blind Ambition: The White House Years* (London: W.H. Allen, 1977), p. 254. The UK Security Service was apparently asked by the White House to find out if Ellsberg had had any contact with the KGB while he was at Cambridge University. J.T. Richelson and D. Ball, *The Ties That Bind* (Boston: Unwin Hyman, 2nd edition, 1990), p. 237.
40. Final Report of the Committee on the Judiciary, supra (note 37), pp. 243–4.
41. Justice D.C. McDonald, *Commission of Inquiry Concerning Certain Activities of the RCMP*, Second Report: *Freedom and Security under the Law* (Ottawa: Minister of Supply and Services, 1981), pp. 54–72; J. Sawatsky, *Men in the Shadows: the RCMP Security Service* (Toronto: Doubleday, 1980), pp. 191–4. For early development of security intelligence in Canada see also G.S. Kealey, 'The Surveillance State: The Origins of Domestic Intelligence and Counter-Subversion in Canada, 1914–21', *Intelligence and National Security*, 7(3), July 1992, pp. 179–210.
42. McDonald, ibid, Part III. The report of the Quebec inquiry, chaired by Jean Keable has not been translated into English: *Rapport de la Commission d'enquête sur des opérations policières en territoire québécois* (Québec: Ministère des communications, 1981).
43. Special Committee of the Senate on the Canadian Security Intelligence Service, *Delicate Balance: a Security Intelligence Service in a Democratic Society* (Ottawa: Minister of Supply and Services, 1983). For a detailed critique of the first Bill see P.H. Russell, 'The Proposed Charter for a Civilian Intelligence Agency: An Appraisal', *Canadian Public Policy*, 9, 1983, pp. 326–37.

44. Canadian Security Intelligence Service Act, 1984, s.38(a).
45. Ibid, s.2.
46. Notes for a Speech by the Honourable Pierre Blais, Solicitor General of Canada to the CASIS Conference, *Accountability and Effectiveness: National Requirements for Security Intelligence in the 1990s*, Ottawa 29 September, 1989, pp. 3–4.
47. The Hon. Doug Lewis, Solicitor General of Canada, *Statement on National Security*, 19 March 1992.
48. R.J. Spjut, 'Defining Subversion', *British Journal of Law and Society*, 6(2), Winter 1979, p. 254.
49. McDonald, supra (note 41), p. 447.
50. Ibid, pp. 73–7 in which the 1975 Directive is quoted. Richelson and Ball discuss in general why the security intelligence agencies of the UKUSA countries engaged in repressive actions, supra (note 39), pp. 296–8.
51. Quoted in McDonald, ibid, pp. 76–7.
52. Ibid, pp. 438–40.
53. Ibid, p. 441.
54. Russell, supra (note 43), p. 329.
55. Ibid,
56. Special Committee of the Senate, supra (note 43), §§39–40.
57. R.D. Crelinsten, 'Terrorism, Counterterrorism and National Security', in P. Hanks and J.D. McCamus (eds), *National Security: Surveillance and Accountability in a Democratic Society* (Cowansville, Québec: Les Editions Yvon Blais, 1989), pp. 215–16.
58. SIRC, *Annual Report 1986–87* (Ottawa: Minister of Supply and Services, 1987), pp. 34–40.
59. For a detailed account of this see P. Gill, 'Defining Subversion: The Canadian Experience Since 1977', *Public Law*, Winter 1989, pp. 617–36.
60. James Kelleher, Solicitor General of Canada, *Notes for a Speech to the Conference on 'Advocacy, Protest and Dissent'* Queen's University, Ontario, 25 February 1988, p. 7, emphasis in original.
61. SIRC, *Amending the CSIS Act: Proposals for the Special Committee of the House of Commons 1989* (Ottawa: Minister of Supply and Services, 1989), p. 1.
62. Report of the Special Committee on the Review of the CSIS Act and the Security Offences Act, *In Flux But Not In Crisis* (Ottawa: Canadian Government Publishing Center, 1990), pp. 23–4.
63. Solicitor General, *On Course: National Security for the 1990s*

(Ottawa: Minister of Supply and Services, 1991), pp. 40–41. These ministerial directives dated from 1987 when the Counter-Subversion Branch had been closed.

64. F. Cain, 'Accountability and the Australian Security Intelligence Organization: A Brief History', in A.S. Farson *et al.* (eds), *Security and Intelligence in a Changing World: New Perspectives for the 1990s* (London: Frank Cass, 1991), pp. 104–8. This account is based on ibid, pp. 104–25.

65. See also C. Andrew, 'The Growth of the Australian Intelligence Community and the Anglo-American Connection', *Intelligence and National Security*, 4(2), April 1989, pp. 242–3.

66. Ibid, pp. 246–7. This article was written with the benefit of a sight of Justice Hope's unpublished Fifth Report. See p. 254, note 46.

67. Cain, supra (note 64), p. 113.

68. Justice R.M. Hope, *ASIO*, Fourth report (Canberra: Australian Government Printing Service, 1977), §§62–6.

69. Justice R.M. Hope, *Report on the ASIO* (Canberra: Commonwealth of Australia, 1985), pp. 69–70.

70. This is part of s.3 of the ASIO Amendment Act, 1986.

71. P. Hanks, 'National Security – a political concept', *Monash University Law Review*, 14, 1988, p. 131 and see discussion of 'terrorism' below.

72. Hope, supra (note 69), pp. 60–61.

73. Church Committee, supra (note 33), pp. 394–5.

74. Ibid, p. 400.

75. Quoted in J.T. Elliff, *The Reform of FBI Intelligence Operations* (Princeton: Princeton University Press, 1979), p. 196.

76. Church Committee, Final Report, Book II, *Intelligence Activities and the Rights of Americans* (Washington DC: US Government Printing Office, 1976), p. 319.

77. Ibid, p. 320.

78. 392US1, quoted in ibid, p. 318, note 44.

79. Ibid, p. 320.

80. J.T. Elliff, 'The Attorney General's Guidelines for FBI Investigations', *Cornell Law Review*, 69, 1984, pp. 785–815 discusses in detail the 1983 guidelines. It has also been argued that Reagan's 1981 Executive Order regarding intelligence activities licensed the CIA to perform internal security functions contrary to the National Security Act, 1947. S.J. Conrad, 'Executive Order

12333: "Unleashing" the CIA Violates the Leash Law', *Cornell Law Review*, 70, 1985, pp. 968–90.
81. Quoted in R. Godson, *Intelligence Requirements for the 1980s: Domestic Intelligence* (Lexington: D.C. Heath, 1986), p. 258.
82. Ibid, pp. 251–2.
83. I. Leigh and L. Lustgarten, 'The Security Service Act 1989', *Modern Law Review*, 52(6), 1989, p. 803.
84. Quoted in Lord Denning's Report of his Inquiry into the Profumo affair: (HMSO: Cmnd 2152, September 1963), §236.
85. Paragraph 2, reproduced in ibid, §238.
86. Ibid, §230.
87. F. Kitson, *Low Intensity Operations: Subversion, Insurgency, Peacekeeping* (London: Faber and Faber, 1971), p. 3.
88. House of Lords Debates, 26 February 1975, col. 947.
89. House of Commons, Home Affairs Committee, *Special Branch*, Minutes of Evidence, L. Brittan, Home Secretary, 30 January 1985, pp. 108, 114.
90. House of Commons, Fourth Report from the Home Affairs Committee, *Special Branch*, HC Paper 71, 1985, p. xxi.
91. Ibid, p. viii.
92. D. Hurd, HC Deb., 17 January 1989, col. 218.
93. Ibid, col. 219.
94. HC Deb., 2 March 1978, col. 650.
95. R. H. Schultz and R. Godson, *Dezinformatsia: Active Measures in Soviet Strategy* (New York: Berkley Books, 1986), p. 2.
96. In December 1980 the Heritage Foundation issued a report on US intelligence activities which argued that 'clergymen, students, businessmen, entertainers, labour officials, journalists and government workers all may engage in subversive activities without being fully aware of the content, purpose, or control of their activities'. Quoted in J. Shattuck, 'National Security a Decade After', *Democracy*, 3(1), 1981 p. 59.
97. For a specifically Canadian version of this argument see J. Starnes, 'Canadian Security', *International Perspectives*, Sept./Oct. 1984, pp. 23–6. Generally on 'agents of influence' see A.N. Shulsky, *Silent Warfare: Understanding the World of Intelligence* (Washington: Brassey's (US), 1991), pp. 79–80.
98. For example, see E. Grace and C. Leys, *The Concept of Subversion*, paper for SIRC Conference, Queen's University, Ontario, February 1988, pp. 27–8.

99. F.J. Donner, *The Age of Surveillance: The Aims and Methods of America's Political Intelligence System* (New York: Vintage Books, 1981), pp. 455–60 discusses this with respect to the US. Richard Morgan advocates just the kind of very broad definition of 'terrorism' – for example, including civil disobedience – which will be most convenient for authorities and most likely to bring about this result. *Domestic Intelligence: Monitoring Dissent in America* (Austin: University of Texas Press, 1980), p. 135.

100. SIRC, *Annual Report for 1987–88* (Ottawa: Minister of Supply and Services, 1988), p. 29.

101. SIRC, *Annual Report for 1989–90* (Ottawa: Minister of Supply and Services, 1990), pp. 43–9.

102. CSIS Act, 1984, s.2.

103. Report of the Special Committee, supra (note 62), p. 23.

104. Solicitor General, supra (note 63), pp. 37–9.

105. Crelinsten, supra (note 57) p. 208.

106. Ibid, p. 213.

107. T. Hadden, 'Daggers Drawn in the Legal Dark', *The Guardian*, 28 April 1992, p. 19.

108. Church Committee, supra (note 76), p. 320.

109. Richelson and Ball, supra (note 39), pp. 68–73.

110. McDonald, supra (note 41), p. 443.

111. S.17A, quoted in Hanks, supra (note 71), p. 132.

112. J.M. Oseth, *Regulating US Intelligence Operations* (Lexington: University Press of Kentucky, 1985), p. 98.

4

Penetration I:
Gathering Information

The extent to which states are able to penetrate their societies can be seen as a major indicator of their modernity. However, the state is only one of a large number of institutions attempting to exercise control via surveillance. It is an important, but not the only, player responsible for the movement towards what has been described as 'a total surveillance system'[1] or a 'maximum security society'.[2] Security intelligence agencies are part of the inner circle of the Gore-Tex state and here and in Chapter 5 their penetration of other levels of the state and society is analysed in terms of an 'intelligence process'. This consists of five main elements: planning and direction; collection; production and analysis; dissemination, and countering. This idea of a 'process' or 'cycle' has been most often applied to the analysis of foreign intelligence but it provides a useful framework also for the analysis of domestic security intelligence; for example, it is used in CSIS's first public annual report.[3]

In using such a framework as an analytical device there is always a danger that the process under review appears to be far more rational and coherent than it really is. The idea of a process is used here because it gives us a means of discussing the different aspects of security intelligence. There is much to be said for Arthur Hulnick's suggestion that, in 'reality', it 'is much more useful to consider the intelligence process as a matrix of interconnected, mostly autonomous functions'.[4] Either way it is important to keep in mind the variety of ideological and organisational distortions that infect the process.[5] First, however, in the light of the discussion in the last chapter of the problems of defining the key terms with which security intelligence agencies

135

operate, we must consider what they actually do; specifically, how surveillance relates to action.[6]

WHAT SECURITY INTELLIGENCE AGENCIES DO

This has been extensively discussed in North America and Australia, but not in the UK. In the Security Service Act, 1989, we are told that the function of the Security Service:

> 1(2) . . . shall be the protection of the national security and, in particular, its protection against threats from espionage, terrorism and sabotage, from the activities of agents of foreign powers and from actions intended to overthrow or undermine parliamentary democracy by political, industrial or violent means.
> 1(3) It shall also be the function of the Service to safeguard the economic well-being of the United Kingdom against threats posed by the actions or intentions of persons outside the British Islands.

Thus the function of the Service is to protect national security and safeguard economic well-being. In the last chapter we examined the problems caused by the use of such vague concepts as 'national security' and 'economic well-being'; here we concentrate on 'protect' and 'safeguard'. Bearing in mind earlier discussions of different interpretations of power, the central issue is whether this involves the security intelligence agency solely in the collection of information, meaning that the agency will be more like a 'domestic intelligence bureau' (see Chapter 2) with its exercise of power being relatively limited, or whether it may engage also in countering actions, which move it towards being a 'political police' with more extensive potential for exercising power. The Act itself provides no real enlightenment on this issue, but there was a hint that the second is more likely to be the case in the Minister's introduction of the Bill in the Second Reading debate:

> The main responsibilities of the Service for the protection of national security are clearly set out in the Bill. In addition, the Security Service must be able *to act* if necessary against any substantial threat to the nation as a whole.[7]

Elsewhere more explicit attention has been given to this question. For example, the Australian Security Intelligence Organisation Act 1979 specifies that 'it is not a function of the Organisation to carry out or enforce measures for security . . .'[8] ASIO describes its own functions as being to:

> *obtain*, *correlate* and *evaluate* intelligence relevant to security;
> *communicate* security intelligence as appropriate;
> *advise* Ministers and Commonwealth authorities on matters relating to security;
> *advise* Ministers and Commonwealth authorities and some others on protective security; and
> *obtain* within Australia foreign intelligence using special powers granted to it under warrant, and *communicate* the intelligence as appropriate.[9]

ASIO reiterates that it is not a police force and has no powers to arrest, detain or interrogate people[10] but a certain ambiguity remains since there are other forms of action which the Organisation might contemplate, even officially. For example,

> Where insufficient evidence exists to recommend expulsion of an individual suspected of engaging in activities prejudicial to security, ASIO may take suitable lawful steps to discourage or inhibit the activity. Such a step may be the simple expedient of signalling in some way that ASIO is aware of the individual's plans or intentions.[11]

Thus it must be remembered that police powers of arrest and detention are not the only forms of countering potentially available to security intelligence agencies.

In Canada, the McDonald Commission similarly recommended that the essential function of the security intelligence agency that it proposed should be the collection, analysis and reporting of intelligence and that it should not be authorised to enforce security measures. McDonald considered that a better check for civil liberties was provided if executive enforcement responsibilities were dealt with by other agencies.[12] The Canadian Security Intelligence Service Act 1984 set out the basic mandate:

> The Service shall collect, by investigation or otherwise, to the extent that it is strictly necessary, and analyse and retain information and intelligence respecting activities that may on reasonable grounds be suspected of constituting threats to the security of Canada and, in relation thereto, shall report to and advise the Government of Canada.[13]

In addition, CSIS is to provide security assessments (s.13), information and advice in support of government citizenship and immigration programmes (s.14) and to assist in the collection of foreign intelligence in Canada (s.16). As McDonald had recommended, the statute did not include the functions of 'deterring, preventing and countering' that had appeared in the 1975 Cabinet Directive to the RCMP Security Service[14] (discussed above in Chapter 3) and addressed specifically the question of disclosure of information. This has always been one of the prime methods of countering (see discussion in Chapter 2 of 'education' and 'deception') and the CSIS Act clearly leaves room for this: 'The Service may disclose information . . . for the purposes of the performance of its duties and functions under this Act'.[15] Other forms of countering are not explicitly excluded from the Act, except in so far as they do not appear in s.12. Neither do CSIS officials have police powers, the primary responsibility for the enforcement of any security offences remaining with the RCMP (s.61(1)) within the Security Offences Act 1984.

From 1985 onwards, the Inspector General established by the CSIS Act as one part of the oversight structure attempted to develop an agreed clarification of the s.12 mandate, for example, the practical meaning of terms such as 'investigation or otherwise' and 'strictly necessary'; but by the time of the parliamentary review of the Act during 1990, six years after its passage, there had been no comprehensive ministerial direction.[16] In its response to the Parliamentary Report, the government issued such a direction and said it would be made public later that year.[17]

In the United States, the Church Committee investigation of the FBI commenced on the same basis as did McDonald in Canada: that is, the agency concerned was both a federal police force and a domestic security intelligence agency. Whereas McDonald examined in great depth the question of whether these

two functions should be separated, the Church Committee did not
– at least there is no sign of such discussion in the conclusions
and recommendations in the Committee's Final Report. Church's
recommendations concentrated more upon the way in which
investigative techniques linked with law enforcement, on the
one hand, and civil rights on the other. Compared with Hope
and McDonald, Church reflected little consideration of the role
of a security intelligence agency in gathering information for the
purpose of advising and informing government.

Thus, without specifying precisely what the FBI was to do, the
Committee stated that:

> the ultimate goal is a statutory mandate for the federal
> government's domestic security function that will ensure
> that the FBI, as the primary domestic security investigative
> agency, concentrates upon criminal conduct as opposed to
> political rhetoric or association.[18]

This goal has not been achieved and the Committee accepted that
a strict 'criminal standard' might be inappropriate since it saw
the need for the FBI to have the authority to conduct 'intelligence
investigations' of conduct which had not reached the stage 'of a
prosecutable act'.[19] Therefore it confined its recommendations
to a series of proposals as to what countering activities the FBI
should be prohibited from employing:

(a) Disseminating any information to the White House,
    any other federal official, the news media, or any other
    person for a political or other improper purpose, such
    as discrediting an opponent of the administration or a
    critic of an intelligence or investigative agency.
(b) Interfering with lawful speech, publication, assembly,
    organisational activity, or association of Americans.
(c) Harassing individuals through unnecessary overt in-
    vestigative techniques such as interviews or obvious
    physical surveillance for the purpose of intimidation.[20]

The Attorney General's guidelines issued in 1976, before the
publication of the Church report, were less precise as is discussed
in Chapter 5.

Since information-gathering may amount to a form of countering activity, for example as in (c) above, the importance of attempting to define very specifically just what security intelligence agencies may and may not do can be seen. Again, this is not because of a naive assumption that such agencies will interpret their mandates minimally but because, without that specific mandate, any attempt to provide some external check on their activities will be doomed from the outset.

PLANNING AND DIRECTION

'Targeting' by police and internal security agencies can be examined at various levels. These vary in the degree of generality or specificity on the one hand; and in the degree of formality/ informality on the other.

At the most general level, decisions regarding who or what is to be targeted will be based on the definitions examined in Chapter 3, that is whether particular individuals constitute a threat to 'national security' or are, in terms of the prevailing definition, 'subversive'. As we saw, these definitions operate in a very general sense and are unlikely, on their own, to provide adequate guidance to an operative. Furthermore, while the procedures for establishing the priorities and targets for foreign intelligence-gathering are relatively formalised in the UK, those for domestic security intelligence are far less so.

Before examining the latter in more detail it is useful to consider the overall structure of the security intelligence network in the UK, and the main relationships are summarised in Figure 4.1. Information gathered by the security intelligence agencies is channelled into the Joint Intelligence Organisation (JIO). This is part of the Cabinet Office and consists of staff who draw up assessments. The JIO is divided into Current Intelligence Groups assigned to different geographical areas. The Joint Intelligence Committee (JIC) consists of the heads of the Security Service, SIS, GCHQ, Chief of Defence Intelligence Staff (DIS) and the chair of the JIO. But it is said that the dominance of the Foreign and Commonwealth Office plus representation from other ministries – the Treasury and Defence – and the Cabinet Office itself ensures that the collection agencies are in

140

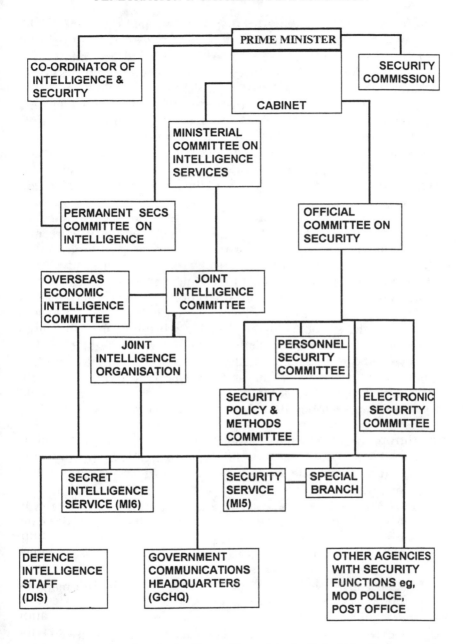

Figure 4.1 Security Intelligence Network in the United Kingdom

141

a minority and in no way control the assessment process.[21] The JIC meets weekly to consider the summary assessment prepared by the JIO and then reports are forwarded to ministers – the Prime Minister, Defence, Home, Foreign Ministers, the Chancellor of the Exchequer, and, where appropriate, the Secretary of State for Northern Ireland. Security Service reports are circulated separately. The other main committee concerned with the preparation of assessments is the Overseas Economic Intelligence Committee, which is chaired by a Treasury official and includes representatives of departments responsible for Trade, Industry and Energy as well as the heads of the collection agencies.

The Permanent Secretaries Committee on the Intelligence Services (PSIS) is chaired by the Cabinet Secretary, currently Sir Robin Butler, and includes the permanent secretaries of the Foreign Office, Ministry of Defence, Treasury, Home Office, and the Chief of Defence Staff. It meets quarterly, discusses general priorities and budgets, but not operations. It has been described as 'the supreme entity in the intelligence mandarinate'[22] and reports to the Prime Minister directly. The job of the Ministerial Committee on Intelligence Services (MIS) is 'to keep under review policy on the security and intelligence services'[23] and it makes the final budget decisions on the basis of what it is told by the Prime Minister. The Co-ordinator of Intelligence and Security, Gerald Warner since October 1991, has the following responsibilities:

1   to prepare an annual review of intelligence for presentation to PSIS. This looks at the intelligence of the previous year and suggests the broad lines of future requirements and priorities;
2   to scrutinise the annual financial estimates and five-year forecasts of the agencies and present them to PSIS with his recommendations;
3   to conduct enquiries on various intelligence subjects which he, the Cabinet Secretary or PSIS deems necessary; and
4   'generally act to lubricate Cabinet Office involvement in intelligence and security matters'.[24]

Concerning 'security' matters specifically, the Security Service is the main agency involved and the committee structure to which it works is centred on the Official Committee on Security. Like the PSIS this is chaired by the Cabinet Secretary and has three subordinate committees: the Security Policy and Methods Committee is concerned with the physical security of property and with the classification of documents; the Personnel Security Committee, also chaired by the Cabinet Secretary, supervises the positive vetting system and inquiries into leaks, and the Electronic Security Committee is concerned with the protection of computer and related information networks. The Security Commission is established at the behest of the Prime Minister to investigate particular security lapses. It consists of a panel of seven members drawn from judges, retired military officers and civil servants, three of whom will normally be selected for any particular investigation (see further below in Chapter 7).

The JIC/JIO network was established in 1939 and there was a suggestion from the JIC towards the end of the war that it should co-ordinate the work of the Security Service and the SIS, but this did not occur and such co-ordination of *domestic* security intelligence as occurred was done by the Security Service itself. This situation seems to have continued into the post-war era; while the advent of 'terrorism' as a security intelligence problem affecting both foreign and domestic areas in the 1970s may have modified this somewhat, it appears still that the Security Service dominates the establishment of domestic security intelligence priorities. This is suggested by, for example, the distribution of Security Service reports to ministers separately from those of the JIC. Thus there appears to be a different structure for 'intelligence' (JIO/JIC) than for 'security' (OCS/PSC) Since the Security Service is crucially involved in both security and intelligence domestically, there would not appear to be any co-ordination mechanism *from outside* of the Security Service's activities.[25] A similar situation prevailed in Canada during the 1980s.[26]

At the next level, that is the individual agencies, there will be operational guidelines, or standing orders. These may be either published or unpublished; in fact it is likely to be the case that there are both. In the UK no guidelines have been published regarding the Security Service. Those used by police Special Branches had existed since 1970 but they were not published until 1984 following the establishment of

143

an inquiry into Special Branch by the House of Commons Home Affairs Committee. How far these differed from the previously unpublished ones is not known in detail, but the main change publicly acknowledged by then Home Secretary, Leon Brittan, was that the 1984 guidelines provide more detailed guidance to chief officers on the need for accurate and relevant records.[27]

Similarly, external inquiries into domestic security intelligence agencies in North America and Australia have focused greater attention on the internal rules of those agencies also. ASIO, for example, during 1987–88, started on the preparation of a consolidation of its administrative and operational procedures.[28] This can be a long process. In Canada, SIRC reported in 1991 that most sections of the CSIS Manual had been updated to take into account the changes in the 1984 CSIS Act. SIRC reports each year in general terms on the main amendments made to the CSIS Manual, for example, that during 1990–91 CSIS had incorporated the ministerial direction on the use of informers into the Manual, and also had made a number of other minor changes regarding CSIS involvement in security aspects of immigration, and regarding the dissemination of information.[29] We have already seen that new guidelines were issued to the FBI in 1976 and 1983.

Some guidelines, not normally published, may sometimes reach the light of day. The following extracts from Merseyside Police standing orders do not relate particularly to Special Branch but to uniformed patrol officers and collators. Collators (two per Division) were responsible for the collection, analysis and dissemination of all kinds of information within the force, that is, criminal intelligence. Regarding the job of the Resident Beat Constable:

> 43. To obtain information, it is useful for the area constable to make himself known to local officials, shopkeepers, tradesmen, garage proprietors and other reliable persons who regularly visit or reside in each road or street in the area. He should aim at having a contact who is confident in him in every road and street . . .
> 47. The amount of information passed to the Collator by the area constable will indicate his effectiveness.

Regarding the duties of a Collator:

> 52. All items, however insignificant, will be recorded and indexed and will be available to all personnel at all times . . .
> 62. It should always be borne in mind that the Collator's Office should be an Information Bureaux [*sic*] in addition to a Criminal Intelligence Office and *information of all kinds should be encouraged on the premises* [*sic*] that we do not know today what we will need tomorrow.[30]

The last part quoted – the 'logic of intelligence-gathering' – indicates the difficulties faced by attempts at controlling excessive intelligence-gathering.

Yet there is another level to consider, that is the actual 'working rules' of operatives which may frequently diverge considerably from their guidelines, whether published or not, as was discussed in Chapter 2. For example, with respect to the use of informers, where the police claim to exercise strict control because of the dangers of corruption, one report indicated that 60 per cent of London detectives persistently broke the rules regarding dealing with informants.[31]

Therefore there are a number of questions which need to be asked about the domestic targeting process in the UK. Since the process is clearly less formalised than for foreign intelligence-gathering, it would be mistaken to view the process as a 'rational' one in which policies made at the top are implemented by those below; rather it is ideological orthodoxies, organisational routines, sub-cultures, bureaucratic politics and working rules that will actually determine who is targeted at any one time.

In 1977 the South Australian Cabinet appointed Justice White of Adelaide to ascertain the extent to which Special Branch records there genuinely related to security matters and to consider the suitability of the criteria on which records were based. White's *Initial Report* referred to 'a hard core of genuine security intelligence material' but he found also 'a mass of records (indeed, the greater part of Special Branch records) relating to matters, organisations and persons having no connection whatsoever with genuine security risks'.[32] Outside of the 'hard core' about half of the records related to communist activities,

The other half of 'non-terrorist' records relate to organisations and persons conceived to be 'left-wing', and suspected by Special Branch of holding or supporting 'subversive' views by reason only of the fact that such organisations or persons adopted policies or opinions which were 'radical', or 'to the left' of an arbitrary centre point fixed by someone in Special Branch. I have no doubt that the arbitrary centre point was established by Special Branch with the assistance of ASIO, either by means of information fed into Special Branch by ASIO as being relevant to security, or by ASIO's periodical training sessions of State Special Branch officers at seminars.[33]

These files resulted from targeting procedures in which:

Such persons were selected because the organisation or situation, in which they were when they came under notice, was considered by Special Branch to be potentially subversive *per se*, a judgement made upon unsound criteria, which were laid down long ago, and continued uncritically, without review by higher ranking officers sensitive to policy matters.[34]

Per se targeting, sometimes referred to as 'targeting-by-category', in which any members of an organisation classified within a particular targeted category would themselves become a target simply by reason of that membership, was standard practice in domestic security intelligence agencies. Such internal organisational practices, however, can be highly resistant to outside efforts at change, as, for example with the first effort to clarify the security intelligence mandate in Canada in 1975 (see Chapter 3 for details).

The CSIS Act 1984 which separated out the Security Service from the RCMP and established the first statutory, and narrower, security intelligence mandate did not have much immediate effect on targeting procedures. During 1986–87 the SIRC carried out a study of CSIS counter-subversion activities and concluded that CSIS intruded too widely on the lives and activities of too many Canadians.[35] SIRC recommended that the Subject Evaluation Reports prepared by investigators should discuss explicitly the magnitude and imminence of the threat posed, and also that the Target Approval and Review Committee (TARC) should target by individuals rather than by categories on the *per se* principle. As we saw in Chapter 3, the counter-subversion branch was abolished in 1987. A few of the branch's former targets were considered sufficiently serious threats to merit reallocation to either the counter-terrorism or counter-intelligence branches while the majority of files were left in what was called the 'residue'. These were to be maintained by the CSIS Analysis and Production Branch (RAP) which relied entirely on non-intrusive, open collection methods. Should any individual appear to require more intrusive surveillance then ministerial permission would have to be sought.[36] Subsequently, SIRC found that this procedure had not worked because RAP had not succeeded in showing that any of the 1,400 individuals being monitored in the residual counter-subversion category posed a threat to the security of Canada as defined in section 2[d] of the CSIS Act. They were still on file because of traditional targeting by category. Since RAP was not able to devote sufficient resources to the kinds of investigation that would be necessary to produce threat assessments on individuals, SIRC proposed that the residue be eliminated entirely. All files would be subject to the more thorough assessment of individual threats as conducted within the counter-terrorism or -intelligence branches or would be closed.[37]

Cathy Massiter provided some insight into the working of targeting procedures in the UK Security Service, from which she had resigned in 1984. When Joan Ruddock became chair of CND in 1983 the Security Service wished to record her activities but had initial difficulty finding a pretext. This was provided when she gave an interview to a Soviet journalist who was actually a KGB officer, although Ruddock did not know that, and thus a file could be opened on the premise that she had been a 'contact of a hostile intelligence service'. Other CND members were similarly brought within the system.[38] In earlier years when CND itself was classified as a subversive organisation this problem would not have arisen because of *per se* targeting procedures.

The Security Service Act 1989 in the UK appears to have legalised this longstanding practice of *per se* targeting which has been criticised in the North American and Australian inquiries.

If a person complains to the Tribunal under the Act that he or she has been the subject of inquiry by the Security Service, then if the individual had been targeted because of membership of a category 'regarded as requiring investigation' the Tribunal

> shall regard the Service as having reasonable grounds for deciding to institute or continue inquiries about the complainant if the Tribunal consider that the Service had reasonable grounds for believing him to be a member of that category.[39]

There is just one small potential avenue for changes to be brought about: if the Tribunal think that the Service may not be justified in regarding all members of a particular category as requiring investigation they shall refer it to the Commissioner (s.7(1)) who *may* make a report on this to the Home Secretary who *may* take such action as is thought fit (s.7(3)). Since there is no provision in the Act for ministerial *direction* of the Security Service, it is not clear what, if any, impact this will have on traditional targeting procedures.

In general, another way in which greater controls have been applied to targeting practices has been to distinguish levels of targeting and to require different levels of authorisation for each. In the United States the new guidelines laid down for the FBI in 1976 permitted 'preliminary investigations' into an individual or group if allegations or information were received regarding violence and a breach of the law relating to, for example, the overthrow of government. Such an investigation would be limited to an examination of FBI indices and files, public sources, federal, state and local records, inquiry of existing sources of information, use of previously established informants, physical surveillance and interviews for the limited purpose of identifying the subject of the investigation. Such an investigation would normally terminate after 90 days unless a 'limited' or 'full' investigation had been authorised by then.[40] The 1983 guidelines extended somewhat the potential scope of preliminary inquiries.[41]

Since 1988 CSIS targeting policy designates three collection levels, each with specified investigative techniques and approval procedures. Level One investigations, like the FBI's preliminary investigations, are for short durations and limit investigators to open sources and records held by other police and security intelligence agencies. Level Two investigations may be more intrusive, and include for example, physical surveillance and interviews. They may be approved initially at a regional level, but can be renewed only under the authority of the Target Approval and Review Committee (TARC), which is chaired by the Director. Level Three, involving the most intrusive techniques, will require court warrants under the CSIS Act, and go through a process of approval involving lawyers external to the Service and the Deputy Solicitor General before the court is approached.[42]

It is not clear that this problem has been addressed in the UK or, if so, what internal procedures are in place. For example, Special Branch Guidelines, section 5, reads:

> A Special Branch gathers information about threats to *public order*. Such information will enable the Branch to provide assessments of whether marches, meetings, demonstrations and pickets pose any threat to public order and help the chief officer to determine an appropriate level of policing.[43]

Clare Short MP pointed out to the then Home Secretary, Leon Brittan, that this made it legitimate to carry out widespread surveillance of trades unions to see if there *might* be public disorder. Brittan denied this on the grounds that the section talks of 'threats', not something that 'might become a threat', arguing that such a distinction was regularly made by lawyers[44] but not indicating just how this provided guidance for Special Branch officers!

Jean-Paul Brodeur has pointed to the numerous difficulties involved in targeting: for example, the known impossibility of predicting which few individuals in the population will actually constitute security threats. Brodeur suggests it is the covert character of suspicious behaviour which is likely to indicate that it might be illegal rather than legal political action, but if this is so, then the more serious the threat, the harder it will be to detect. Therefore, under pressure to have something to show for their efforts, security services have tended to concentrate their efforts on dissent, which is conspicuous and easily studied.[45] As was seen in Chapter 3 with the RCMP's reaction to the 1975

Directive, security services have tended to implement this via the targeting of groups whose public positions proclaimed their opposition to prevailing political arrangements. But even after the passage of the CSIS Act, SIRC noted the same phenomenon still at work in the residue of counter-subversion files during 1989–90 which included a great deal of information on activities in federal and provincial elections.[46]

Another example of the same problem is provided by the FBI's investigation during 1983–85 of the Committee in Solidarity with the People of El Salvador (CISPES). The initial targeting was not under the FBI domestic security/terrorism guidelines but under those covering international terrorism. These require that the target be someone who knowingly engages or assists in international terrorism. Since the FBI was intending to investigate whether CISPES was a front organisation for such activities, the investigation should have focused on those people suspected of acting illegally. But what actually took place was a much broader investigation in which the FBI undertook to locate every CISPES group and member in the country. This led to the compilation of information on hundreds of CISPES demonstrations, protests and boycotts. The FBI itself collected no information relevant to the original targeting and yet in over two years showed no signs of voluntarily winding down the inquiries from the kind of all-embracing investigation of lawful political activity which had been common under Hoover. The new oversight structures can take some credit, however, in that it was a (delayed) review by the Justice Department which led to the abandonment of the investigation in 1985.[47] Subsequently six FBI employees were disciplined and the Senate Intelligence Committee concluded that the the case 'was a serious failure in FBI management'.[48]

Given the future orientation of intelligence and the consequent uncertainty as to just what will or will not be relevant to the specific parts of security intelligence agencies' mandates, it has to be questioned whether the substantive effect on an organisation or movement will be much different whether domestic security intelligence agencies are formally targeting *individuals* within the organisation or the organisation *per se*. But even if there is little difference, particularly from the perspective of those under surveillance,[49] it does not mean that the effort to make the distinction is a waste of time as far as attempting to minimise the intrusiveness of a security intelligence agency is concerned. The impossibility of providing an unambiguous security intelligence mandate and the resistance of security intelligence agencies to change mean that only a continuous process of oversight regarding the suitability of operational guidelines and practices can enhance both organisational effectiveness and propriety within the overall context of statutory definitions.

INFORMATION-GATHERING TECHNIQUES

It is at this point of the security intelligence process that the penetrativeness of security intelligence agencies becomes concrete. In their consideration of the future of security intelligence in Canada the McDonald Commission established the following five principles to be applied to the use and limitation on gathering techniques. First, there should be no violations of the criminal law; if the use of certain techniques which would violate the law is considered necessary for reasons of national security, then the law should be changed to accommodate that. Second, the investigative means to be employed should be proportionate to the threat posed and the probability of its occurrence. Third, the need to use various information-gathering techniques, even if lawful, must be balanced against the possible damage they cause to civil liberties, for example to avoid the 'chilling' effect of surveillance on the freedom of association. Fourth, the more intrusive the technique, the higher the authority that should be required to approve its use in some cases authorisation would be from inside the security intelligence agency, in others it should be from outside, specifically from the judiciary. Finally, except in emergencies, less intrusive techniques should be employed before more intrusive techniques.[50] These principles provide a set of benchmarks by which current practices may be judged.

Open sources

Most of the information accumulated by security intelligence agencies is from open sources; this is true of all forms of intelligence, particularly with respect to background information relating to resources and capabilities. Where it may not be adequate is in the assessment of intentions/motivations. It has been estimated that 75 per cent of all the information monitored by Special Branch officers is either publicly available or freely given. Press reports, petitions, political groups, publications, meetings and information passed on knowingly or unknowingly provide the bulk of this.[51] There are other, less 'open', sources as well: visits to lecturers and teachers, searches carried out in pursuance of warrants under the Official Secrets Acts. The UK Prevention of Terrorism Act (PTA) provides police with a number of powers aimed at information-gathering: for example, people may be 'examined' at ports on less than reasonable suspicion and the completion of landing cards provides the basis for many thousands of checks each year against Special Branch records.[52]

Similar estimates have been provided with respect to the sources of foreign intelligence. Sir Reginald Hibbert, a former British diplomat and intelligence officer, has suggested that a diplomatic mission might gather 50 per cent of its information from open, published sources, a further 10–20 per cent which is not classified but derives from the privileged sources available to diplomats, and a further 20–25 per cent which is classifiable but which is imparted deliberately to diplomats, for a variety of reasons. Finally there is probably less than 10 per cent of the information gathered about a country which comes from secret intelligence sources, the primary value of which is often short term and tends to confirm what has already been calculated from the other varieties of non-secret information gathered.[53] On the other hand, Michael Herman has suggested that Hibbert underestimates both the quantitative and qualitative importance of covertly gathered material regarding defence and national security.[54]

In general there would appear to be a tendency within security intelligence agencies to invest greater credibility in information gathered from covert sources than that gathered from open sources. Extensive security and secrecy procedures regarding the gathering and assessment of covertly gathered information can lead, via processes of paranoia and group-think, to an inability to challenge the credibility of the information, and to assumptions that it will be more accurate than that gathered openly. There is little evidence for these assumptions.[55] Consequently, in Canada, for example, SIRC has continued to monitor the implementation by CSIS of McDonald's recommendation that greater use should be made of open source material.[56]

State records

What access does the Security Service have to information in the possession of other state agencies? Having examined this question in the US, the Church Committee recommended that, as far as intelligence investigations were concerned, tax returns, medical or social history records, confidential records of private institutions and confidential records of federal, state and local government agencies should not be used unless the person was the target of a full investigation. Additionally, the Attorney General must make a written finding that less intrusive techniques had been considered and rejected and that he believes the information to be necessary.[57] In Canada, the McDonald Commission recommended that the heads of federal government institutions could release basic biographical information to a security intelligence agency upon a written request which stated that the information was necessary to locate/identify an individual suspected of constituting a statutorily defined threat to the security of Canada. Any further information should only be accessible to the agency by means of a judicial warrant, excluding census information which should be exempt.[58]

The Church recommendation was not followed; as we saw above, these techniques are still available as part of a preliminary investigation. In Canada, the CSIS Act permitted CSIS to enter into arrangements with federal and provincial governments and police agencies. During 1988–89 SIRC developed a framework for monitoring and auditing information exchanges under these agreements and, in a limited spot check, found that most exchanges were relatively mundane, for example, checking birth records as part of security vetting, but SIRC admitted to concern that neither CSIS nor themselves were able to check adequately on the type and sensitivity of information exchanges. During 1989–90 SIRC carried out further study of both foreign and domestic information exchanges. Regarding the former, SIRC recommended that CSIS adopt a more comprehensive framework of policy and procedures, specifically to prevent information about Canadians falling into the wrong hands. Regarding the latter, SIRC made several recommendations, including that CSIS maintain a log of all exchanges and be required to obtain a court warrant before being given access to medical records.[59]

In the UK if any such procedures have been established they certainly have not been published. It would appear, for example, that the Security Service makes regular use of DSS records at Newcastle, initially by means of having officers working there undercover, latterly by means of computer links.[60] Wider governmental computer links are now being developed to include the Home Office, DSS, Customs and Excise and the Inland Revenue in the Government Data Network. A report from the National Audit Office in 1989 said that none of the initial user departments had any plans to exchange information via the network with other users (so why have a network?) but since there appear to be no standard procedures governing the exchange of information between departments in any case,[61] it is likely that the traditional forms of informal contact will facilitate agencies' access to other departments' information. The Data Protection Registrar has not progressed very far in his attempt to have the contributing departments discuss and possibly publish the rules of data transfer – for example, circumstances of transfer, levels of authorisation and arrangements for checking and review.[62] In his 1992 Report he cited 'data matching' whereby departments share information in order to build up profiles of individuals as a new threat to personal privacy.[63]

Informers

Of all the methods by which security intelligence agencies obtain information covertly, this is both the most productive and most problematic, respectively in terms of agency effectiveness and civil rights. It is also the one that has been least discussed and is, possibly, least subject to internal organisational control. Different types present varying degrees of penetration. The McDonald Commission gave four main categories of 'human source', in ascending order of penetration: first, the 'volunteer source' who may be no more than an ordinary citizen offering information on a once only basis, but this might include also people offering information in return for some favour, for example, intervention with the prosecuting authorities. Second is the 'undeveloped casual source' in which there is some encouragement of a person to provide information which they come by in the ordinary performance of their job, for example, a taxi driver, maintenance personnel, and telephone company employees. The sources receive no payment. The equivalent in the FBI was the 'confidential source', used in 50 per cent of the domestic intelligence investigations analysed by the General Accounting Office (GAO) in its study of the Bureau.[64]

Third in McDonald's classification was the 'developed casual source' in which there will be more frequent contact with the source, who will be paid and is more likely to be given active information-gathering tasks. Fourth, and most penetrative of all, is the 'long-term deep cover operative' who is part of an extensive, lengthy and often elaborate operation. The source may be someone who was a member of the target organisation who was subsequently 'turned' into providing information, or may be an officer of the security intelligence agency who adopts a false identity – a 'legend' – and infiltrates the target organisation.[65] The GAO study of the FBI found that 'paid and directed' sources – roughly the equivalent of McDonald's third and fourth categories – were used in 85 per cent of domestic intelligence cases, compared with the use of electronic surveillance in just five per cent of cases.[66]

The productivity of informers cannot be measured just in terms of their information-gathering potential. Recalling the earlier discussion of the coincidence of processes of power and information, the significance of informers is that their presence, or even the suspicion of their presence may be highly disruptive. For Brodeur, one of the four distinguishing features of 'high policing' was that it did not just make use of informers but acknowledged its willingness to do so in order to create disruption.[67] Indeed, the threat to tell the organisation that a person is an informer may be used as a means of forcing people to become so.[68] It is likely that the smaller the organisation, the more disruptive will be the effect of an informer;[69] one reason for organising in cells is to minimise the impact of informers. Mark Urban has estimated that around one in 30 or 40 of PIRA's frontline membership were informers between 1976 and

1987.[70] In some cases organisations have maintained apparent significance for longer than was really the case because of the continued involvement of informers. For example, the influence of the Communist Party of the United States (CPUSA) was overstated in part because of Hoover's personal dogma, but also because of the activity of an army of FBI informers; by the end of 1956 'many' of the CPUSA's 4–6,000 membership were FBI informers,[71] the ratio of informers to members reaching more than one to six at some point.[72] In other cases, while the genuine members of an organisation may evolve towards lawful action, a paid informer within the group may cast doubt on their change and ensure that they remain under suspicion.[73]

For the security intelligence agencies the advantages of an informer over technical means of surveillance are many: depending on the mode of recruitment, informers are likely to be cheaper and they are more flexible and 'active' as information-gatherers compared with the relatively passive bug or tap. In June 1975 the FBI was using over 1,500 domestic intelligence informers and its budget for payments for Fiscal Year 1976 was $7.4 million. On average informers were paid about $100 per month, with the more productive ones receiving $300–400 monthly.[74] Most informers in Northern Ireland receive only £10 to £20 per week, with bonuses of £200 to £300 for successful tip-offs, and much larger payments to those in high places.[75]

The risks involved in their use are, however, many. First, since they are giving information in exchange for benefits, for example money or immunity from prosecution, they are like all private entrepreneurs and will tend to overvalue what they have to sell.[76] Informers' motives may be any mixture of fear, insecurity, revenge, envy, remorse or money;[77] therefore, compared with the technical source, there are enormous problems in assessing the validity of the information provided. Second, handlers are prone to be optimistic about the reliability of their sources in order to enhance their own position.[78] Third, as McDonald pointed out, the use of informers involves the security intelligence agency in deception and betrayal which may have deleterious effects on the moral characters of both handlers and sources.[79] This may strike the 'realist' as rather quaint, but the consequences can be as bad for the effectiveness of the agency as for its morality. The dilemma is obvious where handlers find themselves developing close working relationships with those they suspect or know to have killed their colleagues.[80]

A particular aspect of this is the way in which security intelligence agencies recruit informers. Police most often recruit informers by striking a bargain with someone who has been arrested, but if the security intelligence agency does not have police powers, for example CSIS or the UK Security Service, then it may have to use other techniques. The main leverage available is the process of making security assessments in the context of positive vetting or immigration procedures. The case of Issa Mohammed, discussed in Chapter 6, shows how inimical the use of such pressures can be to civil rights.[81]

The relationship between handler and source may well be long-term and become very close. One side-effect of this is that agencies and officers become very secretive and reluctant to share sources. This may well have a negative effect on the co-ordination of operations within an agency, and even more so between different agencies. In Northern Ireland two handlers might be assigned to an informer. If the two are from different agencies a Tasking and Co-ordination Group (TCG) would decide who they were to be. The TCGs were established in the late 1970s as 'police primacy' was introduced and are headed by an RUC Special Branch officer. The RUC tried to reduce the Army's use of informers to a minimum, but both Army and Security Service resisted this since, they said, it would place too much power into the hands of the many Protestant 'hard men' within Special Branch.[82]

Another potential abuse is that an informer may actually behave as an *agent provocateur* and become even more of a countering factor than is represented by their presence and possible 'chilling' effect within an organisation. One relatively well-documented case in Britain concerns Kenneth Lennon who had infiltrated an IRA team in Luton on behalf of the Special Branch in the early 1970s and had even been prosecuted in order to maintain his cover. He was acquitted and several days later alleged to officers of the National Council for Civil Liberties (NCCL) that he had been coerced into operating as an *agent provocateur*. He was found dead three days later, apparently having been shot by the IRA. The internal police inquiry by

Deputy Commissioner J. Starritt of the Metropolitan Police concluded that there was no support for the allegation that Lennon was pressured into becoming an informer, or, later, that he acted as an *agent provocateur*; there was nothing to suggest that Special Branch officers had departed from the Home Office guidelines, nor that they had any direct or indirect responsibility for Lennon's death; and there was nothing to support the contention that Special Branch improperly influenced Lennon's arrest and trial.[83]

Geoffrey Robertson's account of the case concludes differently at almost every point:

> The Special Branch had absolved [Lennon] of all responsibility for serious crimes he had confessed to committing. They had suppressed any suspicion that he might have acted as an *agent provocateur* to incite political agitators to criminal activity that they might not otherwise have contemplated. They had permitted the police to arm a fanatical youth, and had encouraged elaborate security precautions against jail-break plots that they knew were being fomented by their own agents. They allowed the press to publish false information that may have had the effect of prejudicing a trial and endangering life. They withheld evidence from lawyers at two major criminal trials, thereby preventing the emergence of a complete picture necessary to do justice to the defendants. They used the procedures of the criminal law to bolster the cover of their informant, but when the plan misfired and he was exposed they failed to protect him.[84]

Part of the difference in these accounts might be explained by the limited nature of Starritt's inquiry: examination of the case papers and police records and discussions with *senior* police officers involved. Given the 'sanitisation' of information as it moves up the police hierarchy, such an inquiry would be unlikely to reveal departures from guidelines by the actual case officers.

The question of how these problems might be dealt with has been tackled in depth only in North America. In 1976 Attorney General Levi issued and published guidelines for the FBI's use of informers in domestic security and criminal investigations.

The FBI was to instruct them that they should not participate in violence, use unlawful techniques to obtain information, initiate a plan to commit criminal acts, or participate in criminal activities in so far as the FBI determined this was necessary for the purposes of a federal prosecution. If the FBI learned that an informer was involved in a crime then it should tell the relevant law enforcement agency or, if that was deemed inadvisable, the Justice Department.[85]

The Church committee proposed more rigorous standards: the FBI could not recruit new informers or direct existing ones against a new target for *intelligence* purposes unless the Attorney General made a written finding that less intrusive techniques had been considered and rejected and the informer was necessary to obtain the information. The Committee considered and rejected the argument that judicial warrants should be required for the use of informers, in part because it would place judges so close to the heart of the investigative process that it amounted to a step toward an inquisitorial system.[86] The same position was taken by the McDonald Commission.[87] The Commission recommended that administrative guidelines be developed, to be approved by the minister and published. These should include, that informers should dissociate themselves from unlawful activities, should not act as *agents provocateurs* or be used for disruption except in cases involving espionage, sabotage or foreign interference.[88]

Since the passage of the CSIS Act guidelines have been developed by CSIS, in consultation with the SIRC but they have not been published. The government announced that they were based on the following criteria:

– Human sources are to be used only when and to the extent it is reasonable and necessary to do so in meeting the Service's statutory responsibilities.

– The need to use a source must be carefully weighed against possible damage to civil liberties.

– Given the intrusiveness of this investigative technique, the use of sources must be centrally controlled.

– Sources are to carry out their tasks without engaging in illegal activities. They should conduct themselves in such a manner as not to discredit the Service or the Government of Canada.

– Sources are to be managed so as to protect both the security of the Service's operations and the personal safety of sources.

– Sources should be treated ethically and fairly in their handling and compensation.[89]

Given the large challenge that these criteria pose to traditional security intelligence, and police, practices, it is easy to be cynical as to how effective they will be. This is aggravated by the fact that, unlike the interception of communications, where there is in Canada and the US some judicial involvement in approvals, in the case of informers approval and supervision procedures remain entirely internal to the security intelligence agencies. Furthermore, agencies have resisted outside attempts to audit the effectiveness of informers.[90]

If there are guidelines in the UK Security Service then they have not been made known to ministers or permanent secretaries in the Home Office. Those relating to the police use of informers were developed only after criticism from the Court of Appeal in 1969[91] and published in Starritt's report on the Lennon case.[92] They do not apply to the RUC.[93]

The problem of the use of informers in security intelligence operations where prosecution is not even a distant objective remains intractable and apparently immune from serious inquiry. This is well illustrated by the case of the Kincora Boys' Home in Northern Ireland. By 1975 it was known by the RUC, Army Intelligence and the Security Service that boys at the home were being subjected to sexual abuse by, among others, the leader of a Protestant paramilitary group, TARA, who worked at the home. Three men were arrested and charged in 1980. Several official inquiries into the case have taken place, but almost all of them with terms of reference which precluded any investigation of the allegation that from 1975 to 1980 the Security Service was using this information, and allowing the abuse to continue, in order to control TARA or, at least, to monitor developments among Protestant paramilitaries. In the one inquiry which in 1982 appeared to address this issue the Security Service refused to

160

respond to police questions. This case is at the heart of Colin Wallace's allegations. The Calcutt inquiry into Wallace's dismissal was the latest of a long line of inquiries with narrow terms of reference, but its support of Wallace's allegation that his own dismissal had been engineered is likely to lend further support to demands for a fuller inquiry into the case. It was reported that some senior civil servants also supported this demand.[94]

'Surreptitious entries' and break-ins

Entrance onto property may be deemed necessary by a security intelligence agency for a number of reasons, for example, in order to obtain documents, or to install some form of electronic surveillance, a 'bug'. The most preferred form of entry will be via some trusted intermediary, but this will often not be available. The most frequent method will be the 'surreptitious entry' in which, say, a 'telephone engineer' will gain admittance by subterfuge. But where this is not practicable then a break-in may be necessary. In Canada the McDonald Commission examined 47 cases in which the Security Service had made surreptitious entries and found that this method was used primarily in cases involving targeted individuals suspected of espionage or foreign interference or of links with terrorist groups. The Commission said it had found no evidence that the technique was used 'significantly' in domestic subversion cases.[95]

In the US the Church Committee reported:

> Warrantless break-ins have been conducted by intelligence agencies since World War II. During the 1960s alone, the FBI and CIA conducted hundreds of break-ins against American citizens and domestic organisations. In some cases these break-ins were to install microphones; in other cases, they were to steal such items as membership lists from organisations considered 'subversive' by the Bureau.[96]

During 1966 FBI policy changed when Hoover forbade any further use of 'black bag' techniques for searching and copying records for domestic intelligence purposes, though they might still be used against foreign targets and break-ins to install microphones were still allowed. This was one of Hoover's self-imposed restraints which the Huston Plan was intended to reverse. The Justice Department continued to assert the constitutional right of the President to authorise break-ins without a court warrant where the search was related to foreign espionage or intelligence, arguing that there was no real difference, in privacy terms, between a burglary and a wiretap. The Church Committee recommended that all government search and seizures should be subjected to judicial warrant procedures.[97]

As in other areas, information regarding the behaviour of the UK Security Service and Special Branches in this respect is more sketchy. In 1977 during the months leading up to the ABC trial – the prosecution of Crispin Aubrey, John Berry and Duncan Campbell under the Official Secrets Act – there were a series of break-ins to the cars or homes of those involved in the ABC defence committee in which papers were rifled but nothing of value stolen.[98] Peter Wright describes how

> for five years we bugged and burgled our way across London at the State's behest, while pompous bowler-hatted civil servants in Whitehall pretended to look the other way.[99]

Section three of the Security Service Act 1989 now requires the security intelligence agencies to obtain a warrant before carrying out any 'interference with property'; to what extent these new procedures will restrict traditional security intelligence activities remains to be seen. The precedent of warrants in the area of interception of communications suggests that the impact will not be great.

Interception of communications

The Church Committee found that:

> Since the early 1930s intelligence agencies have frequently wiretapped and bugged American citizens without the benefit of judicial warrant.[100]

Unusually full information was published as to the extent of interceptions by Justice Hope in his 1985 Report. To support his finding that a relatively small proportion of ASIO resources were devoted to counter subversion, he gave the annual figures for telephone interceptions relating to subversion for the previous six years

Table 4.1 Telephone Interceptions Regarding Subversion, Australia, 1978–84

	1978–79	1979–80	1980–81	1981–82	1982–83	1983–84
New	6	3	5	3	3	1
Renewals	20	15	11	10	12	3
TOTAL	26	18	16	13	15	4

Source: Justice Hope, *Report on the ASIO* (Canberra: Commonwealth Government Printer, 1985), p. 80.

Numbers of warrants have been published elsewhere, but since they may cover any number of telephone lines, they are not always very illuminating. But Hope went on to report that the total number of telephones covered during this period was about 30, and that during 1981–84 the total number of individuals subjected to ASIO surveillance for the purposes of 'subversive studies' was 37.[101] Canadian inquiries have tended to address the questions of telephone intercepts and electronic surveillance together and their main findings are discussed in the next section.

In the UK the practice of intercepting the mail was acknowledged in a series of Post Office Acts, but nowhere was statutory authority for the practice actually granted to the government. This remained the situation when technological advances meant that the executive started to tap telephones. The argument that the whole process relied on the traditional royal prerogative power was endorsed by the Report of the Birkett Inquiry in 1957:

> We favour the view that [the right to intercept communications] rests on the power plainly recognised by the Post Office statutes as existing before the enactment of the statutes, by whatever name the power is described.[102]

This Inquiry had been established after the revelation that the transcripts of telephone conversations between a barrister and his client had been made available to the Bar Council, but it made few dramatic proposals for change.[103] The Report did for the first time give detailed information as to the procedures established for the authorisation of taps, though it excluded consideration of those granted by the Foreign Secretary. As far as national security cases were concerned, it said that there must be a major subversive or espionage activity that was likely to injure the national interest and that the material likely to be obtained must be 'of direct use' to the Security Service in carrying out its tasks; it is worth bearing in mind that the Maxwell-Fyfe Directive remained unpublished at this time and therefore it was not known what the tasks of the Security Service were! Further, the Report said, as with the police and customs, normal methods of investigation must have been tried and have failed, or must, from the nature of things, be unlikely to succeed.[104]

This Report was consistent with the general pattern of events in the UK regarding the powers of the security intelligence agencies: the state would continue to use those techniques made available by technological advances and to the extent that resources permitted. Questions of legality would arise only if and when an operation became public and the resulting controversy could not be dealt with by denials or refusals to comment. If inquiries were established, or, as later on, adverse European Court decisions were received or anticipated, then any criticism from these official sources would be dealt with by minimal changes aimed, as far as possible, at legalising the *status quo* and minimising the impact on security intelligence operations.

No effort was made to provide statutory authorisation for telephone tapping subsequent to the Birkett Report, but in 1977 a series of events was set in train which, eight years later, culminated in legislation outlawing unauthorised telephone tapping and providing a statutory basis for taps by security intelligence agencies, police and customs. The disclosure to the defence that the telephone conversations of James Malone, charged with receiving stolen property, had been tapped by the police led Malone to challenge the legality of the interception.[105] The Vice Chancellor of the Chancery Division, Sir Robert Megarry, rejected Malone's case, on a number of grounds. First, there was no right of property in a telephone conversation; second, privacy was not a concept recognised in English law; third, the European Convention was not enforceable in English courts; and, finally, the notion that tapping was illegal because there was nothing to render it legal was anathema to English law. However, the Vice Chancellor also said that tapping was a subject which cried out for legislation.[106] The then Home Secretary initiated a review of telephone tapping after this judgment, and in 1980 a White Paper was published consequent upon this review. In essence this reiterated the adequacy of the time-honoured procedures and, since Megarry had not found tapping to be illegal, concluded that there was no need for legislation to make authorised interception legal.[107]

Home Secretary William Whitelaw announced, however, that a continuous review of the interception of communications would be instituted, to be carried out by senior judges, the first of whom was Lord Diplock. Somewhat curiously it was said that the first report of the monitor would be published but that subsequent reports would not. The first was published in March 1981 and concluded that the procedures established in the White Paper of 1980 were working satisfactorily and with the minimum interference with individual rights. Having examined a random selection of warrant applications, Diplock said he was satisfied that the agencies had been candid with the minister and that the procedures adopted were appropriate to detect and correct any departure from the proper standards.[108]

Through the early 1980s the government maintained its position that legislation was unnecessary and undesirable, but others disagreed. The Royal Commission on Criminal Procedure echoed Megarry's view that interception should be based on a statutory footing[109] and during the committee stage of the British Telecommunications Bill in 1981 an amendment to this effect was inserted. The government reversed this at Report stage, Whitelaw arguing that the government's case was based on the essential incompatibility between, on the one hand, the requirement that interception must be secret if it were to be effective and, on the other hand, a statute which would make interception subject to litigation in the (non-secret) judicial process.[110]

In December 1982 the European Commission of Human Rights upheld Malone's case that his rights to privacy (Article 8 of the Convention) and to a domestic legal remedy (Article 13) had been contravened. In May 1983 the case was referred to the European Court of Human Rights, which in August 1984 unanimously upheld the verdict that there had been an Article 8 violation but did not rule on the Article 13 violation. The Court's main criticism was that the rules regarding tapping and the disclosure of metering records to the police were imprecise and inadequate, leaving too much discretion to the executive. A White Paper outlining the government's proposed response was published and debated on 7 February 1985[111] and a week later a bill was introduced to Parliament. When debate on this began in March it did so in the context of the row about the *20–20 Vision* programme which had broadcast Cathy Massiter's allegations of investigative activities by the Security Service, including telephone tapping, which went outside its duties under the Maxwell-Fyfe Directive.

The first section of what was, in July, to become the Interception of Communications Act created the offence of unlawfully intercepting telephone or postal communications. No effort was made to deal with 'metering'[112] or electronic surveillance – 'bugging'. Interceptions in pursuance of a warrant issued by a secretary of state will not be unlawful, nor will they be when the consent of an occupier is obtained. Section 2 lays down the conditions for the issue of a warrant: if the secretary of state considers it necessary in the interests of national security, for the purpose of preventing or detecting serious crime or for the purpose of safeguarding the economic well-being of the UK. Warrants in respect of economic well-being will relate only to people outside the UK.

Sections 3 to 6 enshrined in the statute essentially those procedures which had been in operation since 1980 regarding the scope of warrants, their renewal, modification and arrangements for safeguarding and limiting the use of intercepted material. This included provisions which meant that the number of warrants would bear no necessary relation to the number of lines tapped, and also provided legal authority for 'trawling' methods of interception made use of by GCHQ as well as taps directed against particular names or addresses.[113]

Section 7 established a tribunal to investigate whether the powers of the secretary of state were being correctly exercised, should anybody complain that their communications were being intercepted. The tribunal is able to quash warrants, order the destruction of material and award compensation if warrant powers have been exercised improperly, but the check is a procedural one and complainants would receive confirmation of their complaint only where there has been procedural irregularity. The Tribunal's decisions are not subject to appeal or judicial review; indeed in section 9 it is enacted that in any Court proceedings 'no evidence shall be adduced and no question shall be asked' which suggests that any Crown employee has intercepted communications, whether authorised or not. Thus by a splendid irony the Act makes impossible the very sequence of events which brought it about! Finally, section 8 incorporates the position of judicial monitor in the role of Commissioner with the task of reviewing the warrant arrangements and assisting the Tribunal as necessary.[114]

The most obvious criticisms to be made of the Act are, first, the exclusion of electronic surveillance, and, second, the restriction of 'oversight' procedures 'to ensuring executive compliance with bureaucratic procedure'.[115] It is not part of the terms of reference of either the Tribunal or the Commissioner to investigate unauthorised interceptions.

There remains an apparently extremely large gulf between official explanations of the extent of and controls on the use of interception and unofficial disclosures. On the one hand, the information regarding the capacity of police, customs and security intelligence agencies to intercept telephone calls suggests the *potential* for a great deal of tapping, for example, 60 full-time tapping operatives in AES 9 of British Telecom installing taps where System X direct dialling exchanges[116] either do not exist or are considered inadequate, and 80 higher grade engineers maintaining and servicing tapped lines. At the BT centre at Gresham Street there are more than 1,000 lines plus switching mechanisms, meaning it can deal with many thousands of incoming intercepts. In addition there are centres for use by the Security Service and the SIS, to which calls are automatically transferred. More than 100 transcribers work at Gresham Street, though many calls are never transcribed but scanned by computers examining for keywords.[117] Additional transcribers work at MI5 on the material directed there.[118] If one adds to this the possibility that GCHQ 'trawling' techniques via word and voice recognition may be being applied to domestic interceptions,[119] then the potential is clearly great.

In contrast, the official view is one of highly limited use of a technique which is also highly effective. No assessment of effectiveness for security intelligence has been published, but the police maintain that between 1975 and 1985 interceptions had made possible the arrest of 5,000 people and the recovery of £100 million worth of drugs and stolen goods.[120] The fact that this figure was produced by the Home Secretary during the second reading debate on the Interception of Communications Bill may raise some questions as to its validity. Official figures on the extent of tapping have remained constant for 20 years with Home Secretaries issuing between 350 and 470 warrants a year since 1969 while the number of telephone lines has increased from 8 million to over 20 million. Both the customs and the police, including special branches operate with quotas of a certain number of taps at a time, although the Security Service has no quota.[121] As to the numbers involved in transcription, in the case of the Met's Criminal Intelligence Branch (C11), 16 officers are engaged in listening to taps 'from time to time'. This all presents a rather different picture from that painted in the previous paragraph.

Can these accounts be reconciled? There are a number of possibilities: first, it might be that the higher estimates of the amount of interception are too high because they calculate the technological *potential* for interception and then assume that this is the *actual* extent to which it is carried out. Alternatively, it is possible that this technological potential is actually used and that the structure of ministerial warrants and judicial monitors which has subsequently developed is intended to present a form of legal cover for the security intelligence agencies. Thus if and when interceptions are exposed the political and legal process can be wheeled out to stave off any serious inquiry into the extent or authorisation of interception. Such a process could exist either with the knowledge of the relevant ministers and monitors or, alternatively, they could be unwitting stooges in the process. This may all sound rather conspiratorial but the possibility that this explains the gulf cannot be entirely excluded.

A third possible explanation is also the simplest. A single warrant may cover an organisation and, following the logic of *per se* targeting, may include all its members or adherents. At different times, therefore, one warrant would have been enough to intercept the communications to and from all offices of the Communist Party, another one for NCCL, another for CND, and it is not difficult to see how this could, thereby, rapidly require large numbers of transcribers more in line with the unofficial projections based on technological capacity. Given the extensive interception which might flow from just one warrant, therefore, it is not obvious that the security intelligence agencies need, or would have the resources, to indulge in unauthorised tapping. It must be remembered that the interception of telephones and the mail are the only forms of information-gathering which involve co-operation with other agencies, specifically British Telecom and the Post Office. Before 1989 they were also the only ones to be subjected to any kind of authorisation by outsiders. Therefore it would have made a great deal of sense for the security intelligence agencies to be careful that they were not exposed on the issue. Wright, for example, was happy to admit to the cavalier way in which he and his colleagues had 'bugged and burgled' their way across London while noting that procedures for obtaining interception warrants were adhered to.[122] Ministers also acknowledged that while they dealt regularly with interception warrants they were never consulted about the use of other techniques.[123]

The interception of mail takes two main forms: the mail-cover and mail-opening. In the former, all the information on the outside of the envelope is recorded – date, place of posting, name and address of sender, etc. In the latter, mail to a target address is opened. Both the FBI and the CIA at various times carried out large-scale programmes of mail-opening. In 1970, during discussions of what became the Huston Plan, they told the President it was illegal, falsely stated it had been discontinued and proposed that it be 'restarted'. The President eventually demurred but the CIA went on doing it anyway![124]

McDonald carried out a detailed review of RCMP Security Service operations in this area between November 1970 and December 1977. A total of 94 were identified of which 66 involved the actual opening of mail, mostly involving persons either known or suspected of political violence in Quebec, international terrorism, espionage or foreign interference.[125]

Wright discusses the procedures used during his time in the UK Security Service – sometimes steaming kettles, sometimes the split-bamboo technique – but, he laments, the Post Office technicians carrying out the work could never open covertly an envelope which had been sealed at each edge with Sellotape![126]

Electronic surveillance

If checks on the use of telephone and mail intercepts seem slight, then those on the use of electronic surveillance in the UK are even less. In the US efforts have been made to involve the courts, as with taps, in the authorisation process, but in the UK the courts are effectively excluded by the fact that electronic surveillance is not illegal. Illegality will only arise if burglary is necessary in order to plant a bug. This was a potential problem for the Security Service until it was removed by the 1989 Act which legalises such activity if done on the authority of the Home Secretary's warrant (s.3).

The McDonald Commission found that both internal authorisation procedures within the RCMP Security Service and, after 1974 when Privacy and Official Secrets legislation came into effect, ministerial authorisation by the Solicitor General did not really distinguish between telephone intercepts and electronic surveillance. McDonald found that both techniques had been used frequently, though, interestingly, during the 1966–69 Royal Commission on Security the Security Service placed a moratorium on break-ins looking for documents and objects.[127] During 1974 and 1979 the numbers of warrants issued to the Security Service fluctuated between 299 and 517, though each year's total would include a high proportion of renewals.[128] Section 21 of the CSIS Act now requires the CSIS to apply for a judicial warrant in any case in which it requires entry, or a telephone intercept or to install some electronic surveillance device.

It is not known what internal guidelines and authorisation procedures exist within the UK Security Service, but guidelines have been issued to the UK police which set out the following criteria:

a) the investigation concerns serious crime (plus the investigation of malicious/obscene phone calls);
b) normal methods of investigation must have been tried and failed, or must, from the nature of things, be unlikely to succeed if tried;
c) there must be good reason to think that the use of the equipment would be likely to lead to an arrest and

a conviction, or where appropriate, to the prevention of acts of terrorism;

d) use of equipment must be operationally feasible.[129]

The technology relating to surveillance advances at a rapid pace; for example, the 'infinity' bug requires a transmitter to be placed in a telephone in the target room. Once in place, conversations in that room can be eavesdropped at any time from anywhere by simply dialling the target number. The phone does not ring but all conversations in the room can be monitored. Visual surveillance also becomes ever more sophisticated with image-intensifiers making it possible whether night or day.[130]

CONCLUSION

The evidence is incomplete as to the extent to which practice in the UK approaches the McDonald principles. First, the warrant procedures established in the Security Service Act 1989 have legalised the use of techniques that would have been illegal before then. Second, there are some police guidelines indicating that more intrusive techniques should not be authorised until less intrusive ones have been tried. But fundamental problems remain; for example, the lack of a bill of rights in the UK means that there are no positive civil rights, such as privacy, to be 'chilled'. Moreover there is a simple lack of relevant information. Little research in the UK has been carried out into the information-gathering practices of uniformed patrol officers and even less on targeting by detectives and their use of informers. Less still is known about the rules (if any) and practices of security intelligence officials in the UK but, from what emerged in inquiries elsewhere, it would be unwise to assume that they have avoided targeting on the basis of political stereotypes and unnecessary invasions of privacy.

NOTES

1. C. Dandeker, *Surveillance, Power and Modernity* (Cambridge: Polity Press, 1990), p. 40.
2. G.T. Marx, *Undercover* (Berkeley: University of California Press, 1988), p. 219.

3. CSIS, *Public Report 1991* (Ottawa: Minister of Supply and Services, 1992), p. 11.
4. A.S. Hulnick, 'Controlling Intelligence Estimates', in G. Hastedt (ed.), *Controlling Intelligence* (London: Frank Cass, 1991), p. 84.
5. The former were discussed in Chapter 3, the latter are discussed in Chapter 6. Although he analyses foreign and military rather than domestic intelligence, Robert Mandel provides a useful and systematic review of 'distortions' in 'Distortions in the Intelligence Decision-Making Process', in S.J. Cimbala, *Intelligence and Intelligence Policy in a Democratic Society* (Ardsley-on Hudson; Transnational Publishers, 1987), pp. 69–83.
6. L.K. Johnson, 'Making the Intelligence "Cycle" Work', *International Journal of Intelligence and Counter-Intelligence*, 1(4), 1986, pp. 1–23.
7. D. Hurd, HC Deb., 15 December 1988, col. 1113, emphasis added.
8. ASIO Act, 1979, s.17(2).
9. ASIO, *Report to Parliament 1987–88* (Canberra: Australian Government Publishing Service, 1989), p. 1, emphasis in original.
10. Ibid, p. 9.
11. Ibid, p. 23.
12. Justice D.C. McDonald, *Commission of Inquiry Concerning Certain Activites of the RCMP* Second Report, *Freedom and Security Under the Law* (Ottawa: Minister of Supply and Services, 1981), p. 613.
13. CSIS Act, 1984, s.12.
14. McDonald, supra (note 12), p. 613.
15. CSIS Act, 1984, s.19(2).
16. Report of the Special Committee on the Review of the CSIS Act, *In Flux But Not In Crisis* (Ottawa: Minister of Supply and Services, 1990) pp. 25–6.
17. Solicitor General of Canada, *On Course: National Security for the 1990s* (Ottawa: Minister of Supply and Services, 1991); SIRC, *Annual Report for 1991–92* (Ottawa: Minister of Supply and Services, 1992), pp. 74–7.
18. Church Committee, Final Report, Book II, *Intelligence Activities and the Rights of Americans* (Washington DC: US Government Printing Office, 1976), p. 316.
19. Ibid. This issue is discussed further in Chapter 9 below.
20. Ibid, p. 317.

21. M. Herman, 'Intelligence and Policy: A Comment', *Intelligence and National Security*, 6(1), January 1991, p. 234.
22. P. Fitzgerald and M. Leopold, *Stranger on the Line: The Secret History of Phone Tapping* (London: The Bodley Head, 1987), p. 54.
23. *The Guardian*, 20 May 1992, p. 2.
24. *The Guardian*, 6 April 1988, p. 4.
25. This description of the UK security intelligence network has been drawn from: ibid; *The Independent*, 3 December 1986, p. 17; R. Norton-Taylor, *In Defence of the Realm?* (London: Civil Liberties Trust, 1990), pp. 57–9; Fitzgerald and Leopold, supra (note 22), pp. 53–4; J.T. Richelson and D. Ball, *The Ties That Bind* (Boston: Unwin Hyman, 2nd edition, 1990), pp. 26–9; and K.G. Robertson, 'Accountable Intelligence: the British Experience', *Conflict Quarterly*, VIII(1), Winter, 1988, pp. 17–19.
26. S. Farson, 'Propriety, Efficacy and Balance', in P. Hanks and J.D. McCamus (eds), *National Security: Surveillance and Accountability in a Democratic Society* (Cowansville, Québec: Les Editions Yvon Blais, 1989), pp. 144–6.
27. House of Commons, Home Affairs Committee, *Minutes of Evidence, Special Branch*, 30 January 1985, p. 108.
28. ASIO, supra (note 9), p. 10.
29. SIRC, supra (note 17), 1991, p. 4.
30. Merseyside Police Standing Orders, Section 2, *Functions and Duties of Each Rank*, 1983, unpublished.
31. *The Observer*, 3 August 1986, p. 3, and see further discussion below.
32. Honourable Mr. Acting Justice White, Initial Report to The Honourable D.A. Dunstan, Premier of the State of South Australia, *Special Branch Security Records* (South Australia: Government Printer, 1978), §1.2.1..
33. Ibid, §2.8. See also A.T. Turk, *Political Criminality* (Beverly Hills: Sage, 1982), pp. 123–4 regarding the widespread application of such targeting.
34. White, supra, §8.4.
35. SIRC, *Annual Report for 1986–87* (Ottawa: Minister of Supply and Services, 1987), pp. 34–7.
36. SIRC, *Annual Report for 1987–88* (Ottawa: Minister of Supply and Services, 1988), p. 13. For full discussion see P. Gill,

'Defining Subversion: the Canadian Experience since 1977', *Public Law*, Winter 1989, pp. 617–36.

37. SIRC, *Annual Report for 1989–90* (Ottawa: Minister of Supply and Services, 1990) pp. 46–9.
38. *The Observer*, 24 February 1985, p. 1.
39. Security Service Act, 1989, Schedule 1, §2(4). This Act is discussed more fully in Chapter 8.
40. J.T. Elliff, *The Reform of FBI Intelligence Operations* (Princeton: Princeton University Press, 1979), pp. 196–8.
41. These guidelines are reprinted in R. Godson, *Intelligence Requirements for the 1980s: Domestic Intelligence* (Lexington: D.C. Heath, 1986), pp. 245–64.
42. Solicitor General of Canada, supra (note 17), pp. 59–62.
43. *Guidelines on the Work of a Special Branch*, Home Office, mimeo, December 1984. Emphasis in original.
44. House of Commons, supra (note 27), p. 113.
45. J.-P. Brodeur, 'On Evaluating Threats to the National Security of Canada and to the Civil Rights of Canadians', paper for SIRC seminar, October 1985, pp. 7–9.
46. SIRC, supra (note 37), p. 46.
47. G.M. Stern, *The FBI's Misguided Probe of CISPES* (Washington DC: The Center for National Security Studies, 1988), pp. 2–16.
48. J.K. Davis, *Spying on America: The FBI's Domestic Counterintelligence Program* (New York: Praeger, 1992), p. 180.
49. R. Whitaker, *Left Wing Dissent and the State: Canada and the Cold War Era*, paper for SIRC Conference, Queen's University, Ontario, February 1988, p. 19.
50. McDonald, supra (note 12), pp. 513–14.
51. T. Bunyan, *The History and Practice of the Political Police in Britain* (London: Quartet, 1977), pp. 135–7.
52. For example, see C. Walker, *The Prevention of Terrorism in British Law* (Manchester: Manchester University Press, 2nd edition, 1992), pp. 213–29.
53. R. Hibbert, 'Intelligence and Policy', *Intelligence and National Security*, 5(1), January 1990, 112–13. Similar estimates of the quantitative significance of covertly gathered material have been provided elsewhere, for example, K.G. Robertson, 'The Study of Intelligence in the US', in R. Godson (ed.), *Comparing Foreign Intelligence* (Washington DC: National Strategy Information Center, 1988), p. 30.

54. Herman, supra (note 21), pp. 232–3.
55. McDonald, supra (note 12), pp. 516–17; H.L. Wilensky, *Organizational Intelligence: Knowledge and Policy in Government and Industry* (New York: Basic Books, 1967), pp. 66–74.
56. SIRC, *Annual Report for 1985–86* (Ottawa: Minister of Supply and Services, 1986), p. 25; SIRC, supra (note 37), p. 25.
57. Church Committee, supra (note 18), p. 329.
58. McDonald, supra (note 12), p. 592.
59. SIRC, *Annual Report for 1988–89* (Ottawa: Minister of Supply and Services, 1989) pp. 8–9; SIRC, supra (note 37), pp. 35–41.
60. P. Wright, *Spycatcher* (New York: Viking Penguin, 1987), p. 360; D. Campbell and S. Connor, *On The Record: Surveillance, Computers and Privacy – The Inside Story* (London: Michael Joseph, 1986), pp. 284–5.
61. National Audit Office, *Mangement of Administrative Telecommunications*, NAO Publication No. 112, January 1989, §57.
62. Letter from Assistant Registrar, Office of the Data Protection Registrar, 27 September 1990.
63. *The Guardian*, 16 July 1992, p. 4.
64. Church Committee, Final Report, Book III, *Supplementary Detailed Staff Reports on Intelligence Activities and the Rights of Americans* (Washington DC: US Government Printing Office, 1976), p. 228.
65. McDonald, supra (note 12), pp. 296–9.
66. Church Committee, supra (note 64), p. 228.
67. J.-P. Brodeur, 'High Policing and Low Policing: Remarks About the Policing of Political Activities', *Social Problems*, 30(5), June 1983, pp. 514–15.
68. M. Urban, *Big Boys' Rules* (London: Faber and Faber, 1992), p. 104.
69. O. Kirchheimer, *Political Justice: The Use of Legal Procedure for Political Ends* (Princeton: Princeton University Press, 1961), pp. 234–7.
70. Urban, supra (note 68), p. 244.
71. R.G. Powers, *Secrecy and Power: The Life of J. Edgar Hoover* (New York: Free Press, 1988), p. 340.
72. Richelson and Ball, supra (note 25), p. 289.
73. Brodeur, supra (note 45), p. 14.
74. Church Committee, supra (note 64), pp. 260–61.
75. Urban, supra (note 68), pp. 105–6.

76. Brodeur supra (note 45), pp. 13–14.
77. Wilensky, supra (note 55), pp. 67–8.
78. For example, Urban, supra (note 68), p. 107.
79. McDonald, supra (note 12), p. 536; including, if deemed necessary, deception of courts. Urban, supra (note 68), p. 245.
80. Urban, ibid, p. 106.
81. J.-P. Brodeur, 'Criminal Justice and National Security', in Hanks and McCamus, supra (note 26), pp. 64–5. See Urban, ibid, pp. 104–5 for other examples.
82. Urban, ibid, pp. 93–8, 108–10; M. Dillon, *The Dirty War* (London: Arrow Books, 1990), pp. 367–8.
83. J. Starritt, *Report to the Home Secretary from the Commissioner of the Metropolis on the Actions of Police Officers Concerned with the Case of Kenneth Joseph Lennon* (London: HMSO, 1974), §§108–14.
84. G. Robertson, *Reluctant Judas: The Life and Death of the Special Branch Informer, Kenneth Lennon* (London: Temple Smith, 1976), p. 196.
85. Full guidelines are reprinted in Elliff, supra (note 40), pp. 215–19.
86. Ibid, pp. 123–7. For the Church Committee's consideration of cases and issues involving informers see supra (note 64), pp. 225–70.
87. McDonald, supra (note 12), pp. 538–9.
88. Ibid, pp. 549–51.
89. Solicitor General of Canada, supra (note 17), p. 14.
90. See T. Poveda, *Lawlessness and Reform: the FBI in transition*, (Pacific Grove, CA: Brooks/Cole Publishing, 1990) p. 83 regarding the FBI's refusal of a request from the GAO to carry out such an audit.
91. Robertson, supra (note 84), pp. 184–6.
92. Supra (note 83).
93. Urban, supra (note 68), p. 107.
94. *The Guardian*, 23 October 1989, p. 24. For full details of the case see P. Foot, *Who Framed Colin Wallace?* (London: Pan, 1990), esp. pp. 115–46, 298–319, 399–425.
95. McDonald, supra (note 12), p. 142.
96. Church Committee, supra (note 18), p. 13.
97. Church Committee, supra (note 64), pp. 365–71. The procedures eventually adopted in the US are discussed in the section on judicial oversight in Chapter 8 below.

98. *New Statesman*, 15 February 1980, p. 236.
99. Wright, supra (note 60), pp. 54–5.
100. Church Committee, supra (note 18), p. 12.
101. R.M. Hope, *Report on the ASIO* (Canberra: Commonwealth Government Printer, 1985), pp. 80–81.
102. *Report of the Committee of Privy Councillors appointed to Inquire into the Interception of Communications*, Cmnd 283 (London: HMSO, September 1957), §50.
103. For full discussion of background to this inquiry see Fitzgerald and Leopold, supra (note 22), pp. 116–27.
104. Cmnd 283, supra (note 102), §§67–8.
105. Fitzgerald and Leopold, supra (note 22), pp. 133–8.
106. Quoted in ibid, p. 135.
107. HC Deb. 1 April 1980, col. 205.
108. *The Interception of Communications in Great Britain: Report of the Rt. Hon. Lord Diplock*, Cmnd 8191 (London: HMSO, March 1981), pp. 6–7.
109. The Royal Commission on Criminal Procedure, *Report*, Cmnd 8092 (London: HMSO, 1981), §3.57–3.60.
110. HC Deb. 1 April 1981, col. 335.
111. *The Interception of Communications in the United Kingdom*, Cmnd 9438 (London: HMSO, February 1985).
112. Modern computerised exchanges record automatically the date, time, duration and destination of all calls made from any given telephone. Police and security agencies do not need a warrant to ask BT for such information, for example see Fitzgerald and Leopold, supra (note 22), pp. 205–10. A recent example of this practice was exposed by a break-in and theft of metering records from an Edinburgh police station. *New Statesman and Society*, 7 August 1992, p. 17.
113. See Fitzgerald and Leopold, supra (note 22), pp. 145–9 for full discussion.
114. For general discussion of the Act see further I.J. Lloyd, 'The Interception of Communications Act, 1985', *Modern Law Review*, 49, January 1985, pp. 86–95.
115. Fitzgerald and Leopold, supra (note 22), p. 151.
116. These computerised exchanges allow for the interception of calls without requiring any physical intercept to be placed.
117. *The Observer*, 30 October 1988.
118. 20/20 Vision, *MI5's Official Secrets*, broadcast, 8 March 1985.

119. Fitzgerald and Leopold, supra (note 22), pp. 110–11; Norton-Taylor, supra (note 25), p. 53.
120. HC Deb., 12 March 1985, col.158.
121. Report of the Commissioner for 1986, *Interception of Communications Act*, Cm 108 (London: HMSO, January 1987), §§53–4.
122. Wright, supra (note 60), pp. 46, 54–5.
123. Interviews with Merlyn Rees (10 July 1990) and William Whitelaw (13 June 1990) (both former Home and Northern Ireland Secretaries) and a former Permanent Secretary in both those departments (14 June 1990).
124. Church Committee, supra (note 18), p. 12.
125. McDonald, supra (note 12), p. 210.
126. Wright, supra (note 60), p. 45.
127. McDonald, supra (note 12), p. 110.
128. Ibid, pp. 152–4.
129. Home Office, *Guidelines on the Use of Equipment in Police Surveillance Operations*, mimeo, 1984, §4.
130. For fuller discussion see Fitzgerald and Leopold, supra (note 22), Ch. 8; see also Marx, supra (note 2), pp. 207–19.

5

Penetration II:
Producing Intelligence

This chapter is concerned with what security intelligence agencies do with the information which they gather. There are numerous possibilities but they will all involve some way of determining what, if anything, the information means and, second, what should be done with it. Should it be communicated elsewhere, should it be acted upon and, if so, in what way?

PRODUCTION AND ANALYSIS

The early part of this process may be almost entirely technical, for example, transcribing tapes from telephone intercepts and preparing material for storage and retrieval; but it may be also evaluative, for example, translating documents and interpreting photographs.[1] It is at the analysis stage that 'information' is converted into 'intelligence'. Since 'facts' rarely, if ever, speak for themselves, the analysts' ability to draw defensible conclusions from variously sourced information is centrally important. Yet it lacks the glamour of clandestine activities and the high-tech of exotic collection systems and a tendency to underestimate its significance has been noted in many intelligence agencies. For example, the CIA rapidly moved after its inception into covert activities contrary to what many had expected of the new agency and this resulted in future years in a relative downgrading of the status of analysts.[2]

When disseminating its product to other agencies which may be required to act on it, the security intelligence agency needs to be able to state clearly what it thinks the information means and to present it in a way which will attract the attention of 'customers'. One key role for analysts is to evaluate the information received, for example attempting to eliminate any 'disinformation' intended to mislead the agency. Regarding foreign intelligence it seems to be accepted that, in principle, competitive approaches between analytic groups will produce the best product; for example, they will be best at challenging 'groupthink' (for discussion of this see Chapter 6). Yet the requirements of policy-makers for guidance may mean that in practice the structure which develops is aimed at the production of a consensus assessment. An example of this is the production of National Intelligence Estimates (NIE) in the US, where agencies may register their dissent from any memoranda via footnotes.[3]

McDonald's main criticism of the way in which analysis had been conducted within the RCMP Security Service was that the product concentrated too much on providing covertly collected material on specific groups and individuals, and that it had been weakest in providing strategic, longer-term analysis which requires attention to both overt and covert sources of information.[4] Three years after the separation out of the CSIS, SIRC noted in its annual report that the Service still appeared to be too dominated by the case approach of 'street-wise' intelligence officers rather than the longer term analysis recommended by McDonald. This was aggravated by the persisting tendency of CSIS to recruit intelligence officers from the ranks of former police officers.[5] Three years later, however, the Commons Special Review Committee commended CSIS for the progress it had made in improving its strategic analytical capacity.[6]

Other problems can arise from the different personalities attracted to analysis rather than policy or executive roles. Policy-makers are said to enjoy possessing and using power rather than being contemplative. They dislike ambiguity and complexity, do not like being criticised and do not like being reminded of the limits to their power. Conversely, analysts tend to distrust power and those who use it; they believe that the world is ambiguous and uncertain and they enjoy questioning, and identifying problems rather than making decisions aimed at their solution.[7] To the extent that such differences of approach occur systematically and are reinforced by the structural differences between analytic and executive branches within security intelligence agencies, obtaining some institutional balance between information and action (knowledge and power) will be difficult.

Therefore there are different schools of thought on how analysts should relate to policy-makers. On the one hand the dominant argument in the UK[8] and in the US until the 1970s is that analysts should concentrate on description and the preservation of their 'objectivity' which requires a degree of insulation from the policy-making process. On the other hand, a more recently influential group argue that analysts must be more integrated with policy, for example by relating their analysis to the future opportunities which policy-makers might have and being much more self-conscious about the models and theories which underlie their analysis.[9]

Although most of this discussion has been in terms of foreign intelligence, the costs and benefits apparent here are not without relevance to domestic security intelligence. If analysts are isolated from the policy process, then their product may be uncontaminated by policy-makers' preferences, but if they are equally unaware of the policy *problems* then their product may be unhelpful and simply ignored. Conversely, analysts will be aware of the problems if they are integrated in the policy process but there is a greater danger that they will skew their analysis to what they perceive the policy-makers want to hear. Robert Gates, appointed as Director of the CIA in 1991, is, for example, a proponent of the second school. In 1989 he wrote:

> Contrary to the view of those who are apprehensive over a close relationship between policy-makers and intelligence, it is not close enough. More interaction, feedback, and direction as to strategies, priorities, and requirements are critical to better performance.[10]

Therefore it is not altogether surprising that, during his confirmation hearings before the Senate Intelligence Committee, allegations were aired that during his time as Deputy Director Gates had suppressed dissent among the CIA's Soviet analysts in order to deliver assessments more in line with the Reagan administration's public positions.[11]

Examination of security intelligence agencies in the UK would need to include an examination of the efficacy of the analysis process; For example, are analysts within the agencies valued, or subordinate in status to the more exotic gatherers? Do the consumers of the security intelligence product believe that the intelligence they are provided meets their needs? Indeed, is the product disseminated to all those within government who might benefit from it?

DISSEMINATION

The issue here is what the security intelligence agency does with its intelligence. Since information is the currency of police and security agencies, they will spend some to get some. In dealing with potential informers and other agencies the agency will use information as 'leverage' in order to obtain more.[12] How widespread the official dissemination of intelligence is within government will depend on the nature of the intelligence. General economic data is likely to be distributed more widely than military data.[13] In some cases intelligence agencies will supply intelligence to other departments, in others it will be to their own operational arms, for example, from the Directorate of Intelligence in the CIA to the Directorate of Operations, or within the police from the Collator to uniformed patrol officers. In the case of an organisation like the Security Service in the UK the question that needs to be asked is to what extent, if at all, other departments of state benefit from the intelligence produced by the Service.

One of the reasons for the proliferation of intelligence-gathering agencies is that each executive agency prefers to have its own intelligence gatherers (see discussion in Chapter 6). The shooting of three IRA members by members of the SAS in Gibraltar in March 1988 provides an illustration of why this is so. The inadequate inquiry into this event, that is the inquest held in September 1988, has left many questions unanswered. Broadly speaking, the two main views of the shooting are, first, the official one as reflected in the evidence that was given at the inquest, and, second, an unofficial view which is based additionally on an examination of the issues and evidence excluded from the inquest. The first view is that surveillance of the three people by SAS and Security Service watchers was suddenly disrupted two days earlier than the planned bombing when the three were alarmed by an accidentally sounded police siren, appeared to be reaching for weapons and/or detonator buttons and were consequently shot by the SAS to prevent greater loss of life. The second view is that the shooting was in fact the culmination of a military plan to 'take-out' the three.[14] This view is based on a number of major problems with the first version, for example the changing official story regarding the presence or absence of surveillance of the three in Spain as far as the Gibraltar border and the fact that the Gibraltar police had handed over control of the operation to the military just before the 'surprise' shootings occurred. The conflict between the two accounts could only be resolved by the widest inquiry.

For present purposes, however, let us assume that the official view is correct. What is significant then is the evidence given by Security Service officers to the inquest. Seven in all gave evidence, the most senior, 'Mr O', being the officer responsible for briefing those concerned in the operation, including the Gibraltar Commissioner of Police, military officers and the colony's governor (himself shot by the IRA in October 1990). Although 'O' had been responsible for the briefing, he had himself not gone to Gibraltar and the delivery was by a colleague who was not called to give evidence. 'O' admitted that the briefing had been mistaken in three main respects. First, based on the assessment of a bomb found in a car in Brussels in January 1988, it was assumed that a remote control detonating device would be used, rather than a timer as was eventually found, despite the fact that the terrain in Gibraltar would have rendered a remote control device unreliable. Second, it had not been anticipated that the car which was driven into Gibraltar two days early would be just a blocking car to save a parking space and third, soldiers were briefed that the three would be armed. In the event they were unarmed when shot.[15] Therefore, it would not be surprising if the SAS soldiers were less than pleased with the quality of the intelligence they had been provided with, a secondhand, by MI5, particularly since it ended up with a number of them giving evidence at the inquest. This is, of course, if the official story is correct; if it is not, then these 'intelligence errors' would be explained differently as part of a *post hoc* rationalisation of events which could present a plausible story to the inquest.

As noted earlier, one of the problems with the dissemination of information by a security intelligence agency is that it will be primarily concerned to protect the integrity of its own sources of information. This is particularly a problem when information may be used to support a prosecution; indeed, prosecutions may be dropped or courts deceived in order to preserve the secrecy of sources. On the other hand, to the extent that security intelligence agencies are part of a wider structure of state and government institutions, they will have an interest in the dissemination of their product to other agencies as indicators of the 'value-for-money' being given by the agency. At a conference in Ottawa in September 1989 on 'Security and Intelligence Needs for the 1990s' a number of panellists referred to the need for 'entrepreneurship' and the 'selling' of the intelligence product both to operational people within agencies and to often sceptical outside agencies.[16]

Such a process will not, of course, be immune from the wider political process within which security intelligence agencies operate. In the US, for example, the tendency of intelligence agencies, particularly military ones, to orient and time their dissemination of intelligence to crucial points in the congressional budgetary process has been well documented.[17] Hoover also used his files for broader purposes. When Senator Joseph McCarthy shot to national prominence in February 1950 with his allegations of varying numbers of communists in the US State Department, he turned to Hoover for assistance. Hoover first recommended to McCarthy that he appoint a former FBI agent, Don Surine, as an investigator, and then they agreed a further strategy by which Hoover could assist without risk of exposure. In essence this involved McCarthy's presenting the information which he received from the FBI as if it had come from the investigative files of the Civil Service Commission.[18]

There is also a general tendency among security intelligence agencies to seek to discredit or smear any outsiders who seek to investigate or to criticise their operations. Information from the FBI's central files plus personal information sent to Hoover by field agents was available to discredit those who criticised the Bureau. It also maintained a 'not to contact list' which by

184

1972 contained 332 names of 'individuals known to be hostile to the Bureau'. Before anyone was placed on this list a summary of the information held about that person would be prepared for Hoover. Such information would be utilised also in any bureaucratic fights that the Bureau had, and files were prepared on all newly elected members of Congress and Governors, and kept in the Crime Records Division for use in 'congressional liaison'. Hoover's long immunity from congressional criticism has been put down partly to his use of such material.[19] Hoover did not normally have to use the information at all; according to the 'law of anticipated reactions' members of Congress would refrain from criticising the Bureau for fear of what he might leak about them.

Similar disinformation operations are not unheard of in Britain. During April and May 1977 the legal moves to deport Philip Agee and Mark Hosenball coincided with the appearance in court of the three ABC defendants. A disinformation campaign was directed primarily at Philip Kelly, a journalist not directly implicated in either case but certainly known to all those involved. This combined a variety of facts, half-truths and fantasies to present a picture of an all-encompassing conspiracy traceable back to the KGB. The strategy was primarily aimed at detaching from the defence campaigns the support they had received from 'respectable' people so that the defendants could be isolated as disloyal radicals; and the campaign was partially successful, though, eventually, the prosecution's case under section 1 of the Official Secrets Act collapsed.[20] During one of the *Spycatcher* court hearings in Britain Sir Robert Armstrong conceded that MI5's legal adviser routinely briefed a number of Fleet Street editors.[21] Although most of the victims of smears, as in the ABC case, were on the political Left, people on the Right have apparently not been immune. In addition to the legal attempts made to prevent Anthony Cavendish from publishing his book *Inside Intelligence*, which were discussed in Chapter 1, he was apparently subjected also to an attempt by the Security Service to discredit him through the use of three government-supporting newspapers.[22] In these examples the dissemination of intelligence amounts to a form of countering activity and is discussed further in the next section.

Another aspect of dissemination is the extensive contacts which exist between state agencies and the private sector. David Leigh discusses

> the existence of a surprising network of contacts between MI5 officers, journalists, businessmen and Conservative MPs, which belies the claim that MI5 is a passive 'secret' organisation. The City Golf Club in Fleet Street, the Special Forces Club in Knightsbridge, and the Carlton Club in St James were the venues for this secret side of British life.[23]

A particular aspect of this is the relationship between serving officials and former colleagues now working in the private security sector. This can be seen in both the US and the UK, for example in the establishment of private security firms by ex-SAS members and ex-police officers. In some cases contact is in the form of information-trading, but there is also some 'sub-contracting' between government and private agencies. For example, a 'private client' commissioned Zeus Security Consultants in 1983 to gather information about objectors to the proposed Sizewell nuclear-processing plant. Zeus in turn sub-contracted the work to Contingency Services, run by Vic Norris, who gathered the information and claimed also to have established three 'dummy' protest groups which could be used for disruptive purposes. Peter Hamilton of Zeus denied any Whitehall involvement with this scheme,[24] but in general the company aims 'to provide security services of all kinds to government and other authorities'. Hamilton himself is a former army intelligence officer who claims to have been seconded to the Security Service at some point. Lord Chalfont and Sir James Starritt, former head of the Metropolitan Police Special Branch, were members of the Zeus Board during the 1980s.[25]

In at least one case more precise links between the Security Service and the private sector have been established. This is the case of the Economic League whose officials have been known to work within the Security Service's premises and lecture on their courses. The League was founded in 1919 (although it was known as the National Propaganda Committee until 1925), the prime mover being Admiral Sir Reginald 'Blinker' Hall who had just retired as Director of Naval Intelligence. At this time he was co-operating also with Basil Thomson, head of Special Branch, to advocate the establishment of a new co-ordinated domestic security intelligence agency for the UK, which was intended to supplant Kell's MI5 (see Chapter 6). From 1925 onwards the League built up its information dossiers on socialist and 'subversive' organisations. By the mid-1930s card indexes of individuals were being compiled and the information passed on to companies. The formal vetting system was established after the war in the context of the 'Red scare' when requests for information about individuals increased rapidly. The service was started in the London region based on records supplied by a senior Special Branch officer.[26]

By the mid-1980s the League had over 2,000 subscribing companies, files including the names of 30,000 people and, in 1986, for example, carried out 200,000 name checks.[27] It retained its contacts with the police; in the words of the League's Director-General

> . . . the police and Special Branch are interested in some of the things that we are interested in. They follow the activities of these groups in much the same way as we do and therefore they do get in touch with us from time to time and talk to us and say 'Were you at this demonstration or that?' Obviously we help them where we can. If we come across things that we think will be of particular interest to them we send it to them. Now obviously, in the course of discussions, there is an exchange of information, just in the ordinary course of talking.[28]

The fact that both the League and the Security Service make use of people's national insurance numbers as identifiers would facilitate information exchanges between the two.[29]

Private security and investigative agencies are, of course, growing far more rapidly than State services.[30] In 1985 Hamilton was a member of the Institute of Professional Investigators along with 850 others, mostly former police and intelligence officers but including some serving police and Post Office investigators.[31] Between 1986 and 1989 the British Security Industry Association grew from 80 to 150 member companies employing some 70,000 staff. Estimates of the total numbers employed in the private security industry are as high as 250,000. Alongside this rapid growth go increasing numbers of contacts with state agencies, partly as a result of privatisation during the 1980s. Sixteen contracts have been awarded by the MOD to private security firms to guard 44 military establishments, and Protective Security Systems have been authorised by the Home Office to appoint 'special constables' with stop, search and arrest powers in Harwich docks.[32] In the context of the need for 'deniability' in security intelligence operations, the proliferation of such firms and personal contacts between serving and former security intelligence officers can only make the question of sub-contracting loom larger in future.[33]

In some cases the 'dissemination' of intelligence will amount to no more than the storage of information in the organisational memory. The amount and range of political intelligence held on citizens in the US and UK can only be estimated, but firmer information does exist concerning past practices. With respect to the US the Church Committee concluded:

> Intelligence agencies have collected vast amounts of information about the intimate details of citizens' lives and about their participation in legal and peaceful political activities.

These included:

> – 300,000 individuals indexed in a CIA computer system and separate files created on approximately 7,200 Americans and over 100 domestic groups between 1967 and 1973.
> – Approximately 100,000 Americans the subject of US Army intelligence files created between mid-1960s and 1971.
> – 26,000 individuals catalogued on an FBI list of persons to be rounded up in the event of a 'national emergency'.[34]

The systems by which files and associated indexes are developed can become highly elaborate. Hoover was fully aware of the illegality of many FBI information-gathering operations. His concern, however, was not to limit them but to maintain tight bureaucratic control of the practice and to prevent discovery by outsiders, whether by court orders or congressional subpoenas.[35] In 1942, for example, he devised a special filing procedure for documents relating to break-ins. Memoranda requesting his permission to conduct a burglary were to be captioned 'Do Not File' and were therefore neither serialised nor indexed in the Bureau's central records system. Once Hoover had approved the operation the memoranda were filed in the office of whichever assistant director had supervisory responsibility and were destroyed every six months. Similarly the field office copies of such requests were kept in the office safe and destroyed after every yearly visit by the Bureau's inspectors.[36]

Ironically, it was Hoover's meticulous record-keeping which eventually led to the exposure of this system. His 1966 order prohibiting further domestic security break-ins (see above Chapter 4) was written on a memorandum summarising the 'Do Not File' procedure so when, in 1971, he decided to preserve the former he kept also the latter, and told his administrative assistant to transfer the memo from his 'Personal and Confidential File' to the 'Official and Confidential File'. Both these files were kept in Hoover's office and neither was integrated into the central records system. After his death and on his instructions, the 'Personal' files were all destroyed, but the 'Official' files were integrated into the central system and the 'Do Not File' practice emerged during the Church Committee investigation in 1975. Although most of the records had been destroyed in line with the policy, the Church Committee was able to reconstruct the scope and political purposes of FBI break-ins when it discovered that all the records of the New York field office for the period 1954 to 1973 had not been destroyed.[37]

In the UK, the Special Branch had 1.15 million names on index during 1974 and of these 300,000 had personal files. Since then these will have gone to make up the major part of the storage on the Metropolitan Police's 'C' Department computer which includes also drugs, immigration, serious crimes, and fraud intelligence.[38] As far as MI5 is concerned Peter Wright reports that in 1955 there were about two million Personal Files in the Registry, a number which remained fairly static until the late 1960s and early 1970s when 'it began to rise dramatically . . . with the onset of student and industrial militancy'.[39]

The issue of file retention was the only one dealt with in any detail by the Commissioner (Lord Justice Stuart-Smith) under the Security Service Act in his second report issued in May

1992.[40] It was Harriet Harman and Patricia Hewitt's case to the European Commission of Human Rights that had been one of the precipitators of the Act and, in 1991, when they were pursuing the case with the Tribunal, it appeared that their files had not been destroyed.[41] Stuart-Smith described the Security Service's procedure. If the criteria for opening a permanent file (on which Stuart-Smith did not elaborate) do not exist then a temporary file may be opened for up to three years. When a 'permanent' file is opened it will be coded green and for whatever period this lasts active inquiries will be made about the subject. The file may then change to amber for some period during which no active investigation will be conducted but information received may be added. Presumably, for example, no new informers would be recruited during this period but information from those already in place would be added to the file. Once a file becomes coded red then neither active inquiries nor the addition of further information is permitted. Finally, after some period, the index entry for the file will be transferred from the Live to the Research Index, the file microfilmed and the hard copy destroyed.[42] This is curious since the process of computerising files apparently began in the mid-1970s and the Service's computers have the capacity for 20 million separate files[43] but Stuart Smith makes no reference to computer files.

Stuart-Smith notes that the general policy of the Service is to retain records indefinitely and endorses this central principle of security intelligence agencies but then says that, before the 1989 Act, certain categories of files had been destroyed, specifically, temporary files that had not been converted into permanent ones and permanent files which subsequently appeared to have been opened in error. The Service said that they no longer destroyed these files in case they were required for an investigation under the Act, and he agreed with this procedure.[44] Apart from the issue of whether the destruction of files did not contradict the central principle of 'not knowing today what might be useful tomorrow', there is an important question here. As long as files exist within the organisational memory they will be available and, if they have been developed improperly, their continued existence constitutes a continuing abuse of power against the people concerned. But against their undoubted interest in having those files destroyed there is a competing interest in their retention. It has become clear from foreign inquiries and oversight procedures that access to agency files is the only sure way of establishing precisely their practices; therefore there is a broader public interest in ensuring that files are not destroyed, although they should not remain indefinitely within the control of the originating agency. The ability of people to obtain access to their files is discussed in Chapter 8.

COUNTERING

Finally, and perhaps potentially the most penetrative aspect of security intelligence agency operations, is when the intelligence process culminates in some decision to act. Before active countering activities are considered, however, it is important to recall the point made earlier that surveillance itself may amount to a form of countering. For Brodeur, one of the four distinguishing features of high policing is that the police do not just make use of informers but that they acknowledge their readiness to do so in order to disrupt the activities of target organisations.[45] For example, the McDonald Commission examined cases in which the RCMP Security Service approached suspected members of the FLQ in 1971 and 1972.

> The objective was to recruit them as sources of information about FLQ groups and individuals. If recruitment failed, it was hoped that knowledge in the milieu that the suspect had been approached by the RCMP might cause the suspect to be distrusted and cause members of the group he was associated with to be concerned about the extent to which the RCMP knew their affairs.[46]

Other surveillance techniques, for example, openly taking photographs, and intercepting communications in such a way that the targets know precisely what is happening, may also be used overtly as a means of disruption.

The Church Committee found that covert countering actions had been used by the FBI to disrupt the lawful political activities of individuals and groups and to discredit them, 'using dangerous and degrading tactics which are abhorrent

191

in a free and decent society'.[47] Between 1956 and 1971 the FBI carried out a series of counter-intelligence programmes (COINTELPRO) which, concluded the Church Committee, were explicitly intended to deter citizens from joining groups, neutralising those who were already members and preventing or inhibiting free expression. Some of the tactics used risked, and sometimes caused, serious emotional, economic or physical damage.[48] The COINTELPRO directed at black nationalists was started in 1967 and field offices were instructed to exploit conflicts within and between groups, to use the media to ridicule and discredit groups and to gather information on the 'unsavoury backgrounds' of group leaders. Once the Black Panther Party emerged as a group of national stature, field offices were instructed to develop measures aimed at 'crippling' it, for example by aggravating conflicts between the BPP and other groups.[49]

Not surprisingly, given the lack of any definition of the 'New Left', this was the most haphazard of the COINTELPROs after its launch in May 1968. Agents were instructed to gather information on the 'immorality' and the 'scurrilous and depraved' behaviour of members of targeted groups and then, in June 1968, to use a number of countering measures: creating the impression that leaders were informants (known as the 'snitch jacket' technique), having members arrested on marijuana charges, sending anonymous letters about New Left staff (signed 'A Concerned Taxpayer') to the media and university authorities, and disrupting activities by notifying members that events had been cancelled.[50] Other tactics used included actions designed to break up marriages, to finish funding or employment and to encourage gang warfare between rival, violent groups. The most infamous of the FBI's COINTELPROs was that deployed against Martin Luther King over a number of years, culminating in the attempt to bait him into committing suicide.[51]

Since, unlike CSIS and ASIO, the FBI is a police force its powers gave it a continuing potential for a wider range of countering actions. The 1976 guidelines attempted to prevent a return to COINTELPRO by limiting the right of the Bureau to disseminate information just to other state agencies and to informers and potential victims if it would prevent or safeguard against violence. The guidelines did not include the specific provisions recommended by the Church Committee (for details see Chapter 4). Attorney General Levi proposed that this could encompass 'deterrent interviewing' of those believed to be planning violence and interventions in order to prevent access to weapons or to render them inoperative.[52]

In Canada, the activities of the RCMP which in part led to the establishment of the McDonald Inquiry included the burning of a barn in which a meeting of a 'subversive' group was to be held, issuing a communiqué to the media that would be regarded as a call to arms, and providing misinformation to the media. The McDonald report observed that not only did these methods violate the law and precepts of democracy but also that they had a corrupting effect on the Service itself, and resulted in a loss of respect for the agency following their disclosure.[53]

The most controversial countering practices in the UK relate to Northern Ireland. From 1981 onwards the RUC developed a form of legal countering against paramilitaries by means of 'supergrasses'. Between 1981 and 1983, 25 supergrasses were responsible for nearly 600 people being arrested and charged with offences connected with paramilitary activities. Fifteen supergrasses retracted their evidence before the trials in which they were involved began or were concluded; in the other ten trials the conviction rate was 42 per cent, allowing for the fact that most who appealed were successful.[54] The effectiveness of the supergrass strategy as measured by prosecutions was not therefore very high, but viewed by the authorities as a means of 'internment by remand'[55] or judged by its production of information and disruptive impact upon paramilitary organisations rather than convictions then the system may have been more productive.[56]

Fred Holroyd's account of countering was summarised in Chapter 1. Colin Wallace makes complementary allegations relating to his army job of fomenting a disinformation campaign during the 1970s. As we saw in Chapter 1 also, following the transition from SIS to Security Service control of intelligence in Northern Ireland in 1973, Wallace became involved in a new campaign, inspired by MI5, which was aimed at dealing with the apparently deteriorating security situation. This was called 'Clockwork Orange'. Initially the main targets were paramilitary commanders, but soon Wallace was increasingly inundated with material relating primarily to British politicians, particularly with reference to their financial, moral and political vulnerabilities. By the autumn of 1974 he was becoming concerned at the drift of the operation and it appears that by expressing his concerns to a Security Service officer he may have precipitated his removal from Northern Ireland. This allegation is of a countering operation of large proportions; it may have started as an attempt to disrupt and demoralise paramilitary organisations, but appears then to have moved far beyond that into actually countering the policies of the elected governments of the period – both Labour and Conservative – because, it is alleged, those policies appeared to be appeasing the Catholic population at the expense of the Protestant hegemony.[57]

Another sight of countering came through John Stalker's investigation of the most extreme form of all, assassination. John Stalker was Deputy Chief Constable of the Greater Manchester Police when, in the Spring of 1984, he was appointed to investigate the shootings of six men in Northern Ireland, late in 1982, by a specialist squad of officers from the RUC Special Branch. In September 1985 Stalker submitted his interim report to the RUC Chief Constable. This recommended the prosecution of 11 RUC officers for a variety of offences including conspiracy to pervert the course of justice, and perjury. He also requested access to a tape-recording from the surveillance of a barn in which two of the men had been shot, one of whom had died. Stalker understood the tape to be in the possession of the Security Service and believed that this might provide evidence to sustain further prosecutions of perjury and possibly murder. There was a delay of five months before the RUC Chief Constable passed on the report to the Northern Ireland DPP. Stalker was about to return to Belfast to continue his quest for the tape when, on 28 May 1986, he was removed from the investigation, first, through being sent on leave and then through being suspended while allegations against him of corrupt associations with alleged criminals in Manchester were investigated.

Stalker himself wrote later that he was convinced that his removal from the investigation was a government decision taken at the highest level because of the embarrassment that was likely to be caused by his intended investigation of senior officers of the RUC and his quest for the tape.[58] The circumstantial evidence for this conclusion was reinforced subsequently by the failure of the prosecution of Kevin Taylor, the 'criminal' with whom Stalker was alleged to have had a corrupt association. Taylor and three others were charged in 1989 with attempting to defraud the Co-op Bank of £254,000 but the prosecution withdrew the charges 16 weeks into the trial after accepting defence contentions that police officers had misled a judge in order to gain access to Taylor's bank accounts.[59] The Director of Public Prosecutions called for a police inquiry into the collapse of the prosecution and eventually announced that no police would be charged as a result of their conduct of the Taylor investigation.[60]

There is an alternative hypothesis, however, which is that Stalker was removed from the investigation, not to derail it but to safeguard it. It was feared that the growing allegations against Stalker might discredit the inquiry at any time and therefore he must be removed.[61] Evidence for this proposition is provided by the fact that Stalker's team of detectives was kept intact by the man who replaced him, Colin Sampson, Chief Constable of West Yorkshire, and that Sampson's report ultimately made the same recommendations regarding the prosecution of both RUC officers and Security Service officers for conspiracy to pervert the course of justice.[62] This hypothesis has also been supported by a 'senior civil servant' who worked with the RUC in Belfast during 1981–85, who concluded that Stalker's removal constituted 'Rotten judgement, but no conspiracy'.[63] Similar alternative hypotheses have been advanced in other situations in which the Security Service was seen to be trying to protect itself against investigations or allegations by outsiders – for example, that MI5 investigations of those around Harold Wilson were carried out in order to *protect* the government, not to destabilise it.[64]

Even with full access to people and papers, an inquiry would have some difficulty in determining which of these two hypotheses was nearer to the truth, but either way, the Stalker affair to date raises serious issues. For one, when the Northern Ireland DPP considered Stalker's interim report and Sampson's three subsequent reports made between October 1986 and April 1987, he concluded that there was evidence of attempts or conspiracies to pervert the course of justice. The Attorney General, however, having considered whether prosecution would be in the public interest, particularly 'considerations of national security', advised the DPP accordingly and it was agreed that no prosecutions would take place.[65] The following month, another inquiry was set up into disciplinary charges against RUC officers involved in the original shootings and just over a year later disciplinary hearings were held into charges against 20 officers; after two days, 18 were reprimanded, one was cautioned and the case against the last was dismissed.[66]

As a result of his investigation Stalker concluded:

> The circumstances of those shootings pointed to a police inclination, if not a policy, to shoot suspects dead without warning rather than to arrest them.[67]

Others have commented on the use by security forces in Northern Ireland of 'set pieces' in which circumstances are created when suspects can be 'taken out' rather than arrested.[68] Therefore the affair does throw into sharp relief a number of fundamental questions regarding, first, 'the effectiveness of the political controls, and supervision exercised over' the RUC;[69] second, as with Wallace's Kincora and Clockwork Orange allegations, it appears that the Security Service can remain immune from any form of external accountability for its intelligence or countering activities; and, third, more broadly, present arrangements for the investigation of police and intelligence abuses are patently inadequate.

Finally, though briefly, mention needs to be made of perhaps the most extraordinary countering operation of all – the campaign by the Security Service, or at least elements within it aided and abetted by others in the CIA, over 30 years from the end of the Second World War to discredit Harold Wilson and other of his ministers on the basis that they were, at best, communists and at worst Soviet agents. Since they were therefore totally unfit for office, the argument continued, they should be discredited in order to hasten their removal. The main accounts of this were referred to in Chapter 1.[70] They make the point that the seeds of the campaign against Wilson were planted in the immediate post-war period when Wilson was at the Board of Trade and sought to encourage East–West trade. This involved him in several journeys to the Soviet Union and in a variety of contacts with East Europeans. However, no clear evidence of disloyalty was ever found against Wilson or his immediate colleagues.[71] The point is, however, that there was nothing that the suspects could have done which would have persuaded the Security Service, especially counter-intelligence, that they were not security risks. In part this was because MI5 applied a ludicrous 'absolute standard' of security risk, for example, the existence of *any* contact with the USSR, which it would never have applied to its own people.[72] But it was also the consequence of the counter-intelligence methodology developed by James Angleton in the CIA and his disciple, Wright, in MI5.[73]

Soviet penetration, they argued, rested on strategies of disinformation which were perpetrated in part by 'agents of influence'. These were of two types: knowing and unknowing. The former could be discovered from their regular contacts with their handlers, but the latter had no handlers in the traditional sense. Often the only 'evidence' that people were 'agents' was the fact that they took public positions on policy issues which were consistent with the goals of the Soviet Union. Maximising trade with the West was a Soviet objective for a variety of financial, political and intelligence reasons; any Western politician favouring such trade was therefore an unknowing agent of influence on behalf of the Soviet government and thus a security risk. QED.[74] With such a methodology, notions of 'evidence' and 'proof' take on whole new meanings. Only in highly secretive and autonomous security intelligence organisations could such beliefs become so significant.

Thus the point that at least some part of the UK security intelligence network thought Wilson was a security risk can hardly be contested, but the question remains as to what, if anything, they did about it. Specifically, was there a plot to discredit and bring about the downfall of Harold Wilson as Prime Minister? Dorril and Ramsay identify three distinct versions of the plot as reported by Peter Wright. The first and earliest version was that described by Chapman Pincher in *Inside Story* in which Wright, then unnamed, would have exposed Wilson as a security risk and then would have resigned from the Security Service.[75] The second version, chronologically, was that given by Wright in *Spycatcher* in which he said he had been approached for help by a group of Security Service officers who wanted to leak files in order to discredit Wilson between the two 1974 elections.[76] The third version was given by Wright himself in his interview on *Panorama* in July 1988 in which he admitted that his account in *Spycatcher* was wrong, and said that the plan was that he and a group of eight or nine colleagues from K Branch, responsible for counter-espionage, would go to Wilson with the relevant files and persuade him to resign in order to minimise the scandal of his treachery.[77] For their part Dorril and Ramsay conclude that part of the second version is the nearest to what actually happened,[78] despite Wright's subsequent change of mind.

There are numerous threads to this story and this analysis cannot do justice to the complexity with which they are interwoven. For example, Labour Party politicians were not the only ones to fall foul of smear tactics; they were also directed at major figures throughout the 'liberal-left' of British politics.[79] The international network of security intelligence agencies meant that such activities were not necessarily confined to the UK. For example, at about the same time as the 'Wilson Plot' was gathering momentum, in Australia there was great controversy surrounding the removal of the Whitlam government in 1975 by the Governor General. This happened at the time of a constitutional crisis concerning the inability of the government to have its budget passed through the Senate, but the government had also fallen foul of its own security intelligence agencies and, most importantly, of the CIA. The 'Murphy Raid' on ASIO in March 1973 (see above p. 113 for details) raised fears that were compounded when the Labour government discovered that the Pine Gap SIGINT station in central Australia was actually run by the CIA. Fearing that, having discovered the deception the government might compromise the operation, the CIA embarked on a disinformation campaign against the Whitlam administration. When the government was removed from office a few days later it was, to say the least, happy timing from the point of view of the UKUSA network.[80] Nor was the CANZAB network necessarily limited in its effect to those countries formally constituting it. For example, Willy Brandt's resignation in a security scandal in 1974 was precipitated by British analysis of decrypted material spiced with then current counter-intelligence logic that Brandt's involvement with communists in the resistance against Nazism probably made him a communist.[81]

198

But one aspect of Dorril and Ramsay's analysis is particularly central to the present concern with analysing the structure, policies and practices of the security intelligence agencies in the United Kingdom with particular respect to their autonomy and penetration. It is worth quoting Dorril and Ramsay's conclusions at some length:

It is now apparent that the covert operations against the politicians of this country in the late sixties and early seventies were woven into, and became a tool in a fierce bureaucratic conflict between MI5 and MI6.

The background to that conflict was the shrinking overseas post-war British Empire. By the time Labour took office in 1964, relative economic decline and the forces of colonial liberation in the Empire, where both MI5 and MI6 had been operating, was producing pressure on overseas budgets and the security services. MI5 found their imperial security role being reduced and MI6 moving into some of what had been their territory, notably in Africa. In this process, it was always MI5 who were on the defensive, and their apparently incompetent handling of the various security scandals of the Macmillan era did nothing to help. The trans-Atlantic dissatisfaction with MI5 eventually produced the secret American Grey-Coyne inquiry into British security procedures in 1965. While the CIA's Angleton failed in his attempt to use the report to engineer a CIA takeover of MI5, MI6 were more successful, subsequently getting themselves on to joint MI5/MI6 operations like the Fluency Committee and the counter-intelligence unit K5.

This erosion of MI5's bureaucratic 'turf' continued when MI6 was put in overall charge of the intelligence war in Northern Ireland in 1971 by Edward Heath. Insult was added to injury when IRD (the Information Research Department), a Foreign Office/MI6-oriented outfit, was added in 1971, to run the psychological war. On the mainland UK, MI6's incremental expansion into MI5's territory continued with the formation of the nominally 'freelance' anti-subversive activities of the Institute for the Study of Conflict, largely staffed by former IRD employees, and its rapid penetration of the institutions of the state – the military and police, for example – where once MI5 had the exclusive franchise. The ensuing vicious faction fight in Northern Ireland has been described by two of its victims, Colin Wallace and Fred Holroyd.[82]

As these authors acknowledge, however, the tale is yet more complex, in part because these agencies were not necessarily homogeneous. Within the Security Service, for example, Angleton's allegations about Wilson in 1965 were embraced by some officers who wished to place him under surveillance, while others were appalled at the idea that the Service would spy on a prime minister. Continued attention therefore needs to be paid to factional disputes *within* the security intelligence agencies as well as *between* them.[83]

There was no official response to the allegations until 1987 when Prime Minister Margaret Thatcher denied everything:

> The Director-General [of MI5] has advised me he has found no evidence of any truth in the allegations . . . He has given me his personal assurance that the stories are false . . . The then Director-General has categorically denied that he confirmed the existence within the Security Service of a disaffected faction with extreme right-wing views. He has further stated that he had no reason to believe any such faction existed. No evidence or indication has been found of any plot or conspiracy against Lord Wilson by or within the Security Service.[84]

Whether such personal assurances from within the Security Service are an adequate form of 'oversight' will be examined in Chapter 7.

CONCLUSION

The significance of the discussion at the beginning of Chapter 4 can now be seen. One way of achieving a security intelligence agency which approximates to the model of the domestic intelligence bureau (see Chapter 2) would be to grant it legal authority solely to gather information. It should not be given a more general mandate to 'protect' or 'safeguard' since that will ensure its involvement in countering operations. A limited information-gathering mandate will not eliminate the possibility of abuse – processes of surveillance and dissemination, as we have seen, still provide ample opportunities for the use and abuse of power. More active countering measures will need to be sub-contracted to other agencies, which takes us beyond the confines of this analysis, but poses two major problems. First, there is a clear need, in this age of privatisation, for careful checking of tendencies for 'delicate' surveillance and countering tasks to be contracted out to the private sector. Second, there is the question of the legitimacy of a variety of countering techniques, whether carried out by state or private agencies. In the context of serious political violence there may be few objections to mild deceptions or 'spiking' arms caches, but summary killings and disinformation campaigns against elected ministers raise major questions about the organisation, control and oversight of security intelligence agencies, to which we now turn.

NOTES

1. A.N. Shulsky, *Silent Warfare: Understanding the World of Intelligence* (Washington DC: Brassey's (US), 1991), pp. 37–48 for summary.
2. J. Ranelagh, *The Agency: The Rise and Decline of the CIA* (New York: Simon & Schuster, 1987), pp. 112–17. Also, see M. Herman, *Evaluating Intelligence: a British Perspective*, paper for International Studies Association Conference, Vancouver, March 1991, p. 5.
3. V. Marchetti and J.D. Marks, *The CIA and the Cult of Intelligence* (New York: Dell, 1980), pp. 72–3; Ranelagh, ibid, pp. 170–83. See also ibid, pp. 622–4 for a discussion of the 'A' Team/'B' Team competition in 1976 regarding Soviet intentions.
4. McDonald, Second Report, *Freedom and Security Under the Law* (Ottawa: Minister of Supply and Services, 1981), pp. 600–2.
5. SIRC, *Annual Report for 1986–87* (Ottawa: Minister of Supply and Services, 1987), pp. 13, 42–3; and see S. Farson, 'Old Wine, New Bottles, and Fancy Labels: The Rediscovery of Organizational Culture in the Control of Intelligence', in G. Barak (ed.), *Crimes by the Capitalist State: An Introduction to*

State Criminality (Albany: State University of New York Press, 1991), especially pp. 199–205.

6. Report of the Special Committee on the Review of the CSIS Act and the Security Offences Act, *In Flux But Not In Crisis* (Queen's Printer for Canada, 1991), p. 59.

7. L.K. Gardiner, 'Squaring the Circle: Dealing with Intelligence-Policy Breakdowns', *Intelligence and National Security*, 6(1), January 1991, pp. 141–2.

8. M. Herman, 'Intelligence and Policy: A Comment', *Intelligence and National Security*, 6(1), January 1991, p. 229.

9. For example, R. Godson, 'Intelligence for the 1990s', in R. Godson (ed.), *Intelligence Requirements for the 1990s* (Lexington: D.C. Heath, 1989), pp. 4–11.

10. Quoted in Gardiner, supra (note 7), p. 150.

11. *The Guardian*, 27 September 1991, p. 10.

12. A.T. Turk, *Political Criminality* (Beverly Hills: Sage, 1982), pp. 126–7.

13. For example, Robin Robison, who had worked in the JIC reported that GCHQ intercepts relating to Robert Maxwell were disseminated to the Bank of England, *Financial Times*, 15 June 1992, p. 1.

14. *Private Eye* report, *Rock Bottom: The Gibraltar Killings, Government and Press Cover-Up* (London: Pressdram, February 1989).

15. *The Guardian*, 8 September 1988, p. 3; 28 September 1988, p. 6; H. Kitchin, *The Gibraltar Report* (London: Liberty, 1989), p. 11,

16. The public conference was organised by CASIS. In the subsequent volume of published papers, that by Robert Jervis is particularly relevant: 'Strategic Intelligence and Effective policy', in A.S. Farson *et al.* (eds), *Security and Intelligence in a Changing World* (London: Frank Cass, 1991), pp. 165–81. See also R. Mandel, 'Distortions in the Intelligence Decision Making Process', in S.J. Cimbala, *Intelligence and Intelligence Policy in a Democratic Society* (Ardsley-on-Hudson: Transnational Publishers, 1987), pp. 69–83.

17. For example see Marchetti and Marks, supra (note 3), pp. 266–73.

18. A.G. Theoharis and J.S. Cox, *The Boss: J.E. Hoover and the Great American Inquisition* (London: Harrap, 1989) pp. 283–7.

19. Church Committee, Final Report, Book II, *Intelligence Activities and the Rights of Americans* (Washington DC: US Government

Printing Office, 1976), pp. 239–40; see also R.G. Powers, *Secrecy and Power: The Life of J. Edgar Hoover* (New York: Free Press, 1987), pp. 266–7.

20. *New Statesman*, 15 February 1980, pp. 234–6; see also D. Hooper, *Official Secrets* (London: Secker & Warburg, 1987), pp. 104–22.
21. *The Observer*, 29 November, 1987, p. 16.
22. A. Cavendish, *Inside Intelligence* (London: Collins, 1990), pp. xxii–xxiii; see also S. Dorril and R. Ramsay, *Smear!* (London: Fourth Estate, 1991), p. 114.
23. D. Leigh, *The Wilson Plot* (London: Heinemann, 1988), p. xvi.
24. *The Observer*, 27 January 1985. A few weeks later *The Observer* ran another story quoting two private investigators, Dennis Byrne and Gary Murray, on the prevalence of contacts between the Security Service, special branches and private agencies: 3 March 1985.
25. R. Norton-Taylor, *In Defence of the Realm?* (London: Civil Liberties Trust, 1990), p. 70,
26. M. Hollingsworth and C. Tremayne, *The Economic League* (London: Liberty, 1989), pp. 1–7.
27. Norton-Taylor, supra (note 25), p. 72.
28. *World In Action*, Granada TV, broadcast 8 February 1988.
29. D. Campbell and S. Connor, *On The Record* (London: Michael Joseph, 1986), pp. 288–90.
30. For a survey of the organisation and activities of private police see L. Johnston, *The Rebirth of Private Policing* (London: Routledge, 1992), Chs. 4–5.
31. P. Fitzgerald and M. Leopold, *Stranger on the Line* (London: Bodley Head, 1987), p. 191.
32. *The Guardian*, 27 September 1989, p. 2.
33. G.T. Marx, 'The Interweaving of Public and Private Police in Crime and Undercover Work', *Crime and Justice System Annuals*, 23, 1987, pp. 172–93. See also N. South, *Policing for Profit* (London: Sage, 1988), *passim*; G. Murray, *Enemies of the State* (London: Simon and Schuster, 1993), *passim*.
34. Church Committee, supra (note 19), pp. 6–7.
35. Ibid, p. 55.
36. Ibid, pp. 61–2.
37. Theoharis and Cox, supra (note 18), pp. 11–13.
38. Campbell and Connor, supra (note 29), pp. 263–9.
39. P. Wright, *Spycatcher* (New York: Viking Penguin, 1987), p. 38.
40. Rt. Hon. Lord Justice Stuart-Smith, *Security Service Act 1989*,

Report of the Commissioner for 1991, Cm 1946 (London: HMSO, May 1992) (although cover is incorrectly dated May 1991).
41. *The Guardian*, 7 December 1991, p. 4.
42. Stuart-Smith, supra (note 40), 19.
43. Wright, supra (note 39), p. 358; Norton-Taylor, supra (note 25), p. 45.
44. Stuart-Smith, supra (note 40), §§18, 22–3.
45. J.-P. Brodeur, 'High Policing and Low Policing', *Social Problems,* 30(5), June 1983, pp. 514–15; see also Turk, supra (note 12), pp. 129–60 for a wide-ranging review of 'neutralisation' and 'intimidation' as active policies of political police which complements their 'information control'.
46. McDonald, Third Report, *Certain RCMP Activities and the Question of Governmental Knowledge* (Ottawa: Minister of Supply and Services, 1981), p. 220.
47. Church Committee, supra (note 19), p. 211.
48. Ibid.
49. Ibid, pp. 87–8.
50. Ibid, pp. 88–9.
51. Church Committee, Final Report, Book III, *Supplementary Detailed Staff Reports on Intelligence Activities and the Rights of Americans* (Washington DC: US Government Printing Office, 1976), pp. 79–184; see also K. O'Reilly, *Racial Matters: the FBI's Secret File on Black America 1960–72* (New York: Free Press, 1989), pp. 125–55.
52. J.T. Elliff, *The Reform of FBI Intelligence Operations* (Princeton: Princeton University Press, 1979), pp. 127–31 discusses the issues involved.
53. McDonald, supra (note 4), pp. 267–75.
54. S, Greer, 'The Supergrass System', in A. Jennings (ed.), *Justice Under Fire: The Abuse of Civil Liberties in Northern Ireland* (London: Pluto, 2nd edition, 1990), pp. 73–4.
55. Ibid, p. 73.
56. See also D. Bonner, 'Combating Terrorism: Supergrass Trials in Northern Ireland', *Modern Law Review* 51, 1988, pp. 23–53; M. Urban, *Big Boys' Rules* (London: Faber and Faber, 1992), pp. 133–7.
57. For full discussion see P. Foot, *Who Framed Colin Wallace?* (London: Pan, 1990), pp. 37–114, on which this summary is based. See also Urban, ibid, pp. 77–8.

58. J. Stalker, *Stalker* (London: Harrap, 1988), pp. 264–5.
59. Kevin Taylor provides his own view of these events in K. Taylor with K. Mumby, *The Poisoned Tree* (London: Pan, revised edition, 1991).
60. *The Guardian*, 20 December 1991, p. 3.
61. P. Taylor, *Stalker: the Search for Truth* (London: Faber and Faber, 1987), p. 160.
62. *The Guardian*, 14 June 1991, p. 3.
63. P. Buxton, 'Book Review' *Criminal Justice*, 6(2), May 1988, pp. 6–7. Steve Dorril discusses these alternative hypotheses in *Lobster*, 23 (June 1992), pp. 21–5.
64. S. Dorril and R. Ramsay, supra (note 22), p. 120.
65. HC Deb. 25 January 1988, col. 22.
66. *The Guardian*, 18 February 1988, p. 6; 15 March 1989, p. 20.
67. Stalker, supra (note 58), p. 253.
68. C. Campbell and F. Ni Aolain, 'Answering for Necessary Force', *Civil Liberty Agenda* (London: Liberty, Winter, 1992), pp. 6–7.
69. Stalker, supra (note 58), p. 264.
70. Dorril and Ramsay, supra (note 22); D. Leigh, *The Wilson Plot* (London: Heinemann, 1988).
71. Leigh, ibid, p. 254.
72. Dorril and Ramsay, supra (note 64), p. 120.
73. See T, Mangold, *Cold Warrior* (New York: Simon & Schuster, Touchstone Edition, 1992), pp. 57–62 for a brief description of Angleton's significance for post-war Western counter-intelligence.
74. R.H. Shultz and R. Godson, *Dezinformatsia* (New York: Berkley Books, 1986), p. 2.
75. C. Pincher, *Inside Story* (London: Book Club Associates, 1978), pp. 16–18.
76. Wright, supra (note 39), pp. 367–70.
77. Dorril and Ramsay, supra (note 22), p. 246.
78. Ibid, pp. 246–7.
79. Ibid, p. 273.
80. J.T. Richelson and D. Ball, *The Ties That Bind* (Boston: Unwin Hyman, 2nd edition, 1990), pp. 266–8.
81. Leigh, supra (note 70), pp. 230–32; S. Dorril, 'Willy Brandt: the "Good German"', *Lobster*, 22, November 1991, pp. 12–15.
82. Dorril and Ramsay, supra (note 22), p. 328.
83. Ibid, pp. 115, 328, and see discussion in Chapter 6. Chapman Pincher's view is that this entire story was a fantasy of Wilson's

and, subsequently, of the political Left in general, and that he played a key role himself in disseminating the idea of the Wilson Plot: *The Truth About Dirty Tricks* (London: Sidgwick & Jackson, 1991), pp. 141–51.

84.   HC Deb. 6 May 1987, col. 1726.

6

Autonomy I: Organisation and Control of Security Intelligence Agencies

In the light of the analysis in the last two chapters of what security intelligence agencies typically do, here we consider questions of organisational structure and process. Specifically, should there be a domestic security intelligence agency separate from the police, how should the agency be controlled by elected ministers and what are the major issues of organisational resources and culture?

Figure 6.1 summarises aspects of the analysis so far. As we saw in Chapter 3, it is important to consider first the nature of the threats to the state and society rather than starting with some pre-existing institutional framework. Threats may be assessed, first, by reference to their origin. All states collect foreign intelligence, but not all have a specific agency for the covert gathering of HUMINT such as a SIS or CIA. There are several arguments as to why foreign and domestic threats should be assessed by separate agencies, for example, that one depends on willingly breaking the laws of other countries while the other is based on the defence of domestic law. Another argument is that abuses of power would be more likely and more damaging if agencies covered both foreign and domestic threats. Yet the opposite has been argued regarding counter-intelligence work because it is not divisible by borders. CSIS may gather both domestic and foreign intelligence. A proposal for a new counter-intelligence agency with both domestic and foreign mandates was made to the Reagan administration, but it did not bear fruit.[1] 'Foreign' and 'domestic' threats may not be clear-cut. Further, states will perceive threats that do not derive originally from abroad, but in which there is some foreign attempt to make use of or subvert

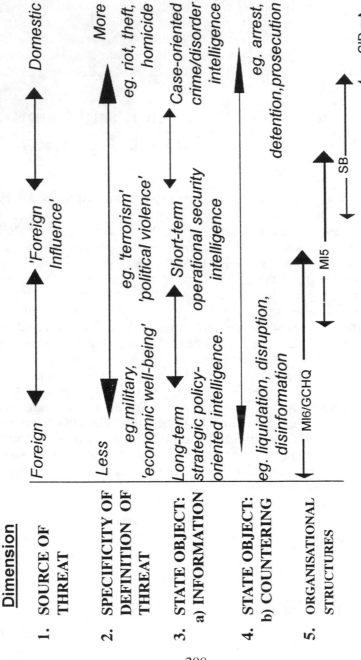

Figure 6.1 Dimensions of Security and Crime Intelligence

domestic political groups, as more serious than 'purely' domestic threats and this is reflected in placing 'foreign influence' at the centre of the first dimension in Figure 6.1. Clearly there is a danger that the search for 'foreign influence' may be simply a pretext, as, for example, it appeared to be in the launching of the Huston Plan discussed in Chapter 3.[2]

As we also saw in Chapter 3, 'national security' threats tend to be enumerated in much more general terms, and often not with respect to particular legal offences, certainly when compared with the threats that are more specifically enshrined within the criminal law. The second dimension in Figure 6.1 reflects the general rule that domestic threats to security tend to be reflected in laws which, while still inherently ambiguous, are more specifically defined than such notions as 'economic well-being'. The third and fourth dimensions in Figure 6.1 reflect the state's response to threats: to gather information and then to act as we saw respectively in Chapters 4 and 5. There is a difference between information which is gathered for the purposes of developing strategic intelligence which is provided to foreign-policy-makers and that which is gathered by police with respect to the commission of a serious crime. In terms of state action, the former may well be directed to policies which aim not only to counter threats, but also to reduce the state's vulnerabilities.[3] In the latter, the state's preferred action will be the arrest, charge and conviction of the perpetrators. Short-term operational security intelligence reflects something of a mid-point between these two ends of the intelligence dimension. The concern is with relatively immediate threat assessments and security concerns, which often seem to squeeze out any longer-term contemplation of security trends. Yet, in comparison with criminal intelligence, there is far less concern with developing information which can be used in court as part of a prosecution.

The fifth dimension reflects, schematically, the relationship of the main security intelligence agencies within the UK at present. At the foreign end where threats are defined most broadly in terms of national interest, the concern is with generating a variety of long- and short-term intelligence which can be supplied to policy-makers or used to conduct covert countering operations. The agencies primarily concerned are the SIS and GCHQ. Their operations spread some way into the domestic sphere, though precisely how far is matter of debate.[4] Certainly there is overlap with the Security Service which is primarily responsible for domestic security but whose counter-espionage and counter-intelligence work will clearly bring it into contact with threats emanating from abroad. MI5 overlaps also with police special branches. Partly this is because MI5 officials do not possess police powers and therefore arrests for security-related offences will be made by Special Branch officers. Until 1992 another source of the overlap derived from the historical responsibility of the Metropolitan Police Special Branch for dealing with Irish Republican paramilitary activities on the British mainland, while the Security Service was responsible for Loyalist paramilitaries (see further below, p. 216). Special Branch in turn will overlap to some extent with normal CID squads, of which they are formally a part.

A SEPARATE SECURITY INTELLIGENCE AGENCY?

Figure 6.1 is intended to illustrate that threats, types of information and forms of countering do not fall into neat pigeon-holes. The real differences which do exist shade into one another at various points on each dimension.[5] This is the context within which appropriate organisational structures must be considered, although those for foreign intelligence-gathering are beyond the scope of this discussion.

Regarding domestic threats, it is argued that the main difference between a police and a security intelligence agency is in their goals: the police aim to obtain convictions, the security intelligence agency aims to gather information and produce intelligence.[6] For police and prosecutors, who are primarily interested in 'making cases', anything which smacks of research or intelligence is afforded low status within the organisation.[7] For security intelligence agencies, the fact that an operation ends up in a prosecution may actually indicate 'failure' since they would have preferred to convert the person into an intelligence asset rather than see them in court. This reduces dramatically their value as an informer. However, we must be aware that there is not just one model of policing and it is possible to exaggerate the significance to police of convictions. First, the fundamental goal of the police

210

is order-maintenance, to which end obtaining convictions is only marginally related.[8] Second, policing has become more similar to security intelligence. Traditional histories of the development of policing in the UK have made much of the distinction between its constabulary nature, for example the 'citizen in uniform', and notions of 'high police' as developed in eighteenth-century France by Joseph Fouché in which protection of the state was the pre-eminent goal. This and the fact that scholarship on the police in the UK has tended to concentrate on the uniformed, constabulary functions rather than the plain-clothes, undercover, sometimes political, functions has led to an unjustified exaggeration of this distinction.

Since the 1960s UK police have moved some way from reliance on the preventive value of uniformed patrolling by police towards increasing reliance on more 'positive' forms of policing with respect to both crime and disorder. Initially this was reflected in the adoption of unit beat policing and the increased use of vehicles. Introduced under the pressure of shortages of police, it eventually degenerated into 'fire brigade' policing which was widely criticised both within and outside police forces.[9] As that approach was seen to fail, while levels of recorded crime rose, fresh emphasis was given to aspects of policing which more closely resemble the security intelligence process. These included the use of stop and search, detention for purposes of interrogation, and attempts to develop local intelligence systems based on sub-divisional collators and divisional intelligence officers which would then be applied to 'targeting' those groups seen as particularly 'crime-prone'.[10] More specialist 'intelligence units' such as those for drugs[11] and football violence have been developed at the national level, coming together in 1992 in the National Criminal Intelligence Service (NCIS). This is staffed by police and customs officers and has targeted its initial efforts on 50 'leading criminals', including preparing intelligence 'packages' for local forces.[12] The other main managerial innovation of the 1980s was 'policing by objectives' which is based on research, the analysis of information, the establishment of policy objectives, and the collection and evaluation of information relating to the achievement or otherwise of those objectives.[13] This strategy can be characterised as a model of policing more akin to the security intelligence process.

Police Special Branches provide the organisational link between policing and security intelligence work in the UK. The Branch mandate indicates that it is much more concerned with information-gathering than with seeking 'the enforcement of law' and convictions. It does have more normal police 'executive' functions, for example VIP protection, and arrests for security offences, but predominantly it seeks information: for example, it 'gathers information about threats to public order'; 'effort is devoted to the study and investigation of terrorism'; and it 'provides information about extremists and terrorist groups to the Security Service'.[14]

This police–security intelligence link can be more usefully seen as a spectrum from 'high' to 'low' policing. Brodeur identifies four basic features of high policing. First, it is 'absorbent' – it aims to control by storing intelligence which is all-encompassing. In the terms of this analysis, it might be described as being more penetrative. Second, it does not just enforce law and regulations passed elsewhere, but has the power to 'create' the rules which it then enforces. Third, crime control is not an end in itself, but may be used as a tool of coercion, such as blackmailing suspects into becoming informers. Fourth, as discussed in Chapter 5, high police do not just make use of informers but acknowledge their willingness to do so because of the disruptive effect that this can have on targeted groups.[15] Clearly police and security intelligence agencies will vary in the extent to which such techniques are used (and will be located at different points on the dimension in Figure 6.1), but the important point is that the differences between agencies will be of degree not kind. For example, Ron Crelinsten notes

> that there is a close similarity between security intelligence operations and what is known as pro-active policing. This resemblance highlights the similarity between investigating covert, clandestine activities of a subversive nature and those of a purely criminal nature, such as drug traffic or organised crime.[16]

Stuart Farson points out that where security intelligence and police agencies have the same goal, say the prevention of serious political violence, then there is no real difference between what might be called 'criminal intelligence' and 'security intelligence'.[17]

On Brodeur's second point it might be argued that whereas an 'independent security state' (see Chapter 2) may be in a position to create rules as it goes along, a security intelligence agency operating within a liberal democratic framework will not be in a position to usurp the legislative assembly or political executive. But careful attention must be paid to the specificity with which security laws are constructed; if, as is the case in the UK with 'subversion' and 'terrorism' (see discussion above in Chapter 3), the official definitions are very broad, then the greater is the opportunity for the security intelligence agency to 'create' rules in particular cases.

The case for establishing a security intelligence agency separate from the police has been most extensively considered by the McDonald Commission. The main arguments presented were, first, in favour of the recruitment of a wider variety of better-educated people and more participatory management and, second, that security intelligence agencies need direction and control by government to an extent that might be considered improper in a police force.[18] It should be noted, however, that McDonald made these points in the specific context of removing security intelligence from the paramilitary RCMP,[19] though they can be applied to some extent to most police forces. Another argument for separation is that a security intelligence agency with police powers has a greater potential for repression and coercion than one without:[20] that is, to become more penetrative.

There are arguments, however, against the creation of a separate security intelligence agency. One is that it institutionalises the concept of political policing and permits the development of a vested bureaucratic interest in its continuation, even if the threats pass. Particularly in a situation such as that in the UK, where there has been no clear debate about just what are the threats to domestic security against which the security intelligence agency is supposed to be gathering information, it will find it quite easy to justify its continued existence by the discovery of new 'threats', especially when one of the guiding principles of intelligence work is that 'you never know today what information you might need tomorrow' (see Chapter 4).

Another argument is that separating intelligence 'heads' from executive 'arms' can create organisational difficulties. For example, being unwilling to trust the agency from which it is supposed to receive intelligence, the 'arm' might develop its own information-gathering structure. After the removal of the Security Service from the Canadian RCMP in 1984 and the creation of CSIS to gather information, the RCMP retained responsibility for the enforcement of security offences. Jean-Paul Brodeur suggested:

> Since a police apparatus strives to establish the closest possible link between information and action, there is a strong possibility that the RCMP will grow another intelligence 'head' of its own to guide its striking arm and will not be content to rely exclusively on the CSIS for information.[21]

This prediction proved to be accurate when it was revealed in 1989 that the RCMP had established a National Security Intelligence Directorate.[22]

At times the relations between separate agencies, within either the same or different states, can degenerate into 'turf wars'. When CSIS was established in Canada, its relationship with the RCMP in the early years gave rise to a number of such problems. One concerned the story of Mahmoud Mohammed Issa Mohammed which became public in February 1988 when the RCMP's attempt to spirit him out of Canada became public amid accusations that CSIS had publicised the operation. Issa Mohammed had been active in the PFLP in the 1970s, including involvement in plane hijackings, and his subsequent attempt to resettle in Canada suggests, at the least, a clash of organisational interests between the RCMP, the Immigration Service and CSIS. CSIS interviewed Issa Mohammed in Madrid before he entered Canada in 1987, interviewed him regularly after his arrival and in January 1988 abducted him to a hotel for three days. Meanwhile the RCMP determined to remove him from the country and made a deal with his lawyers before the official deportation hearing was completed; CSIS officials happened to be present at Toronto airport as the RCMP prepared to place Mohammed on his flight.[23] SIRC's report on the episode failed to deal with a number of serious questions, including the way immigration hearings are used to recruit informers, and, to put it mildly, was minimalist:

> We found that CSIS did not slip up in the entry into Canada of . . . Mohammed; someone did, but it was not CSIS. Nor did it compromise his attempt to leave the country.[24]

Similar tensions between the FBI and the CIA in the United States were noted by Marchetti and Marks, particularly in the area of counter-espionage where the two agencies have overlapping responsibilities. The general view within the CIA was that the FBI agents were 'rather unimaginative police-officer types' while the FBI saw CIA counter-intelligence operators as 'dilettantes who are too clever for their own good'.[25] One structural consequence of this kind of friction was the establishment within the CIA of the Domestic Operations Division with its headquarters not at Langley, the main CIA centre, but in Washington on Pennsylvania Avenue.[26] For his part, Hoover was unwilling to co-operate with any other agency unless the Bureau was in charge. This was one factor behind the hatching of the Huston Plan (see Chapter 3).

An inquiry by New Zealand's chief ombudsman into the domestic security intelligence agency there, the Security Intelligence Service (SIS), heard complaints from the police that the SIS was not passing them the information it needed regarding terrorist groups. The SIS maintained that it told the police just what they needed to know and feared leaks from within the force. In some cases the SIS had persuaded foreign police officers to pass information direct to it, by-passing the New Zealand force.[27] In Australia, there appear to have been particularly bad relations between ASIO and the Joint Intelligence Organisation. The JIO was established in 1969 with responsibility for the collation and assessment of information within the Department of Defence, but over the years, on occasions, its staff were placed under surveillance by ASIO who also spread rumours that JIO officers had been responsible for various leaks.[28] Again, there is a structural element to this since ASIO is responsible for security assessments (vetting) in the Australian public service, which would require on occasions some degree of investigation of all personnel in agencies such as the JIO. ASIO's role is, however, advisory; decisions as to the granting of access to material are made by departmental heads, and it is clear from ASIO's published comments that it is not happy with the security procedures and consciousness in some departments.[29]

In the UK, during 1991–92, the JIC carried out a review of the role of the security intelligence agencies. The most publicised conclusion of this review has been a shift of the prime responsibility for intelligence regarding PIRA activities in Britain from the Metropolitan Police Special Branch to the Security Service. To judge from the competitive briefings of the press being carried out by the two agencies, this decision reflected the outcome of a classic turf war. On the one hand, the lack of Special Branch success against PIRA active service units and the escape of alleged members from Brixton in 1991 after a bungled branch operation were noted. On the other hand, the Security Service's search for a new post-cold war role and the lack of relevance of much of its information were quoted.[30] Merely shifting this responsibility from one agency to the other will not, of itself, eliminate these contests. In this case, specifically, the Security Service will still have to rely on the Branch's police powers for legal countering operations. Indeed, it has been reported subsequently that police are providing training for Security Service staff in gathering evidence for use in court,[31] but if intelligence was to be gathered solely in order to prepare prosecutions, there was little sense in removing the role from the police at all. The logic of this switch would be to give a wider variety of countering options, including, presumably, 'extra-legal' operations (see discussion in Chapter 5).

Given the well-documented problem of turf wars and poor ' co-ordination between security intelligence agencies, aggravated beyond the normal wear-and-tear of bureaucratic politics by secrecy, it might be considered a sound principle to have as few separate agencies as is consistent with adequate information collection and countering action regarding serious threats. Some overlap between these agencies is inevitable but, as can be seen in Figure 6.1, the overlap between present UK agencies is considerable. Figure 6.1 is highly schematic and does not contain a detailed analysis of precisely the degree of overlap or complementarity between these agencies, but it does pose the question, to which we shall return in the final chapter, of whether both the Security Service and police Special Branches are necessary.

THE MINISTERIAL ROLE: DIRECTIVES AND DENIABILITY

A fundamental condition of the maintenance of security and intelligence agencies and their participation in co-operative arrangements with allied agencies must be, given the extraordinary powers and capabilities of these agencies and the increasingly pervasive nature of their operations, that they be subject to firm, continuous and responsible oversight and direction. Unfortunately the management structures and processes for the provision of such oversight and direction have proved to be deficient to greater or lesser extents in all of the UKUSA countries.[32]

'Oversight' and 'direction' are two distinct senses in which the autonomy of the security intelligence agencies can be discussed. The former concerns whether the agency is subject to some form of review or oversight by a body outside of the executive branch, and will be dealt with in Chapter 8. The latter concerns the extent to which the agency is independent from political or ministerial direction by the executive branch of the government and is dealt with here. These two are broadly synonymous with, respectively, Keller's 'insularity' and 'autonomy'[33] (see Chapter 2, p. 81).

There are two extreme possibilities with respect to ministerial control, both of which pose considerable dangers: either a complete lack of control or ministerial direction in the partisan interests of the governing party. The first of these was seen as inevitable by Sir Findlater Stewart who (as chairman of the Home Defence Committee) said that 'except on the very broadest lines' there should be no ministerial direction:

. . . having got the right man (as Director General) there is no alternative to giving him the widest discretion in the means he uses and the direction in which he applies them . . .[34]

217

There is, of course, nothing inevitable about this at all, but certainly elected ministers have often preferred to remain in ignorance, Echoing Findlater Stewart, Canadian Prime Minister Pierre Trudeau said in 1977:

> I have attempted to make it quite clear that the policy of this government, and I believe the previous governments in this country, has been that they . . . should be kept in ignorance of the day to day operations of the police force and even of the security force. I repeat that is not a view that is held in all democracies but it is our view and it is one we stand by. Therefore, in this particular case it is not a matter of pleading ignorance as an excuse. It is a matter of stating as principle that the particular minister of the day should not have a right to know what the police are doing constantly in their investigative practices, what they are looking at, and what they are looking for, and the way in which they are doing it.[35]

Acknowledging that a recent amendment to the Official Secrets Act had required the Solicitor General to be informed of some security operations, in order that he could sign the necessary warrant, Trudeau continued:

> I would be much concerned if knowledge of that particular investigative operation [tapping] by the security police were extended to all their operations and, indeed, if the Ministers were to know and therefore be held responsible for a lot of things taking place under the name of security or criminal investigation.[36]

The McDonald inquiry examined the extent to which ministers had given tacit assent to the RCMP to engage in illegal surveillance activities after the October Crisis of 1970. McDonald concluded that senior members of the RCMP had tried to have the question of illegal acts discussed by the Cabinet but that ministers had failed to resolve the question one way or another; that is, they had neither directed the RCMP to continue nor instructed them to desist from such activities.[37]

In the United States, once Hoover had his authorisation for the surveillance of 'subversive activities' from Roosevelt and Secretary of State Hull in 1936, he neither troubled attorneys general (his formal superiors) with further requests for authorisation nor did he inform them of what the FBI was doing unless *he* decided that there was some particular reason for doing so. At the same time he safeguarded his direct access to successive presidents with judicious use of the information gathered by the Bureau so that he became the real 'untouchable' in Washington. Only one Attorney General, Robert Kennedy, was able to prevent Hoover's by-passing him,[38] but this lasted only as long as his brother was in the White House. Immediately after President Kennedy's assassination, Hoover reverted to his usual practices.

In his testimony to the Church Committee, Nicholas Katzenbach, who was Attorney General during 1965–66, made clear the problems he faced in office. He argued that without the clearest proof of the utmost impropriety on the part of the FBI director, no attorney general could have won a political fight with him. Furthermore, Hoover's formal subordination worked in his favour in two ways: if criticised, Hoover was always able to rely on public support from his superior, even from Robert Kennedy,[39] while he was protected by his public reputation from interference by his superior. Katzenbach referred to his inability to control Hoover as one of the reasons why he resigned as attorney general after a relatively short time – 20 months – in the office.[40]

Several presidents were prepared to make use of the Bureau to gather information on political opponents, yet it was the lack of a clear legal basis for many FBI operations and Hoover's forced reliance on vague presidential directives that led him to become 'violently defensive' whenever the Bureau's authority for secret operations was questioned.[41] Again, the problem we come back to here is the vagueness of the mandate: it allowed presidents to benefit from political intelligence whether or not they had actually directed its accumulation. The difficulty of achieving meaningful ministerial control is reinforced both by 'need to know' and the doctrine of 'plausible deniability'.

'Need to know' is a basic organising principle of all security intelligence agencies and is aimed at minimising the chance that operational information will leak in such a way that operations, or sources are compromised. As we shall discuss below (see pp. 236–7), this also causes problems both within and between agencies, but it is used particularly against outsiders, including ministers. In general, security intelligence officers are nervous of politicians and their propensity to indiscretion. This principle was institutionalised in the UK first in the 1945 Findlater Stewart memorandum and then in the Maxwell-Fyfe Directive to the Director General of the Security Service, which superseded it in 1952:

> You and your staff will maintain the well-established convention whereby Ministers do not concern themselves with the detailed information which may be obtained by the Security Service in particular cases, but are furnished with such information only as may be necessary for the determination of any issue on which guidance is sought.[42]

The only issues on which regular guidance would appear to have been sought from Home Secretaries before 1989 were Security Service applications for warrants for the interception of telephone or mail communications, a procedure that was placed on a statutory footing in 1985 with the passage of the Interception of Communications Act. This was extended by the 1989 Security Service Act to cover other 'interferences with property' (s.3). Before then it did not appear that ministers were regularly consulted about the use of any surveillance technique apart from telephone or mail intercepts.[43]

More controversial is 'plausible deniability'. In essence this refers to an operation which involves illegality or political embarrassment but which the security intelligence agency considers necessary. Should the operation become public knowledge (some will, by their very nature, many will not) it is considered essential that ministers are able to deny any knowledge of the operation in such a way that they can be believed. This doctrine encourages the invention of false information which will be acceptable to other government agencies, the courts and the public.[44] The best way of achieving this is if ministers *do* know nothing of the operation, and this 'principle' has been written into legislation. In C-157, the first attempt to legislate after the

McDonald Report in Canada, the government proposed that the minister could give only general directions to CSIS and could not override particular decisions by the Director of the Service as to the groups or individuals to be targeted. This proposal was much criticised and was changed in the subsequent Bill which became the CSIS Act, so that plausible deniability was not 'erected into a statutory principle'.[45] The ASIO Act 1979 contained similar limitations on ministerial direction to those of C-157, but in 1986 the independence of the Director General of ASIO was preserved only in the matter of the advice given by ASIO to other agencies.[46]

The ignorance of ministers may be utilised by security intelligence agencies as part of a structure of deniability. For example, on several occasions in the UK during recent years the Attorney General appears to have been drawn into government disinformation campaigns with respect to security intelligence matters. One of these was the Zircon affair of 1987. In November 1985 BBC Scotland commissioned Duncan Campbell to make a series of six programmes to be entitled *Secret Society*. One of these concerned the government's secret plans to construct an independent British SIGINT satellite, on which subject, the programme alleged, ministers had misled Parliament. The government's initial attempts to prevent the broadcasting of the programme involved seeking a civil injunction, but when this was delivered to Campbell too late to prevent the publication of an associated article in the *New Statesman*, the government's strategy switched to criminal procedures under the Official Secrets Act. According to constitutional doctrine in the UK, at this point government decision-making should have switched from any collective Cabinet discussion to the individual decisions of the Attorney General regarding criminal investigation and possible prosecution.[47] This, according to the Home Secretary in the subsequent emergency debate, is what happened.[48] The police obtained search warrants, first for the offices of the *New Statesman* and the homes of those who researched the programme, and, a week later, for the offices of BBC Scotland from which the police eventually removed all the material relating to all six programmes in the series. When the question was raised as to why the Security Service's legal adviser,

Bernard Sheldon, had been involved in discussions of the police's action, the Solicitor General denied it.

> The Hon. Gentleman also mentioned Mr. Sheldon in connection with the recent searches of BBC Premises. I am informed that neither that official nor the Security Service had any involvement at all in any decisions or actions relating to this matter.[49]

On the face of it this is an extraordinary statement. Faced with what the government saw as a major breach of national security and the Official Secrets Act, the Security Service, with the prime responsibility for such matters, had no involvement in any of the decisions relating to that breach!

The most likely hypothesis for the role played in these proceedings by the law officers – the Attorney General and Solicitor General – is that of the 'cut-out'; either witting or unwitting. A cut-out is often required to appear as the originating agency in order to preserve the identity of the real originating agency. The latter in this case were clearly the security intelligence agencies and the Prime Minister. However, the rhetoric of the rule of law does not permit the political direction of the criminal justice process; therefore there is a need for the appearance of independence, and this is provided by the Attorney General. That independence derives, we are told, from the fact that the Attorney General is not a member of the Cabinet and makes independent decisions in criminal matters; but, as an elected politician and a member of the government, has the advantage, from the government's point of view, of being in tune with its overall political objectives. Thus the official doctrine of independent decision-making by the Attorney General in cases such as this should be seen as a presentational device which provides a legitimation for government actions ('independent law officers overseeing the criminal process') rather than as an actual explanation of those actions. A more accurate explanation in this case would be that of the security intelligence agencies and their ministers seeking to stifle embarrassing political disclosures.[50] The role of the law officers in the Westland and *Spycatcher* sagas can be examined for signs of similar use by ministers of the law officers to mount deniable operations.

In other words there are a variety of organisational and political pressures which lead to the situation of large-scale ministerial ignorance of security intelligence operations. The question is whether this is the best way of ensuring either that a government's security intelligence needs are fulfilled or that security intelligence agencies are not engaged in unacceptable or unnecessary operations.

The McDonald Commission recommended a variety of areas which should be covered by ministerial directions, including guidelines regarding investigative techniques and reporting arrangements, review of the agency's progress in establishing personnel and management policies required by government, review of operational decisions involving questions of legality and the mandate, ensuring that the agency's targeting priorities accord with those of the government, approving proposals for applications for judicial authorisation of investigative techniques where required, and approving liaison arrangements with other agencies. In addition the minister should be responsible for developing policy proposals for administrative and legislative changes to be presented to the Cabinet and Parliament.[51] The Commission recommended also that the day-to-day ministerial involvement be exercised at Deputy Minister (a civil service position in Canada) level and this was the essential structure established in the CSIS Act.

Since 1984 over 50 ministerial directions have been issued to CSIS, grouped into seven major categories: arrangements regarding the Director's accountability to the minister, the government's annual priorities, guidance on CSIS's statutory functions, guidance on investigative techniques, management practices, standards for co-operative arrangements with other agencies, and policy on the management of files and records.[52] The Australian legislation not only permits the minister to give ASIO directions, but actually obliges their doing so regarding investigations of 'politically motivated violence'.[53] These were tabled in Parliament in June 1988 before being promulgated within ASIO.[54]

In the UK the situation remained less formalised as far as domestic security intelligence was concerned, at least until the passage of the Security Service Act. In general, ministers and permanent secretaries would leave the security service to get on with what it considered to be its business. Permanent secretaries would brief incoming ministers on the issues likely to be raised by the Security Service, would try to seek out the minister's general attitude on what s/he did or did not want to know and would then act accordingly. This does not differ markedly from the relationship between permanent secretaries and ministers in other policy areas, but would be aggravated in the case of security intelligence by the lack of any direct hierarchical relationship between, say, the Home Secretary and the Director General.[55] In Northern Ireland the situation is different in that the Director and Co-ordinator of Intelligence would report directly to the permanent secretary of the NIO, as well as to the Director General.

Ministerial reluctance to intervene has been reinforced by the general mystification surrounding intelligence matters in the UK.[56] Therefore, the prime determinant of the extent of ministerial interest in the Security Service will be the press of events; for example, some major incident or scandal resulting in public arousal would increase ministerial interest above the normally minimal levels.[57] Therefore it might be suggested that there is a direct correlation between the autonomy of the security intelligence agency and public ignorance or apathy. Of course, to the extent that security intelligence matters remain shrouded in unnecessary secrecy, being publicised normally only through state (dis)information policies, this autonomy will be self-reinforcing.

On the other hand, serious problems may arise if there is either too much ministerial direction, or direction of a particular kind. Since ministers are amateurs, it is said, their guidance should be restricted to a clear enunciation of government intelligence priorities and overall questions of organisation and budgets. Second, it would be quite wrong, so the argument goes, for elected politicians to make use of this particularly sensitive part of the state apparatus to achieve some political advantage for their own party or supporters and officers must be protected from attempts to use them in this way. In the UK, the Maxwell-Fyfe Directive acknowledged this:

> It is essential that the Security Service should be kept absolutely free from any political bias or influence and nothing should be done that might lend colour to any

suggestion that it is concerned with the interests of any particular section of the community, or with any other matter than the Defence of the Realm as a whole.[58]

This might be compared with the 1989 Security Service Act which refers only to a prohibition of work in support of a political party and says nothing about working against parties.[59] However, the issue goes deeper. This official view depends on an assumption that, whereas particular governments may have partisan views, the state reflects some overall consensus about the goals of and threats to society.

This assumption is rarely justified; whatever the view taken of the debate about the partisan nature of the state in general, there can be no doubt that security intelligence agencies in North America and the UK have all behaved in a highly partisan fashion. This has resulted not just from a minister issuing orders to an otherwise neutral agency but also because shared assumptions between particular governments and their security intelligence agencies have made formal partisan direction unnecessary.

In the UK, before the 1983 general election, Michael Heseltine established DS-19 in the Ministry of Defence to co-ordinate a government publicity campaign against CND, which was gaining in popularity at that time. The Security Service was asked for material and, according to some, refused the request, eventually reaching a compromise that it would provide only material obtained from open sources.[60] However, as Cathy Massiter revealed,[61] a telephone tap was also placed on John Cox, a CND vice-president. This could be done without the Security Service being seen to indulge in partisan activity because Cox was a member of the Communist Party, formally a subversive organisation and therefore within the Maxwell-Fyfe Directive. Of course such a tap enabled information to be gathered on many other CND officials who had nothing to do with the Communist Party.

Morton Halperin, Director of the American Civil Liberties Union (ACLU), has argued that most of the abuses of civil liberties by security intelligence agencies in the US came from presidents seeking to spy on and manipulate their political opponents rather than from career officials. Halperin cites examples of this through several administrations: Franklin D. Roosevelt's orders to the FBI to investigate those wanting to preserve US neutrality in the Second World War, John F. Kennedy's orders to the Bureau to investigate the sugar industries and Lyndon B. Johnson's orders to the FBI to spy on people at the 1964 Democratic Party Convention.[62] Also during Johnson's administration, Attorney General Robert Kennedy proposed to the President that the FBI use its 'special techniques' of information-gathering against the Ku Klux Klan and in 1967, following the Detroit and Newark riots, Attorney General Ramsey Clark instructed the Bureau to 'use the maximum available' intelligence resources to gather information relating to civil disorders.[63] Attempts have been made to protect employees subjected to improper pressure and these are discussed in Chapter 7.

ORGANISATIONAL RESOURCES AND RECRUITMENT

Historically, the resources available to the UK Security Service have ebbed and flowed as between wartime and peace. MI5 was rapidly expanded at the onset of both world wars: at the end of the first its staff was over 800 but by 1925 had fallen to 30. In 1931 civilian intelligence staff were transferred to MI5 from the Metropolitan Special Branch and from 1934 on the Service continued to grow so that by September 1938 it had 30 officers, 120 secretarial and registry staff and a surveillance section – 'Watchers' – of six men. By the outbreak of the Second World War this had grown to 83 officers and 253 support staff (almost all women), and by January 1941 to 234 officers and 676 support staff (of whom 634 were women).[64] A 'large number of its personnel'[65] were again returned to civilian life during 1944–45, but the run-down was never as thorough as after 1918, and the cold war ensured a steadier size. There are now 2,000 people employed in the Security Service, 340 of whom are in the General Intelligence Group working as case officers and analysts. The rest are support staff.[66]

Very little is known about the size of the Security Service budget. Eunan O'Halpin has tried to put together a picture of the funding of the intelligence community in general from various sources. He has had some success with the early decades of the twentieth century, regarding, for example, expenditure on the passport control organisation, the traditional cover for SIS operations, and the Government Code and Cypher School (the forerunner of GCHQ). As far as the Security Service is concerned, O'Halpin notes that 'books on MI5 contain no worthwhile information on financial matters, and very little evidence of its funding has been found'. He observes that the Security Service budget was cut from £80,000 to £35,000 between 1919 and 1920, but acknowledges that these figures are incomplete since some of its staff costs would have been carried on the ordinary War Office vote at this time.[67] During the same period, and in the context of the continuing struggle for influence between the Security Service and the Special Branch, Basil Thomson, head of the latter, proposed a new organisation for the co-ordination of domestic security intelligence gathering and, to ensure its autonomy from the future possibility of an unsympathetic Labour government, proposed also that £1 million be invested, the income from which would provide a secure and independent budget. There is no evidence that this proposal was implemented.[68] More recent attempts at estimating the size and costs of security intelligence agencies in the UK are summarised in Table 6.1.

The size of police Special Branches has fluctuated similarly: between 1883 and 1909 membership fluctuated up to 38, by 1913 it had risen to 72 or more, and by November 1918 to about 700.[69] By 1920 this had dropped to 120 but in 1934 was increased again up to about 200.[70] Apart from an increase during 1939–45, the size remained at this level through the 1950s. From 1961 small Special Branches were established in some provincial forces, but

Table 6.1 Estimated Security Intelligence Budgets and Staff, UK

| | 1985* | | 1990** | |
	Budget	Staff	Budget	Staff
Police Special Branches	£40m	1,500	£20m	2,000
Security Service (MI5)	£160m	2,000	£200m	2,000
Secret Intelligence Service (MI6)	£140m	3,000	£160m	3,000
GCHQ	£600m	11,500	£260m–750m	7,000

*   D. Leigh and P. Lashmar, *The Observer*, 3 March 1985.
** R. Norton-Taylor, *In Defence of the Realm?* (1990), pp 42, 46, 50, 52.

by 1968 there were fewer than 50 in these squads, alongside about 300 then in the Metropolitan Police.[71] By 1984 there were 446 in the Met (including 73 on port duties and 67 on personal protection) and about 870 elsewhere in England and Wales, many of whom would also have been in port units – for example, 73 out of 108 in Merseyside.[72] By this time there were also other police squads, established as 'offshoots' of Special Branch, such as the Illegal Immigrants Intelligence Unit and the Anti-Terrorist Branch.

As far as Special Branch budgets are concerned, the Association of Metropolitan Authorities collated information in 1984 on those branches within the six metropolitan counties and City of London, see Table 6.2.

More information is available about domestic security intelligence agencies elsewhere. For example, as of June 1988 ASIO had 735 staff and its budgetary allocation for 1987–88 was $Aus35.73 million.[73] CSIS's expenditure for the same year was $Can136.86 million, and its estimated expenditure for 1991–92 was $Can214 million. SIRC noted that the rapid increase in expenditure on CSIS during 1989–92 was due to major capital expenditure on new headquarters and computers, rather than reflecting any increase in operations.[74]

Security intelligence agencies have always resisted publishing more detailed breakdowns of budgets and staff allocations, on the grounds that the information would help their targets to take their own countering measures against the agencies' penetration efforts. This leaves a central question unanswered: to what extent do the size of staffs and their internal distribution between the main organisational branches reflect a realistic appraisal of the threats to the domestic security or, alternatively, a misallocation of resources based on misperceptions? A number of factors may

Table 6.2   Special Branch Budgets, 1984

	GMC	City	Mersey-side	Northumberland	W. Mids	S. Yorks	W.Yorks	Total
Total Officers	53	4	108	35	73	19	39	331
(Port Unit)	24	–	73	6	21	–	8	132
Total cost (£m)	1.14	0.1	2.2	0.5	1.3	0.3	0.7	6.3

Source: AMA Police Panel Working Party on Accountability.

combine to produce a considerable lag between the agency and the world with which it relates. These include 'grooved thinking' where officials respond to new cases in terms of previously established organisational rules and working practices.[75] Also, agencies may fail to distinguish between real and imagined threats – bearing in mind the fact that the state might actually 'need' enemies[76] – and changes in the allocation of resources only tend to occur incrementally. Also, there is pure manipulation. When William Sullivan, then third in seniority in the FBI, was publicly critical of Hoover's ability to understand the changing nature of the internal security threat in the US, specifically that unrest had nothing to do with the Communist Party, he later told Senate investigators that 'all hell broke loose'. 'How do you expect me to get my appropriations if you keep downgrading the [Communist] Party?' asked Hoover.[77]

Once ASIO Annual Reports started to be published officially, the information in the published version was less comprehensive than their previously unpublished reports had been. For example, their 1979–80 Report was leaked including information on the functional allocation of staff:

Table 6.3 Allocation of ASIO Staff
Members, October 1980

	%
Management	4.5
Administration	16.0
Collection	44.5
Information Management	16.0
Assessment	10.5
Protective Security	1.5
Security Checking	4.5
Liaison	1.5
Training	1.0

Source: Richelson and Ball, *The Ties That Bind* (1990), p. 50.

Additional information provided on the allocation of staff to the different sections of the mandate make it possible to calculate that 11.9 per cent of the organisation's staff resources were allocated to the collection and assessment of information relating to 'subversive studies' and 9.7 per cent to 'politically motivated violence'. This is similar to the 10 per cent found to be allocated

229

to counter-subversion by CSIS in SIRC's counter subversion study.[78] In 1993 the Security Service published its first pro-motional literature, which included the information that 70 per cent of its resources were allocated to counter-terrorism, 25 per cent to counter-intelligence and 5 per cent to counter-subversion.[79] (See Figure 6.2.)

The question of recruitment to security intelligence agencies is particularly important because, if it merely reflects the political dominance of certain classes or groups, partisan direction by ministers will not be a problem since it will usually be unnecessary. For example, in the FBI the only black agents for many years were Hoover's personal servants and the Director's racism permeated the Bureau.[80] In Canada the RCMP, including its security service, was dominated by anglophones, and the issue of the status of francophone agents continued to dog the new CSIS in its early years.[81] Some of the greatest controversies surrounding the FBI and the RCMP concerned their respective investigations of the black civil rights movement in the US and the separatist movement in Quebec.

A central feature of modern states is that recruitment to its administrative apparatuses becomes based less on patronage and more on impersonal and competitive educational criteria.[82] Until the late 1970s the UK Security Service was apparently able to resist this trend. Recruitment between the wars was by personal introduction which was believed to be the best guarantor of loyalty and integrity, and most recruits were middle-aged retired men from the public services, whose pensions cushioned them against the low salaries.[83] During the post-war period most recruits were ex-police officers, armed forces personnel and former officials from the declining colonial service. A number of criticisms of recruitment have been voiced, even by conservatives: Lord Carver has criticised procedures which seemed to him to operate 'on the basis that, provided the man or woman is a friend of a friend of a friend, he or she must be all right' and Lord Beloff perceived that the Service was 'employing people whose degree of political sensitivity was rather low'.[84] Regarding recruitment to MI5, Porter concludes his historical survey:

> They had always been an odd bunch . . . socially and politically entirely untypical of the nation as a whole,

Figure 6.2 Structure of Security Service

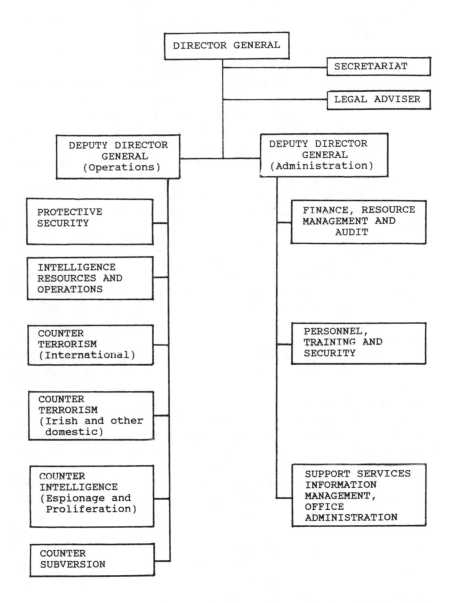

Source: adapted from Home Office, *The Security Service* (London: HMSO, 1993), p.11.

eccentric and often not very bright. This does not seem to have changed appreciably by the 1970s.[85]

This autonomy from developments in the rest of the state was both cause and effect of a certain 'backwardness' in the Security Service. In 1976, in an effort to broaden the recruitment base to MI5, James Callaghan and Merlyn Rees insisted that the Service go through Civil Service Commission procedures, and that appears to have had some impact.[86] More recently, faced with recruitment problems, the Security Service commissioned a private personnel firm to examine its policy and sought ways of discreetly advertising for recruits.[87] ASIO has made use of an advertising agency[88] and CSIS has recruited openly via over 100 newspapers.[89]

Because the FBI is primarily a highly public police force, we know more about its recruitment procedures than about domestic security intelligence agencies elsewhere. 'Special agents' are recruited from those who have a first degree. They then sit a variety of written examinations, attend a formal interview, and then undergo the US equivalent of positive vetting, including possibly a polygraph test. If successful at all these stages the candidate then attends for 15 weeks' basic training which incorporates a further series of physical and academic examinations.[90]

In common with the rest of the state sector, women have been under-represented in security intelligence agencies and have tended to be concentrated in clerical and administrative jobs. Women comprised 39.4 per cent of ASIO staff in 1988 but, whereas three-quarters of clerical staff were women, only 17.5 per cent of intelligence officers were.[91] CSIS has been attempting to detach itself from the white, anglophone, male image of the days of the RCMP. The Commons Special Review Committee reported that the proportion of francophones recruited to CSIS had increased significantly since 1984, although it also noted continuing complaints of discrimination against francophone employees.[92] The proportion of women in CSIS increased from 36 to 43 per cent between 1984 and 1991, and from seven to 20 per cent among intelligence officers[93] but the Parliamentary Committee was critical of the minimal improvement in the representation of women at supervisory levels.[94]

With regard to recruitment from minorities, federal privacy requirements in Canada prevent ethnic monitoring,[95] but CSIS reported that between 1988 and 1991 'visible minorities' increased from 0.6 to 2.45 per cent of employees.[96] In Australia, ASIO reported that 7.2 per cent of its employees were from non-English-speaking backgrounds, compared with 12.1 per cent in the Australian Public Service as a whole.[97] Under Hoover the FBI was notoriously an organisation dominated by white men and when William Webster became Director in 1978 there were still only 91 women agents.[98] Table 6.4 shows the changes which occurred in the FBI during the 1980s.

By comparison, we have virtually no information on the gender and ethnic mix within the UK security intelligence agencies. Based on the general criticisms of recruitment that were referred to above, the likeliest hypothesis is that the recruitment of ethnic minorities has been minimal, and that of women has been predominantly to clerical grades. Peter Wright gives us some indication of the Security Service view of the role of women:

> The Registry employed enormous numbers of girls to maintain efficient delivery of files within the building, as well as the massive task of sorting, checking and filing the incoming material. In Kell's day (ie until 1940) the Registry Queens as they were known, were recruited either from the aristocracy or from the families of MI5 officers. Kell had a simple belief that this was the best vetting of all. The debutantes were often very pretty, as well as wealthy, which

Table 6.4 Minorities and Women in the FBI 1978–89

| | Numbers and percentages of Special Agents | | | | | | | | | | |
| | Native-American | | Asian-American | | African-American | | Hispanic-American | | Women | | Total |
	No.	%	No.	%	No.	%	No.	%	No.	%	No.
1978	23	0.3	40	0.5	185	2.3	173	2.2	147	1.9	7,900
1989	39	0.4	120	1.2	432	4.5	482	5.0	910	9.4	9,650

Source: adapted from Hearings before the Subcommittee on Civil and Constitutional Rights, Committee on the Judiciary, House of Representatives, *FBI Oversight and Authorization Request for Fiscal Year 1991* (1990), p. 475.

accounts for the large numbers of office marriages, to the point where it became something of a joke that the average life expectancy of a Registry Queen was nine months – the time it took her to get pregnant.[99]

The other group most discriminated against historically in terms of recruitment to the security intelligence agencies has been homosexuals. Until the 1980s in the UK homosexuality remained an absolute bar to receiving the positive vetting clearance required for work in the security intelligence agencies and other areas of the state sector. The effectiveness of the security intelligence agencies at enforcing their own policy does not appear to have been conspicuously successful, however. For example, Anthony Cavendish, in his book written to defend his old friend Maurice Oldfield against smears deriving from Oldfield's homosexuality, comments that there were'numerous . . . active homosexuals in MI6'.[100] More recently there has been some sign of change in the official position. The House of Commons Defence Select Committee held an inquiry into positive vetting in 1983 and were told by the MOD that they followed guidelines established by the Security Commission in 1982, which said that each case should be judged on its merits. Stable and acknowledged homosexual relationships would not necessarily lead to a vetting failure; however, subsequently a number of civil servants approached the First Division Association because they had been denied clearance even though they were celibate or in stable relationships.[101] In July 1991 the Prime Minister announced a further change in the rules, saying that no longer would homosexuality represent an automatic bar to the highest levels of security clearance, except in the armed forces where homosexual acts remained disciplinary offences.[102]

Positive vetting is one thing, but recruitment is another. There is some distance between formal declarations of shifts in official policy and actual changes in agencies' recruitment policies where questions of organisational sub-culture are so important (see below). In the US in the mid-1980s intelligence agencies were still not recruiting homosexuals, although there had been a case at the National Security Agency in 1980 when officials allowed a man who said he was homosexual to keep the job he already had.[103]

The Security Commission inquiry into the Bettaney case heard considerable evidence which was critical of the internal organisation and management within the Security Service. Its report published in May 1985 noted that most senior managers did not accept those criticisms, but the Security Commission itself clearly did.[104] Noting that such training in personnel management as there was took place in-house, the Security Commission could not accept that the reliance on 'massive and indigestible volumes' of Conditions of Service and Section Duties actually constituted a personnel policy, and required that practices be revised in the light of the Cassels Report on Personnel Work in the Civil Service (1983).[105]

In Canada the McDonald Inquiry considered a range of personnel matters: the kinds of personnel required in a security intelligence agency, methods of recruiting, policies relating to secondments, career paths, training, whether employees should be public servants, the issue of unionisation, and counselling, discipline and grievance procedures. Numerous recommendations were made on these matters; for example, that people should be recruited from a wider variety of backgrounds (not too many ex-RCMP officers), greater attention be given to career paths and secondments, employees should not be public servants and should not be able to unionise, and that confidential employee-counselling be established.[106] There is no evidence that such matters have received more than piecemeal consideration in the UK.

ORGANISATIONAL CULTURE AND COMMUNICATIONS

In Chapter 2 we identified a number of information-control processes which contributed to our model of the relationship between security intelligence agencies and society. Here we are concerned briefly with similar processes within such agencies. Robert Mandel discusses four 'clusters of distortions' to which the intelligence process is prone. One of these – the insuperable difficulties of targeting and evaluation – has already been discussed in Chapters 4 and 5. A second cluster concerns the proficiency and personality limitations of individual officials.[107] For example, problems will result from people's self-imposed conformity in the face of some perceived organisational 'dominant ideology' as referred to by Miranda Ingram.[108] On the other hand, Stephen Emerson shows how such conformity may be imposed from above, as in the CIA's analytical directorate in the 1980s.[109]

Another, more subtle, process is 'group-think' to which security intelligence agencies might seem to be particularly vulnerable:

> The more amiability and *esprit de corps* among the members of a policy-making in-group, the greater is the danger that independent critical thinking will be replaced by group-think, which is likely to result in irrational and dehumanising actions directed against out-groups.[110]

This might even degenerate into the kind of paranoia that seems to have inflicted the UK Security Service at various times, most notoriously in giving rise to the mole-hunts against senior members of the Service.[111]

Mandel's third cluster was of internal bureaucratic obstacles such as compartmentalisation and organisational politics. Some of the reasoning behind the need-to-know principle and its impact on the ministerial role has already been discussed. However, it has wider ramifications. The McDonald Commission examined the operation of the principle within the RCMP Security Service and the problems to which it could give rise. These could include employees excluded from knowing certain things becoming frustrated and fearing that their exclusion reflected on their competence, that teamwork and co-operation between different units could be hampered, that the quality of decisions might be adversely affected because the number of people able to comment is minimal, and, finally, it might be used as a rationale to cover up some abuse.[112] Bearing in mind what was said in Chapter 2 about the operation of information-control processes both within and between 'social units', it is not difficult to see how security intelligence agencies, being quite small, operating secretly and having these restrictions on internal communication can become seedbeds for a variety of organisational pathologies.

The Bettaney case highlighted the problems which can occur in security intelligence agencies when the genuine needs of security and secrecy become overlaid with unnecessary levels so that the genuine requirement for 'need-to-know' restrictions acts as a brake on communication within the agency and normal personnel management is impossible. Even within ordinary police agencies the problems of supervisors are considerable because of the wide discretion available to patrol officers and because of the low visibility of their actions. Thus much supervision is carried out on the basis of written reports by officers,[113] reports which can normally be relied upon to tell a plausible story. The problems of supervisors in security intelligence agencies are not exactly the same, but because of the 'need-to-know' practice might actually be worse.

Personal and bureaucratic factors can be combined within the concept of organisational sub-cultures. Their relevance to explaining what organisations actually do has been most clearly demonstrated in research into policing. In his overview of police research Robert Reiner concludes:

> An understanding of how police officers see the social world and their role in it – 'cop culture' – is crucial to analysis of what they do and their broad political function. It is a commonplace of the now voluminous sociological literature on police operations and discretion that the rank-and-file officer is the primary determinant of policing where it really counts – on the street.[114]

As was discussed in Chapter 2, it would be a mistake to see cop culture as leading to an 'abuse' model of police deviance in which the problem is solely that cop culture deviates from the requirements of due process; rather, given the permissive nature of the law, it is cop culture which accounts for the ways in which police occupy the space left by formal legal enactments. Security intelligence agencies are sufficiently similar to police (in some cases they are 'police' agencies), to enable us to consider it highly likely that sub-cultures play a similar role there. Stuart Farson, for example, examines in some detail the dangers of examining security intelligence agencies without bearing this in mind. He points out that the McDonald Commission in Canada and the subsequent legislation rested their analyses of what had 'gone wrong' in the RCMP, and how future problems might best be prevented, on formal organisational models constructed from new legal rules and oversight structures. In comparison, equally important questions of organisational culture in the security intelligence agency were relatively ignored until subsequent inquiries demonstrated how resistant the agency had been to the formal changes.[115]

There is one aspect of the difference between police and security intelligence agencies which is important here and adds another dimension to the consideration of organisational culture. Police forces may be very large and are organised hierarchically, with the added rigidity that derives from uniforms, ranks and internal disciplinary codes. This is the context within which the rank-and-file cop culture thrives and protects itself by passing only sanitised reports of incidents and events up the hierarchy, so that the most misinformed member of the organisation may well be the Chief Constable.[116] Security intelligence agencies, by comparison, are small, and hierarchies minimal, with the different levels of junior and senior officers relating primarily to salary rather than position or job.[117] The main restrictions on internal organisational communications, therefore, are less those characterising the police hierarchy and more those based on the 'need-to-know' regarding specific operations. This does not mean that organisational culture will be unimportant, but that it will operate differently in security intelligence than in police agencies. Specifically, there is less likely to be an essentially rank-and-file culture, a major part of which is 'protecting' the bosses from knowledge of what happens on the street, than that there will be a shared organisational culture incorporating both senior and junior officials.

One indicator of this is the extent to which they share a view of the agency's 'mission'. A sense of mission is one central aspect of cop culture[118] but, given the multiple and often conflicting goals of police,[119] the sense of mission may be fractured into competing views of what police should be doing, and one of the main fractures may be between rank-and-file and supervisory officers. Compared with the 'low' police, the goals of security intelligence agencies – 'high' police – are *relatively* unambiguous, centring as they do on the protection of the state uncomplicated by those service and regulatory functions which accrue to police. Put another way, compared with police, it is likely that there will be a relatively homogeneous acceptance of the dominant political mission throughout security intelligence agencies,[120] which does produce fertile ground for 'group-think'.

Another indicator of this phenomenon will be the way in which actions taken by the agency which are illegal but which are deemed to be necessary to achieve organisational objectives, will be dealt with by senior managers. Few, if any, will invoke sanctions on every occasion. Research would suggest that technically illegal behaviour will be condoned by senior managers to the extent that it is consistent with organisational objectives and will only be sanctioned if, for example, it is carried out in opposition to organisational objectives or for personal gain.[121] Clearly, this has great significance for proposals as to the reform of oversight of security intelligence agencies, which will be discussed in Chapters 7 and 8.

The possibility of conflicts between different groups which reflect in part different 'sub-cultures', should not be excluded, however. These might best be analysed from the perspective of policy analysts. Graham Allison, for example, provides a model of 'bureaucratic politics' which seeks to explain governmental actions as the result of bargaining 'games' among 'players' in different positions within bureaucracies, who have varying parochial priorities, perspectives, goals and interests.[122] Allison's model can be criticised for ignoring the important structural constraints upon bureaucracies[123] but it does alert us to the role that might be played by 'micro-politics' in the practices of security intelligence agencies. The conflicts between different sub-cultures has been discussed, for example, in the case of the CIA by William Colby.[124]

Applying such a model might appear to contradict the idea of 'group-think', which rests on the notion of conformity rather than conflict. In fact it can be seen how security intelligence agencies might be prone to either or both of these: the point of such models is to use them to suggest profitable lines of inquiry. Therefore the question to be asked is: under what conditions and organisational structures is organisational effectiveness hindered either by 'group-think' or by bureaucratic politics, or by both?

Mandel's fourth cluster of distortions related to 'the absence of effective external guidance both from governmental sources outside the intelligence community and from non-government sources.[125] We have considered the first part of this in the section on the ministerial role; in the next chapter we examine questions of external oversight.

CONCLUSION

The main theme of this chapter has been to suggest that the links between different types of security intelligence are continuous and that there should be no automatic assumption of the need for a security intelligence agency separate from the police. There are arguments for separating the two, but the problem of turf wars and poor (or non-existent) co-ordination is a strong argument for minimising the number of different agencies engaged in the security intelligence process. Similarly, an agency with police powers may pose more of a potential threat to liberties, but one without these powers does not have to face the limited discipline of having to rationalise its information-gathering and countering activities within the context of the criminal justice process.

Whatever type of agency is finally considered to be appropriate, the next key question is how autonomous of political control it should be. Inquiries into security intelligence have shown how, left to their own devices, agencies tend to become more like 'political police' or even 'independent security states' (see Chapter 2) and the trend in the last 20 years has been to try to check the autonomy of agencies. Since this raises, in turn, the opposite problem, that agencies become subject to direction for partisan purposes, safeguards must be developed which break down the isolation of agencies in other ways, for example protecting the rights of whistleblowers.

Historically, the autonomy of security intelligence agencies in the UKUSA countries has been maintained by highly restrictive recruitment. It is not simply that they have been the preserve of white males – other state agencies have been so also – but that recruitment from particularly narrow social groups has led to the highly partial definition of targets, as we discussed in Chapter 3. Recruitment from a broader social base is a necessary, though not a sufficient, condition for agencies to act in defence of a broader conception of the public interest than has been the historical case in the UK.

The phenomenon by which organisational culture (and clashing sub-cultures) determine what organisations actually do is well-known. In the case of security intelligence agencies its role is reinforced by secrecy and autonomy to such an extent that it can amount to organisational paranoia. This cannot be tackled by structural and legal changes alone; it requires the widest attention to control, recruitment, training and oversight.

NOTES

1. J.T. Richelson and D. Ball, *The Ties That Bind* (Boston: Unwin Hyman, 2nd edition, 1990), p. 281.
2. J. Shattuck, 'National Security a Decade After', *Democracy*, 3(1), 1983, p. 67.
3. Cf B. Buzan, *People, States and Fear* (Hemel Hempstead: Harvester Wheatsheaf, 2nd edition, 1991), pp. 112–14.
4. For example, see R. Norton-Taylor, *In Defence of the Realm?* (London: Civil Liberties Trust, 1990), p. 53 regarding GCHQ and surveillance regarding 'subversion'.
5. Cf the 'zones of ambiguity' identified by R. Crelinsten, 'Terrorism, Counterterrorism and National Security', in P. Hanks and J.D. McCamus, *National Security: Surveillance and Accountability in a Democratic Society* (Cowansville, Québec: Les Editions Yvon Blais, 1989), pp. 207–25.
6. An official statement of this view is given in the Report to the Solicitor General by the Independent Advisory Team on the CSIS, *People and Process in Transition* (Ottawa: Minister of Supply and Services, 1987).
7. F.T. Martens, 'The Intelligence Function', in P.P. Andrews Jr. and M.B. Peterson (eds), *Criminal Intelligence Analysis* (Loomis, CA; Palmer Enterprises, 1990), pp. 4–10.
8. The research evidence on this point is summarised in R. Reiner, *The Politics of the Police* (Hemel Hempstead: Harvester Wheatsheaf, 2nd edition, 1992), pp. 139–46.
9. R. Baldwin and R. Kinsey, *Police Powers and Politics* (London: Quartet, 1982), pp. 30–51; M. Weatheritt, *Innovations in Policing* (Beckenham: Croom Helm, 1986), pp. 88–98.
10. Baldwin and Kinsey, ibid, pp. 59–103.
11. N. Dorn, *Intelligence Development, The National Criminal*

Intelligence Service, and the Ascendancy of the Intelligence Officer over the Detective in the Centralisation of Policing in Britain, paper for British Criminology Conference, University of York, July 1991.

12. *The Guardian*, 23 July 1992, p. 8. T.G. Poveda, *Lawlessness and Reform* (Pacific Grove, CA; Brooks/Cole, 1989), p. 151 refers to similar changes in the US.

13. Weatheritt, supra (note 9), pp. 118–24.

14. Home Office, *Guidelines on the Work of a Special Branch*, mimeo, December 1984.

15. J.-P. Brodeur, 'High Policing and Low Policing', *Social Problems*, 30(5), June 1983, pp. 513–15.

16. Crelinsten, supra (note 5), p. 218. A.T. Turk, *Political Criminality* (Beverly Hills: Sage, 1982) makes the same point, pp. 122–3.

17. S. Farson, 'Criminal Intelligence Versus Security Intelligence: A Re-evaluation of the Police Role in the Response to Terrorism', in D.A. Charters (ed.), *Democratic Responses to International Terrorism* (Ardsley-on-Hudson, NY: Transnational Publishers, 1991), especially pp. 198–9.

18. McDonald, Second Report, *Freedom and Security under the Law* (Ottawa: Minister of Supply and Services, 1981), pp. 754–8.

19. Farson, supra (note 17), p. 212.

20. McDonald, supra (note 18), p. 614.

21. J.-P. Brodeur, 'Criminal Justice and National Security' in Hanks and McCamus, supra (note 5), p. 66.

22. Cf discussion of the SAS in Gibraltar in 1988 in Chapter 5 pp. 182–3.

23. For full details see R. Cleroux, *Official Secrets: The Story Behind the CSIS* (Scarborough, Ontario: McGraw-Hill Ryerson, 1990), pp. 1–30 and J.L. Granatstein and D. Stafford, *Spy Wars: Espionage and Canada from Gouzenko to Glasnost* (Toronto: Key Porter Books, 1990), pp. 245–51.

24. SIRC, *Annual Report* for 1987–88, (Ottawa: Minister of Supply and Services, 1988), p. 2.

25. V. Marchetti and J.D. Marks, *The CIA and the Cult of Intelligence* (New York: Dell, 1980), pp. 178–9.

26. Ibid, pp. 191–3.

27. Report by Chief Ombudsman, *Security Intelligence Service* (Wellington: Government Printer, 1976), pp. 69–70.

28. Richelson and Ball, supra (note 1), p. 246.

29. ASIO, *Report to Parliament 1987–88* (Canberra: Australian Government Printing Service, 1989), pp. 33–5.
30. *The Guardian*, 15 April 1992, p. 3; 23 April 1992, p. 2.
31. *The Observer*, 21 June 1992, p. 5.
32. Richelson and Ball, supra (note 1), pp. 307–8.
33. W.W. Keller, *The Liberals and J. Edgar Hoover* (Princeton: Princeton University Press, 1989), p. 21.
34. Quoted in Lord Denning, *Report of the Inquiry into the Profumo Affair* (HMSO: Cmnd 2152, September 1963), §263.
35. Quoted in J.Ll.J. Edwards, *Ministerial Responsibility for National Security* A study prepared for the McDonald Commission, (Ottawa: Minister of Supply and Services, 1980), p. 94.
36. Ibid.
37. McDonald, supra (note 18), pp. 63–8.
38. A.M. Schlesinger, Jr., *Robert Kennedy and His Times* (London: André Deutsch, 1978), p. 259.
39. Church Committee, Hearings, *FBI*, Volume VI (Washington DC: US Government Printing Office, 1975), p. 201. Poveda, supra (note 12), pp. 84–6 and pp. 141–2 shows how the central theme in the FBI after Watergate was the attempt to reduce the autonomy of the Bureau by integrating it into the executive branch.
41. R.G. Powers, *Secrecy and Power* (New York: Free Press, 1987), p. 274.
42. 1952, §6 reprinted in Denning, supra (note 34), §238.
43. Interviews with Merlyn Rees (10 July 1990) and William Whitelaw (13 June, 1990). In 1989 the then Home Secretary claimed that the Interception of Communications Act 1985 had brought him into closer contact with the Security Service than his predecessors had been before the Act. HC Deb., 16 January 1989, col. 108.
44. M. Raskin, 'Democracy Versus the National Security State', *Law and Contemporary Problems*, 40(3), 1976, p. 206.
45. P.H. Russell, 'The Proposed Charter for a Civilian Intelligence Agency: An Appraisal', *Canadian Public Policy*, 9, 1983, p. 334.
46. P. Hanks, 'Accountability for Security Intelligence Activities in Australia', in Hanks and McCamus, supra (note 5), p. 48.
47. Edwards, supra (note 35), pp. 41–54.
48. HC Deb., 3 February 1987, col. 823.
49. HC Deb., 6 February 1987, col. 1295.
50. See P. Gill, "'Allo! 'Allo! 'Allo! Who's In Charge Here Then?'

Liverpool Law Review, 9(2), 1987, pp. 189–201, for detailed discussion.

51. McDonald, supra (note 18), pp. 876–7.
52. Solicitor General, *On Course: National Security for the 1990s* (Ottawa: Minister of Supply and Services, February 1991), pp. 11–16.
53. ASIO Act 1979, s.8A(2).
54. ASIO, supra (note 29), p. 12.
55. I. Leigh and L. Lustgarten point out that the Security Service Act 1989 had only minimal impact on this, 'The Security Service Act', *Modern Law Review*, 52(6), pp. 810–14.
56. C. Andrew, *Secret Service* (London: William Heinemann, 1985), pp. 500–6.
57. Interviews with two former permanent secretaries of Home and Northern Ireland offices, 13 and 14 June 1990. Interview with CSIS official, 4 May 1988.
58. 1952, 4, reproduced in Denning, supra (note 34), §238.
59. S.2(2)(b).
60. Interview with Rupert Allason MP, 10 July 1990.
61. 20/20 Vision, *MI5's Official Secrets*, broadcast 8 March 1985.
62. J.N. Moore *et al.*, 'National Security and Civil Liberties, *Center Magazine*, 18, May–June 1985, p. 52.
63. J.T. Elliff, 'The President and the FBI', *The Bureaucrat* 3(1), 1974, pp. 46–7.
64. F.H. Hinsley and C.A.G. Simkins, *British Intelligence in the Second World War*: Vol. 4, *Security and Counter-Intelligence* (London: HMSO, 1990), pp. 9, 69.
65. N.West, *A Matter of Trust* (London: Coronet, 1983), p. 17.
66. Home Office, *The Security Service* (London: HMSO, 1993), p. 9.
67. E. O'Halpin, 'Financing British Intelligence: the Evidence up to 1945' in K.G. Robertson (ed.), *British and American Approaches to Intelligence* (Basingstoke: Macmillan, 1987), p. 198.
68. Ibid, pp. 208–9. See also Andrew, supra (note 56), pp. 229–32.
69. B. Porter, *Plots and Paranoia* (London: Unwin Hyman, 1989), pp. 113, 119, 130, 135.
70. T. Bunyan, *The History and Practice of Political Police in Britain* (London: Quartet, 1977), p. 122.
71. *The Guardian*, 17 April 1984.
72. Home Office Memorandum, *Police Special Branches*, Home Affairs Committee, Minutes of Evidence, 30 January 1985, p. 96.

73. ASIO, supra (note 29), pp. 40, 46.
74. SIRC, *Annual Report for 1990–91* (Ottawa: Minister of Supply and Services, 1991), p. 50. CSIS, *Public Report 1991* (Ottawa: Minister of Supply and Services, 1992) did not include any expenditure figures.
75. For example, see J. Steinbruner, *The Cybernetic Theory of Decision* (Princeton: Princeton University Press, 1974), pp. 125–8.
76. Buzan, supra (note 3), p. 140.
77. Church Committee, Final Report, Book II, *Intelligence Activities and the Rights of Americans* (Washington: US Government Printing Office, 1976), p. 962.
78. SIRC, *Annual Report for 1986–87* (Ottawa: Minister of Supply and Services, 1987), p. 35.
79. Home Office, supra (note 66), p. 12.
80. Powers, supra (note 41), pp. 323–4, 367.
81. SIRC, *Closing the Gaps: Official Languages and Staff Relations in the CSIS* (Ottawa: Minister of Supply and Services, 1987).
82. C. Dandeker, *Surveillance, Power and Modernity* (Cambridge: Polity Press, 1990), pp. 53–4.
83. Hinsley and Simkins, supra (note 64), p. 10.
84. Porter, supra (note 69), p. 213.
85. Ibid.
86. M. Ingram, 'Trouble With Security', *New Society*, 31 May 1984, p. 349. Home Office, supra (note 66), p. 10.
87. J. Simpson, 'The New Espionage', *The Spectator*, 22 February 1992, p. 10.
88. ASIO, supra (note 29), p. 40.
89. SIRC, *Annual Report for 1989–90* (Ottawa: Minister of Supply and Services, 1990), p. 51.
90. D.A. Phillips, *Careers in Secret Operations: How to Be a Federal Intelligence Officer* (Bethesda: Stone Trail Press, 1984), pp. 41–3. Following the conviction of Geoffrey Prime the Security Commission recommended polygraph testing in the UK security intelligence agencies, but the government did not implement this: I. Linn, *Application Refused: Employment Vetting by the State* (London: Civil Liberties Trust, 1990), p. 14.
91. ASIO, supra (note 29), p. 44.
92. Report of Special Committee on the Review of the CSIS Act, *In Flux But Not In Crisis* (Ottawa: Queen's Printer for Canada, September 1990), pp. 54–6.

93. CSIS, supra (note 74), pp. 24–5.

94. Special Committee, supra (note 92), p. 56.

95. SIRC, supra (note 89), p. 52.

96. CSIS, supra (note 74), p. 25.

97. ASIO, supra (note 29), p. 44.

98. Phillips, supra (note 90), p. 74.

99. P. Wright, *Spycatcher* (New York: Viking Penguin, 1987), p. 39.

100. A. Cavendish, *Inside Intelligence* (London: Collins, 1990), p. xii.

101. Linn, supra (note 90), pp. 28–9.

102. HC Deb., 23 July 1991, col. 476.

103. Phillips, supra (note 90), pp. 74–5. See also L.J. Moran, 'The Uses of Homosexuality: Homosexuality for National Security', *International Journal of the Sociology of Law*, 19, 1991, pp. 149–70.

104. *Report of the Security Commission on the Case of Michael John Bettaney* (London: Cmnd 9514, HMSO, May 1985), pp. 2–3.

105. Ibid, pp. 25–7.

106. McDonald, supra (note 18), pp. 705–32.

107. R. Mandel, 'Distortions in the Intelligence Decision Making Process', in S.J. Cimbala, *Intelligence and Intelligence Policy in a Democratic Society* (Ardsley-on-Hudson, NY: Transnational publishers, 1987), pp. 69–71.

108. Ingram, supra (note 86), pp. 349–50.

109. S. Emerson, *The CIA and the Politicization of Intelligence in the 1980s*, paper for International Studies Association Conference, Vancouver, April 1992.

110. J.L. Janis, *Victims of Groupthink: a Psychological Study of Foreign Policy Decisions and Fiascos* (Boston: Houghton Mifflin, 1972), p. 13.

111. P. Knightley, *The Second Oldest Profession: The Spy as Bureaucrat, Patriot, Fantasist and Whore* (London: Pan, 1986), Ch. 14; see also T. Mangold, *Cold Warrior* (New York: Simon & Schuster, Touchstone edition, 1992), Ch. 22.

112. McDonald, supra (note 18), pp. 745–7. The Rockefeller Commission on the CIA commented on how these procedures hampered the work of legal and inspector general staffs within the CIA: J.M. Oseth, *Regulating US Intelligence Operations* (Lexington: University of Press of Kentucky, 1985), p. 82.

113. D.J. Smith and J. Gray, *Police and People in London, IV The Police in Action* (London: Policy Studies Institute, 1983), p. 274.

114. Reiner, supra (note 8), p. 107.

115. S. Farson, 'Old Wine, New Bottles, and Fancy Labels', in G. Barak (ed.), *Crimes By The Capitalist State* (Albany: State University of New York Press, 1991), pp. 185–217.
116. D. Bradley *et al.*, *Managing The Police* (Brighton: Wheatsheaf, 1986), p. 23.
117. Cavendish, supra (note 100), p. xvi.
118. Reiner, supra (note 8), pp. 111–14.
119. Bradley *et al.*, supra (note 116), pp. 62–83.
120. Cf N. Steytler, 'Policing Political Opponents: Death squads and cop culture', in D. Hansson and D. van Zye Smit (eds), *Towards Justice: Crime and State Control in South Africa* (Capetown: Oxford University Press, 1990), pp. 106–33. At pp. 110–14 he analyses the 'dominant political discourse' in the culture of both senior and junior officers in the 'high policing' activities of the South African Police.
121. Farson, supra (note 115), pp. 187–8.
122. G. Allison, *Essence of Decision* (Boston: Little, Brown, 1971), pp. 162–81.
123. L. Freedman, 'Logic, Politics and Foreign Policy Processes: A Critique of the Bureaucratic Politics Model', *International Affairs*, 52(3), July 1976, pp. 434–49.
124. W.E. Colby and P. Forbath, *Honorable Men: My Life in the CIA* (New York: Simon & Schuster, 1978), pp. 462–5.
125. Mandel, supra (note 107), p. 74.

7

Autonomy II: Principles and Institutions of Oversight

In North America and Australasia the last 20 years have seen a range of inquiries into domestic security intelligence agencies and various new oversight mechanisms were developed. In the UK during the same period governments put up staunch resistance to any similar proposals. Even when the government introduced the Security Service Act it denied that it was a review or oversight measure (see below) and a major impetus behind the Bill was to head-off demands for greater democratic control.

After John Major's 1992 election victory there was an apparent shift when he announced that the peacetime existence of the SIS was to be officially recognised in a statute. A Cabinet Committee was then formed to examine options for some form of parliamentary review of the SIS and other security intelligence agencies. The early indications were, however, that this would involve just a small committee of privy councillors with limited access to information.[1]

The object of this chapter is to consider the variety of oversight mechanisms that have developed outside the UK, so that whatever detailed proposals emerge from the UK government in 1993 can be properly evaluated.

GENERAL PRINCIPLES OF OVERSIGHT

The debate in Britain regarding oversight mechanisms has been unnecessarily polarised in terms of the objective of oversight. For some, the only thing that appears to matter is the effectiveness of security intelligence agencies. Michael Mates MP, for example, concluded his recent survey by canvassing a number of alternatives, making clear that their objective should 'not be to assuage media or parliamentary concern, but to allow for better internal management'.[2] In 1992, Sir John Wheeler MP, former chair of the Home Affairs Committee, announced his support for 'a carefully defined and limited form of parliamentary oversight, to provide for better efficiency and effectiveness'.[3] Alternatively, Richard Norton-Taylor's recent contribution to the debate acknowledges the necessity for the foreseeable future for security intelligence agencies to protect democracies by means of gathering advance information of threats,

> But experience has shown that without a robust system of independent oversight, the system is wide open to abuse. Security services· are unable to resist the temptation to indulge in activities that have no place in a democracy. The cure can be as dangerous as the disease.[4]

While Mates and Wheeler seem to dismiss the importance of oversight as a means of reassuring the public against the abuse of power by security intelligence agencies, Norton-Taylor does not acknowledge the part it can play in improving effectiveness. If it is decided that a separate domestic security intelligence agency is required, it seems most sensible to generate oversight structures which seek to ensure that the agency is effective in achieving agreed objectives while not abusing political rights.

An important consideration in any discussion of structural, legal or institutional changes is the significance of political will and the danger of faith in the 'structural fix'.[5] Elegant structures of control and oversight may be erected but may be quite worthless if those responsible for them see their role as providing no more than a modicum of public reassurance that previous problem-areas of government are now under control. The general propensity of reforms to be directed in part at 'symbolic reassurance' has been noted by Murray Edelman;[6] in an area of government operations as secretive and intrinsically difficult to control as security intelligence, this is an even greater danger. This should alert us to the possibility that some of those working inside security intelligence agencies may embrace reform as a means of staving off more thorough changes.

Whatever oversight structures are developed, the preconditions for them to have some real rather than purely symbolic impact are that they have adequate resources, including full access to information, and the political will to use them.[7] Oversight structures lacking the necessary resources and will are worse than just useless, however. By providing an apparent channel for accountability they may provide an extra protective layer for the inner state as it resists democratic penetration. Even in the USA, for example, where oversight would seem to be at its strongest, there are suggestions that the Congress may have been pulling its punches in the case of the Iran-Contra deals,[8] perhaps for fear of the consequences for the US system as a whole if the President and Vice President were found to be implicated so soon after Watergate.

Given the enormous resources expended on security intelligence agencies and the potential for power that they possess, the area of security intelligence should not be exempted totally from normal democratic processes simply on production of the 'national security' totem. But before examining the various institutions which might perform oversight roles, it will be useful to develop some underlying principles that take into account the major aspects of the analysis so far. These can be used to construct a model of the different levels at which both the managerial control and external oversight of security intelligence agencies should be practised.

These principles are not intended to be cast in stone; they should rather be treated as hypotheses which might be used heuristically. It is possible to find current examples of practices which depart from all these principles, but that is useful because it provides comparative information necessary to consider whether the principles could be usefully applied in the UK. First, both managerial control and external oversight are required at each of the different levels which were identified in Chapter 2 as constituting the Gore-Tex state. The three distinct levels within the state are the security intelligence agency itself, the executive branch, and outside the executive branch. A fourth level of analysis is that between the state and the people.

Second, the same positions should not be responsible for both control and oversight. This is not to say that those responsible for the control of security intelligence agency operations should not consider the desirability that those operations are carried out properly and without infringing the law and civil rights, but, rather, that it is naive to believe that ministers or officials will be able to subject their own actions to effective oversight. This scepticism forms the basis of political control of bureaucracy in general in liberal democracies.

Third, those positions responsible for control of security intelligence agencies should draw up standards and guidelines which will be public in so far as is compatible with fundamental security needs, and which will increase in specificity the nearer the level of control is to the agency itself.[9] At the highest level of generality will be the positions taken by outside groups and political parties which are likely to cover questions of overall oversight structures as well as security intelligence mandates. Next will be the statutory mandate as established by the legislative assembly (see discussion in Chapter 3). Also relevant at this level will be those court decisions which, if they occur at all, establish case law regarding the basic powers of security intelligence agencies. Based on the statutory mandate, more specific guidelines and directions should be issued by the relevant (politically appointed) minister; and, finally, the most specific guidelines of all will be those generated internally by the agency to give effect to ministerial guidelines and directions.

Fourth, each control position will be accountable or responsible to that at the next level moving away from the agency, in conformity with the usual principle of political control. Fifth, the primary role of each oversight institution will be to report to the control institution at the same level. For example, an oversight institution which is outside the security intelligence agency itself but within the executive branch should report initially to the minister who is responsible for control at that level. In addition, in order to augment the accountability of each control position to that at the next level, each oversight institution should make as much of its findings as possible available also to the oversight institution at the next level. The relationship between these principles is shown in Figure 7.1.

This model will provide a framework for the consideration here of the main alternative institutions and structures which perform various control and oversight roles. It also provides a context within which to conduct the major debates; for example, precisely

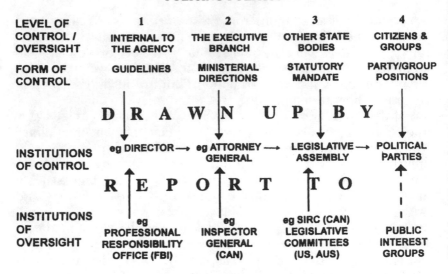

LEVEL OF CONTROL / OVERSIGHT	1 INTERNAL TO THE AGENCY	2 THE EXECUTIVE BRANCH	3 OTHER STATE BODIES	4 CITIZENS & GROUPS
FORM OF CONTROL	GUIDELINES	MINISTERIAL DIRECTIONS	STATUTORY MANDATE	PARTY/GROUP POSITIONS

D R A W N U P B Y

| INSTITUTIONS OF CONTROL | eg DIRECTOR → | eg ATTORNEY → GENERAL | LEGISLATIVE → ASSEMBLY | POLITICAL PARTIES |

R E P O R T T O

| INSTITUTIONS OF OVERSIGHT | eg PROFESSIONAL RESPONSIBILITY OFFICE (FBI) | eg INSPECTOR GENERAL (CAN) | eg SIRC (CAN) LEGISLATIVE COMMITTEES (US, AUS) | PUBLIC INTEREST GROUPS |

Figure 7.1 Model of Control and Oversight of Security Intelligence Agencies

how specific or not should the rules for security intelligence agencies be at each level? A central feature of the debate in the United States was the question of whether there should be a legislative mandate (or 'charter') for the FBI and, if so, how detailed it should be. This reflected very different perceptions of the amount of discretion which the executive branch and the agency itself should be allowed, and, indeed, the extent to which institutions outside of the executive branch (level three) should be involved in not just writing detailed operational guidelines but also approving specific operations.[10] The course of this debate in the US was of course determined partly by the political context of a system best described as one of 'separated institutions sharing powers'[11] but the same issues require resolution in the UK.[12]

In the parliamentary debate on the Security Service Act 1989 the government resisted all suggestions that there should be some element of parliamentary oversight. It argued that there is an inevitable 'barrier of secrecy' around the Security Service which prevents this so that, for example, if people were taken inside the barrier and able to scrutinise security intelligence operations they would be unable to make any of their knowledge public.[13] While some degree of secrecy regarding security intelligence operations is clearly necessary, this argument of a simple dichotomy between those who know and those who do not holds little water. It is contradicted by existing information control practices. Specifically, 'need-to-know' procedures are intended to ensure that as few people as necessary know about any specific operation and this applies inside security intelligence agencies as well as outside. Therefore, rather than erecting some imaginary barrier between 'insiders' and 'outsiders', the issue that should be discussed is what information should be available to institutions of control and oversight at the various levels, given their role in ensuring that security intelligence agencies operate both effectively and with propriety. Control institutions must have sufficient access to security intelligence information to be able to make valid judgements as to whether the principles and rules that they have laid down are being adhered to. Oversight institutions at levels two and three must have full access to security intelligence files and operatives. In practice, neither control nor oversight institutions will access the totality of security intelligence information, but they must have the potential to do so.

LEVEL ONE: THE AGENCY

Internal inspection

We have already seen that domestic security intelligence agencies have tended to be left alone by ministers and officials elsewhere in the executive branch of the state for various reasons, some more defensible than others. Historically the weakness of external control and oversight mechanisms has meant that if any checks were to be found on the activities of agencies they would be found within the agencies themselves. Yet it is clear that such internal oversight mechanisms as did exist had low status and made very little impact. Within the CIA, for example, there were a variety of offices with internal auditing functions including the Office of Inspector General which was to investigate anything from affirmative action complaints from employees to allegations of unlawfulness and impropriety. Yet the Office was unaware of any of the wrongdoings disclosed by the Church

Committee, and the later Iran-Contra affair. As the Agency became embroiled in congressional investigations of its history, William Colby, Director of the CIA at the time, indicated the importance of the Inspector General by reducing its staff from 14 to five.[14] The significance of internal oversight can be further gauged by the failure of a number of detailed histories of the CIA even to mention the Office in their indexes.[15] As a consequence of the Iran-Contra affair, Congress established an independent inspector general for the CIA in 1989.[16]

Regarding the FBI, the autonomy of the Bureau from outside constraint or review during Hoover's directorship was legendary,[17] and it would appear that the major objective of internal review procedures was to secure the compliance of Bureau personnel with the Director's wishes. Under Hoover, the Inspection Division conducted annual audit-inspections of all field offices and headquarters divisions. Officially, these were to report on the compliance with 'applicable laws, regulations and instructions', the efficient use of resources and the attainment of objectives. However, in practice they were often a matter of bargaining to the point of collusion between the inspectors and the Special Agent in Charge (SAC) of the office. The Inspection Division was implicated in some of the Bureau's illegal activities, for example in reviewing all the memoranda relating to illegal break-ins before they were destroyed under the 'Do Not File' procedure.[18] Clarence Kelley, who became Director of the FBI in 1977, reformed the inspection system into part of a Management By Objectives system which could play some part in monitoring compliance with new guidelines regarding investigations but would not of itself be an adequate mechanism for uncovering improper or illegal behaviour. In 1976 a Professional Responsibility Office was established within the FBI mainly to handle complaints of misconduct by Bureau personnel falling short of criminal behaviour, but there was initial uncertainty as to its precise role.[19]

Internal audit with respect to the propriety of operations was only instituted within the RCMP Security Service in 1978, that is after the McDonald Commission was established. The Commission recommended that the new Service should have a small internal investigative unit for handling complaints but that the major auditing responsibility should rest with an outside body.[20]

Whistleblowers

The propensity for state agencies to abuse the genuine justifications for some degree of secrecy in order to protect themselves from embarrassing disclosures was noted in Chapter 2. There is therefore a need to incorporate some protection for what might be described as informal mechanisms for 'internal oversight', specifically 'whistleblowers', alternatively described as 'ethical resisters'.[21] Those working within security intelligence agencies face two main hurdles should they be concerned that secrecy is operating against the public interest. The first is specific legal requirements that they do not disclose official information. In the UK this position has had statutory force since the first Official Secrets Act 1889, and section 1 of the 1911 Act, aimed at preventing espionage, still applies. The US Espionage Act 1917 provides a similar enactment. Section 2 of the UK Official Secrets Act 1911 represented the broadest restriction with its criminalisation of the unauthorised disclosure of any official information, but the clear evidence of the unworkability of this blunt instrument of government led to its being replaced by the Official Secrets Act 1989. This criminalises disclosure of six named areas of information, including that relating to security intelligence (section 1). Other official information will remain protected by internal civil service regulations.

As the old section 2 proved unreliable, or in cases where it was inapplicable, the UK government relied more on the contractual obligation of an employee to retain for ever the confidences gained by reason of employment. This is the second hurdle facing the prospective whistleblower and was the basis of the government's case against Peter Wright and Heinemann, author and publisher respectively of *Spycatcher*. Even after the European Court of Human Rights ruled in November 1991 that the House of Lords ban on British newspapers disclosing the contents of *Spycatcher* had been a breach of the European Convention, the government maintained that the lifelong duty of confidentiality on security intelligence officers remained.[22]

In the US, after the Supreme Court upheld and developed this common law idea in the case of Frank Snepp, who did not submit his book *Decent Interval*[23] (which was highly critical of CIA activities in Vietnam) for pre-publication review, the Reagan administration required hundreds of thousands of federal employees with access to classified data to sign non-disclosure agreements and thousands of others with higher access to Sensitive Compartmented Information (SCI) to sign even more stringent agreements, including pre-publication review. The classification method underlying the system was widened in 1982 and gave ten categories of information, disclosure of which 'reasonably could be expected to cause damage to the national security'.[24] A Report of the US General Accounting Office indicated that between 1984 and 1989 around 3.35 million federal employees and 1.75 million government contractors signed non-disclosure agreements. During the six months from October 1989 to March 1990, 48 federal agencies conducted about 10,000 pre-publication reviews.[25]

What protection has the whistleblower in such circumstances? It varies between states: in the US, for example, it has always been difficult to prosecute civil servants for leaking information, except in the relatively narrow case of espionage, because of the first amendment protection of the freedom of speech. In 1978 the US Congress passed the Civil Service Reform Act which set out to protect whistleblowers who leaked information which they believed revealed 'mismanagement, a gross waste of funds, an abuse of authority, or a substantial and specific danger to public health or safety'.[26] In other countries, notably the UK, prosecuting public officials has been far easier. But, short of prosecution, the main hazard faced by civil servants everywhere has been the variety of internal administrative 'punishments' that might be inflicted upon them. Colin Wallace was first moved from his post in Northern Ireland and then dismissed from his MOD job after he expressed concern at the Kincora case (see Chapter 5). When Wallace appealed against his dismissal the Civil Service Appeal Board was, first, misled by the MOD about the nature of Wallace's job and then the Chair was privately contacted by 'unnamed MOD officials' in an attempt to uphold the dismissal. Sir David Calcutt, who inquired into the dismissal in 1990, recommended £30,000 compensation for

Wallace,[27] although his report, based on restrictive terms of reference, begged many more questions than it answered. It has since been suggested that Calcutt himself did not receive full details of Wallace's job description during his inquiry.[28] Wallace formally complained to the police about this apparent attempt to pervert the course of justice, but Scotland Yard's Organised Crime Branch were reluctant to go ahead until they had consulted the Crown Prosecution Service, and the Director of Public Prosecutions decided in April 1991 that the evidence did not justify a police inquiry.[29]

Fred Holroyd's allegations of a variety of countering operations by the security forces in Northern Ireland, up to and including assassination, during 1974–75 (see Chapter 1, pp. 21–21), connect in numerous ways with Wallace's revelations. In Holroyd's case, he was taken under guard to the Army psychiatric hospital in Netley.[30] Cathy Massiter, who joined MI5 in 1970, complained during 1983 to the head of her section, her assistant director and then the personnel branch that her work in providing briefing material to DS-19 in the MOD on CND was outside the Maxwell-Fyfe Directive. She was told to see a psychiatrist, who had clearance to see members of the Security Service, and eventually it was made clear to her that she would have to resign. She left the Service in February 1984.[31] Similarly, Pamela Lamble, a secretary in SIS in the 1970s, was referred to a psychiatrist after she complained of lax security and subsequently resigned. She later wrote to the Soviet Embassy, knowing the letter would be intercepted, and was charged under Section 1 of the then Official Secrets Act. Subsequently the charges were dropped.[32]

This question also needs to be considered in the wider context of freedom of information legislation, if any, and also of public officials viewed as citizens rather than merely as employees.[33] Particularly in the case of security intelligence agencies, where both the formal and informal pressures to maintain secrecy are greatest, some systematic provision for whistleblowers is needed, in order both to assist the general oversight of such agencies and to reduce the likelihood of leaks being even more damaging if they go directly to the media. In Canada, the McDonald Commission proposed that security intelligence employees should be encouraged to disclose questionable activities to the independent review body which they proposed and also that no punishments should attach to employees who did this,[34] but the CSIS Act only places an obligation on the Director of the Service to disclose to the Solicitor General and Attorney General unlawful activities (s.20). These reports will be passed to the Security Intelligence Review Committee. Under Attorney General Levi, FBI officials and agents were ordered to report any requests made to the Bureau or practices within the Bureau 'which may be improper or which present the appearance of impropriety'.[35]

A minor reform was made in the UK in this respect when Sir Philip Woodfield was appointed as Staff Counsellor for the Security Service in 1988. Employees unhappy about any aspect of their work could go to see him. It is not known to what extent officials have made use of his services. Although his location in the Cabinet Office may not inspire enormous confidence in his independence, he apparently holds surgeries around the country.[36] But, however effective these reforms, they can deal only with those situations in which there is conflict between ministers and officials.[37] Whenever, as often, they share organisational assumptions about what the agency should do, the only check against any impropriety will be some form of external oversight (see Chapter 8).

LEVEL TWO: THE EXECUTIVE BRANCH

Ministerial 'oversight'

A shorthand way of describing this level of oversight and control would be 'ministerial'. The relevant institutions here are Attorney General (United States and Australia), Solicitor General (Canada) and Home Secretary (UK). The second principle proposed above was that the same institution should not be responsible for both oversight and control. In parliamentary systems, the idea of ministerial responsibility rests on the notion of an administrative hierarchy in which subordinate officials are simply the instruments of the minister and, therefore, should not themselves be held responsible.[38] This can be seen to be a weakly based doctrine with respect to contemporary British government in general, but with respect to security intelligence agencies it has never been adequate because neither the Security Service nor the police have ever been members of an administrative hierarchy. Clement Attlee, Labour Prime Minister from 1945 to 1951, described the Security Service as being 'under the direct control of the Prime Minister'[39] but there is little evidence that it actually was. According to the Maxwell-Fyfe Directive, the Director General of the Security Service was personally responsible to the Home Secretary, although the Service was not a part of the Home Office.[40] The Security Service Act 1989 describes the Service as being 'under the authority of the Secretary of the State' (s.1(1)). Similarly, with respect to those security intelligence aspects of policing, the doctrine of 'constabulary independence' as developed during the twentieth century, however weakly grounded it might be,[41] has certainly meant that only Chief Constables have been in a position to direct police officers.[42]

However, the government has continued to maintain, in the face of the evidence, that the present UK system of ministerial responsibility for security intelligence agencies can achieve both goals of effective ministerial direction and adequate oversight of those agencies. For example, less than three weeks after the TV programme based partly upon Cathy Massiter's allegations was first scheduled for transmission and then withdrawn by the Independent Broadcasting Authority (IBA), the then Home Secretary, Leon Brittan told the House of Commons:

> . . . since these allegations came to the fore I have taken steps to examine the allegations that the Security Service has operated improperly in carrying out investigations and surveillance in relation to subversive activity.
>
> I have concluded, in the light of the allegations and my inquiries into them, *that the security service has carried out no operation, investigation, surveillance or action against any individual otherwise than for the purposes laid down in its directive and with the propriety which successive Governments have rightly demanded of it*, and which this Government will continue to demand.[43] (Emphasis added)

Such an inquiry, to be carried out properly, would have taken many researchers many months. At the close of the Second

Reading debate on the Security Service Bill, John Patten, Minister of State at the Home Office, reiterating the government view that external oversight was impossible, said: 'In practice, the effective oversight of the Security Service is inseparable from overall responsibility for the Security Service'.[44] A variation on this theme is the suggestion that a minister of state, attached to the Cabinet Office, could provide oversight, having full access to relevant information and answering questions in the House.[45] Since the minister would be a member of the governing party and participate in all the Cabinet Committees it is clear that this would provide nothing approximating to independent oversight.

However, since ministers do not have the time, even if they have the inclination, to oversee the operations of security intelligence agencies, efforts have been made to find some way of providing them with an oversight capacity which does not detract from their responsibility to Parliament. What needs to be questioned is how far such methods are intended to provide genuine oversight of security intelligence agencies, or whether they are intended primarily to protect ministers from political embarrassment.

Security Commission

The Security Commission was established in the UK in 1964, to meet only when asked to do so by the Prime Minister in response to some security problem. It has therefore produced only random reviews with fairly narrow terms of reference. There is a panel of members, of whom three or four will normally work on a specific investigation; the chair is a law lord and the rest of the membership is drawn from those who are retired from high public positions in the civil and military services. It is difficult to gauge what impact the Commission has had on the internal policies of the Security Service but, judging by the relatively frequent recurrence of problems since 1965, perhaps not a great deal.

The example of the limited nature of the Security Commission's inquiry in the Prime case was given in Chapter 1 (p. 33), and it seems that their report had little impact. Jock Kane maintained in 1988 that the new procedures recommended by the Security Commission regarding the removal of documents from GCHQ had not been implemented four years later.[46] Michael Bettaney was convicted under the Official Secrets Acts in April 1984. He had offered to provide information to the KGB but they, fearing Bettaney was a Security Service 'plant', exposed him. The Security Commission was convened to investigate, it being the first time that the Security Service itself had been the subject of an investigation.[47] By the time of their first meeting, ten days after their inquiry was called for, the Commission members had received 'a great deal of written material' from the Security Service and at their second meeting they took initial oral evidence from the Director General, his deputy and the director of the Counter-Espionage Branch in which Bettaney was working at the time of his arrest. They then asked for and received 'a great deal of further written material' from the Security Service, plus police reports on Bettaney's arrest, a full transcript of the trial, and further papers relating to personnel management policies; they also took oral evidence from 60 people including members of the Service at all levels, particularly those who had worked with Bettaney.[48] The four members of the Security Commission completed their report by February 1985.

On the face of it a thorough job was done and, as was noted in Chapter 6, major criticisms of personnel policies were made, but there still remains doubt as to the depth into which the Commission was able, or chose, to delve. For example, the comment that the written evidence was 'prepared especially for us'[49] is a trifle ambiguous. It seems rather quaintly British that an investigating commission should be prepared to accept as written evidence from the agency under investigation material which it had 'prepared especially'!

Before the Security Commission as such was established, groups of privy councillors had sat on security issues, for example Radcliffe in 1962 regarding vetting and security procedures within the civil service.[50] The extent to which such commissions might be misled or, alternatively, be used to present official misinformation, is illustrated by the report in March 1956 which said that one of the chief problems of security was 'to identify the members of the British Communist Party, . . .'[51] Since we know now that in 1955 the Security Service had broken into a flat in Mayfair and removed for filming the entire membership records of the British Communist Party, this is somewhat hard to credit![52] It should be noted that there is an alternative explanation of these events. Steve Dorril and Robin Ramsay suggest either that the burglary occurred after the 1956 Report, though this does not fit the dates given in other sources, or that the whole story was a piece of disinformation by Peter Wright to cover the other clandestine methods by which the UK security intelligence agencies had built up its list of CP members.[53] Maybe so, but since Wright was perfectly happy to discuss those methods in various places, it is not clear why he should have been concerned to conceal them in this case.

President's Foreign Intelligence Advisory Board (PFIAB)

One of Michael Mates's suggestions is that the Security Commission, could be reconstituted to perform a similar function to the US President's Foreign Intelligence Advisory Board (PFIAB), emphasising that its main contribution would be to the efficiency of the Service rather than reassurance of the public.[54] Given Mates's overall concern with effectiveness and his dismissal of oversight concerns, this is a logical proposal in that the PFIAB itself was never intended as an oversight body; rather it was intended to concern itself with the efficiency and effectiveness of intelligence-gathering in the US. The Rockefeller Commission, which reported in 1975, recommended, among other things, that the PFIAB's role be expanded into oversight of the CIA, but President Ford created instead an Intelligence Oversight Board. PFIAB consisted of the personal nominees of each President and reviewed the performance of all agencies concerned in the intelligence process. It concerned itself with the adequacy of management within the agencies and co-ordination between them.[55] The traditional close ties of PFIAB members with defence contractors had resulted in recommendations for ever bigger and more expensive collection systems, which, in turn, contributed to the accentuation of quantity over quality as the solution to intelligence problems.[56] President Carter in 1977 abolished the PFIAB because of this and the Board's traditional support for covert action.[57] Following a recommendation of his transition team, the PFIAB was reconstituted under Reagan. Overall, however, it has been seen as being just as ineffective as the Intelligence Oversight Board (see below), and for the same reasons: a part-time membership of dignitaries and inadequate staff.[58]

Inspectors General

The main method by which more systematic oversight on behalf of ministers in parliamentary democracies has been sought has been by the development of Offices of Inspectors General. These must be distinguished from those which, as with the CIA until 1989, are internal to the security intelligence agency itself.

One of the major departures made by the Canadian government from the McDonald Commission's recommended structure for oversight of the new CSIS was to reduce the extent of external (level three) review and increase the element of (level two) review on behalf of the minister. Whereas McDonald had proposed two (level three) oversight bodies, an Advisory Committee on Security and Intelligence (ACSI) to conduct general oversight and a Security Appeals Tribunal (SAT) to hear appeals against refusals of security clearances, the government proposed an Inspector General (IG) at level two and the Security Intelligence Review Committee (SIRC) at level three combining the roles of ACSI and SAT (see further below). In its report on the government's first bill to implement McDonald, the Senate Committee noted:

> The obvious intent . . . is that the Inspector General should provide, for the political masters of the agency, ongoing information as to its functioning. If the Solicitor General is to be politically responsible he must know what is going on in the agency, through his deputy. The Inspector General will be the ministry's 'eyes and ears' on the Service.[59]

The IG is appointed by the government, is responsible to the Deputy Solicitor General and is required to monitor and review the operational activities of CSIS with particular reference to their compliance with ministerial policies, legality and reasonableness.[60] He has access to all the information under CSIS control, subject to the same exclusion as SIRC regarding Cabinet confidences (s.31), a point criticised by the Senate Committee,[61] and provides one link in the reporting chain set up by the Act (see Figure 7.2). The CSIS director must make his annual report to the minister (1) and give a copy to the IG (2). As soon as practicable, the IG must submit to the minister his report, known as a Certificate, stating his satisfaction or otherwise with the director's report and giving the minister the result of his monitoring activities (3). A copy of this Certificate and the director's report is forwarded by the minister to SIRC (4). SIRC then takes this report and Certificate into account in the preparation of its annual report which goes to the Solicitor General (5) and thence to Parliament (6).

Until 1988 there were problems of understaffing, despite the first Inspector General – Dick Gosse – commenting in his first Certificate that there was no point in having an IG unless he had adequate resources.[62] The reporting chain therefore took some time to come together: SIRC's first report went to the minister having been produced without the benefit of either the CSIS or the IG's reports. Now the Office operates with a staff of 12 divided into two streams, one for monitoring and review and the other for policy and standards, most of the resources being in the former.[63]

In terms of the formal reporting chain (see Figure 7.2) the annual report of the CSIS director is a major focus for the IG's review and Gosse was critical of the director's earliest reports for concentrating on the good news and being generally unhelpful.[64] However, the Inspector General showed that he was well aware that the director's reports alone, even if more comprehensive, would not be capable of providing the basis for adequate review. As he noted:

> Various practices have evolved at operational levels which appear to be as determinative of investigative decisions, or more so, than the policies developed by the Service and published, for that purpose, in its Operational Manual.[65]

Since his resources were limited, and a full audit of CSIS operations would not be possible, the knowledge and reports of the Inspector General tended to develop out of particular investigations. For example, during 1986 the minister asked the IG for a report on the shooting of a Punjabi State cabinet minister

Figure 7.2 Review of Canadian Security Intelligence Service

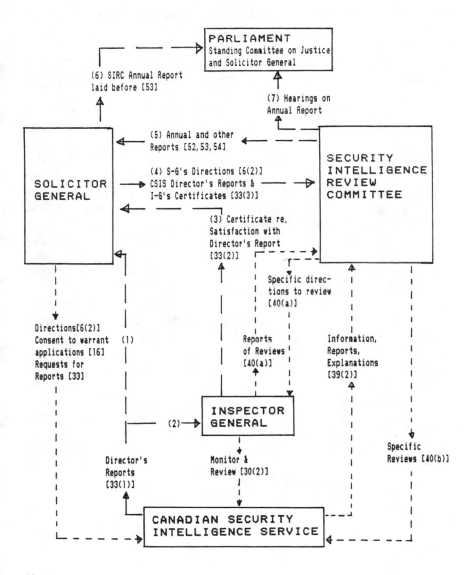

Notes:
1. Figures in [] refer to relevant sections of the Canadian Security Intelligence Service Act, 1984.
2. ——— —— indicates the main reporting chain.
3. − − − − − − indicates the main routes for the direction and review of CSIS by external agencies.

265

on 25 May on Vancouver Island, specifically, the extent to which CSIS had information which might have been passed sooner to the RCMP.[66]

Formal and informal dealings with SIRC have also played a crucial part in determining the IG's workload. Formally, the IG is part of the ministerial secretariat (level two), while SIRC is outside the executive structure (level three); therefore it might be expected that a good part of the IG's work would be responding to ministerial requests. That did occur, for example, in the case of the Vancouver shooting, but it is clear that under Dick Gosse the agenda for the office was set more by the IG than it was by the minister – to the extent that the minister was expected to appoint someone more responsive to his particular needs as Gosse's successor.[67] Judging by the critical comments in the Commons Special Committee's Report as to the reluctance of the next IG, Richard Thompson, to provide them with information regarding the Office,[68] it seems as though the minister might have succeeded.

In the early years, because of the pressure on resources felt both in SIRC and the IG's office, considerable efforts were made to avoid the duplication of effort, for example by discussing future work programmes.[69] Even in cases where SIRC issues the IG with a formal direction to carry out a review, there is prior consultation as to the scope and wording of the direction and interchange will continue throughout on refining the scope of the study as new information emerges.[70] The issue of overlap between SIRC and the IG is discussed below.

The Commons Special Committee concluded its review of the Inspector General's performance by noting that it had been unable to obtain much information relating to the impact the IG had had on CSIS, and by making a number of recommendations intended to give the IG greater independence from ministerial influence in determining his priorities.[71] The government dismissed the Special Committee's concerns as being without foundation and proposed no change in the role of the Inspector General.[72]

Part of the reason for the Special Committee's doubts as to the independence of the Inspector General is that his overview covers compliance with ministerial and agency policies as well as with the law; in other words it appears to cover both control and oversight functions. In Australia, Justice Hope recommended the establishment of an Inspector General in his second report into security intelligence and made it clear that he should concentrate on the oversight function:

> What is needed is an independent person with power to maintain a close scrutiny of ASIO's performance of its functions, and to look into complaints, in order to give greater assurance to the Attorney General, and through him Parliament and the public, that ASIO is acting with propriety and within its charter.[73]

The subsequent legislation, the Inspector General of Intelligence and Security Act, 1986, placed the Inspector General clearly within the executive branch (level two), and gave the office a potentially wider remit than that in Canada. In Australia it covers not just the domestic security intelligence agency, ASIO, but also ASIS, DSD, JIO and ONA. At the instigation of a minister, a complainant, or on his own volition the IG, can inquire into compliance of the agencies with the law and ministerial guidelines, and the propriety of their activities as well as employee grievances, though his powers are more restricted with respect to the last two agencies. The IG has full access to documents and may compel responses from officials, overriding secrecy provisions in other statutes. All his reports go to the responsible minister, and he can only respond to a complainant in terms approved by the minister. His annual report goes to the Prime Minister and is to be laid before Parliament.[74] On paper, therefore, the Australian Inspector General appears to combine the review functions of the Canadian Inspector General and SIRC.

However, whereas they cover just one agency and have between them 24 staff, the Australian IG covers five agencies and has three staff! In the first four-and-a-half years the office received 46 complaints, all against ASIO, and 'the vast majority' were said to be unfounded.[75] He also investigated some allegations which appeared in the media but most of the workload concerned employee grievances. Although the office has carried out spot-checks into records where ASIO has conducted intrusive surveillance with a ministerial warrant, its agenda would seem to be primarily reactive compared with the greater element of a proactive oversight agenda in Canada.

In the United States, Attorney General Levi established within the Justice Department an Office of Professional Responsibility (OPR) in 1975 which was intended to ensure the maintenance of professional standards in the FBI. An early assessment of the OPR's performance pointed out that the definition of its duties was unclear, as was the way its work would interact with the FBI's own Professional Responsibility Office established in 1976 (see above) and the Intelligence Oversight Board (IOB) (see below). There was an attempt to insulate the work of the OPR from the other divisions of the Justice Department and from the Bureau, by having it operate by means of task forces created for specific purposes. One of its initial tasks was to work on the process of notifying those people who had been 'caused actual harm' by COINTELPRO operations and who remained unaware that they had been targeted.[76]

Finally, in February 1976, President Ford announced the establishment of the Intelligence Oversight Board (IOB), composed of three people, who would report serious questions about legality to the Attorney General and important issues of propriety to the President. The IOB covered the whole field of domestic and foreign intelligence agencies, but it had no mandate to review operations on its own initiative; rather it was to review periodically the internal (level one) channels of oversight.[77] Assessment of the performance of the IOB has been scathing. People have been appointed to it, and to its complementary 'control' institution, PFIAB, much more on the basis of closeness to the incumbent president than for any expertise in intelligence. Meeting bi-monthly and normally enjoying a staff of one, oversight has been reduced to 'a part-time hobby for itinerant dignitaries'.[78] When the inexperienced IOB attorney learned of the Iran-Contra operation he began an inquiry which consisted of a five-minute conversation with Oliver North and a 30-minute meeting with the legal counsel from the National Security Council.

> Assured by these individuals that there was nothing to worry about, he ended his 'investigation'. The Intelligence Oversight Board: three blind mice and a lamb.[79]

CONCLUSION

The issue here is clear. The structural autonomy of security intelligence agencies has meant that the only historical checks upon the propriety of their activities were those which were self-imposed. The frequent absence of these resulted in widespread abuse of power. For the future, it is crucial that better mechanisms of internal audit and review are developed because of their relative proximity to the 'sharp-end' of security intelligence operations. In turn, if ministers are to be expected to exercise clearer political control of security intelligence, they will require specific means of ensuring that their guidelines with respect to both policy and propriety are followed.

However, oversight at these two levels within the executive branch requires reinforcement. Agencies may treat ministers as a threat to their autonomy; ministers may decide that they do not want to know what agencies do. To guard against these and other dangers, oversight from outside of the executive branch is required.

NOTES

1. *The Guardian*, 24 June 1992, p. 2.
2. M. Mates, *The Secret Services: Is There a Case for Greater Openness?* (London: Institute for European Defence and Strategic Studies, 1989), p. 58.
3. *The Independent*, 26 May 1992, p. 4.
4. Richard Norton-Taylor, *In Defence of the Realm?* (London: Civil Liberties Trust, 1990), p. 129.
5. R. K. Betts, 'American Strategic Intelligence: Policies, Priorities and Direction', in R.L. Pfaltzgraff, Jr. *et al.* (eds), *Intelligence Policy and National Security* (Basingstoke: Macmillan, 1981), p. 248; J.M. Oseth, *Regulating US Intelligence Operations* (Lexington: University Press of Kentucky, 1985), pp. 185–7.
6. M. Edelman, *The Symbolic Uses of Politics* (Urbana: University of Illinois Press, 1976 originally published 1964).
7. For example, see P. Gill, 'Symbolic or Real? The Impact of

the Canadian Security Intelligence Review Committee, 1984–88', *Intelligence and National Security*, 4(3), July 1989, pp. 550–75.

8. S.M. Hersh, Foreword, *The Chronology: The Documented Day-by-Day Account of the Secret Military Assistance to Iran and the Contras*, National Security Archive (New York: Warner Books, 1987), pp. vii–viii.

9. M. Supperstone, 'The Law Relating to Security in Great Britain', in K.G. Robertson (ed.), *British and American Approaches to Intelligence* (Basingstoke: Macmillan, 1987), p. 219.

10. Oseth, supra (note 5), pp. 167–8.

11. R.E. Neustadt, *Presidential Power: The Politics of Leadership* (New York: New American Library, Mentor Book, originally published 1960), p. 42.

12. For example, see Supperstone, supra (note 9), pp. 228–30.

13. For example, HC Deb., 15 December 1988, cols. 1118–19.

14. L.K. Johnson, *America's Secret Power: the CIA in a Democratic Society* (New York: Oxford University Press, 1989), p. 239.

15. R. Jeffreys-Jones, *The CIA and American Democracy* (New Haven: Yale University Press, 1989); J. Ranelagh, *The Agency: The Rise and Decline of the CIA* (New York: Simon & Schuster, 1987).

16. G. Hastedt, 'Controlling Intelligence: Defining the Problem', in G. Hastedt (ed.), *Controlling Intelligence* (London: Frank Cass, 1991), p. 16 and see below for discussion of Inspectors General.

17. Church Committee, Final Report, Book II, *Intelligence Activities and the Rights of Americans* (Washington DC: US Government Printing Office, 1976), pp. 270–74.

18. Ibid, p. 155 and see Chapter 5.

19. J.T. Elliff, *The Reform of FBI Intelligence Operations* (Princeton: Princeton University Press, 1979), pp. 178–88.

20. McDonald, Second Report, *Freedom and Security Under the Law* (Ottawa: Minister of Supply and Services, 1981), pp. 739–43.

21. M.P. Glazer and P.M. Glazer, *The Whistleblowers: Exposing Corruption in Government and Industry* (New York: Basic Books, 1989), p. 4.

22. *The Guardian*, 7 December 1991, p. 5.

23. (London: Allen Lane, 1980.)

24. M.M. Cheh, 'Spies, Leakers, Whistle-blowers, and Bunglers: Real and Imagined Threats to National Security', in P.Hanks and J.D.

McCamus (eds), *National Security: Surveillance and Accountability in a Democratic Society* (Cowansville, Québec: Les Editions Yvon Blais, 1989), pp. 158–66.

25. US General Accounting Office, *Information Security: Federal Agency Use of Nondisclosure Agreements* (Washington DC: GAO, January 1991), pp. 2–3.

26. J. Michael *et al.*, *The Ponting Dilemma: Secrecy, the Civil Servant and the Public Interest* (London: Policy Studies Institute, January 1985).

27. *The Guardian*, 14 September 1990, p. 24.

28. *The Guardian*, 5 April 1991, p. 5.

29. *The Guardian*, 3 April 1991, p. 5.

30. F. Holroyd, *War Without Honour* (Hull: Medium Publishing, 1989), especially pp. 70–105.

31. *The Observer*, 24 February 1985, pp. 1–2.

32. See R. Thomas, *Espionage and Secrecy* (London: Routledge, 1991), pp. 117–18 and note 58 for details.

33. K.P. Swan, 'Whistle-blowing and National Security', in Hanks and McCamus, supra (note 24), pp. 173–4.

34. McDonald, supra (note 20), p. 749.

35. Elliff, supra (note 19), p. 182.

36. I. Leigh and L. Lustgarten, 'The Security Service Act', *Modern Law Review*, 52(6), 1989, p. 833.

37. Fresh advice was given to civil servants after the Ponting case, see G. Drewry, 'The Ponting Case – Leaking in the Public Interest', *Public Law* (Summer 1985), pp. 203–12.

38. K.G Robertson, *Public Secrets* (Basingstoke: Macmillan, 1982), p. 25.

39. 'Foreword', in P. Sillitoe, *Cloak Without Dagger* (London: Cassell, 1955), p. v.

40. 1952, §1.

41. For example, see L. Lustgarten, *The Governance of Police* (London: Sweet & Maxwell, 1986), pp. 53–67.

42. Police Act, 1964, s.5(1).

43. HC Deb., 12 March 1985, col. 154.

44. HC Deb., 15 December 1988, col. 1184.

45. Mates, supra (note 2), p. 57.

46. *After Dark*, broadcast on Channel 4, 16 July 1988.

47. *Report of the Security Commission on the Case of Michael John Bettaney*, Cmnd 9514 (London: HMSO, May 1985), §1.3. See

271

I. Leigh and L. Lustgarten, 'The Security Commission', *Public Law* (Summer 1991), pp. 215–32 for a general discussion of the Security Commission.

48. Cmnd 9514, ibid, §§2.2–2.7.
49. Ibid, §2.3.
50. *Report on Security Procedures in the Public Services*, Cmnd 1681 (London: HMSO, November 1961).
51. *Report of the Conference of Privy Councillors*, Cmnd 9715 (London: HMSO, 1956), §6.
52. P. Wright, *Spycatcher* (New York: Viking Penguin, 1987), pp. 54–6.
53. S. Dorril and R. Ramsay, *Smear!* (London: Fourth Estate, 1991), p. 31.
54. Mates, supra (note 2), p. 58.
55. Ranelagh, supra (note 15), p. 746.
56. V. Marchetti and J.D. Marks, *The CIA and the Cult of Intelligence* (New York: Dell, 1980), pp. 285–7.
57. Ranelagh, supra (note 15), p. 662.
58. Johnson, supra (note 14), pp. 236–8.
59. Report of the Special Committee of the Senate on the CSIS, *Delicate Balance* (Ottawa: Minister of Supply and Services, November 1983), p. 29.
60. CSIS Act 1984, ss.30–3.
61. Supra (note 59), p. 30.
62. *Certificate of the Inspector General, Submitted Pursuant to s.33(2) of the CSIS Act*, September 1985 (Ottawa: Office of the Inspector General, 1985), p. 14.
63. Report of the Special Committee on the Review of the CSIS Act, *In Flux But Not In Crisis* (Ottawa: Queen's Printer for Canada, September 1990), p. 138
64. *Certificate of the Inspector General, Submitted Pursuant to s.33(2) of the CSIS Act* (April 1986), pp. 12–14; April 1987, pp. 49–50.
65. Ibid, April 1987, p. 200.
66. Interview with Dick Gosse, 2 May, 1988.
67. Interview with Ron Atkey, Chair of SIRC, 9 May 1988; interview with officials in Secretariat of Ministry of Solicitor General, 4 May 1988.
68. Supra (note 63), p. 139.
69. Interviews with Gosse, supra (note 66), and Executive Secretary of SIRC, 27 April 1988.

70. Interview with Michael de Rosenroll, Acting Inspector General, 29 April 1988.
71. Supra (note 63), pp. 140–43.
72. Solicitor General, *On Course: National Security for the 1990s* (Ottawa: Minister of Supply and Services, February 1991), p. 21. See also S. Farson, 'Problems of Political Oversight: Difficulties Encountered by the Special Committee During Parliament's Five-Year Review of the CSIS Act', paper for Annual Conference of CASIS, Queen's University, Kingston, Ontario, June 1991, pp. 37–8.
73. R.M. Hope, *Australian Security Intelligence Organization* (Canberra: Commonwealth Government Printer, 1985), §16.84.
74. P. Hanks, 'Accountability for Security Intelligence Activity in Australia', in Hanks and McCamus, supra (note 24), pp. 47–8.
75. R. Holdich, 'The Work of the Australian Inspector General of Intelligence and Security', in *Newsletter No. 16*, CASIS, Université de Montreal, December 1991, p. 13; this account is based on pp. 13–17. See also F. Cain, 'Accountability and the ASIO: A Brief History', in A.S. Farson *et al.* (eds.), *Security and Intelligence in a Changing World* (London: Frank Cass, 1991), pp. 119–23.
76. Elliff, supra (note 19), pp. 160–77 for full discussion.
77. Oseth, supra (note 5), pp. 94–5.
78. Johnson, supra (note 14), p. 237.
79. Ibid, p. 238.

8

Autonomy III: Overseeing the Executive

In this chapter we consider the possibilities for oversight of security intelligence agencies from outside the executive branch of the state. This had barely been contemplated before the inquiries in Canada, Australia and the US in the 1970s demonstrated the inadequacy of internal and ministerial controls. Legislative oversight had existed formally for some time in the US but congressional committees had failed over many years to provide any serious check on the autonomy of the FBI and CIA. Therefore real efforts in this direction are relatively recent and while some have produced energetic new institutions, others have been extremely hesitant.

LEVEL THREE: OTHER STATE BODIES

At this level there are three distinct types of institutions which need to be considered, the first two based respectively on the legislative and judicial functions of the state, and a third, hybrid type such as the Canadian Security Intelligence Review Committee (SIRC).

Legislative oversight

Part of McDonald's recommended structure for review of the security intelligence service in Canada was a joint Senate–Commons committee. It was argued that the existing Commons standing committee on justice matters was too large, its membership too fluctuating and its procedures too restrictive for pursuing security intelligence inquiries. The joint committee should have no more than ten representatives of all political parties and be chaired by a member of the Opposition in the same way as the Public Accounts Committee. The members should not be subject to formal security screening but the security intelligence agency would notify the party leader of any nominee believed to constitute a significant threat to Canadian security. It would be as much concerned with effectiveness issues – for example, it might investigate any security breaches which occurred – as with propriety issues. It would receive annual reports both from the CSIS and the ACSI, the proposed independent review body, and should meet in public as much as possible; whenever it met *in camera* it should publish edited transcripts where possible. The problem of opposition members receiving secret briefings and thereby being prevented from exercising their duty to criticise was acknowledged, but the improved 'education' of members that would result was believed to be preferable to their remaining reliant on leaks for their information.[1]

The Canadian debate showed there were three main strands of argument on this question: the first was that a fundamental principle of liberal democracy was the accountability of permanent bureaucracies to elected representatives in Parliament and that, though security intelligence raises particular problems, it should not be exempted from that principle. The second strand accepted the principle but tended to argue that it was not possible to implement it; while a third strand has argued that external review would actually be *more* effective if carried out by a non-parliamentary body. McDonald took the first line of argument and sought to find answers to the practical problems inherent in parliamentary control of security intelligence services, hence the recommendation for a joint committee to reduce partisanship. In his study for McDonald, Ned Franks concluded that the standing committees were ill-adapted to deal with security intelligence matters:

> The opposition attacks; the government uses its powers to protect witnesses and prevent inquiry; the opposition is frustrated and makes wild accusations; and both sides become upset and bitter.[2]

However, neither the government nor the Senate committee agreed. Using the arguments of partisanship and the risks of leaks, they argued that Parliament could best inform itself by considering SIRC's annual report.[3]

Those who took the same line as McDonald attempted to demonstrate that the practical problems raised in the Senate Report and endorsed by the government were far from insurmountable. On the issue of leaks from legislative committees, for example, the New Democratic Party MP, Svend Robinson, asked Robert Simmons, Staff Director of the US Senate Select Committee on Intelligence, about the US experience and Simmons replied:

> I will not say it is not a problem, because there are those people in Washington who will say it is a problem. I do not feel it is a major problem. I think the security has been pretty good. I certainly do not think the extent to which it has been a problem outweighs the benefits that we obtain from having this system . . . [4]

Importantly, this conclusion was endorsed by Mary Lawton of the Office of Intelligence Policy and Review in the US Department of Justice, who had said herself during the previous session:

> The experience is we seldom find the source, so we cannot say. But I would say we generally have, with some minor exceptions, good confidence in the committees and in the care with which they protect the information.[5]

In the US leaks abound from all quarters of the government; for example, a study by the Senate Intelligence Committee during the first five months of 1986 found 147 newspaper articles divulging classified information, all but 12 of which cited administration sources, including the intelligence agencies themselves, rather than congressional ones.[6] Similarly, in the UK the 'lobby system' is used for the leaking of information, on an unattributable basis, in support of government policies and sometimes this may involve security intelligence information.[7] Therefore arguments about the risk of leaks cannot be used specifically as a reason against legislative review.

But, in Canada, the government prevailed and little improvement in parliamentary and public discussion of security intelligence matters was predicted. The only opportunity for parliamentary discussion was the consideration of SIRC's annual report. It is clear that the present standing committee was not able to escape from the constraints which were predicted, particularly those of time – in the first three-and-a-half years of the Act's operation the committee held just seven hours of hearings spread over four separate occasions.

The Special Committee set up by the Canadian House of Commons to carry out the five-year review of the CSIS Act during 1989–90 represented Parliament's first systematic review of the security intelligence system. Although this committee pursued a non-confrontational strategy towards the government over the question of access to information, it was not successful in obtaining much of the information it sought. For example, neither the IG nor the SIRC would release reports which had been made to the minister and the time pressure on the committee to complete its work ruled out any judicial challenge to the government who, it appears, quite consciously delayed the committee on this issue.[8]

The Special Committee recommended that the Commons Standing Committee on Justice and the Solicitor General establish a permanent sub-committee to deal exclusively with security and intelligence matters. The sub-committee should not attempt to replace SIRC or carry out much by way of direct investigation of CSIS activities, but would review the budgets of the security intelligence agencies, and the work of SIRC and the IG, and undertake more general reviews regarding security intelligence matters. The committee made its proposals quite tentatively, and said that if such a sub-committee was not established then there should be a further review of the CSIS Act in five years' time.[9] The government seized on the committee's hesitance and said it would be 'premature' to create a sub-committee,[10] but the Commons set one up in 1991.

In Australia, both Justice Hope's reports in 1977 and 1985 recommended against a parliamentary committee but the Labour government announced in 1985 that it intended to establish a joint committee of the House of Representatives and Senate to oversee ASIO. Legislation was passed in 1986, and incorporated into the

ASIO Act 1979, but it was August 1988 before the new committee started work. The committee has seven members appointed by each House (three from the Senate, four from the House) after consultation with all party leaders. It is precluded from reviewing certain matters: foreign intelligence, matters which are 'operationally sensitive', matters not affecting Australian citizens or permanent residents and individual complaints (which are the business of the IG, see above). It can require the production of documents and the giving of evidence, but it must give five days' notice and the minister may issue a non-reviewable certificate preventing any person or document from going to the committee.[11] In other words, the committee's powers are highly restricted:

> . . . this committee should be recognised as very much a token gesture from the government to the critics of ASIO from within the Labour Party, for in reality the committee has very little in the way of effective review powers; and is placed firmly under government control in its membership, its agenda and its investigative powers.[12]

In the UK the Commons Home Affairs Select Committee has said that it should have a role in reviewing Security Service budgets and policies, but the government has rejected this option pending future legislation regarding the SIS and GCHQ. Richard Norton-Taylor has proposed, on behalf of the organisation Liberty, a committee in the House of Commons. He suggests a new select committee for security and intelligence which would have 20 members reflecting the party balance in the Commons, be supported by adequate staff, have the final say over security intelligence agencies' budgets, carry out investigations and make recommendations and could draw up guidelines regarding security intelligence activities.[14] This proposal is modelled more on the US congressional intelligence committees rather than on the existing select committees in the Commons. The latter do not exercise the kind of 'executive' functions of budgets and guidelines envisaged here, and this raises major questions. Certainly, it would not be in line with the model proposed here, which separates control and oversight institutions. For example, it can be argued that if a committee has control functions then this can lead to confusion of responsibility with the minister in overall control of the security intelligence agencies. Also, to the extent that the committee becomes implicated in the actual running of the security intelligence agencies it may well compromise its ability to act as an independent and external critic of those agencies.

It can be argued that this has not been a problem for the US congressional intelligence committees, but their relationship to the executive branch is very different from that of legislative committees in either Westminster or 'Washminster' systems, as in Canada and Australia. The congressional committees are not dominated by the executive as a Commons select committee could be and as, for example, the Commons Home Affairs Committee was when it wrote its report on police special branches. Similarly, in 1992 the Commons Trade and Industry Select Committee concluded its report on the Iraqi supergun affair by calling for the intelligence services to be made accountable to Parliament, but the Conservative majority refused to criticise specifically the failure of the services to inform ministers of what they knew.[15]

Yet even in the US the issue of how far congressional oversight committees should be involved in 'control' matters is a matter of constant debate. Some intelligence insiders saw that incorporating Congress would have the advantage of sharing out the burden to be borne in the event of mistakes being made. For example, Stansfield Turner, Director of the CIA during 1977–81, later wrote:

> . . . it is to the advantage of the professionals to have vigorous oversight. To the extent that they are sometimes held retroactively responsible or are unjustly accused in the press, the fact that two congressional committees and the National Security Council are responsible for knowing what is going on helps cushion the impact of public reaction. In addition, oversight, especially by Congress, can give helpful guidance to the CIA as to what is and what is not acceptable conduct in the pursuit of secrets.[16]

But Turner did not support the idea of Congress being notified prior to any covert action.[17] While Congress had tried to achieve such prior notification, presidents sometimes resisted even 'timely' *post hoc* notification, as in the case of the mining of the Nicaraguan harbours in 1984.[18]

There is not the space here to discuss the wisdom of congressional attempts to insert themselves into the control process in the US but, given the facility with which the executive controls the House of Commons, such a course would be unwise in the UK. Given the logic of the overall model that institutions of oversight and control should remain distinct, a proposal to create a parliamentary committee might be better concentrating on the investigative and review functions and ensuring that it acquired sufficient independent powers of access, unlike the Australian example.[19]

Judicial oversight

According to the 'rule of law', government officials are subject to the same rules of law and conduct as are citizens. This should provide one of the main checks on the abuse of power by the state or, more precisely, 'the one means of guarding against the Dual State'. However, continues Raskin:

> The courts are frightened of the Dual State, hoping that the problem will go away if no attention is paid to it. Furthermore, where such cases have been presented to the courts, judges have been reluctant or unable for institutional reasons, to rule against the secret agencies or inquire into their activities.[20]

Judges and courts are involved in pronouncing on the activities of security intelligence agencies on a rather haphazard but ultimately restricted basis. They may be requested to make decisions in press freedom cases or criminal trials in which security intelligence agencies and questions of 'national security' are involved. Alternatively, judges may become involved through specific measures established for the granting of warrants for telephone tapping and bugging, or as part of some scheme for the review of the security intelligence apparatus as in the UK Security Service Act 1989.

The first question is whether the courts are constitutionally capable of dealing with issues of national security. In the US, where there has been a strong tradition of judicial review of executive acts, this has been reflected in some judicial willingness to consider security issues. The Supreme Court, in *US* v. *US District Court* (1972) which concerned the electronic surveillance of domestic political groups, refused to accept that 'national security' was beyond the competence of the courts. Speaking for a unanimous court, Justice Powell said:

> We cannot accept the government's argument that internal security matters are too subtle and complex for judicial evaluation . . . There is no reason to believe that federal Judges will be insensitive to or uncomprehending of the issues involved in domestic security cases . . . If the threat is too subtle or complex for our senior enforcement officers to convey its significance to a court, one may question whether there is a proper cause for surveillance.[21]

Not only did the court reject the competence argument but it also held that domestic security surveillance required a warrant under the Fourth Amendment just as warrants were required in criminal investigation cases (*Katz* v. *US*, *Berger* v. New York, both 1967). The court did not consider whether prior judicial authorisation would be required in foreign intelligence cases. Subsequently the US Court of Appeals considered this in *US* v. *Butenko* (1974); it was held that the court was competent to deal with the issue but it held that warrant requirements could be dispensed with.[22] In 1978 this issue was dealt with by Congress in the Foreign Intelligence Surveillance Act (FISA) (see below).

In the UK the dominant view is that the issue is not for the judges. In 1916 Lord Parker said:

> those who are responsible for the national security must be the sole judges of what the national security requires. It would be obviously undesirable that such matters should be made the subject of evidence in a court of law or discussed in public.[23]

Nothing much had changed by the time the case involving the government ban on trade unions at GCHQ reached the House of Lords. Lord Diplock said:

> National security is the responsibility of the executive government; what action is needed to protect its interests is . . . a matter upon which those upon whom the responsibility rests, they and not the courts of justice, must have the last word. It is *par excellence* a non-judicial question. The judicial process is totally inept to deal with the sort of problems that it involves.[24]

Unlike the USA, where a tradition of judicial review of executive and legislative actions has developed, the UK courts operate in the context of parliamentary supremacy which has come to mean executive dominance through the mechanism of party government. It is clear that during the last 20 years the UK judiciary have become more active in terms of judicial review and have been prepared to invalidate ministerial decisions on the grounds of illegality, irrationality or procedural impropriety.[25] But this has not penetrated far into the area of national security.

For example, Lord Scarman in the GCHQ case was prepared to say that the court would accept the executive's view of what action national security required once the court was satisfied on the facts that national security was at issue, unless it was shown that the opinion was one which no reasonable minister could hold,[26] but in practice little evidence seems to be required to so satisfy a court. A more recent case involved a judicial challenge to a decision of the Home Secretary to deport a Sikh independence campaigner, Karanjit Singh Chahal, who was alleged to be involved in terrorism. Mr Justice Popplewell ruled against the Home Secretary because he showed no sign of having considered a report about the persecution of Sikhs in India, and thus showed some judicial willingness to challenge executive discretion, but the judge did not determine the legal issue of whether an asylum claim might take priority over an expulsion on national security grounds.[27] Supperstone concluded his recent review of this question thus: 'The ambit of judicial review where national security is involved is, in reality, extremely limited.'[28]

There are a number of general factors accounting for the hesitancy of the courts to deal with national security in all countries. Comparing the contribution of courts with that of legislatures and judicial commissions, Peter Hanks suggests a number of structural factors. Commissions such as those by McDonald in Canada and Hope in Australia have had broader terms of reference regarding the organisation and policies of domestic security intelligence agencies, while the courts have been faced with diverse and specific issues – for example, the publication of government information, security intelligence officers' memoirs, and the question of trades unions within security intelligence agencies. Also, a wide variety of views and options are available to commissions whereas courts possess only a limited repertoire of remedies with which to deal with the specific aspects of the case before them. However, concludes Hanks, whether courts' reluctance to become involved in national security questions is because of judicial unwillingness to deal with difficult issues or because of institutional constraints, the consequence of their unwillingness to challenge executive definitions has been to endorse an authoritarian view of the state.[29]

It is important to recall here the discussion in Chapter 2 regarding the double-edged nature of law. This can be seen most clearly in the US where, as exampled above, the courts have restricted executive discretion to use national security as a blanket justification for intrusive surveillance by security intelligence agencies, yet *at the same time*:

> The ultimate effect of much law in this area has been to authorise discretion and flexibility in the management of security practices.[30]

The 'particularistic' nature of case law enables judges to make specific decisions which depart from rule of law principles while maintaining the superiority of those principles.[31] So, for example, 'national security' in a specific case can be cited as a reason why it is necessary to depart from the 'rule of law' *and in order to protect*

283

the rule of law. The main mechanism for this in the UK is the notion of the 'public interest' which incorporates, in the eyes of the judges, upholding the interests of the state.[32]

This is central to analysing not just the capacity of judges to act as 'overseers' of domestic security intelligence agencies, but also the potential impact of legislative changes relating to their organisation and powers. Legislation is prone to two main types of vulnerability. On the one hand it can attempt to be highly detailed in order to try to minimise the room for manoeuvre of those to whom the law will apply. This was broadly the approach of those attempting to pass a comprehensive charter for the FBI through Congress in the later 1970s. It failed partly because of the argument that detailed regulation via statute would not provide a workable framework for security intelligence agencies. On the other hand, a statute enunciating general principles, which may be the only practical way of proceeding, is likely to be particularly vulnerable to having the 'gaps' filled in by those not entirely sympathetic to the intentions of the legislators. The general statute would provide a source of ideological strength, by demonstrating that security intelligence activities were now governed by law, while the actual gaps and ambiguities in that law would be a source of operational strength for the security intelligence agencies.

The following is an example of how 'gaps' may be filled. In *R* v. *Secretary of State for the Home Department, ex parte Northumbria Police Authority* (1988), the Court of Appeal determined that the Home Secretary has the right under the Police Act 1964 to supply CS gas and plastic baton rounds to a Chief Constable, despite the police authority's refusal. However since the more general prerogative power 'to keep the peace' had been used by the Divisional Court to justify their previous decision in the case, the Appeal Court judges considered this also and concluded that the Crown's prerogative includes the general power to take a direct hand in the government and administration of police forces in England and Wales, over and above the Home Secretary's specific statutory powers. A.W. Bradley, commenting on this decision, said:

> . . . it is likely to be remembered as a precedent for use in the future when central government wishes to influence

the front line of policing and has no sure statutory base on which to rely.[33]

Until 1989 the powers of the UK Security Service derived entirely from the prerogative power. The Security Service Act of that year was, in effect, an enabling statute which placed these powers on a statutory footing, aiming thereby to provide some legal protection to the Security Service should it fall foul of, for example, the European Commission of Human Rights or domestic law relating to burglary (see full discussion below). This might be regarded as progress if it could be assumed that the statute replaced the (even vaguer) prerogative powers claimed by the executive, but the Northumbria case suggests it is possible that the prerogative power will be regarded by judges as remaining intact should any gaps appear in the statutory cover. If this is the case regarding police and the peace, then it is not difficult to see it being applied to the 'national security' mandate of the Security Service Act (s.1).[34]

Regarding the specific involvement of the judiciary in overseeing, for example, warrant procedures, in the US a special court sits to hear applications under the Foreign Intelligence Surveillance Act 1978. This Act provided for a procedure that superimposed a requirement for a judicial warrant on the executive approval process which culminated with the Attorney General, and laid down a standard to be applied by the courts which approached, but did not quite meet, the standard used in domestic law enforcement cases. The court, which includes selected judges operating on a rota basis and using secure premises, may issue warrants for one-year surveillance of foreign officials and 90 days for US persons. In its first two-and-a-half years of operation the FISA court issued almost 1,000 warrants and in no case was a government request refused. For some this simply reflects that the new process is a device to legitimise state activities, while there is a contrary argument that the requirement for judicial authorisation has led the executive to be more careful in its screening process.[35] In Canada, federal judges are involved in the procedure for obtaining wiretap warrants under the CSIS Act 1984. There is no information on the refusal rate under the CSIS Act but Brodeur found that during 1974–84 in Canada there were over 10,000 police requests for bugging and telephone tapping authorisations or renewals, of which only 14 were refused by judges.[36]

In the UK these authorisation procedures are contained entirely within the executive branch, first under the Interception of Communications Act 1985 (ICA) regarding mail and telephone intercepts and second, under the Security Service Act 1989 for other 'interferences' with property. Indeed, both statutes specifically exclude the courts from any consideration of these procedures (see above Chapter 5). The only involvement of judges is of those appointed as commissioners under the ICA or SSA or as members of the respective tribunals (see discussion below). Just before the passage of the ICA, Lord Bridge, as a member of the Security Commission, conducted an 'inquiry' into Cathy Massiter's allegations regarding Security Service wiretaps. It was pointed out at the time that Lord Bridge could have carried out only the most formal procedural examination of warrant applications for telephone taps in the six days his inquiry lasted and his conclusion that no warrants had been 'issued in contravention of the appropriate criteria' satisfied nobody.[37]

Special review bodies

In the Franks inquiry into the Falklands war, a group of six privy councillors carried out a full investigation with access to all relevant documents and officials. Although this committee was looking only at one very small part of the intelligence jigsaw some have seen it as a possible precedent for a more permanent body.[38] As a proposal, this is somewhat similar to the Security Intelligence Review Committee's (SIRC) five privy councillors established in Canada in 1984 to provide external oversight of CSIS. The privy councillors are appointed by the government but after consultation with other parties. Those appointed are not necessarily privy councillors before their appointment, a practice which can help to avoid such a committee becoming a sinecure for ex-ministers. They work part-time but have the support of a full-time staff of about a dozen in carrying out their dual functions of review of the CSIS and sitting as an appeals body against refusals of security clearances and hearing other complaints against the actions of the CSIS.

The Chair of SIRC from 1984 until 1989, Ron Atkey, had an academic background and had been a government minister briefly during 1979–80. He was also a director of the Canadian Civil Liberties Association and appeared to symbolise a willingness to extract as much mileage as possible from the review process. During its early years SIRC found its resources stretched between developing its own proactive programme of review while reacting to complaints, appeals, and those issues which arose from press publicity. However, there was a good deal of cross-fertilisation between these different aspects of review and it is reasonable to conclude that the committee did have some real impact on CSIS operations. For example, it was SIRC's concern with the breadth of CSIS counter-subversion investigations that led it to recommend the abolition of the counter-subversion branch (see above pp. 110–11). Subsequently this led to an enormous reduction in the number of files maintained under the counter-subversion mandate, as we saw in Chapter 4. Another measure of the impact of the SIRC has been the extent to which it has been prepared to make public its criticisms of CSIS. Certainly this upset a number of 'insiders', but it is clear that the use of publicity was necessary to induce the CSIS to make changes which it was otherwise resisting, for example in terms of improving the status of civilian recruits compared with those entering from the RCMP.[39]

The committee's initial reporting responsibility is to the minister. So, in terms of the oversight model developed in Chapter 7, SIRC, operating at level three, is to report to the minister at level two. This has brought the committee into conflict with Parliament. Since the IG also reports to the minister, the question arises as to how far SIRC and the IG cover much of the same ground in terms of reviewing CSIS. This issue became quickly apparent to the Special Committee on the Five Year Review of the CSIS Act which reported in 1990. The Committee requested access to both the IG's certificates and those reports which SIRC had made to the minister, but which had not been made public. In both cases access was denied to the Special Committee, in the first case because the certificates were said to constitute confidential 'advice' to ministers[40] and in the second, because SIRC believed it could report only to the minister, except for those reports which it chose to make public.[41] Since the Special

Committee could perceive no difference between the IG and SIRC in their unwillingness to assist Parliament's oversight role it is not surprising that it considered whether one of them might be redundant. Finally, the Special Committee did not recommend the abolition of the IG only because it proposed additional powers for SIRC and that SIRC should report directly to Parliament rather than through the minister.[42] Some members of SIRC itself clearly felt that they should be able to report directly to Parliament.[43] Given the structural location of SIRC 'between' Parliament and the minister, it is inevitable that each side will fear that the committee is too close to the other. On a number of occasions SIRC has been subjected to parliamentary and public criticism because of its alleged closeness to the minister.

This occurred, for example, in connection with a CSIS investigation into what was termed 'native extremism'. During 1988 there were a number of examples of direct action by native Canadians, including sit-ins by Innu in Labrador in protest at low-level training flights by NATO over their traditional hunting grounds. In December, CSIS embarked on an investigation, which was carried out using non-intrusive methods and was concerned to find out what if any potential existed for serious political violence (s.2(c) of the mandate) and whether there was any indication of foreign involvement (s.2(b)). This investigation ended in March 1989, and SIRC was alerted to it by an MP when the committee appeared before the Justice and Solicitor General Standing Committee on May 30, 1989. In June SIRC commenced an inquiry which included examination of the relevant files between 1986 and 1989 and interviews with CSIS officials. In its report to the Solicitor General in November, SIRC concluded that CSIS had the authority to carry out an investigation and that it was conducted properly. But, given the sensitivity of the issues surrounding native Canadians, the Committee was critical that the investigation was not authorised at the highest level where the CSIS Director would be involved, that is the Target Approval and Review Committee (TARC), and that the targeting was essentially open-ended regarding the native community rather than relating specifically to individuals and organisations. SIRC also said that an interview carried out by a CSIS official with a missionary working with the Innu, just before the investigation formally started, amounted to a breach of regulations, though CSIS contested this.[44] When there was subsequent violence in native communities between March 1989 and July 1990, SIRC reviewed CSIS activities in relation to that violence. SIRC reported that there was no evidence of CSIS investigation of this violence since it was considered to be a criminal matter and outside the CSIS mandate.[45]

However, when the minister published a version of SIRC's report, with significant portions missing for reasons of national security or privacy, the Solicitor General's accompanying press release appeared to mislead. SIRC later said:

> It will be seen that a statement in the Solicitor General's news release, namely that we found no evidence of any misconduct by Service employees, does not reflect our conclusions.[46]

This comment was published in September 1990. When SIRC had earlier appeared before the Special Commons committee reviewing the CSIS Act, the new Chair, John Bassett, had declined to tell MPs whether or not the committee had challenged the minister's misleading statement.[47] As a result of this episode SIRC announced that it would in future prepare two versions of any special reports it made to the minister under s.54 of the Act, a full version for official consumption and a second version without sensitive information which the minister could make public.[48]

The fact that the Commons review committee was unable to get a sight of SIRC's s.54 report on the CSIS 'native extremism' inquiry, or, indeed, any of the others made since 1984, clearly led to a great sense of frustration on the part of MPs and the conclusion among some of those involved that the idea that SIRC was Parliament's surrogate in the oversight of the CSIS was unsustainable.[49] Stuart Farson, who was Research Director to the Review Committee, has argued that this idea was specifically negated by the very provision for a five-year *parliamentary* review of the CSIS Act,[50] but there is a great deal of difference between the kind of oversight that can be provided by an ongoing committee such as SIRC with a staff of 12 and by a quinquennial parliamentary committee with a smaller staff. Therefore the Commons committee's final recommendations for the establishment of a permanent parliamentary subcommittee and a direct reporting relationship between SIRC and Parliament (level three) rather than the minister (level two) did represent a logical step forward in terms of the model developed here. The government did not follow this suggestion, preferring that the minister continue to receive both SIRC's and IG's reports. This reflected the preference of the executive to control as far as possible the oversight process.

In Australia, after the first Hope Commission, the most radical innovation at this level was the establishment of a Security Appeals Tribunal (SAT), chaired by a judge, who could hear appeals against and overrule security assessments of individuals in terms of their eligibility for work in the civil service. In 1983 the SAT determined that being a communist was not necessarily a bar to employment in the public sector, thus reversing what had been official policy and the basic assumption for most ASIO operations since 1917. Citing the Australian Tribunal, Judge McDonald recommended the establishment of a similar body in Canada,[51] but the CSIS Act placed this appeals function within the mandate of the Security Intelligence Review Committee.

The Security Service Act 1989

It has already been noted that the UK government's motives for introducing this legislation were primarily to augment the legitimacy of the Security Service and to legalise those of its operations which were otherwise unlawful. The reason for doing so at this particular time was a combination of the heightened public awareness of the Service in the wake of the *Spycatcher* fiasco and the likelihood of an adverse decision from the European Court of Human Rights. In the Swedish case of *Leander* in 1987 the Court had established the precedent that citizens must have some means of redress against domestic security services.[52] This is important in understanding the Act and comparing it with changes made elsewhere. The legislation in Canada and Australia, and the executive changes in the United States, came about after extensive judicial or legislative inquiries into the activities of the domestic security intelligence agencies. Those inquiries had exposed a variety of abuses of rights and inefficiencies and the subsequent reforms were aimed at better political control of the security intelligence agencies and more effective means of external oversight and review.

The Security Service Act was preceded by no inquiry at all, and was a surprise to all when announced in the Queen's Speech in November 1988. For the first time it provided a legal basis for the existence of the Security Service and, as we saw in Chapter 3, an extremely broad mandate for its operations. In terms of ministerial control it inaugurated a formal reporting chain in which the Director-General will make an annual report to the Prime Minister and the Home Secretary (see Fig. 8.1 (*18*) below. Parenthetical numbers in the remainder of this section all refer to Fig. 8.1.) No provision was made for the publication of any part of this report, as is now the case with an annual report from both ASIO and CSIS.

In one sense it is inappropriate to discuss the Security Service Act in this chapter on the variety of institutions involved in the review and oversight of domestic security intelligence agencies because the government made clear that it did not view its proposals for a commissioner and a tribunal as institutions for providing such oversight. Douglas Hurd, then Home Secretary, described his proposals as catering for the 'aggrieved outsider' to complement the Staff Counsellor who had been introduced in 1987 to cater for the 'aggrieved insider'.[53] On two separate occasions in his speech introducing the Bill in the second reading debate, Hurd contrasted the government's proposals with others 'who have argued for a system of oversight and review'.[54]

The commissioner/tribunal structure and their respective functions imitate directly those introduced to deal with mail and telephone interceptions in the Interception of Communications Act 1985. The Tribunal may consist of three to five people and is to investigate complaints about the Security Service, while the Commissioner is to assist the Tribunal and deals specifically with the question of warrants. Similarly under the ICA the Commissioner has the function of assisting the Tribunal (s.8(1)(b)) but as of 1990 he had had no contact with the Tribunal in implementing any of the Act's procedures.[55] The Security Service Act establishes two main chains of 'review', one covering specifically warrants and the other concerning complaints about other Service activities. The Secretary of State may issue warrants to the Security Service authorising

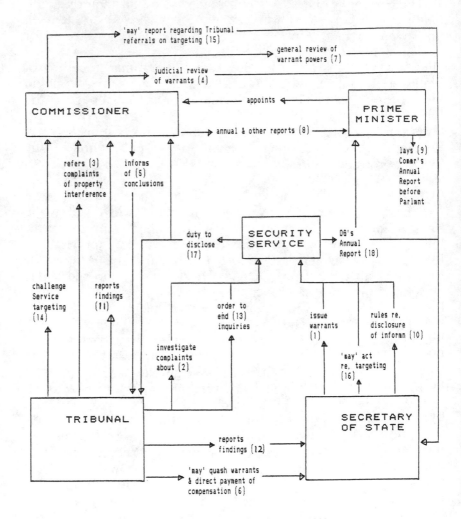

Figure 8.1 Security Service Act, 1989

'interference with property' (*1*) if it is 'thought necessary' to enable the Service to gain information which is 'likely to be of substantial value' in assisting the Service (s.3). Any complaint made to the Tribunal (*2*) regarding some 'interference with property' will be forwarded to the Commissioner (*3*) If the Commissioner finds that a warrant had been issued then s/he applies judicial review principles regarding the reasonableness of the Secretary of State's decision (Schedule 1, §4(1) (*4*) and informs the Tribunal of the decision (*5*). If the Commissioner finds in the complainant's favour (that is that a warrant had been improperly issued), the Tribunal will inform the complainant of the favourable 'determination' (Schedule 1, §5(2)), may order the quashing of the warrant and may, if the Commissioner thinks compensation should be made, direct the Secretary of State to make payment (Schedule 1, §6(2)) (*6*).

The Act is silent on what happens if the Commissioner finds that no warrant has been issued. Given his resources, it is unlikely that he will investigate whether some 'interference with property' took place without a warrant. In a similar situation, the Commissioner under the Interception of Communications Act has made clear that if he suspects interception has taken place without a warrant, an offence under section 1 of the ICA, it is the responsibility of the police, not the Commissioner to investigate.[56] Therefore, assuming that the Security Service will not volunteer the information that they have acted without a warrant, the complainant will simply be told by the Tribunal that no favourable determination has been made (Schedule 1, §5(3)).

The Commissioner is also to 'keep under review' the exercise by the Secretary of State of his warrant powers (s.4(3)) (*7*). This is an interesting use of the term 'review' in the Act considering the Home Secretary's concern to deny that the government was establishing a 'review or oversight' structure. The Commissioner is also to make an annual report to the Prime Minister (that is, in terms of the model, level three reporting to level two) (s.4(5)) (*8*), and this report, like that of SIRC in Canada, will then be laid before Parliament, subject to the exclusion of any sections, whose publication would be considered prejudicial to national security (s.4(6)) (*9*).

The second chain relates to other complaints. If a person complains that the Security Service has 'made inquiries' about them, the Tribunal may determine whether that is so and whether the Service had reasonable grounds for their inquiries (Schedule 1, §2(2,3)). Where the Tribunal finds that the complainant was investigated because s/he was a member of 'a category of persons' regarded as a proper target by the Security Service, then the tribunal will regard this as reasonable grounds for investigating the person if they find that the Service reasonably believed the person to be in such a category (Schedule 1, §2(4)). This is important because it institutionalises *per se* targeting. As was discussed in Chapter 5, this has been the main cause historically of over-extensive surveillance of legitimate political activities by domestic security intelligence agencies. In Canada, for example, there has been a major effort by the review bodies to ensure that individuals are targeted only as a result of an individual threat assessment, and not simply as a result of being a member or supporter of some group.

If a complainant alleges that information gathered in a vetting inquiry has been disclosed by the Security Service then the Tribunal's concern is only with whether the Service had reason to believe the information was true (Schedule 1, §3). If so then the complaint will not be upheld. If the Tribunal determines that the Service did not have reasonable grounds for their actions, then it shall tell the complainant of the favourable determination and report its findings to both the Commissioner (*11*) and the Secretary of State (*12*) (Schedule 1, §5(1)). If the complaint concerned Service investigative activities then the tribunal may order them to be ended and any relevant records destroyed (*13*) (on the issue of file retention see Chapter 5). If the complaint was about the disclosure of information then compensation may be awarded (Schedule 1, §6(1)).

Finally, the Tribunal may report to the Commissioner if it believes that the Service may not be justified in regarding all members of any particular group as requiring investigation (*14*), or, even if a complaint is not upheld, the Tribunal thinks that an investigation into the reasonableness of the Service's actions may be required (Schedule 1, §7(1–2)). In these cases the Commissioner, having investigated, may report to the Secretary of State (*15*) who may take such action as is thought fit (*16*). The Tribunal gives no reasons for its decisions, makes no public report of its actions and its decisions cannot be challenged in court.[57]

It is clear that this structure for 'aggrieved outsiders' has been constructed neither for elegance not for impact. Apart from being needlessly complex, its pre-eminent objective is clearly to provide a minimalist review structure that would pass muster before the European Court of Human Rights. It can be argued that the breadth of the mandate for the Security Service itself contained in Section 1 of the Act would make it very difficult for almost any oversight structure to be able to draw a line on permissible security intelligence activities, but the 'mandates' for the Tribunal and Commissioner are restricted almost entirely to procedural questions. Therefore, although Security Service officers have a 'duty to disclose' (s.4(4)) information to both Commissioner and Tribunal (*17*), it is clear that neither the mandate nor the resources of these will enable them to carry out any systematic review of the range of organisational issues, policies and practices discussed in Chapters 4, 5 and 6.

That this inelegant structure is designed primarily as a legitimating mechanism for the Security Service is evidenced further by the contemporaneous passage of the Official Secrets Act 1989. This replaced Section 2 of the 1911 Official Secrets Act with a series of provisions aimed at more effectively preventing the disclosure of official information in six areas.[58] Section 1 of the Act relates to security intelligence information and makes it an absolute offence for any security intelligence officer to disclose any information which is about or which purports to be about security intelligence. Therefore, it might be asked, how will potential 'aggrieved outsiders' find out that they have been the subject of inquiries or that their property has been interfered with? Only if some security intelligence officer is ultimately prepared to risk two years' imprisonment by telling them! The Security Service and the Official Secrets Acts of 1989 may well represent the first occasion on which a government has established a structure for investigating complaints against a state agency at the same time as specifically criminalising any disclosures of the very information upon which the ability to make complaints rests!

The early product of the new structure has done nothing to contradict the contention of its minimalist intent. For example, the Act states that complaints about Security Service inquiries which began before the implementation of the Act (18 December

1989) and which had not been discontinued by then could be investigated, but the Tribunal has subsequently told one complainant that it would consider only that aspect of his complaint which had occurred after the implementation date.[59] In his first report, Lord Justice Stuart Smith, the Commissioner, admitted that it did not contain much information beyond what was in the Act itself. He detailed the procedures by which warrants are issued by the Home and Northern Ireland Secretaries , and said that he had examined all the applications for the year. His first two annual reports referred to his examination of files and interviews with Security Service officers in relation to a sample of the warrants. He said that he did not think it was in the public interest to publish the number of warrants because of their relatively small number and the limited purposes involved. He reported his satisfaction that the Secretaries of State had properly exercised their powers. He reported that the Tribunal had received 55 complaints in 1990, 22 of which had been forwarded to him because they alleged property interference (3 in Figure 8.1). Investigations were completed in 52 cases and no complaints were upheld. A further 29 complaints were investigated in 1991, none being upheld. Both reports were four-and-a-half pages long.[60]

LEVEL FOUR: CITIZENS' OVERSIGHT

It is clear that the normal level of public discussion of security intelligence matters is slight compared with areas of state policy such as the economy, housing and education. However, this is hardly surprising given the strenuous efforts made by the state to prevent any information about security intelligence becoming available and because it rarely intrudes directly into people's lives. These general factors are compounded in the UK where secrecy is particularly stringent and there is a general lack of consciousness of 'rights' *vis-à-vis* the state, certainly when compared with states possessing more republican constitutions such as the US.

As we saw in Chapter 2, Dahl argues that for a country to be governed by polyarchy its military and police agencies must be controlled by civilians who are themselves subject to control by the 'institutions of polyarchy'.[61] Organised groups and political parties represent the main such institutions at this level; in the terms of this analysis, how far towards the innermost levels of the state do parties and groups penetrate? The answer is: not very far. Still, it is important to consider briefly what examples there are of, respectively, political party, group and more *ad hoc* action.

Loch Johnson identifies a number of areas in which the political parties in the US have debated intelligence controversies, for example the role of the CIA in Vietnam, Watergate and Iran-Contra, and that of the FBI in domestic political surveillance. During the 1980s the aggressive foreign policies of the Reagan administration led to more clear-cut party divisions in the congressional intelligence committees.[62] In the UK, the political parties took no obvious position over security intelligence matters until the 1980s when both the Labour and (then) Liberal parties published extensive discussion documents. The former proposed, first, an Information and Privacy Act to replace the Official Secrets Act and aiming to provide freedom of information and data protection. Second, a Security Act was proposed which would provide a statutory mandate for each of the security intelligence agencies, clarify ministerial responsibility and provide for an annual parliamentary debate on the agencies' annual reports. A parliamentary select committee would be established and security intelligence budgets would be scrutinised by the Public Accounts Committee. There would be a general prohibition on unauthorised surveillance and greater regulation of the interception of communications.[63] In 1991, the Labour Party's Charter of Rights incorporated most of these proposals, although they were presented in outline only. The main innovation was that the select committee would be assisted by an Inspector General, who would have a wide-ranging remit to investigate individual complaints and check that the agencies conformed to their statutory role.[64] Unlike the Canadian IG, this one would operate at level three.

The Liberal Party's proposals were broadly similar: a statutory charter for the Security Service and SIS (but not, apparently, GCHQ), a parliamentary select committee of privy councillors, a code of conduct and discipline for Special Branch and Security Service officers relating to information-gathering activities, and outlawing unauthorised wiretapping and surveillance.[65] All these proposals foundered in the 1980s on the rocks of Thatcherite majorities in the Commons, except for damage-limitation measures such as the Security Service Act. Under John Major, the strength of the arguments regarding the need for further reforms including a modicum of parliamentary oversight appear to have borne fruit, but there is still a significant difference between the minimalist measures emanating from the government and the more rights-oriented proposals advanced by Labour and the Liberal Democrats.

Elsewhere, as we have seen, the clearest party view was to be found in Australia where the Labour Party sought to bring about change via the Hope commissions and subsequent legislation. In Canada the divisions between the two main parties, the Progressive Conservatives and the Liberals, are based far more on historical and regional rather than ideological factors and the only consistent party position – one of scepticism towards the need for a separate domestic security intelligence agency – was provided by the New Democratic Party.

There are few organised groups contributing to the security intelligence debate. Those that there are have developed in the context of particular controversies and some have continued to campaign. In the United States the 1975 investigations spawned a group advocating in defence of the CIA, the Association of Former Intelligence Officers, and the Center for National Security Studies, funded as a project of the American Civil Liberties Union. The former, emphasising the importance of 'effective intelligence',[66] publishes a series of monographs, the Intelligence Profession Series, as part of an education project. The latter was established 'to resist incursions against civil liberties justified on national security grounds';[67] it publishes *First Principles* which covers major developments in the courts and Congress and includes articles dealing with particular issues, It also publishes research reports and conducts litigation on behalf of people and groups whose rights are perceived to have been violated in the name of national security. The other main group in the US is the Consortium for the Study of Intelligence, a Rightward-leaning group of academics which was established in 1979 under the auspices of the National Strategy Information Center and has sponsored regular research colloquia on various aspects of the US intelligence process. The proceedings of these have been published in an 'Intelligence Requirements . . .'[68] series under the editorship of Roy Godson.

In Canada the most systematic input to the security intelligence debate has come from the Canadian Civil Liberties Association and, since 1985, from the Canadian Association for Security and Intelligence Studies (CASIS). The former played a role in co-ordinating opposition to the government's first attempt in 1983 to pass the CSIS Bill. This included lobbying activities but also involved public rallies addressed by, among others, provincial attorneys general who also opposed the Bill.[69] The latter is a broad church containing academics, journalists, government officials, lawyers, citizens and former intelligence officials. It has provided a forum for the debates and controversies following the creation of CSIS. For example it hosted a conference in 1989 at the start of Parliament's five-year review of the CSIS Act at which on-the-record discussions covered a wide political spectrum. It was addressed by the then Solicitor General and some of its sessions were attended by the CSIS Director.[70]

In the UK campaigns have arisen similarly; for example, a Campaign for the Limitation of Secret Police Powers was set up in 1956 and produced two reports on the activities of the Security Service and other agencies, mainly in the context of the vetting procedures introduced into the civil service from 1948 onwards.[71] Out of the campaigns surrounding the deportation of Philip Agee (former CIA) and Mark Hosenball (journalist) and the ABC case in 1977 developed the publication of *State Research Bulletin* which continued regularly until 1982 and has now been resurrected as *Statewatch*. Since 1991 this has provided a bi-monthly bulletin and a computerised information base for subscribers,[72] in both of which policing and security intelligence provide a major component. Similarly, *Lobster* is published by two journalists and, describing itself as a journal of parapolitics, produces well-researched articles into diverse aspects of secrecy and intelligence.[73] The UK has no equivalent of CASIS but, mirroring perhaps the secrecy of the British state, an informal group of academics, the Study Group on Intelligence, produces a members-only newsletter.[74]

Liberty (formerly the National Council for Civil Liberties) has provided the main source and support for litigation contesting specific aspects of security intelligence operations in the UK. As we have seen, the main case which has been pursued through the British courts and then onto the European Commission of Human Rights is that relating to the surveillance of Harriet Harman and Patricia Hewitt while they worked for NCCL. In general the conditions for public interest litigation in the UK are poor. A recent comparative survey argues that in the US, Canada and Australia

> constitutional litigation is an integral part of the dialogue by which constitutional standards are shaped and reshaped under changing conditions.[75]

As we have seen, this dialogue is somewhat curtailed in the area of 'national security' but in the UK, by contrast, judges tend to see constitutional litigation 'as an illegitimate interference with the political process'.[76]

Publicity is a significant weapon in the struggle to control bureaucracies in general,[77] and access to files is the very centre of attempts to exercise real control over security intelligence agencies. In the United States the first major inroads into the files of the FBI were made by the Church Committee and many were reprinted as part of their hearings. Further documents have been obtained by various means. In 1973 the Socialist Workers Party and the Young Socialist Alliance filed a lawsuit seeking damages for the illegal acts they had suffered and an injunction to halt any further FBI countering actions. Pre-trial proceedings lasted eight years and produced hundreds of thousands of pages from FBI files. The trial itself lasted three months in 1981 and the decision was announced in 1986. The FBI was found guilty of violations of the plaintiffs' constitutional rights, and ordered to pay $264,000. A year later an injunction against any further use of FBI files on the SWP or YSA was granted. The Justice Department did not appeal.[78]

Also, there have been many requests under the Freedom of Information Act. These have been so extensive that in 1984 the FBI's Office of Congressional and Public Affairs published a guide to researchers wishing to access FBI records.[79] Material which has already been processed under the Freedom of

Information Act can be read and copied at the FBI Headquarters Reading Room and staff will assist with the making of further FOI requests where necessary. Researchers are even advised that the previous 'Do Not File' memoranda may now be accessed through the central records system![80] These files have formed the basis of a number of biographies of Hoover and other studies.[81]

On the other hand, much material has been deleted from the released documents because it is covered by one of the exemptions permitted by the legislation. In the case of the FBI this is likely to be either 'national security' or 'law enforcement', and in some cases has led to the deletion of entire files – for example, 95,000 pages relating to the Rosenberg case in the 1950s. The strengthening of the FOI in 1974 and President Carter's Executive Order 12065 issued in July 1978 combined to erect more stringent tests before exemptions could apply and made it possible for federal district courts to determine whether classification of documents was appropriate; but President Reagan's EO 12356 in April 1983 made it far easier for the FBI and other intelligence agencies to withhold documents.[82] Nevertheless, complaints were still made from some quarters as to the damaging impact of the FOI Act on Bureau operations and the cost of responding to FOI and Privacy Act requests for information, said to be $11.5m in 1980.[83] Also, in 1977 the FBI adopted a policy of destroying some investigation files over five years old. This policy was successfully contested in court and the Bureau may now not destroy records without their being reviewed by government archivists.[84]

More recently, similar struggles over access have taken place in Canada. An Access to Information Act was passed in 1980 which has granted rights of access to citizens and shifted the burden of proving that material falls within exempted categories to the government. As far as security intelligence information is concerned the main exemptions are s.13 regarding information obtained in confidence from foreign governments or international organisations, and s.15 which exempts the disclosure of information

> which could reasonably be expected to be injurious to the conduct of international affairs, the defence of Canada

or any state allied or associated with Canada or the detection, prevention or suppression of subversive or hostile activites . . . [85]

These categories are enumerated in more detail in the Act, and s.16 further exempts certain information relating to law enforcement and investigative methods. Appeals against any refusals of access may be made to the Information Commissioner, and subsequently to the courts. Cabinet documents are excluded entirely, but only until they are 20 years old. In 1987 the passage of the National Archives of Canada Act provided stronger powers to the archivist to prevent the destruction and take control of records which the archivist believed to be of importance, and since the National Archives normally takes a stronger view on accessibility than the originating agencies this is seen as a development which will work in the interests of scholars, especially if they support the archivist in any battles with the agencies over disposition of their documents.[86] A number of Canadian scholars have benefited from this greater access; for example, Reg Whitaker and Greg Kealey tried and failed to gain access to the RCMP Security Service's historical counter-subversion files, but were able to obtain access to the RCMP internal intelligence bulletins for the period from the early 1920s to mid-1950s.[87]

Under the Australian Freedom of Information Act 1982 all ASIO documents are exempt, although if information supplied by ASIO to other agencies is incorporated into their documents it is not automatically exempt and ASIO has to argue its case. However, the Archives Act, 1983 – permitting access to records over 30 years old – concerns ASIO more, although some of its material is excluded: for example, informers' identities and information provided by foreign agencies. ASIO argued for a general exemption but, after a report from the Parliamentary Committee, the government decided that the Attorney General should arbitrate in any disputes about the release of ASIO records.[88]

Whatever the variations in practice throughout North America and Australia,[89] they present a clear contrast with the situation in the UK. The review in Chapter 1 gave some indication of the entirely haphazard way in which security intelligence information has become available to scholars in the UK; and the reform of the Official Secrets Act in 1989, whatever else it was, was not a freedom of information measure. Since then William Waldegrave, the minister responsible for the Citizen's Charter, has announced a government intention to increase the flow of information to the public, including even an invitation to historians to make proposals for the release of intelligence material such as JIC assessments.[90] However, a *right* of access to information is still rejected, and reliance on ministerial intentions is more likely to reinforce than challenge traditional information control processes in the UK.

Even in the United States where, it might be argued, there are important examples of oversight being exercised at level four, it is clear that the 'polyarchical' processes of organised group politics do not penetrate very often into the secret state and do not constitute democratic control over intelligence policy.[91] Finally, there is always the possibility that the absence, or failure to be effective, of oversight institutions will provoke more dramatic and direct forms of 'oversight'. The breaching of the Berlin Wall remains the best remembered symbol of the collapse of the East German regime in 1989 but equally significant was the invasion and occupation of offices of the MfS (Stasi) in Berlin, Leipzig and elsewhere in January 1990. The subsequent liberation of the agency's files under the control of a special commission headed by Joachim Gauck, a Lutheran minister, has proved highly controversial. Hundreds of thousands wrote in to seek access to their files but the subsequent identification of Stasi informers has proved extremely painful for many people and the extensive exposures have been contrasted with the treatment of Nazi supporters.[92]

Western states have not been immune from similar direct action. In March 1971 a group presumed to be anti-Vietnam war activists broke into the FBI office in Media, Pennsylvania, and stole about 1,000 classified documents detailing COINTELPRO operations. Calling themselves the Citizens' Commission to Investigate the FBI, they subsequently copied the documents in batches to the news media and legislators. The full story of COINTELPRO subsequently emerged from the SWP legal action against the FBI, but the Media burglary has been credited with causing Hoover to cancel all COINTELPRO shortly thereafter.[93] Such commissions are the ultimate form of oversight.

CONCLUSION

Unless the secret state is to be allowed complete autonomy from other institutions, that is, in terms of Chapter 2, it becomes an 'independent security state', questions of control and oversight must be considered at several different levels. In this chapter we have considered the possibilities for oversight outside the executive branch, that is at the third level in our model. The major controversy in parliamentary systems has been whether there should be special committees for security intelligence in the assembly. The trend is clearly towards these, but their precise mandate is crucial. It is important that there are parliamentary committees because they are a symbol of the importance of democratic control, but because they are such a symbol it is equally important that their role is not purely decorative. If it is, then they may simply provide an extra cover of legitimacy to the operations of the secret state. Therefore great care must be given to the membership, powers and resources of any such committee. If it is concluded that it cannot be provided with adequate resources then serious consideration should be given to the creation of a special review body which would be able to carry out more systematic review and which would report to the parliamentary committee.

The judiciary has been the main alternative institution considered to be capable of carrying out oversight. This is entirely logical to the extent that there is a greater effort to subject security intelligence agencies to legal checks, but involving judges is no panacea. If they are too 'executive-minded', for example, their contribution to real oversight may be as little as a parliamentary committee consisting solely of ex-ministers. Some of the arguments regarding judicial involvement are explored more thoroughly in the next chapter.

Processes of oversight operate at their weakest and most haphazard at level four. In the UK the strengthening of these would require political changes far beyond the confines of this analysis. For example, the ability even to construct an accurate history of security intelligence is hampered by the lack of access to historical records. The lack of positive rights, such as to privacy, means that there is no basis on which to mount legal challenges to security intelligence operations. Overall, however, the dominance of government by the executive apparently ensures that any changes to these will reinforce rather than weaken the government's control of information processes.

NOTES

1. McDonald, Second Report, *Freedom and Security Under the Law* (Ottawa: Minister of Supply and Services, 1981), pp. 896–905.
2. C.E.S. Franks, *Parliament and Security Matters, A Study Prepared for the McDonald Commission* (Ottawa: Minister of Supply and Services, 1980), p. 36.
3. Report of the Special Committee of the Senate on the CSIS, *Delicate Balance* (Ottawa: Minister of Supply and Services, November 1983), p. 32.
4. Canada, House of Commons, *Minutes of Proceedings and Evidence of Standing Committee on Justice and Legal Affairs*, 11 May 1984, p. 23.
5. Canada, House of Commons, *Minutes of Proceedings and Evidence of Standing Committee on Justice and Legal Affairs*, 10 May 1984, p. 68.
6. Congressional Quarterly, *Weekly Reports* (Washington DC: Congressional Quarterly Inc., 7 March 1987), p. 416.
7. The rules of the Lobby, 1969 version, were published in *Lobster*, 23, June 1992, pp. 27–8.
8. S. Farson, 'Parliament's Capacity to Conduct a Comprehensive Review: Weak Link in the Chain of Accountability', paper for SIRC Seminar, Vancouver, February 1991 discusses in general the experience of the parliamentary review committee. See also S. Farson, 'Problems of Political Oversight', paper for Annual Conference of CASIS, Queen's University, Kingston, Ontario, June 1991.
9. Report of the Special Committee on the Review of the CSIS Act, *In Flux But Not In Crisis* (Ottawa: Queen's Printer for Canada, September 1990), pp. 191–7.
10. Solicitor General, *On Course: National Security for the 1990s* (Ottawa: Minister of Supply and Services, February 1991), p. 79.
11. F. Cain, 'Accountability and the ASIO: A Brief History', in A.S. Farson *et al.* (eds), *Security and Intelligence in a Changing World* (London: Frank Cass, 1991), p. 123; P. Hanks, 'Accountability

for Security Intelligence Activities in Australia', in P.Hanks and J.D. McCamus, *National Security: Surveillance and Accountability in a Democratic Society* (Cowansville, Québec: Les Editions Yvon Blais, 1989), pp. 51–3.

12. Hanks, ibid, p. 52.

13. Home Affairs Committee, *Accountability of the Security Service*, HC 265 (London: HMSO, 1993); Home Secretary, *Accountability of the Security Service*, Cm 2197 (London: HMSO, 1993).

14. R. Norton-Taylor, *In Defence of the Realm?* (London: Civil Liberties Trust, 1990), p. 133.

15. Similarly, in 1992 the Conservative majority on the House of Commons Select Committee on Trade and Industry took a more deferential stance towards the intelligence services in its report on the Iraqi supergun affair. *The Guardian*, 14 March 1992, p. 1, 17 March 1992, p. 1.

16. S. Turner, *Secrecy and Democracy: the CIA in Transition* (London: Sidgwick & Jackson, 1986), p. 219.

17. Ibid, p. 169.

18. L.K. Johnson, *America's Secret Power* (New York: Oxford University Press, 1989), pp. 119–20.

19. I. Leigh and L. Lustgarten, 'The Security Service Act, 1989', *Modern Law Review*, 52(6), 1989, pp. 814–19 discusses the main arguments regarding parliamentary oversight in the UK context.

20. M. Raskin, 'Democracy Versus the National Security State', *Law and Contemporary Problems*, 40(3), 1976, pp. 205–6.

21. Quoted in M. Supperstone, 'The Law relating to Security in Great Britain', in K.G. Robertson, *British and American Approaches to Intelligence* (Basingstoke: Macmillan, 1987), p. 221.

22. J. M. Oseth, *Regulating US Intelligence Operations* (Lexington: University Press of Kentucky, 1985), p. 55.

23. Quoted in D. Pannick, 'State of Silence', *The Guardian*, 28 July 1986, p. 11.

24. Quoted in Supperstone, supra (note 21), pp. 224–5.

25. J.A.G. Griffith, *The Politics of the Judiciary* (London: Fontana, 4th edition, 1991), p. 125.

26. Supperstone, supra (note 21), p. 226.

27. *The Guardian*, 3 December 1991, p. 2.

28. Supperstone, supra (note 21), p. 226.

29. P. Hanks, 'National Security – A Political Concept', *Monash University Law Review*, 14, 1988, pp. 132–3.

30. J. Shattuck, 'National Security a Decade After', *Democracy*, 3(1), 1983, p. 69.
31. D.J. McBarnet, *Conviction* (Basingstoke: Macmillan, 1983), p. 161.
32. Griffith, supra (note 25), pp. 278–82.
33. A.W Bradley, 'Police Powers and the Prerogative', *Public Law*, Autumn 1988, p. 302.
34. See also Leigh and Lustgarten, supra (note 19), pp. 826–8.
35. Oseth, supra (note 22), pp. 108–10.
36. J.-P. Brodeur, 'Criminal Justice and National Security', in Hanks and McCamus, supra (note 11), p. 63.
37. *The Guardian*, 7 March 1985, p. 1.
38. For example, C. Andrew, *Secret Service* (London: Heinemann, 1985), p. 505. Former Prime Minister James Callaghan, however, accused Franks of throwing a 'bucket of whitewash' over his report: P. Hennessy, *Whitehall* (London: Secker & Warburg, 1989), p. 586.
39. For full discussion see P. Gill, 'Symbolic or Real? The Impact of the Canadian SIRC, 1984–88', *Intelligence and National Security*, 4(3), 1989, pp. 550–75.
40. Farson, 'Problems of Political Oversight', supra (note 8), pp. 35–6.
41. Special Committee, supra (note 9), pp. 155–60.
42. Farson, 'Problems of Political Oversight', supra (note 8), pp. 34–6.
43. Farson, 'Parliament's capacity . . .', supra (note 8), p. 23.
44. SIRC, *Annual Report for 1989–90* (Ottawa: Minister of Supply and Services, 1990), pp. 27–31.
45. SIRC, *Annual Report for 1990–91* (Ottawa: Minister of Supply and Services, 1991), pp. 25–7.
46. SIRC, supra (note 44), p. 28.
47. Farson, 'Parliament's capacity . . .', supra (note 8), pp. 25–7.
48. SIRC, supra (note 44), p. 33.
49. Farson, 'Parliament's Capacity . . .', supra (note 8), p. 9.
50. Farson, 'Problems of Political Oversight', supra (note 8), p. 11.
51. McDonald, supra (note 1), pp. 809–11.
52. C. Andrew, 'The British View of Security and Intelligence', in Farson *et al.* (eds), supra (note 11), pp. 17–18.
53. HC Deb., 15 December 1988, col. 1117.
54. Ibid; see also col. 1119.
55. Interview with Lord Justice Lloyd, Commissioner, 10 July 1990.

56. Ibid.
57. See further Leigh and Lustgarten, supra (note 18), pp. 834–5.
58. S. Palmer, 'Tightening Secrecy Law: the Official Secrets Act 1989', *Public Law*, Summer 1990, pp. 243–56.
59. *The Independent*, 27 June 1990.
60. Cm 1480, March 1991; Cm 1946, May 1992 (1991 on cover).
61. R. Dahl, *Modern Political Analysis* (Englewood Cliffs, NJ: Prentice-Hall International, 5th edition, 1991), p. 82.
62. L.K. Johnson, 'Strategic Intelligence: An American Perspective', in Farson *et al.*, supra (note 11), pp. 59–60.
63. *Freedom and the Security Services* (London: Labour Party, 1983).
64. *The Charter of Rights* (London: Labour Party, 1991), p. 9.
65. Report of the Liberal Party's Intelligence Services Working Group, *Liberty and Security* (Hebden Bridge: Hebden Royd Publications, 1986).
66. Published from 6723 Whittier Avenue, Suite 303A, McLean, Virginia 22101, USA.
67. Published from 122 Maryland Avenue, NE, Washington DC, 20002, USA.
68. Published in Lexington Books by D.C. Heath and Company, Lexington, MA.
69. *Toronto Globe and Mail*, 24 June 1983, p. 8.
70. Papers subsequently published in Farson *et al.* (eds), supra (note 11.
71. T. Bunyan, *The History and Practice of Political Police in Britain* (London: Quartet, 1977), p. 166.
72. Published from PO Box 1516, London N16 0EW, UK.
73. Published from 214 Westbourne Avenue, Hull, HU5 3JB, UK.
74. Secretary of the Group is Ken Robertson, Department of Sociology, University of Reading, Whiteknights, Box 218, Reading RG6 2AA, UK.
75. D. Feldman, 'Public Interest Litigation and Constitutional Theory in Comparative Perspective', *Modern Law Review*, 55(1), January 1992, p. 56.
76. Ibid.
77. B.G. Peters, *The Politics of Bureaucracy* (New York: Longman, 2nd edition, 1984), pp. 242–3.
78. M. Jayko (ed.), *FBI On Trial: The Victory in the SWP Suit against Government Spying* (New York: Pathfinder, 1988), pp. 5–7.
79. Research Unit, Office of Congressional and Public Affairs,

Conducting Research in FBI Records (Washington DC: FBI, 1984).

80. Ibid, p. 6.
81. For example, W, Churchill and J. Vander Wall, *Agents of Repression: the FBI's Secret War against the Black Panther Party and the American Indian Movement* (Boston: South End Press, 1990); J.K. Davis, *Spying on America: the FBI's Domestic Counter-intelligence Program* (New York: Preager, 1992); W.W. Keller, *The Liberals and J. Edgar Hoover* (Princeton: Princeton University Press, 1989); R.G. Powers, *Secrecy and Power: The Life of J. Edgar Hoover* (New York: Free Press, 1987); A.G. Theoharis and J.S. Cox, *The Boss: J.E. Hoover and the Great American Inquisition* (London: Harrap, 1989).
82. W. Churchill and J. Vander Wall, *The COINTELPRO Papers: Documents from the FBI's Secret Wars Against Dissent in the United States* (Boston: South End Press, 1990), pp. 23–32.
83. A.S. Regnery, 'What Kinds of Federal Laws and Attorney General Guidelines are Needed?' in R. Godson (ed.), *Intelligence Requirements for the 1990s: Domestic Intelligence* (Lexington MA: D.C. Heath, 1986), pp. 185–9; see also S. Katz, 'National Security Controls, Information and Communication in the US', *Government Information Quarterly*, 4(1), 1987, pp. 63–81.
84. T.G. Poveda, *Lawlessness and Reform: the FBI in Transition* (Pacific Grove, CA: Brooks/Cole, 1989), p. 83 and note 17, p. 88.
85. R. Whitaker, 'Access to Information and Research on Security and Intelligence: The Canadian Situation', in Hanks and McCamus, supra (note 11), p. 185.
86. Ibid, p. 192.
87. R. Whitaker, *Left Wing Dissent and the State: Canada in the Cold War Era* paper for SIRC Conference, Kingston, Ontario: Queen's University, February 1988, p. 18, note 26.
88. ASIO, *Report to Parliament 1987–88* (Canberra: Australian Government Publishing Service, 1989), pp. 15–18. F. Cain, 'The Right to Know: ASIO, Historians and the Australian Parliament', *Intelligence and National Security*, 8(1), 1993, pp. 87–101.
89. P. Birkinshaw, *Freedom of Information: The Law, the Practice and the Idea* (London: Weidenfeld & Nicolson, 1988), pp. 36–60 provides a good summary of overseas experience for those in the UK.

90. BBC Radio 4, broadcast 25 June 1992. See also *The Guardian* 26 June 1992, p. 8.

91. L.K. Johnson, 'Controlling the CIA: A Critique of Current Safeguards', in G. Hastedt (ed.), *Controlling Intelligence*, (London: Frank Cass, 1991), p. 59; see also Oseth, supra (note 22), pp. 184–5.

92. *The Guardian*, 30 December 1991, p. 6; 3 January 1992, p. 7. See J. Gauck, *Die Stasi-Akten* (Reinbek bei Hamburg: Rowohlt, 1991). (In German)

93. Davis, supra (note 81), pp. 1–24.

9

The Future of Security Intelligence

The analysis so far has attempted to highlight the major themes of what is known or alleged about the security intelligence agencies in the UK. First, that there has been inadequate political or ministerial control of the agencies so that they have been able to operate autonomously; second, that the complete lack of effective external review of security intelligence operations has led to serious abuses of civil rights. Much use has been made of the findings of major inquiries elsewhere. Given the similarities between the organisational and ideological imperatives of security intelligence agencies in the Western liberal democracies, it is reasonable to hypothesise that the problems illuminated in those inquiries in North America and Australasia would be found to have occurred also in the UK. However, this cannot simply be assumed; rather, those inquiries, together with what is known about the UK, enable us to construct an agenda for a full inquiry here.

The objective of this final chapter is to suggest what that agenda might look like and to consider also what kind of inquiry would be necessary to establish a thorough understanding of security intelligence policies and practices. In the previous chapter a number of alternative institutional innovations regarding the external review of security intelligence were considered and a number of suggestions have already been made as to how one or more of these might be incorporated into the UK system. The concern here is not to argue for or against any of those suggestions; rather, it is to point to the need for a careful evaluation of how those institutions might work, or not, within the somewhat peculiar circumstances of the UK political and legal processes.

It would be dangerous for any reform-minded government simply to opt for one or other or even a combination of these alternatives without holding a thorough inquiry first. In most areas of state action a political party, whether in government or opposition, can develop fairly informed ideas of what changes might be made since the policy process is relatively accessible, though not, in the UK, as accessible as it might be. In the area of security intelligence policy, however, this is not the case. This can be seen, for example, in the recent responses of those who were Home or Northern Ireland Secretaries in the 1970s and who now see just how little they really knew about security activities. When allegations against the Security Service were first made by Harold Wilson in 1977, Merlyn Rees and James Callaghan professed themselves to be content with what was happening at that time under their stewardship. Callaghan issued the following statement:

> The Prime Minister has conducted detailed inquiries into the recent allegations about the Security Service and is satisfied that they do not constitute grounds for lack of confidence in the competence and impartiality of the Security Service or for instituting a special inquiry.[1]

In 1978 Home Secretary Rees told Tony Benn:

> By the way, Tony, I want to make the point again that I control all the security services [sic] personally. I check and review everybody whose phone is tapped and I assure you that it is completely under my control.[2]

With the revelations of the 1980s, however, both joined with those calling for a full inquiry into the events of those years, admitting that they had actually been ignorant of them at the time.[3]

Therefore it is doubtful if any party, at least any that wants to bring about change, is in a position to know that its preferred solutions will work. But there is a further danger. It is not just that quickly introduced changes might not work but that they might actually make the problem worse. Resolving the issue of control and oversight of security intelligence agencies in the UK is particularly difficult because any specific reforms have to be considered within the unpromising context of existing political and legal structures. As we have seen, there are a number of aspects of British government which might mean that specific reforms fail. These include the concentration of political power within the central executive of a unitary state, the culture of secrecy with its assumption that it is the state which decides what information is to be divulged, a system of legislative committees which, ultimately, is in thrall to the majority party, and a judiciary which is particularly executive-minded on issues of security and order.

Therefore there is much to be said for considering the reform of state security intelligence within the wider context of constitutional reform. In terms of the previous chapter, levels three and four need strengthening. This is what happened in Canada where the period during which the McDonald Commission met, reported and was translated into the Canadian Security Intelligence Service Act, 1984, also saw the adoption of the Charter of Rights and Freedoms in 1982, and Access to Information and Privacy Acts in 1983. Recently, significant efforts have been put into framing comprehensive proposals for constitutional reform in the UK, first by Charter 88. During 1991, the Institute for Public Policy Research published a draft constitution and Liberty (formerly the National Council for Civil Liberties) published a draft bill of rights called *A People's Charter*.[4] There is not the space to do justice to the full debate here regarding the desirability of extensive constitutional change, but from the discussion so far it must be clear that real change in the state security intelligence network is far more likely to come about to the extent that the political autonomy of the state executive is curtailed.

The paramount need is for information. For example, if some form of parliamentary committee were to be introduced on the basis of the extent of present public and parliamentary knowledge about the security intelligence process in the UK, there is a danger that the committee would make little genuine progress. Without some yardstick of information on previous practices and procedures, and given the time-pressure on members who, in any event, have inadequate staff resources, the committee would be unable to do more than a superficial job. Any number of briefings from senior security intelligence officials are not enough,[5] and the end result might be that the committee would succeed only in giving the security intelligence agencies greater legitimacy. Such a result would not be a problem if it were based on thorough knowledge, but it would be if it were the result of the committee's remaining in blissful ignorance. While Commons select committees have tried to maintain bipartisan resistance to executive dominance in a number of areas since 1979, the security intelligence area is one in which many MPs are, like judges, particularly deferential to claims of executive dominance.

Enough serious allegations as to ineffectiveness, inefficiency and abuses of power by the UK security intelligence agencies have been made to justify the establishment of a wide-ranging inquiry in order to establish as far as possible just which of these allegations have a factual basis. Its investigation of the past must be carried out with a view not to finding low-level scapegoats for past abuses, but to general public education with respect to this area of state activities and to the construction of a system which is capable of providing information about real threats without abusing civil rights.

THE CASE AGAINST AN INQUIRY

This proposal for an inquiry is acknowledged to involve problems. As noted in Chapter 2, the relationship between knowledge and power is symbiotic. Information control processes are means by which dominant groups seek to minimise the influence of outsiders. Equally, inquiries constitute one kind of potential threat to the autonomy of the 'secret state'. The allegations made against security intelligence agencies in the UK could be argued to constitute a legitimacy crisis for the state, though this is clearly more evident in Northern Ireland than in Britain. Burton and Carlen examined how, in the context of such crises, inquiries become one of the 'legal instruments'[6] mobilised by the state to maintain its hegemony. The 'Official Discourse' which is produced by state inquiries is, therefore, the proclamation of the state's legal and administrative rationality. So when 'discreditable episodes' occur the job of the inquiry is to maintain confidence in the state's rationality by reconstructing those episodes as, for example, temporary failures or aberrations.[7]

Similarly, Phil Thomas has challenged the assumptions of state neutrality and just rules upon which the mechanism of the Royal Commission is grounded, and maintains that commissions could be used not only to defuse embarrassment but also as a mechanism of social control. Thus they are 'a mechanism to encourage people's belief in the existence and effectiveness of democratic pluralism . . .'[8] Even those who would probably not accept an overall Gramscian perspective agree that 'an' if not 'the' objective of inquiries is reassurance. For example, inquiries established in the UK under the Tribunals of Inquiry (Evidence) Act of 1921 are said to be.

> a procedure of last resort, to be used when nothing else will serve to allay public disquiet, usually based on sensational allegations, rumours or disasters.[9]

Similarly, Lord Salmon argued that whenever allegations or rumours are such as to cause a national crisis of confidence they must be investigated in order to establish the truth so that any evil found may be rooted out or to reassure the public that the rumours were groundless. Otherwise no democracy will survive for long. Burton and Carlen would challenge Salmon's idealist notion that inquiries attempt to root out evil, since the state is obliged to deny the material sources of the scandals that erupt. So, is there any point in proposing an inquiry into such a sensitive area of state policy if the outcome will be so predictably limited?

The argument here is that the effort is worth making because of the heterogeneity of the state. Burton and Carlen acknowledge that the legitimacy crises which regularly beset the state derive from the fact that state apparatuses 'are loosely co-ordinated and organisationally distinct'. This, they say, is because of their contradictory functions of capital accumulation and legitimation.[10] Security intelligence agencies are concerned with legitimation rather than accumulation, but our model of the multi-level state suggests that even within this function there are significant contradictions which give rise to different practices and perspectives.

When these contradictions become dramatically apparent, Burton and Carlen argue that the task of inquiries is to re-establish the image of administrative coherence.[11] Indeed, we have seen how, in security intelligence inquiries to date, for example those of the Security Commission, reports have typically asserted that lapses or scandals arose because of individual lapses and that only minor procedural reforms are required to prevent recurrences. Complete secrecy is presented unproblematically as 'obviously' necessary in order to protect 'national security', without any examination of the structural problems inherent within security intelligence agencies. Inquiries, then, exist to paper over the cracks, not to expose them further.

Conversely, the job undertaken here is to suggest the outlines of an investigation which will explore rather than gloss over the contradictions which exist between the different levels of the state. This is so that the changes proposed increase the opportunities for democratic control of security intelligence (especially at levels two, three and four) and do not simply reassert the autonomy of the agencies themselves. So, the argument in this chapter is based on a realisation that inquiries certainly can be, and have been used by state elites as a mechanism for quietening public anger while minimising any real adverse impact on dominant structures of power and interest. However, it does not assume that inquiries will necessarily take that course; rather it is argued that inquiries provide some degree of opportunity for a challenge to those structures in the interest of democratising the state. The discussion here considers how an inquiry needs to be organised to maximise the chance that it can succeed in penetrating the outer membrane of secrecy in the Gore-Tex state.

AGENDA FOR THE INQUIRY

In constructing the agenda for an inquiry the sequence of the foregoing chapters is followed. The discussion in Chapter 2 of information control processes, power and law contributed to the model of the Gore-Tex state. The central issues for the inquiry which follow from this are: how autonomous should security intelligence agencies be and in what circumstances and to what extent should they be permitted to penetrate society? Towards which of the types illustrated in Figure 2.2 (p. 82) should the agencies be organised? In Canada the McDonald Commission, for example, focused on these issues when it examined explicitly what it considered to be the basic principles of security intelligence in a liberal democratic state.[12]

Mandate

It is important that the question of the security intelligence mandate is addressed before questions of organisational structure.[13] Bureaucracies, whether state or private, are excellent at discovering fresh goals as old ones are achieved or become irrelevant. Therefore the question of threats must be answered independently, as far as is possible, of existing organisational structures. In line with the discussion in Chapter 3, it is important that the threats be defined as specifically as possible. This is because the historical abuse of power by security intelligence agencies has been directly proportionate to the vagueness of the 'threat' they purported to investigate. Also, this is in the interests of the effectiveness of the agencies since precise definitions will facilitate the more effective use of resources.

Discussion of the mandate requires specific attention to the primary roles of both 'security' and 'intelligence'. The former requires clear rules regarding the agency's specific responsibilities for the protective security of property and information within the state, and the rules for vetting of state personnel.[14] The intelligence role requires that the agency has sufficient flexibility to respond to changing political conditions at home and abroad, yet is provided with a sufficiently specific mandate that citizens' rights regarding privacy, freedom of expression and association are not illegitimately curtailed. Crucially, it should include a clear statement of both what the security intelligence agencies should be doing and what they should not – for example, the 'lawful advocacy, protest or dissent' exclusion found in the CSIS Act (s.2).

There are further questions relating to the legal framework which need to be considered. There are different types of legal framework within which security intelligence might operate. For example, to use Ned Franks's hunting metaphor, should the approach be 'open season' in which the agency is given extensive powers to act, or 'closed season' in which its legal powers are no greater than those of any other public or police body. In the latter case there is the greater risk of the agency 'poaching' in order to fulfil its need for information. Alternatively, should the agency be granted a 'licence' in the form of particular powers over and above those granted to other bodies?[15] This is the approach that the 1989 Security Service Act appears to take in that the Service is able, with a warrant from the Secretary of State, to 'interfere with property' (s.3). However, when the silences of the Act are also taken into consideration, for example the lack of controls on the use of informers and electronic surveillance, and put together with the very broad mandate and lack of external review, then the approach looks much more like a declaration of 'open season'.

What legal standard should be established regarding the certainty of the information upon which investigations are to be based? The main argument here revolves around the imposition or not of a 'criminal standard'. Should the domestic security intelligence agency be limited to the criminal standard of reasonable suspicion that a specific offence has been or is about to be committed before it is empowered to commence an investigation? For this to be the case the mandate would itself have to be defined purely in terms of criminal offences, for example – as of now, espionage, sabotage and terrorism, but not subversion. But even if the mandate is so defined, there is still an argument that information needs to be gathered about threats which may fall short of the imminent commission of an offence now but which might become so in the longer term.

For example, Abram Shulsky argues that there are two areas in which the criminal standard does not allow the state enough 'leeway' in gathering counter-intelligence. First, he says, the state cannot eliminate members of hostile groups from state employment unless it keeps those groups under surveillance in order to compile membership lists. Second, he points out that the difficulty of penetrating 'terrorist' groups means that apparently peaceful, legal support-groups must be penetrated in order to gain information.[16] Similarly Ken Robertson argues that, if the only purpose of security intelligence is to institute criminal prosecutions, then the criminal standard should apply. If, however, security intelligence is required in order to advise the state on the seriousness or otherwise of potential threats to its security, then that standard is too restrictive.[17]

In order to minimise the risks of abuse, therefore, what is required is that the 'threats' targeted by security intelligence must be defined *either* in terms of the criminal law, in which case the criminal standard of reasonable suspicion of an imminent offence will apply, *or* in specific statutory form where some (non-criminal) threat is deemed to require surveillance, for example 'covert foreign influence' on a domestic political group.

Institutional structures

It would be easier to restrict the investigative standard if the agency concerned were a police one, but there is clearly no necessary connection between a police agency and a 'criminal standard'. The experiences of the RCMP and the FBI before the 1970s show this and, of course, the UK police special branches gather much information now that is not subject to the standard of 'reasonable suspicion'. Even the 'non-political' police make increasing use of general 'criminal intelligence', which will have been gathered upon a looser investigative standard.

In examining institutional structures for security intelligence, the foreign inquiries referred to throughout this analysis varied in the extent to which they provided a partial or comprehensive review of security intelligence arrangements in their respective states. Justice Hope's Royal Commission of 1974–77 in Australia was the most comprehensive, covering the whole range of foreign and domestic security intelligence and resulting, for example, in the establishment of the Office of National Assessments as the overall co-ordinator of all international intelligence.[18] Justice McDonald's Royal Commission in Canada was established to consider only the activities of the RCMP and therefore dealt primarily with the question of domestic security intelligence. It did consider the international dimensions of the issue to the extent that the RCMP security service had maintained foreign liaison officers, and that any domestic agency would need to inform itself about threats emanating abroad. McDonald raised the issue of whether Canada should have its own foreign intelligence-gathering agency, similar to the CIA, SIS or ASIS, but it did not consider at all those Canadian agencies which collected foreign intelligence routinely, such as the Communications Security Establishment (CSE), the Canadian arm of the UKUSA SIGINT network.[19] The Canadian government has proved highly resistant to attempts to subject CSE to any kind of external review, most recently when the Commons Committee for the five-year review of the CSIS Act attempted to question government witnesses.[20] In the United States, the congressional inquiries of 1975–76 concentrated primarily on the the main foreign and domestic intelligence agencies, respectively the CIA and the FBI. The rest of the intelligence network came into the investigations only when their activities took place within the United States. Thus, the aspect of National Security Agency operations that was investigated was its monitoring of cable traffic into and out of the US on the basis of 'watch lists' drawn up in co-operation with other agencies such as the FBI and the Bureau of Narcotics and Dangerous Drugs (BNDD).[21]

The question of the relationship between police, domestic and foreign intelligence organisations is not new in the UK. In 1921 the Cabinet ordered an inquiry into the question of expenditure on the Secret Service. The inquiry, headed by Sir Warren Fisher, was at first sceptical of the need to retain MI5 but eventually concluded that it should retain responsibility for counter-espionage and counter-subversion in the armed forces, while Special Branch should be fully subordinated to the Metropolitan Commissioner of Police. The inquiry was revived in 1925 to examine whether MI5 should be amalgamated with the SIS but concluded that this would not be a change worth making.[22] The issue re-emerged towards the end of the Second World War when it was noted that there was duplication and overlapping between SIS and the Security Service. A Foreign Office committee proposed that the Joint Intelligence Committee (JIC) should co-ordinate both military and civil security. The SIS resisted suggestions that the Security Service might be able to run its own foreign intelligence service, and was not anxious to take over responsibility for domestic counter-subversion. For its part, the Security Service argued against the suggestion that counter-subversion should revert to the police on the grounds that the work required people of higher intellectual calibre than were normally recruited by the police, that police security was not good enough for the protection of information and that the police should be kept out of politics,[23] all points echoed by the McDonald Commission.[24] There have been reports that a merger between the Security Service and the SIS (MI6) is again on the Whitehall agenda.[25]

At a conceptual level, Figure 6.1 (p. 208) would provide a starting place for the consideration by any inquiry as to the best institutional structure for the UK. As we have seen, there is general agreement as to the desirability of separating the collection of information abroad and domestically, for example because of the longer term and less specific nature of many diplomatic and economic threats and the entirely different political and legal context of an agency operating in other countries. The crucial question in relation to domestic security intelligence is whether a separate agency is required, or whether a specialist section within the police would be adequate.

Certainly it is possible to see both models at work. In the United States, the FBI has responsibility for the enforcement of federal law; it is also the domestic security intelligence agency. In Canada, the RCMP performs all the normal policing functions in certain provinces on a contractual basis, and policing related to federal law in those provinces which have their own police, primarily Ontario and Quebec. In addition, until 1984 the RCMP incorporated also the Security Service. The investigations initiated during the 1970s into abuses of power by both the FBI and the RCMP produced different reform suggestions. In the US there was no proposal to separate the security intelligence from the police function, while the McDonald Commission concluded that this should be done in Canada. As we saw in Chapter 6, McDonald suggested a number of reasons for the tension between 'law enforcement' and the 'intelligence process' and CSIS was established in 1984 as a civilian agency to take over the security intelligence function from the paramilitary RCMP. However, the RCMP retained its responsibility for the enforcement of security offences and developed its own National Security Intelligence Directorate accordingly.

In the specific case of domestic security intelligence in the UK, the question that needs to be addressed, then, is whether both the Security Service and police special branches are necessary. Both agencies operate in that space between the collection of information relating to the enforcement of the 'non-political' criminal law at one end and that relating to foreign diplomatic, economic and military matters at the other (see Figure 6.1). They specialise in different aspects of the security intelligence task; for example, the Security Service advises government departments on protective security matters relating to information and buildings, while Special Branches (along with the off-shoot Diplomatic Protection Squad) advise on and provide personal protection for prominent people. However, there are contrary arguments. Separate agencies with similar responsibilities, even, as here, where one of them is clearly junior to the other, provide fertile ground for jurisdictional disputes, as seen in the 'counter-terrorism' field in the UK. Second, the existence of two agencies will aggravate the already difficult problems of ministerial control and democratic overview. For example, a denial of authorisation for an operation to one agency might lead to its being 'sub-contracted' to the other if control is seen to be weaker there. Similarly, information seen as particularly sensitive may be held in whichever agency is seen to be most immune from external review.

Rules and working practices

Whatever institutional structure is recommended, however, it cannot be assumed that simply imposing new sets of rules on to security intelligence procedures will bring about the desired change. Indeed, some have suggested that any legal curbs will ultimately be ineffectual as a control on political policing:

> . . . the process of intelligence-gathering always tends to flow through and around legal restraints, and to be limited only by political considerations and the available technology.[26]

Gary Marx makes a similar point with respect to policing – that legal measures intended to restrict some methods of information-gathering, for example coercion, have resulted in the increase of others, for example deception.[27] However, while it may seem obvious that any state, liberal democratic or otherwise, will, to the extent that it feels seriously threatened, not allow its own legal pronouncements to stand in the way of taking action to defend itself, there is no point in pursuing the argument to the extent of rejecting any structures of control and review. There will be a great many aspects of state behaviour, short of desperate 'self-defence', which can be checked by such structures.

A number of these were discussed in Chapter 6. For example, attention must be paid to the organisational sub-cultures which might subvert any new rules,[28] the way in which new formal rules will interact with existing working and inhibitory rules, and also to the fact that the senior officials of security intelligence organisations may themselves be insulated from full awareness of actions taken by operational officers because of the difficulties of supervision and the requirements of 'need-to-know'. The rules which should be applied to relationships between different agencies within the same state can be dealt with best if the inquiry itself deals with the whole state security intelligence network. If it does not, the problem is that (as in Canada where both the McDonald Commission and the subsequent review structure centred on the domestic security intelligence agency – the RCMP and then CSIS – to the exclusion of other agencies), exchanges of information and co-operation on operations are viewed from one organisational perspective only.

Relationships between the security intelligence agencies of different states are prone to particular complexities. For example, care must be taken that other states (officially 'friendly' or otherwise) are not simply making use of contacts within UK agencies in order to achieve covert policy objectives at the expense of UK residents. In the case of the UK, a particularly pressing aspect of security co-operation concerns the developing European structures. Most public debate has been concerned with the economic aspects of closer co-ordination of member states, specifically within the institutions of the European Community. Questions of policing and security, however, are amongst those in which European states are discussing co-operation outside of the Community institutions; for example, the decision in December 1991 to establish Europol as a centralised exchange point for criminal intelligence between EC member states.[29] This 'democratic deficit' is exemplified by the Trevi Group which, since 1975, has provided the forum in which the internal ministers of the member states discuss policy regarding 'terrorism' and other aspects of crime. The Commission is not represented on this Group and it is in no way accountable.[30]

As regards penetration, the key issue is the way in which investigative measures are to be authorised and controlled. As noted in Chapter 4, the general principle which has been adopted in North America and Australia is that authorisation 'ladders' should exist whereby the more intrusive the investigative technique, the higher is the authorisation that is required. This principle has been applied uniformly to the main investigative techniques: entry and search of premises, seizure of documents, electronic surveillance and interception of communications. There are differences of practice, however, with respect to the level at which authorisation is required. Is it required from outside the agency (level two in Figure 7.1, p. 252) or from outside the executive branch (level three)? In Australia warrants may be granted by the Attorney General (level two) while in both Canada and the United States the agencies must seek approval from a judge (level three).

There is one major exception to this general rule: the use of informers. As we saw also in Chapter 4, this is a technique used by security intelligence agencies far more extensively than other techniques and is one which is arguably far more intrusive than other surveillance measures. However, the level of authorisation required for the use of informers remains lower than its intrusiveness merits. For example, informers are not included under the 'special powers' for the use of which ASIO requires a ministerial warrant[31] and the North American agencies are not required to seek judicial authorisation for their use. The main argument for this exception has been that the varieties of people and circumstances involved defy clear specification, as compared with those involving entries, searches and the use of technical devices.[32] In the US, the use of informers by police has not been subjected by the courts to the same fourth amendment restrictions on 'unreasonable search and seizure' as have tapping and bugging.[33]

The fact that in the UK these questions have not been subjected to comprehensive review and legislation has resulted in a patchwork of rules and practice. Some techniques are subject to level two authorisation, primarily telephone tapping and mail intercepts under the Interception of Communications Act 1985, and 'interferences with property' under the Security Service Act, 1989. The latter covers entry and search of property and seizure of records, but still leaves other methods unchecked. For example, neither of these statutes deals with electronic surveillance (in cases where no trespass is required) and so authorisation remains within the agency itself (level one). In no case is the Security Service required to go to level three for authorisation.

Control and review

A final set of factors to be considered would be the procedures for political control and external review of the security intelligence agencies. The model offered in Figure 7.1 (p. 252) provides a framework within which structures of control and oversight appropriate to the UK can be discussed. The relationship between different institutions at the different levels should be examined: with respect to control, for example, that between ministerial directions and internal guidelines. Similarly, oversight institutions must be studied – from the protection of whistleblowers (at level one) to that of public access to security intelligence files (at level four).

While it would be possible to design structures which appear, in the abstract, to be very strong, the probability that their impact could be minimised by unreconstructed working practices must be borne in mind. Therefore, control and oversight structures, to have some chance of working, require at least some degree of co-operation from those to be overseen. Otherwise, there is the danger that one unintended outcome of increased control and oversight will be simply to increase the use by the security intelligence agencies of internal information security procedures designed to maintain organisational autonomy. Alternatively, resort may be had to sub-contracting delicate operations to private sector agencies[34] or other security intelligence agencies not within the scope of the oversight procedures.

Ken Robertson has argued that internal control questions must be the first priority and that oversight is secondary.[35] He says the organisational means for fulfilling the state's security intelligence requirements must be considered before measures intended to ensure democracy and liberty, in the same way that engineers only build safety measures into machines after deciding on what kind of machine best meets public needs. But this mechanical metaphor is not helpful; in the design of industrial machinery it may well be necessary to *trade-off* the benefits they produce against the threats they pose of harm to the public. Political institutions, however, are not machines; in the long run there is no trade-off between their 'benefits' and 'costs'. In the short run it is possible to identify situations in which security intelligence agencies will have to trade-off requirements of legality or propriety against those of effectiveness; for example the 'watcher' who breaks traffic laws in order to maintain surveillance of a target.[36] In order that institutions protect and enhance democracy in the long run, however, it is necessary that they be designed with efficacy and propriety equally in mind. Neither of these should be emphasised over the other.

In terms of the discussion of power in Chapter 2, overemphasis upon either control (purportedly in the interests of effectiveness) or oversight (purportedly in the interests of propriety) falls into the same Manichean trap as assuming that power is *either* zero-sum *or* non zero-sum. Those who diminish the significance of demonstrable abuses of state power and the importance of oversight structures which might prevent them, assume that power is variable sum. Therefore, they say, any increase in the effectiveness of security intelligence agencies will result in an enhancement of the public interest. Allocating equal priority to oversight questions, as here, accepts that effective security intelligence *can* enhance the general public interest, for example by preventing serious political violence by or against a minority group. But it acknowledges also that state power can be constant sum, for example when it is used to harass a minority engaged in peaceful political activity. The object of this inquiry into structures is to increase the likelihood of state power being variable sum, and to reduce its propensity to be constant sum.

PENETRATING THE STATE

Form of the inquiry

The history of state inquiries in the UK raises important questions as to what they are really intended for. Between 1979 and 1990

Royal Commissions were out of fashion since the Thatcher governments believed in 'conviction politics' and rejected the search for solutions to public problems via commissions of 'the great and the good'. On occasions, however, public concern, or the lack of ready-made answers to a problem, did lead the government to establish other forms of inquiry. The Hillsborough disaster in April 1989 led, for example, to the appointment of Lord Justice Taylor to conduct a departmental inquiry into the event and make recommendations regarding crowd control and safety at sports grounds.[37] In October 1989 the Court of Appeal released the 'Guildford Four' who had been wrongly convicted of bombing offences in 1975 and the Home Office responded by establishing another departmental inquiry, under the chairmanship of Sir John May, a former Court of Appeal judge. In February 1990 it was announced that the inquiry was to be broadened to take into account the convictions of the 'Maguire Seven'. After the convictions of the 'Birmingham Six' had been quashed in March 1991 the government established a Royal Commission on Criminal Justice in June which was asked to make its final report by June 1993.[38]

The device by which insiders have most often sought to maintain the autonomy of security intelligence agencies is the 'internal inquiry'. There is no evidence that these have ever succeeded in dealing with fundamental problems. From the earliest allegations of Special Branch malpractices

> . . . the Home Office went no further than to question the men they [the malpractices] were alleged against. In these instances the details of those 'enquiries' were kept from Parliament, which was merely told that they had been rigorous and exonerating.[39]

Successive British Prime Ministers have told Parliament that they have been assured by internal inquiries that particular problems either did not exist or had been dealt with.[40] As we have seen, a number of those ministers have now changed their view on the adequacy of those internal inquiries. Clearly internal 'inquiries' are a major means by which security intelligence agencies seek to protect themselves against change. In 1987, for example, as the *Spycatcher* row rumbled on it was reported that Whitehall officials were arguing that the time had come to accept a 'discreet and secret inquiry' in order to head off more radical demands.[41]

There are seven main alternatives which might be considered as far as state security intelligence activities are concerned: Royal Commission, departmental inquiry, non-statutory inquiry (of the type carried out by Lord Denning into the Profumo case), Security Commission inquiry, committee of Privy Councillors, parliamentary select committee and tribunal of inquiry under the 1921 Act. Table 9.1 contains a list of post-war inquiries into security intelligence and related matters. The respective merits of different types of inquiry were considered by the Royal Commission established in February 1966 to review the working of the 1921 Act. It was in fact inquiries related to security intelligence matters which set in train the events leading to this Commission. John Vassall was identified as having been working for the Soviet Union on the basis of information given to the CIA by Golitsin, the Soviet defector, and he was convicted under the Official Secrets Act and sentenced to 18 years' imprisonment in 1962. Following closely on the conviction of George Blake, the press speculation about Vassall's relationship with former Civil Lord of the Admiralty Thomas Galbraith, for whom he had worked between 1957 and 1959, led the government to set up a departmental inquiry under a civil servant, Sir George Cunningham, to examine the security implications of Vassall's employment and conviction.

The establishment of this inquiry failed to end speculation. It merely provided an interim report consisting of copies of correspondence between Vassall and Galbraith and his wife.[42] Its work was then taken over by the more prestigious tribunal of inquiry under Lord Radcliffe in November 1962. This inquiry was to examine the specific allegations that Admiralty officials had known about yet not acted upon, allegations about espionage since the Portland case in 1961.[43]

This inquiry had a number of consequences including a reorganisation of security procedures and a recommendation that a standing Security Commission be established to investigate future security lapses. This was implemented in 1964, as we have seen. Furthermore, the procedures under the 1921 Act, which enable a tribunal to report recalcitrant witnesses to the High Court for contempt, were first invoked against three journalists

Table 9.1 UK Inquiries into Security Intelligence and Related Matters

Session	Date	Cmnd No.	Type (see notes)	Subject
55/6	3/56	9715	cpc	Salisbury on Burgess and Maclean
56/7	9/57	283	cpc	Birkett on interception of communications
61/2	11/61	1681	cpc	Radcliffe on Portland case and George Blake
62/3	11/62	1871	di	Cunningham on Vassall
62/3	4/63	2009	t/i	Radcliffe on Vassall
62/3	6/63	2037	–	Minutes – Vassall
62/3	9/63	2152	nsi	Denning on Profumo case
64/5	7/65	2722	sc	Bossard and Allen
64/5	9/65	2773	di	Smith on Bossard and Allen
66/7	6/67	3309	cpc	Radcliffe on D-Notice affair
66/7	6/67	3312	wp	HMG Response to Cmnd 3309
66/7	12/66	3151	sc	Reen
66/7	6/67	3365	sc	Keenan
68/9	12/68	3856	sc	Britten
68/9	3/69	3892	sc	Bland
71/2	1/72	4901	cpc	Parker on interrogation of terrorists
71/2	9/72	5104	di	Franks on s2, Official Secrets Acts
72/3	5/73	5362	sc	Bingham and Hinchcliffe
72/3	7/73	5367	sc	Jellicoe and Lambton
75/6	1/76	6386	cpc	Radcliffe on ministerial memoirs
75/6	8/75	6569	cpc	Diplock on recruitment of mercenaries
76/7	10/77	6677	cpc	Houghton on security of Cabinet documents
80/1	3/81	8191	+	Diplock: interception of communications
80/1	5/81	8235	sc	Diplock on Wagstaff
81/2	5/82	8540	[sc]	After publication of *Their Trade is Treachery*
82/3	1/83	8787	cpc	Franks on Falklands
82/3	5/83	8876	sc	Prime
82/3	7/83	*	sc	Ritchie
83/4	3/84	9212	sc	Bridge on Aldridge
84/5	3/85	**	+	Bridge on Massiter allegations
84/5	5/85	9514	sc	Bettaney
85/6	10/86	9923	sc	9 Signals Regiment in Cyprus
85/6	5/86	9781	nsi	Calcutt on Cyprus interrogations

Notes

*	– not published as Command Paper, but in HC Deb., vol. 46, cols. 517–23, 28/07/83
**	– unpublished; + – 'Communications Interception Standing Inquiry'
cpc	– committee of Privy Councillors
di	– departmental inquiry
nsi	– non-statutory inquiry
rc	– Royal Commission
sc	– Security Commission
t/i	– tribunal of inquiry under 1921 Act
wp	– no inquiry but White Paper published

who refused to divulge the sources of their information. Two were imprisoned for three and six months respectively. The concern at these developments was compounded in the same year by the fast-developing Profumo affair which resulted in the appointment, in June 1963, of Lord Denning to investigate. He reported the following September. This inquiry was not established under the 1921 Act and therefore was held in private; no transcript of evidence was ever published, no witness heard any of the evidence given against her or him, and, throughout, Denning acted as detective, inquisitor, advocate and judge. Although the report was generally accepted at the time, because of the prestige of the judge concerned, serious reservations were expressed about the nature of the procedure[44] and in due course the report was generally discredited.[45] Therefore the problems that had arisen both with the application of the 1921 Act and attempts to avoid it resulted in the appointment of a Royal Commission in February 1966 to review the Act and recommend changes.[46]

The Salmon Royal Commission demolished the case for repeating the kind of inquiry carried out by Lord Denning in the Profumo case: if such an inquiry reported that rumours were unfounded then the fact that it had operated in secret would lead many people simply to disbelieve it, while if reputations were found to be at stake then procedures must allow people to hear and challenge the evidence against them.[47] Also, it is clear that a Security Commission inquiry would not be adequate for the kind of investigation envisaged here. Fourteen were established between 1965 and 1986 on an *ad hoc* basis for the investigation of specific lapses in protective security (see Table 9.1). They sat entirely in private and, as we have seen, depended largely on the support of the Security Service to carry out their work (see Chapter 7). As such this would clearly not be an appropriate mechanism for a thorough and wide-ranging inquiry into the effectiveness and propriety of security intelligence activities in general.

There is little practical difference between Royal Commissions and departmental committees of inquiry. The former are more prestigious because they are appointed by the crown and report to the monarch via Parliament, whereas the latter are appointed by ministers and report accordingly.[48] Both types are normally used for investigating broader concerns of policy and historically they have provided important research bases of data, but they do not have the powers to compel anybody to give evidence or provide documents which, in the case of security intelligence, could be seen as a fatal flaw. Also, because commissioners tend to work part time on such inquiries they have been most often seen as devices by which governments can delay action and obtain a breathing space from public criticism. By the 1980s even some notable participants in commissions through the years were expressing grave doubts about the waste of time and energy they incurred.[49]

An inquiry by a parliamentary select committee provides another option. It was dissatisfaction with the ability of Parliament to investigate allegations of misconduct by officials and politicians that led to the eventual adoption of the 1921 Tribunals of Enquiry (Evidence) Act in Britain. The Salmon Royal Commission pointed out that such reports tended to reflect the partisan views of the members and that the Commons itself would be likely to divide on party lines in discussing the report.[50] Whereas a number of the Commons select committees since 1979 have succeeded in maintaining a bipartisan approach to their work, as we have seen, in the one case of an inquiry into specifically security intelligence questions – the Home Affairs inquiry into police special branches – this was not the case and the committee divided on party lines.

It has been argued elsewhere that, compared with 'the mediocre record of accomplishment' of non-parliamentary inquiries in the UK and of the Presidential Commissions in the United States, the advantage of legislative committees is the fact that the investigators are also the decision-makers and that therefore there is a higher chance of action following an inquiry.[51] The same argument cannot apply to the UK as long as the Commons is organised by a clear party majority which dominates the parliamentary timetable. Here, there is potentially a large gulf between the backbench MPs sitting on the select committee and those within the executive of the 'inner state' who would make decisions regarding the implementation of any changes. The potential of a parliamentary select committee would be greater to the extent that broader constitutional changes occurred to reduce the extensive imbalance between executive and assembly in the UK. Still, it remains an important principle that elected politicians rather than those appointed from the ranks of 'the great and the good' should participate in the governance of security intelligence activities. The inquiry into the working of the 1984 Canadian Security Intelligence Service Act by the Special Review Committee of the Canadian House of Commons indicates some of the possibilities (see above Chapter 8).

One of the issues concerning the involvement of MPs in security intelligence inquiries relates to the feasibility or otherwise of subjecting them to positive vetting. Parliamentarians are unlikely to accept that the executive branch should subject them to positive vetting because of the implications it has for their independence but, consequently, security intelligence agencies under review may prove less than completely forthcoming with information. For example, the Review Committee in Canada during 1989–90 reported

> . . . the reluctance of some elements of the security and intelligence community to provide the Committee with the type of assistance it required to complete its task. This reluctance was manifested in an unwillingness to give the Committee full access to documents, to allow staff to accompany the Committee to all briefings, and to permit staff to visit all premises toured by the Committee.[52]

One way of avoiding this problem would be for all members of such a committee to be made Privy Councillors. Their oath of office is held to do away with the need for positive vetting. In Canada this is the way in which people appointed to the Security Intelligence Review Committee have been formally assured of full access. A Committee of Privy Councillors does provide another option in the UK and one which has already been applied in the security intelligence field (see Table 9.1) including, as we saw in Chapter 8, the Falklands Inquiry.

The final option and potentially the most powerful form of inquiry would be a tribunal established under the 1921 Act. At the time of Lord Salmon's Royal Commission there had been 15 such inquiries, five of them into allegations against the police which, Salmon presumed, would now be pursued under s.32 of the Police Act 1964. Since then there has been Lord

Widgery's inquiry into 'Bloody Sunday' in Northern Ireland in 1972.[53] Salmon argued:

> . . . we are strongly of the opinion that the inquisitorial machinery set up under the Act of 1921 should never be used for matters of local or minor public importance but always be confined to matters of vital public importance concerning which there is something in the nature of a nation-wide crisis of confidence. In such cases we consider that no other method of investigation would be adequate.[54]

Such inquiries are established by resolution of both Houses of Parliament and have the powers of the High Court to summon witnesses and send for documents; and, as in the Vassall case, they may refer cases to the High Court for contempt. They sit in public, except where the inquiry determines this not to be in the public interest. Since 1936, all such inquiries have been chaired by judges on the grounds of their superior prestige in the eyes of the public and their ability to safeguard the rights of individuals against whom damaging allegations might be made in public.[55] The Salmon Royal Commission made a number of recommendations regarding better protection of the rights of witnesses, for example that they be given adequate notice of allegations against them, that they receive adequate time to prepare their case, including public payment of their legal costs, that they have the opportunity to state their case and cross-examine evidence which may affect them, and that they receive immunity from civil or criminal proceedings except perjury to the tribunal itself.[56]

These recommendations were not implemented in the UK but they formed the basis of new legislation in Israel,[57] and provided the basis for the procedures of the McDonald Commission into the RCMP, which was established under the Canadian equivalent of the 1921 Act. It might be argued that the particular problems involved in an inquiry into security intelligence matters in the UK requires the strengths of more than one of these types. Since it would be important for the inquiry to produce comprehensive proposals for the future organisation and policy of security intelligence, a Royal Commission might be seen to be most appropriate. However the involvement of part-time members and lack of powers regarding access to documents and persons would render that inappropriate. This points to a tribunal of inquiry, in which the membership (usually much smaller than a Royal Commission) could work full-time.

In any event there are several key issues which would need to be determined for any such inquiry to have maximum effect. The main ones are the personnel and organisation of the work of the inquiry, the terms of reference and agenda, its gathering of information and the nature of its report.

Membership

As a general rule, reports are more likely to be accepted and acted upon if they are unanimous, and the larger the commission the harder it is to obtain unanimity. Therefore it would seem sensible to keep the membership of an inquiry small: Salmon recommended three as the ideal size for a tribunal of inquiry[58] and this was the number on the McDonald Commission. Apart from judges in the Chair, the members of such inquiries have been disproportionately lawyers.[59] The inquiries into security intelligence matters in Australia and Canada were both chaired by judges, and both Royal Commissions and departmental committees in the UK have been more likely to be chaired by a judge than by any other profession.[60] Apart from the general arguments regarding the esteem and skills of judges, a specific argument in favour of appointing a judge to chair an inquiry is that there is a core of judges which constitutes one of the few groups outside of the security intelligence agencies to have any expertise in such matters. This has developed over the years from their involvement in previous inquiries, the Security Commission, and tribunals and commissions set up under the Interception of Communications and Security Service Acts. Therefore the argument that any security intelligence inquiry would be doomed from the outset by reason of the inevitable ignorance of those responsible could be answered in part by the appointment of judges with relevant experience. However, the question would remain as to precisely how energetic they had been in the pursuit of relevant knowledge in the earlier tribunals.

Comments about the supposed 'independence of the judiciary', or absence thereof, frequently make a basic error as to precisely when and of what the judiciary is supposed to be independent. The judge as 'neutral arbiter' is best exemplified by the typical civil action in, say, contract and tort, where the parties in dispute are usually corporations and, occasionally, state agencies, but where the outcome is seen to have impact only on private interests rather than the public interest. But where cases impact directly on the 'public interest' the judge's role is quite different. We have already seen in Chapter 7 how judges react to cases involving 'national security', specifically how they will defer to executive definitions of problems, and similarly their role with respect to the criminal law is not that of neutral arbiter. In the context of the controversy around the Industrial Relations Act in 1972, Lord Devlin wrote:

> In the criminal law the judges regard themselves as much concerned as the executive with preservation of law and order.[61]

Thus, it might be asked, what is the sense in appointing such figures to head an inquiry into security intelligence activities which reach to the very heart of the state's interest in its own survival? But there is no sense in assuming a determinist answer to this question. Certainly a judge *may* be appointed who will produce a 'snow-job', but it is possible to identify cases in which they have not. For example, the evidence that the McDonald Commission did not simply produce the report preferred by the Canadian government is that two days after the main report (Volume II) was published, the Justice Department released two further legal opinions it had commissioned criticising McDonald's conclusions as to the illegality of the RCMP Security Service's activities.[62] However, it has to be acknowledged that judges in such cases will not step entirely outside of the 'official discourse' and will still seek to reassure wider publics.[63]

In addition, there has been much criticism of the narrow stratum from which people have been recruited for commissions and departmental inquiries in the UK. In 1980 the central 'List of the Great and the Good' consisted of 3,250 names, only 5 per cent were under 40, 16 per cent were women and 80 per cent lived in London and the South East.[64] In 1984 Bernard Donoughue,

who had been a senior adviser to both Prime Ministers Harold
Wilson and James Callaghan, said of those recruited:

> They never take risks and they never introduce any imagi-
> nation. So, in the end, you get the situation which we
> have had in which virtually none of the commissions of
> enquiry . . . come up with anything interesting at all and
> that's why they've become redundant.[65]

Here, there are a range of issues to be investigated which are
not simply reducible to legal language, and therefore an entirely
legal panel should be avoided. The particular experience of those
appointed needs to be considered carefully. While the advantage
of having one or more members with experience of security
intelligence can be seen (in the interests of the inquiry being
able to make rapid progress), the disadvantage is that they might
be far more ready than outsiders to accept the rationales for
actions which would be common within the agencies. Oseth, for
example, notes that the Rockefeller Commission appointed by
President Ford to inquire into the CIA was dominated by men
with long and high-level government service whose perspectives
on the 'problem' would be quite different from many of those
most angered at the alleged abuses of governmental power.[66]
Most appropriate would be the appointment of someone who
has been targeted by the Security Service in the past, perhaps
Joan Ruddock MP or Harriet Harman MP.

Terms of reference

In the establishment of any inquiry the next question, and
probably the most important one, would be the terms of
reference. As was noted above in Chapter 4, a succession of
inquiries were established into allegations about the Kincora
Boys' Home with terms of reference which effectively precluded
the examination of the most serious allegations. To the extent
that state executives establish inquiries in order to limit the
damage of particular allegations, it should be expected that
terms of reference will be drawn up accordingly. For example,
even as congressional investigations were being established into
US intelligence agencies in January 1975, President Gerald

Ford appointed Vice President Nelson Rockefeller to head a Presidential Commission into CIA activities within the United States. Despite the breadth of allegations then appearing with regard to CIA activities (for example assassination plots against foreign leaders), the terms for the commission were established narrowly by reference to the explicit statutory prohibition of CIA involvement in domestic security intelligence matters. William Colby, director of the CIA at the time, later indicated that this was an attempt at damage limitation by the President.[67] The congressional inquiries were established with much more inclusive terms of reference; for example, the Senate committee was to:

> . . . conduct an investigation and study of governmental operations with respect to intelligence activities and the extent, if any, to which illegal, improper or unethical activities were engaged in by any agency of the Federal Government.[68]

The terms given to the Canadian McDonald Commission were broader than Rockefeller's but not so wide as those of Congress. McDonald was limited to the activities of the RCMP, rather than 'any agency', but was to investigate and report on RCMP activities that were 'not authorised or provided by law', which gave room for broader inquiries than simply seeking examples of 'illegal' behaviour.[69] Between 1974 and 1984 Justice Hope carried out a number of inquiries in Australia which were more inclusive of the Australian security intelligence community than McDonald's in Canada. The first Royal Commission on Intelligence and Security was set up in August 1974, under which Hope investigated allegations that had been made concerning the legality and the propriety of the Australian agencies, and also made recommendations regarding the future organisation, control and oversight of the 'community'. Having completed his commission in April 1977, Hope was reappointed in February 1978 to carry out a review of protective security arrangements in Australia, following a bomb incident at the Sydney Hilton hotel. Again this was comprehensive as far as the agencies were concerned, covering civilian police, and military and intelligence components of emergency planning.[70] Finally, in May 1983,

Hope was appointed again as a royal commissioner to examine developments since his previous report, particularly in the context of further controversies around ASIO's surveillance of David Combe, an official of the Australian Labour Party.[71]

Drawing up terms of reference for an inquiry in the UK would have to take account of the ambiguous legal status of the Security Service before 1989. Specifically, there was no law authorising a range of investigative activities such as burglary and an apparent faith in official circles that these were implicitly authorised by reason of the prerogative power. Given the contentious nature of such authority, it would be important that the terms drawn up were not reduced to criteria of legality or illegality but incorporated also notions of propriety.

Further, given the significance of the idea of a security intelligence 'network' or 'community', it would be important not to exclude arbitrarily any particular agency. The main terms of reference for an inquiry should include, at the minimum, the question of the security intelligence mandate, the organisational questions relating to the need for a separate agency, the question of the relation between ministers and the security intelligence agencies, the techniques of information-gathering and the authorisation procedures to be required, and, finally, the question of external oversight.

On the face of it such extensive terms of reference would appear to depart from one of Salmon's main recommendations regarding tribunals of inquiry – that the reference should 'confine the inquiry to the investigation of the definite matter which is causing a crisis of public confidence'.[72] Thus, again, it might seem that the Royal Commission form might be more suitable for the broader examination of the security intelligence process which is being suggested here. But this would depend on the precise nature of the 'definite matter' which the reference identified. If, for example, allegations of the improper dissemination of false information concerning elected politicians and ministers were one 'matter' and allegations of the improper surveillance and harassment of people engaged in lawful political activity were another, then these would seem to be entirely consistent with Salmon's recommendation. Yet a thorough inquiry into such matters would necessarily raise issues of control and oversight which could be written into the terms of reference, as they were in Canada where McDonald was commissioned not only to investigate and report on the prevalence of practices not authorised or provided by law but also 'to advise' regarding the laws, policies and procedures which were necessary and desirable for the future.[73]

The problem with broad terms of reference is that they invite an inquiry to dissipate its energies over a wide field. Lord Salmon, for example, criticised the Warren Commission into the assassination of President John Kennedy for spending so much time hearing testimony into Oswald's life history while paying insufficient attention to the critical ballistics evidence of what shots hit whom.[74] Certainly broad terms will probably require an inquiry to be selective in terms of the specific allegations of abuse which it chooses to pursue. This was the way in which the Senate Select Committee proceeded, given that it had been asked to report within eight months on 14 major areas of US security intelligence.[75] Other aspects of agenda-setting will include the question of how far back investigation will go. The McDonald Commission chose to concentrate on the period since 1969,[76] the date of the previous McKenzie Commission on security intelligence, though its inquiry often did go further back than that. The Church Committee began its work by the construction of chronologies of events which provided its basic methodology for marshalling information,[77] and these later provided the main basis for the detailed reports on the FBI and CIA since their respective origins in 1908 and 1947. If the same approach were taken regarding Special Branch and the Security Service then 1883 and 1909 would be the relevant dates. If, on the other hand, the development of new structures of control and oversight were to be seen as a more crucial task than a detailed historical accounting then some later date might be better. Given the overall significance of the cold war in determining the state's perception of security threats in recent decades and the implications of current political changes in Europe, 1945 would provide a logical starting date.

Organisation and staffing

Tribunals of inquiry in the UK have normally been staffed by civil servants, mainly lawyers from the Treasury Solicitor's department.[78] Similarly, the secretariat for Royal Commissions is derived from the ranks of civil servants; for example, the Phillips Royal Commission on Criminal Procedure derived its secretariat mainly from the Lord Chancellor's department and the Home Office.[79] This secretariat carried out some research for the commission but notably a significant series of outside research studies was commissioned from primarily academic sources.[80] Hope's second Royal Commission in Australia relied on a 'fairly small staff'.[81] North American practice has been somewhat different. Compared with the UK there has been a longer tradition of outsiders being drawn into temporary positions both in the executive and the legislature, and security intelligence inquiries have reflected this. The McDonald Commission, in addition to taking on some experienced police and other government investigators, had 16 research staff and, at various times, 30 lawyers working either full- or part-time.[82] The staff were divided into two main streams, legal and research. This reflected, at least at the outset, a distinction between the investigation of alleged abuses and the consideration of more general policy issues. Although the staff of the Church Committee in the Senate was initially organised in 'task forces' consisting of both lawyers and non-lawyers, one of the factors which led to friction between them was the differing priorities and methods favoured by the two groups.[83] These problems were aggravated in the Senate because of the size of the staffs and the inevitably part-time commitment of the committee members; an inquiry with full-time members would be better able to provide clearer direction and co-ordination of staff work.

Obtaining information

The weight given to different aspects of the agenda will in turn affect the direction of information-gathering by the inquiry, but there are two general issues to be considered whatever the general strategy: first, the question of access and second, the methodology. The extent to which access is granted to the subjects of the inquiry will depend, initially, on the type of inquiry established. As we have seen, tribunals of inquiry have extensive powers relating to access; Royal Commissions and departmental committees of inquiry do not. Research into the activities of the state, or indeed any other powerful bureaucracy, however, faces problems of both formal and informal gate-keeping. Even if questions of formal access are resolved in favour of an inquiry, with a tribunal's powers of access to people and papers, there will remain crucial issues. For example, the McDonald Commission was in possession of such powers but still had some difficulties obtaining access to Cabinet minutes where it was believed that these would shed light on the key question of the extent of ministerial knowledge about the controversial activities of the RCMP security service.[84] Also, even if formal access is granted, there are numerous opportunities for bureaucracies to delay in responding to requests for information; this is a particular danger if an inquiry is known to be constrained by a fixed time limit. This was a problem which faced both the congressional inquiries in the US in the 1970s and the Special Review Committee of the Canadian House of Commons during 1989–90.[85]

Access also depends crucially on the inquiry's understanding of the information-processing practices within the target agencies. Given the ability of bureaucracies to produce quantities of information sufficient to bury outside investigators, the inquiry must beware the 'pragmatic fallacy' that if it collects as much information as possible and applies 'common sense' then solutions will appear.[86] The utility of the information, and answers to questions, provided by security intelligence agencies will depend crucially on what they are asked. This is a prime reason for ensuring that there are people on the inquiry or its staff who understand the agencies' internal information-processing procedures. Only with that knowledge can the inquiry develop methodologies of inquiry that will enable the members not only to obtain relevant information but also to organise it and thereby inform themselves. Different methodologies may well develop, based on different priorities, for example between uncovering abuses and developing future policy, but they should certainly include both the examination of documentation and interviews with agency personnel.

The process of gathering information from the security intelligence agencies themselves must be conducted with the knowledge that such agencies devote a significant amount of effort to preventing outsiders from finding out what they do and how they do it. Putting it bluntly, one of the central findings of external inquiries into security intelligence agencies has been that their officials lie to outsiders. McDonald noted that a common thread running through his inquiry was 'a willingness on the part of members of the RCMP to deceive those outside the Force who have some sort of constitutional authority or jurisdiction over them or their activities'.[87] McDonald did not suggest that RCMP officials had lied to his Commission, but Lord Denning seems to have been less lucky with his Profumo inquiry. Denning did publish for the first time some documents relating to the Security Service in his 1963 report but his conclusion that the service had minimal and wholly proper involvement in the Profumo case has now been discredited. Rather, Denning was effectively 'taken for a ride' by the Security Service, including possibly being shown doctored files.[88] In the case of Hoover's FBI, several special files were maintained outside the central records system as a means of protecting the Bureau from outside scrutiny. For example, additional sets of files were lodged in the offices of some assistant directors, and the personal and confidential file which had been maintained in Hoover's office was destroyed within weeks of his death by his administrative assistant.[89]

Since one of the central problems of security intelligence activities in the UK has been the extent to which they have prospered behind unnecessarily high walls of secrecy, it would be important for an inquiry to take as much as possible of its evidence in public. The significance of this for inquiries in general was noted by Lord Salmon[90] whose arguments were quoted by McDonald in his opening statement in 1977.[91] In any inquiry into security intelligence agencies there are likely to be times when the inquiry will feel it has no alternative to hearing evidence *in camera*, but on such occasions it should prove possible subsequently to release the text of such evidence, expurgated if necessary.[92] The balance of hearings as between public and private will reflect to an important extent the will of the members. The easy route for inquiries into security intelligence agencies is to slip into private session at the first sight of the national security totem, but with some effort procedures can be devised which make this unnecessary and which of themselves mount some challenge to the traditional deadweight of 'national security'. David Calcutt, in the inquiry into the interrogation of servicemen in Cyprus, made use of a number of procedural devices, for example the submission by witnesses of written statements which could be checked in advance. In most cases where classified material appeared it was possible to exclude it without diminishing the value of the statement and this minimised the amount of time in which the inquiry had to exclude the public.[93] There may be reasons other than those of national security why information should not be divulged in documents or public hearings. McDonald identified more general 'public interest' and 'privacy' interests as further reasons for non-disclosure.[94] For example, it would be expected that informants' and agents' names would be excluded, as they were from documents supplied to the Senate inquiry by the FBI and CIA.[95] In any event the inquiry itself must be the final arbiter of what is and what is not released to the public.

At this stage of the proceedings care needs to be taken to safeguard as far as possible the rights of individuals against whom allegations are made in the full glare of a public inquiry. Lord Salmon's Royal Commission of 1966 made a number of recommendations in this respect.[96] These have not actually been legislated into effect but have often been followed as a matter of practice by subsequent inquiries. For example, Calcutt's Cyprus inquiry followed Salmon's recommendation and provided written notice to any witness whose conduct was likely to come under scrutiny. These letters set out the substance of the matters out of which criticism was likely to arise and, as far as possible, witnesses were seen in such an order as to ensure that they knew as much as possible of the evidence against them when they appeared to present their own case.[97]

Reporting

Finally, what should be the nature of the final report? This question is closely bound up with the process of information-gathering by the inquiry. A major aspect of the negotiation process in which the inquiry may become embroiled with the executive branch in general and the security intelligence agencies in particular will concern the destination of information given to the inquiry. Throughout, key decisions will have to be made about precisely who (members and/or staff?) can view what documents and where (at the agency's premises or at the inquiry's?). As far as the final report is concerned, some of the security intelligence inquiries elsewhere have consulted with the agencies concerned as to what might or might not be published. The Church Committee did this in the Senate, although the equivalent committee in the House of Representatives, chaired by Otis Pike, did not. Compared with the relatively accommodating strategy *vis-à-vis* the executive pursued by Church, the Pike Committee adopted a more adversarial approach to the executive branch in its search for information. In January 1976 the House Rules Committee blocked publication of Pike's report unless the President had final authority over the information it contained and the full House upheld the ruling.[98] Shortly thereafter the Pike Report was leaked via CBS correspondent Dan Schorr to the *Village Voice* which published most of the report.[99]

Justice Hope also consulted with ASIO concerning the content of his draft report in 1984, although this was not just to avoid the inadvertent publication of classified material. He also wished to give ASIO management the chance to comment on whether the report 'accurately and fairly represented matters discussed in it'.[100] It might be argued that this is unwise in an area where some hearings may have to be held in secret and some information omitted from reports. Such an action may well give the impression, however unjustified, that the agencies concerned are too influential in the final report on their activities.

CONCLUSION

Given the paucity of hard information relating to the postwar history of security intelligence in the UK, any inquiry established must have full access to files and personnel in order to make any sense of the main allegations. An inquiry organised on the lines suggested here will permit a better assessment to be made of the main alternative explanations of these allegations, in accordance with the research strategy suggested in Chapter 1. This will not be able to establish 'the truth' in the absolute sense that Lord Salmon characterised it in his Lionel Cohen lecture[101] since there are too many contested concepts at the heart of the security intelligence process. For example, even if clear evidence is found that security intelligence officers engaged in disinformation practices towards elected politicians, some will still argue that this is defensible if carried out in the interests of 'national security' or, for example, to 'protect' the integrity of the 'state' or of the 'Crown'. Alternatively, the surveillance of certain groups and individuals engaged in lawful political activity will amount to a clear breach of democratic rights as far as some are concerned, but may constitute necessary action 'in defence of' democratic rights for others.

What any inquiry must attempt to do is to identify clearly the parameters and implications of these arguments as they relate to the activities of the security intelligence agencies. Guidelines as to the legality, propriety and efficacy of those activities must be developed and on that basis a set of proposals must be made which seek to apply basic principles of democratic control and review of state activities to those agencies. Since the reports of commissions and inquiries have too often been ignored in subsequent political debate, it would be important that any government instituting a security intelligence inquiry guaranteed at the time that it would provide a detailed response to, and provide the opportunity for parliamentary debate of, the inquiry's report.[102]

The critical question is whether an inquiry can be designed which will explore rather than cover up the contradictions which are inherent in the security intelligence activities of states claiming to be democratic. Foreign experience, as examined here, suggests there is some potential for this, though the centralisation of state power in the UK provides infertile soil for such a development. The potential of any inquiry is more likely to be realised if that centralisation is challenged by movement towards citizenship based on the possession of political, not just consumer, rights. An inquiry is more likely to close-off serious investigation of the secret state if it is unchallenged by a more general democratisation. Therefore the argument for an inquiry must be pursued within the context of broader arguments for positive rights to security from arbitrary arrest, personal privacy, freedom of information and expression, freedom to organise and to demonstrate, and freedom of movement.[103]

The historical autonomy of the domestic security intelligence agencies in the UK and their ability to penetrate society at will have been based on the unchecked prerogative of the central state. As we have seen, challenges to this have increased in the last 20 years but have achieved only minor procedural changes, for example, regarding telephone tapping. The disappearance of the major justification upon which domestic security intelligence has been based since 1945 – the 'communist threat' – and the lessons from Eastern Europe, South Africa and Northern Ireland as to the possible consequences of unreconstructed and autonomous domestic security intelligence agencies require the most thorough critical examination of the Gore-Tex state.

NOTES

1. Statement published 23 August 1977, reproduced in HC Deb., 8 December 1977, col. 1645.
2. T. Benn, *Conflict of Interest, Diaries 1977–80* (London: Hutchinson, 1990), p. 403.
3. HC Deb., 6 May 1987, col. 725.
4. IPPR, *The Constitution of the United Kingdom* (London, September 1991); Liberty, *A People's Charter: Liberty's Bill of Rights* (London, 1991).
5. Church Committee, Final Report, Book II, *Intelligence Activities and the Rights of Americans* (Washington DC: US Government Printing Office, 1976), p.ix, note 7.
6. S. Hall *et al.*, *Policing the Crisis* (Basingstoke: Macmillan, 1978), p. 234, and see discussion in Chapter 2.
7. F. Burton and P. Carlen, *Official Discourse: On Discourse Analysis, Government Publications, Ideology and the State* (London: Routledge, 1979), pp. 44–51.
8. P. Thomas, 'Royal Commissions' *Statute Law Review* (1982), p. 40.
9. H.W.R. Wade, *Administrative Law* (Oxford: Oxford University Press, 6th edition, 1988), p. 1001. Cf C. Salmon, 'Tribunals of Inquiry', *Israel Law Review*, 2(3), 1967, p. 313.
10. Supra (note 7), p. 48. Cf P. Saunders, *Social Theory and the*

Urban Question (London: Unwin Hyman, 2nd edition, 1986), pp. 304–11 which discusses the fragmentation of the state in the context of distinguishing the 'politics of production' from the 'politics of consumption'.
11. Burton and Carlen, supra (note 7).
12. McDonald, Second Report, *Freedom and Security Under the Law* (Ottawa: Minister of Supply and Services, 1981), pp. 43–7, 407–11.
13. Cf K.G. Robertson, 'The Study of Intelligence in the US', in R. Godson (ed.), *Comparing Foreign Intelligence* (Washington DC: National Strategy Information Center, 1988), pp. 25–6.
14. For example, see I. Linn, *Application Refused* (London: Civil Liberties Trust, 1990), pp. 53–4.
15. C.E.S. Franks, *Parliament and Security Matters* (Ottawa: Minister of Supply and Services, 1980), pp. 3–4.
16. A. Shulsky, *Silent Warfare* (McLean: Brassey's (US), 1991), pp. 152–6, and cf discussion in Chapter 4.
17. Robertson, supra (note 13), p. 20.
18. J.T. Richelson and D. Ball, *The Ties That Bind* (Boston: Unwin Hyman, 2nd edition, 1990), pp. 32–6.
19. McDonald, supra (note 12), pp. 625–6.
20. J.-P. Brodeur (ed.), *CASIS Newsletter*, 16, Université de Montréal (December 1991), pp. 19–26, 29–30.
21. For example, R.E. Morgan, *Domestic Intelligence* (Austin: University of Texas Press, 1980), pp. 73–8.
22. F.H. Hinsley and C.A.G. Simkins, *British Intelligence in the Second World War*, Vol. 4: *Security and Counter-Intelligence* (London: HMSO, 1990) pp. 6–7.
23. Ibid, pp. 177–8.
24. McDonald, supra (note 12), pp. 418–21, 754–74.
25. *The Guardian*, 13 March 1990.
26. A.T. Turk, *Political Criminality* (Beverly Hills: Sage, 1982), p. 123.
27. G.T. Marx, *Undercover* (Berkeley: University of California Press, 1988), p. 47.
28. A.S. Farson, 'Old Wine, New Bottles, and Fancy Labels: The Rediscovery of Organizational Culture in the Control of Intelligence', in G. Barak (ed.), *Crimes By The Capitalist State* (Albany: State University of New York Press, 1991), pp. 185–217; J.M. Oseth, *Regulating US Intelligence Operations* (Lexington: University Press of Kentucky, 1985), pp. 185–6.

29. *Statewatch*, 2(1), London, 1992, p. 1.
30. M. Spencer, *1992 And All That: Civil Liberties in the Balance* (London: Civil Liberties Trust, 1990), p. 22
31. ASIO, *Report to Parliament 1987–88* (Canberra: Australian Government Publishing Service, 1989), p. 11.
32. McDonald, supra (note 12), pp. 538–9.
33. Marx, supra (note 27), pp. 47–8.
34. S. Farson, *The Influence of Criminology on the Study of Security Intelligence*, paper for International Studies Association Conference, Vancouver, March 1991, pp. 20–21. See also, for example, G. Murray, *Enemies of the State* (London: Simon & Schuster, 1993).
35. Robertson, supra (note 13).
36. P. Gill, 'The Evolution of the Security Intelligence Debate in Canada since 1976', in A.S. Farson *et al.* (eds), *Security and Intelligence in a Changing World* (London: Frank Cass, 1991), p. 90.
37. Inquiry by the Rt. Hon. Lord Justice Taylor, Interim Report, *The Hillsborough Stadium Disaster 15 April, 1989*, Cm 765 (London: HMSO, August 1989).
38. *The Guardian*, 11 January 1990, p. 6; 12 July 1990, p. 20; 28 March 1991, p. 37.
39. B. Porter, *The Origins of the Vigilant State* (London: Weidenfeld & Nicolson, 1987), p. 186.
40. S. Jenkins, 'The Oversight of and the Limits on Intelligence Work in a Democracy', Ditchley Conference Report No. D88/11, 1988, p. 4.
41. *The Guardian*, 5 May 1987, p. 36.
42. *Interim Report of the Committee of Inquiry in the Vassall Case*, Cmnd 1871 (London: HMSO, November 1962), p. 3.
43. *Report of the Tribunal appointed to Inquire into the Vassall Case and Related Matters*, Cmnd 2009 (London: HMSO, April 1963), p. iii.
44. Salmon, supra (note 9), pp. 321–3.
45. P. Knightley and C. Kennedy, *An Affair of State: the Profumo Case and the Framing of Stephen Ward* (London: Jonathan Cape, 1987) and see below pp. 341–3.
46. Royal Commission on Tribunals of Inquiry, *Report of the Commission under the Chairmanship of Rt. Hon. Lord Justice Salmon*, Cmnd 3121 (London: HMSO, November, 1966), p. 9.

47. Ibid, §§37–42.
48. M. Bulmer (ed.), *Social Research and Royal Commissions* (London: George Allen & Unwin, 1980), p. 1 and note 2.
49. P. Hennessy, *Whitehall* (London: Secker & Warburg, 1989), pp. 574–82.
50. Cmnd 3121, supra (note 46), §§35–6.
51. L.K. Johnson, *A Season Of Inquiry: the Senate Intelligence Investigations* (Lexington: University Press of Kentucky, 1985), p. 267.
52. Report of the Special Committee on the Review of the CSIS Act, *In Flux But Not In Crisis* (Ottawa: Queen's Printer of Canada, September 1990), p. 8.
53. Tribunal appointed to inquire into the events on Sunday 30 January 1972, which led to the loss of life in connection with the procession in Londonderry on that day, *Report by the Rt. Hon. Lord Widgery*, House of Commons Paper 220 (London: HMSO, April 1972).
54. Cmnd 3121, supra (note 46), §27.
55. Z. Segal, 'Tribunals of Inquiry: A British Invention Ignored in Britain', *Public Law*, Summer 1984, p. 211; Wade, supra (note 9), pp. 1001–2.
56. Cmnd 3121, supra (note 46), §§48–65.
57. Segal, supra (note 55), pp. 208–9.
58. Salmon, supra (note 9), p. 324.
59. For example, see P.E. Sheriff, 'State Theory, Social Science and Governmental Commissions', *American Behavioral Scientist*, 26(5), May/June 1983, pp. 675–6.
60. J.A.G. Griffith, *The Politics of the Judiciary* (London: Fontana, 4th edition, 1991), pp. 42–3.
61. *Sunday Times*, 6 August 1972.
62. M. Mandel, 'Discrediting the McDonald Commission', *Canadian Forum*, LXI(716), March 1982, p. 14.
63. Burton and Carlen discuss the way in which 'common law reasoning and empiricist social research are articulated in ideological practice when judges head official investigations into social situations (crises) . . .' supra (note 7), p. 53.
64. Thomas, supra (note 8), p. 46.
65. Quoted in Hennessy, supra (note 49), p. 578.
66. Oseth, supra (note 28), pp. 25–6.
67. W.E. Colby and P. Forbath, *Honorable Men* (New York: Simon & Schuster, 1978), pp. 398–400.

68. Church Committee, supra (note 5), p. v.
69. McDonald, supra (note 12), pp. 13–22, discusses the Commission's terms of reference.
70. Justice R.M. Hope, *Protective Security Review* (Canberra: Australian Government Printing Service, 1979).
71. R.M. Hope, Royal Commission on Australia's Security and Intelligence Agencies, *Report on the ASIO* (Canberra: Commonwealth Government Printer, 1985).
72. Cmnd 3121, supra (note 46), §78.
73. McDonald, supra (note 12), pp. 14–15.
74. Salmon, supra (note 9), p. 319.
75. Johnson, supra (note 51), p. 27; similarly, Hope, supra (note 71), §1.13.
76. McDonald, supra (note 12), p. 16.
77. Johnson, supra (note 51), pp. 27–8.
78. Cmnd 3121, supra (note 46), §§84–8.
79. The Royal Commission on Criminal Procedure, *Report*, Cmnd 8092 (London: HMSO, January 1981).
80. Ibid, p. 199.
81. R.M. Hope, Royal Commission on Australia's Security and Intelligence Agencies, *General Report* (Canberra: Commonwealth Government Printer, 1985), §1.11.
82. McDonald, supra (note 12), pp. 23, 1213–14.
83. Johnson, supra (note 51), pp. 65–8, 273.
84. For example see McDonald, Third Report, *Certain RCMP Activities and the Question of Governmental Knowledge* (Ottawa: Minister of Supply and Services, 1981), pp. 17–25.
85. S. Farson, *Parliament's Capacity to Conduct a Comprehensive Review*, paper prepared for the SIRC Seminar, Vancouver, February 1991, pp. 30–31.
86. Bulmer, supra (note 48), p. 4.
87. McDonald, supra (note 12), p. 101.
88. Rupert Allason MP, HC Deb., 15 December 1988, col. 1160.
89. See A. Theoharis (ed.), *From The Secret Files of J. Edgar Hoover* (Chicago: Ivan R. Dee, 1991), pp. 3–11 for details.
90. Cmnd 3121, supra (note 46), §§39–40.
91. McDonald, supra (note 12), pp. 1159–60.
92. Ibid, p. 25.
93. Ministry of Defence, *Report by David Calcutt QC on his Inquiry into the Investigations carried out by the Service Police in Cyprus*

in February and March 1984, Cmnd 9781 (London: HMSO, May 1986), §§1.30–1.43.

94. McDonald, supra (note 12), pp. 1161–2.
95. Johnson, supra (note 51), p. 29.
96. Cmnd 3121, supra (note 46), §§48–67.
97. Cmnd 9781, supra (note 93), §§1.23–1.24. In *Mahon* v. *Air New Zealand Ltd and others* (1984), it was determined that the rules of natural justice must apply to any inquiry, including Royal Commissions, which are carrying out an investigation.
98. Johnson, supra (note 51), pp. 180–82.
99. *CIA: The Pike Report* (Nottingham: Spokesman Books, 1977).
100. Hope, supra (note 71), §1.14.
101. Salmon, supra (note 9), p. 313.
102. For example, see Hennessy, supra (note 49), pp. 579–80.
103. See discussion in Liberty, *A People's Charter: Liberty's Bill of Rights* (London: National Council for Civil Liberties, 1991), *passim*.

Appendix

DEFENCE PRESS AND BROADCASTING COMMITTEE

D-NOTICE No. 6

BRITISH SECURITY AND INTELLIGENCE SERVICES

1. The broad functions of the security and intelligence services are widely known. They are responsible for countering threats to the Realm arising from espionage, subversion and terrorism* and for providing HM Government with secret intelligence concerning foreign powers. These services must operate as far as possible in conditions of secrecy. The publication of detailed information about their activities or methods, or the disclosure of identities, is likely to prejudice both present and past operations, and also to make more difficult the day to day work of persons involved.

2. It is requested therefore, that nothing should be published without reference to the Secretary about:

    a. specific operations of the security and intelligence services and those involved with them;

    b. details of the manner in which operational methods, including the interception of communications, are actually applied and of their targets;

    c. the identities, whereabouts and tasks of persons employed by these services, including details of their

---

* 'terrorism' had not appeared in paragraph 1 of the 1989 edition of the Notice.

families and home addresses. Editors are reminded that such disclosures can lead to the identification of other members of the services, and of individuals who have at any time assisted these services; and that the publication of identities or photographs can help a terrorist organisation to identify a target;

d. the addresses and telephone numbers used by these services;

e. the organisational structures, communications networks, numerical strengths, and training techniques of these services, and details of the resources allocated to them;

f. technical advances by the security and intelligence services, in relation to their intelligence and counter-intelligence methods, whether the basic methods are well known or not.

3. Attempts are sometimes made to prompt disclosures about the work of the security and intelligence services by planting stories in the British or foreign press. It is therefore requested that ostensible disclosures of information published about these services should not be repeated or otherwise elaborated upon without reference to the Secretary. This includes information purporting to come from members or former members of these services.

11 May 1992

Index

354

283, 290, 298, 319, 337, 340,
344
Hosenball, Mark, 185, 299
Hulnick, Arthur, 135
HUMINT (human intelligence), 207
Hurd, Douglas, 291
Huston Plan, 101–4, 169
Huston, Tom, 102, 162

ideology, 69, 93, 135, 236, 284
Immigration Act, 1971, UK, 99–100
Independent Broadcasting Authority,
259
information, 48–55; control, 51–5,
83, 303, 314–15; definition, 5;
distortions, 50, 122, 235–40;
gathering, 4, 61, 135–71;
'need-to-know', 50, 219–20;
open sources, 51–3; policy,
81; power and, 61, 66, 180–1;
process, 48–55; state records,
153–4; see also intelligence,
interception of communications
Information Research Department,
199
informers, 30, 52, 61, 144, 145,
154–61, 191, 193–6, 212, 303,
324
Ingram, Miranda, 236
inquiries, access to information,
340–3; departmental
committees of, 327, 330–1;
disadvantages of, 314–16;
internal, 327–8; membership,
334–6; need for in the UK,
4, 17, 161, 196, 311–14;
presidential commissions, US,
331; public hearings, 342–3;
reports, 343–5; role of, 32–4,
314–16, 326–7, 337; royal
commissions, 315, 327, 330,
331, 333–4, 338, 349; staffing,
339–40; terms of reference,
336–9; Tribunals of Inquiry
(Evidence) Act, 1921, 315,
328–30, 332–4; types of, 328
Inspector General, Australia, 267–8;
Canada, 105, 138, 252, 263–7,

277, 287–8, 297; CIA, 253–4,
263
Institute of Professional
Investigators, 187
Institute for Public Policy Research,
313
Institute for the Study of Conflict,
199
intelligence, analysis, 179–81;
collection, 151–71, 213;
definition, 5; dissemination,
182–91; distortions, 135,
235–40; process, 4, 135;
production, 179; storage,
187, 188–91; targeting,
140–51; types of, 208–9; see
also foreign intelligence,
HUMINT, information,
military intelligence, security
intelligence, SIGINT
Intelligence Oversight Board, US,
262, 268
interception of communications,
30, 99; mail, 102–3, 163, 169;
telegrams, 33–4; telephones,
162–9; warrants, 166–8, 220,
281, 285–6, 291–6
Interception of Communications Act,
1985, 166–7, 220, 286, 291, 325
internment, 193
Iran–Contra, 250, 254, 268, 297
Ismay, Lord, 10

Jessop, Bob, 75, 76
Johnson, Loch, 297
Johnson, Lyndon, administration of,
77, 226
Joint Intelligence Committee, UK,
34, 81, 95, 140–3, 216, 303,
320
Joint Intelligence Organisation, UK,
34, 140–3
Jones, R.V., 11–12
judges, 79, 81, 334–5; oversight
of security intelligence,
280–6, 300–2, 304, 312,
335
judicial review, 98, 99–100, 282